The Philosophy of
Schopenhauer

Continental European Philosophy

This series provides accessible and stimulating introductions to the ideas of continental thinkers who have shaped the fundamentals of European philosophical thought. Powerful and radical, the ideas of these philosophers have often been contested, but they remain key to understanding current philosophical thinking as well as the current direction of disciplines such as political science, literary theory, comparative literature, art history, and cultural studies. Each book seeks to combine clarity with depth, introducing fresh insights and wider perspectives while also providing a comprehensive survey of each thinker's philosophical ideas.

Published titles

The Philosophy of Gadamer
Jean Grondin

The Philosophy of Merleau-Ponty
Eric Matthews

The Philosophy of Nietzsche
Rex Welshon

The Philosophy of Schopenhauer
Dale Jacquette

Forthcoming titles include

The Philosophy of Deleuze
Peter Sedgwick

The Philosophy of Derrida
Mark Dooley and Liam Kavanagh

The Philosophy of Foucault
Todd May

The Philosophy of Habermas
Andrew Edgar

The Philosophy of Hegel
Allen Speight

The Philosophy of Heidegger
Jeff Malpas

The Philosophy of Husserl
Burt Hopkins

The Philosophy of Kant
Jim O'Shea

The Philosophy of Kierkegaard
George Pattison

The Philosophy of Marx
Mark Neocleous

The Philosophy of Rousseau
Patrick Riley, Sr and Patrick Riley, Jr

The Philosophy of Sartre
Anthony Hatzimoysis

The Philosophy of Schopenhauer

Dale Jacquette

First published in 2005 by Acumen

Acumen Publishing Limited
15a Lewins Yard
East Street
Chesham
Bucks HP5 1HQ
www.acumenpublishing.co.uk

ISBN: 1-84465-008-1 (hardcover)
ISBN: 1-84465-009-X (paperback)

British Library Cataloguing-in-Publication Data
A catalogue record for this book is available from the British Library.

Designed and typeset in Classical Garamond
by Kate Williams, Swansea.
Printed and bound by Biddles Limited, King's Lynn.

Contents

For Tina, as always, with love

Preface

I came to Schopenhauer indirectly through a prior interest in the philosophy of Wittgenstein. In particular, I wanted to understand what Wittgenstein means in *Tractatus Logico-Philosophicus* 6.4211, when he says that "Ethics is transcendent. Ethics and aesthetics are one." The secondary literature hinted that Schopenhauer's philosophy might provide the key. While this was a tantalizing clue, it did not by itself resolve my uncertainty, but only led to more and more careful reading and rereading of Schopenhauer's works. It was not long in this process before my original motives for studying Schopenhauer ripened into a lasting involvement with all aspects of his thought on its own terms and for its own sake.

As an undergraduate I read Schopenhauer's *Fourfold Root of the Principle of Sufficient Reason* and both volumes of *The World as Will and Representation* in translation. This first exposure to Schopenhauer gave me a rough idea of his philosophy and its relation to the philosophies of Plato and Kant, just as at the time I had only a rough idea of the philosophies of Plato and Kant. It was insufficient background later on to help me clarify what I now see as the early Wittgenstein's debt to Schopenhauer's transcendentalism, not only in the identification of ethics with aesthetics and his concept of the metaphysical subject or philosophical I, but in every aspect of his philosophical semantics and its applications in the *Tractatus*, including the sign–symbol distinction and picture theory of meaning.

What I discovered in reacquainting myself with Schopenhauer is the explanatory power of his dual aspect conception of the world as Will and representation. However useful the study of Schopenhauer has been to my understanding of later episodes in the history of philosophy, it is his philosophical system standing on its own that has meant increasingly more to my own reflections in metaphysics, ethics and aesthetics, and in my efforts to come to terms with all the comedy and tragedy of the human condition. Schopenhauer combines mid-nineteenth-century scientific philosophy with

Eastern mysticism and a penetrating if grotesque insight into the problems of life. The author's captivating philosophical prose, the extraordinary rancour and passion that shine through on every page, and the ingenious fitting together of so many diverse kinds of knowledge from so many different branches of study, contribute to making Schopenhauer's thought a most audacious philosophical enterprise, with an astonishing array of implications for metaphysics, epistemology, ethics, political philosophy, aesthetics, philosophy of logic, mathematics, science and religion. We delve into Schopenhauer's life work not merely as indispensable to a complete understanding of the Western tradition, or of nineteenth-century German idealism, but because Schopenhauer's reflections, if true, no matter how abstruse, offer something that philosophy in our more cynical and still positivistic age has abandoned as beyond the reach of responsible enquiry: a single key to unlock all the philosophical difficulties and religious and psychological mysteries surrounding the facts of life and death.

I approach Schopenhauer critically, as a logician and dyed-in-the-wool analytic philosopher. I do so, however, I believe, with more genuine sympathy for his project and its conclusions than most scientifically trained scholars typically take away from his pages. While there are numerous excellent introductions to Schopenhauer's thought, and new studies on special topics in his philosophy appear every several years, I devote more attention than I have seen in other expositions to Schopenhauer's main and most controversial contribution to metaphysics – the arguments by which he hopes to prove that thing-in-itself is Will. My reason for examining Schopenhauer's reasoning in such detail is that it is specifically by these considerations that he claims to have surpassed Kant as the greatest of all his philosophical precursors. Schopenhauer enthusiastically adopts Kant's distinction between phenomena and thing-in-itself. He nevertheless rejects Kant's attempt to demonstrate the existence of thing-in-itself, and, in the process, more significantly, he denies Kant's conclusion that thing-in-itself is unknowable, merely conceivable, *noumenon*. By offering a glimpse of the hidden nature of thing-in-itself as Will, Schopenhauer goes far, perhaps too far, beyond his teacher. He thereby sets in motion a cascade of implications for other fields of philosophy in the understanding of science, natural history, religion, art and every phenomenal and transcendental aspect of social and political reality. Schopenhauer pursues many of these finer points in his later writings and revised editions of his major works, all of which can be understood as supplements to *The World as Will and Representation*.

The unified synthesis of so many different lines of thought and their sweeping consequences makes Schopenhauer's philosophy, if correct in its principal assertions, one of the most groundshaking, all-encompassing worldviews ever to appear in the history of ideas. It is this elephantine *if*, however, that repeatedly draws readers back to Schopenhauer's writings, to understand more clearly the remarkable chain of inferences by which he proposes to identify thing-in-itself as Will.

Dale Jacquette

Acknowledgements

I am grateful to the series editor, John Shand, for inviting me to contribute this volume on Schopenhauer to Acumen's series on Continental European Philosophy. The material for this book was first presented in seminar lectures on Schopenhauer's philosophy at The Pennsylvania State University in spring 2003. The chapters were drafted in the summer immediately thereafter during the course of a bicycle trip through southern Germany along the Romantische Straße from Würzburg to Fuessen, and completed in the winter of 2004 while serving as Director for Penn State's Athens Abroad Program in Greece. I am indebted to David Cartwright for perceptive suggestions for improvement of an earlier draft of the book, and to Dana Van Kooy and the Center for British and Irish Studies at the University of Colorado, Boulder, for assistance in tracking down elusive sources. I thank my wife and cycling partner Tina for her boundless patience and wise loving counsel.

A note on texts and terminology

Schopenhauer's masterwork, *Die Welt als Wille und Vorstellung*, was published as a single volume in 1818, and reissued in a revised and expanded two-volume second edition in 1844, followed by a third edition the year before his death in 1859. In its English translation as *The World as Will and Idea* or *The World as Will and Representation*, the book's title indicates Schopenhauer's division of the world into two aspects. The world presented to thought and known to empirical science is the world as representation (*Vortsellung*), while as it exists independently of thought it is the world as "Will" (*der Wille*). The world as Will is Schopenhauer's interpretation of the Kantian concept of thing-in-itself, whose hidden inner nature he maintains is revealed for the first time only in his transcendental idealist philosophy. I adopt the convenient English device of marking the distinction between empirical "willing" and the individual empirical or phenomenological "will" or "will to life" (*der Wille zum Leben*) in the phenomenal psychology of individual thinkers in lower-case letters, in contrast with Schopenhauer's concept of the transcendent thing-in-itself, which I capitalize in every instance as "Will". In Schopenhauer's German, all uses of any noun, including *"der Wille"*, with either connotation are capitalized as a matter of orthographic convention. The fundamental distinction between Will as thing-in-itself and phenomenal will in the sense of desire or intention, so important to Schopenhauer's system, is indicated consequently in the original German only by context. The translations of Schopenhauer's writings by E. F. J. Payne similarly do not distinguish between "will" and "Will", but render both without capitalization simply as "will". I have not altered these two uses of the term in quoting from Payne, despite my practice of disambiguating Schopenhauer's concepts as "will" and "Will" everywhere in my own commentary. The Payne translations additionally convert Schopenhauer's expanded phrase for the individual phenomenal will as the "will-to-live". Where I have occasion to discuss this concept in Schopenhauer, I use the literally correct, and I think philosophically more accurate, formula "will to life", treating *"Leben"* with its capitalization in Schopenhauer's original text as a noun rather than as the infinitive form of the corresponding verb. Again, I have not modified Payne's English to fit my preference in quoting from his translations, but ask the reader to recognize throughout the equivalence in meaning of the two phrases wherever they occur.

Abbreviations

BM   Schopenhauer: *On the Basis of Morality* (1995).
CPR Kant: *Critique of Pure Reason* (1965).
FFR Schopenhauer: *The Fourfold Root of the Principle of Sufficient Reason* (1974).
FW   Schopenhauer: *Prize Essay on the Freedom of the Will* (1999).
HN   Schopenhauer: *Arthur Schopenhauer: Manuscript Remains in Four Volumes* (1988).
PP   Schopenhauer: *Parerga and Paralipomena* (1974).
VC   Schopenhauer: *On Vision and Colors: An Essay* (1994).
WN   Schopenhauer: *On the Will in Nature: A Discussion of the Corroborations from the Empirical Sciences that the Author's Philosophy has Received Since its First Appearance* (1992).
WWR Schopenhauer: *The World as Will and Representation* (1966).

Therefore, in a certain sense, it can also be said that the will is knowledge *a priori* of the body, and that the body is knowledge *a posteriori* of the will. (WWR 1: 100)

Schopenhauer's life and times

For when I entered life, my genius offered me the choice of either recognizing truth but then of pleasing no one, or with others of teaching the false with encouragement and approbation; and for me the choice had not been difficult ... Accordingly, I became the [man in the] iron mask ... of the profession of philosophy, secluded from air and light so that no one would see me and my natural claims might not gain authority. But now the man who was killed by the silence of the professors of philosophy, has risen again from the dead, to their great consternation, for they do not know at all what expression they should now assume.

(PP 1: 135–6)

An idealist synthesis

Arthur Schopenhauer crafted one of the most comprehensive philosophical systems the world has ever seen – not that the world paid much attention, at least at first. Schopenhauer weaves together ideas of Plato, Kant and Asian religions into an encyclopedic worldview that combines the empirical science of his day with mystic wisdom in a radically idealist metaphysics and epistemology.

The fundamental distinction in Schopenhauer's philosophy marks a dualistic conception of the world as representation, as it appears to thought, and as thing-in-itself, considered independently of all concepts and categories of mind. Schopenhauer identifies thing-in-itself as Will, which he further characterizes as blind urging or uncaused, unmotivated, objectless and subjectless striving or desire. This alleged discovery and its implications have earned Schopenhauer a unique but often misunderstood place in the history

1

THE PHILOSOPHY OF SCHOPENHAUER

of philosophy. The basis for all of Schopenhauer's system is his theory of knowledge, which he refers to as the fourfold root of the principle of sufficient reason. The principle divides explanations for any occurrence in the world as representation into four types of lawlike generalizations, including all logical, mathematical, causal and moral or motivational phenomena. The fourfold root thereby serves as a criterion demarcating the limits of possible explanation, distinguishing between the represented world, for which any object or event in principle is capable of being explained, and thing-in-itself, which cannot be explained at all by any part of the principle. Schopenhauer's epistemology and idealist metaphysics, finally, underwrites a doctrine of moral pessimism, with a unique perspective on traditional problems of ethics, aesthetics and a reinterpretation of the perennial quest for freedom, salvation and immortality that are distinctively Schopenhauerian.

Schopenhauer's debt to all three main sources, including Plato, Kant and the ancient religions of India, is profound. Above all, in his philosophy he stands as the self-professed successor to Kant. Schopenhauer regards his main contribution to the history of thought as something he achieves by standing on Kant's shoulders, seeing farther and more clearly and consistently than anyone had previously done in a direction toward which Kant had only obliquely pointed. The appeal of Schopenhauer's philosophy is largely due to the simplicity of what Schopenhauer refers to as his "single thought" that the world divides into the two fundamental aspects of representation, as it appears to the thinking subject, and as thing-in-itself (WWR 1: xii, xv–xvi). Schopenhauer believes he surpasses Kant in the most important part of his metaphysics by offering insight into the hidden nature of thing-in-itself as Will.

Biographical sketch

The facts of Schopenhauer's life leading to the period of his greatest philosophical creativity illustrate the culture and times in which late-eighteenth- to mid-nineteenth-century German philosophy flourished. Schopenhauer's middle-class family background was not unusual for a young person aspiring to an academic or literary career in his day, although the story of Schopenhauer's life reveals personality traits that can be seen retrospectively in the later outcome of his philosophy.[1]

Schopenhauer was born on 22 February 1788. His family lived first in Danzig, a mercantile Hanseatic city on the Motlawa River, which was then part of the Prussian Confederation, and has since been restored to Poland as the city of Gdansk. The Schopenhauers moved to Hamburg in 1793, and

2

with the birth of Schopenhauer's sister Adele, in 1797, the household was at least temporarily complete. Schopenhauer's father, Henrich Floris Schopenhauer, a moderately successful merchant of Dutch extraction, is believed to have committed suicide for unknown reasons on 20 April 1805. Schopenhauer's mother, born Johanna Trosiener, later became a popular novelist whose name, to Schopenhauer's chagrin, was more widely recognized in literary circles than his own. Schopenhauer died on 21 September 1860, in Frankfurt am Main, where he had lived for the last 28 years of his life and produced and revised many of his most enduring philosophical writings.

The events of Schopenhauer's life are neither remarkable nor dramatic. When compared, say, with those of other great philosophers, such as Plato, Aristotle, Descartes, Hume or Wittgenstein, Schopenhauer, in keeping with his intellectual predecessor, Immanuel Kant, led the life of a quiet scholar. Unlike Kant, however, Schopenhauer had no need or opportunity to work for a living as a university philosophy professor. Schopenhauer tries to make a virtue of this necessity, having failed to win a permanent place as philosophy instructor at the University of Berlin. He argues, as this chapter's epigraph indicates, that as an independent thinker he was free to pursue the truth without concern for the popularity of his ideas or for pleasing an audience. By living frugally within the means afforded by a modest inheritance from his father's estate, Schopenhauer, who never married, was able to devote all his time and energy to a lifetime of philosophical scholarship.[2] He makes an implicit but thinly veiled comparison between himself and Socrates. Both thinkers were professionally unemployed philosophers engaged in a vigilant search for truth in supreme contempt for the pandering sophists of their day:

> How could philosophy, degraded to become a means of earning one's bread, generally fail to degenerate into sophistry? Just because this is bound to happen, and the rule "I sing the song of him whose bread I eat" has held good at all times, the making of money by philosophy was among the ancients the characteristic of the sophist ... My guiding star has in all seriousness been truth. Following it, I could first aspire only to my own approval, entirely averted from an age that has sunk low as regards all higher intellectual efforts, and from a national literature demoralized but for the exceptions, a literature in which the art of combining lofty words with low sentiments has reached its zenith.   (WWR 1: xx–xxi)

The few anecdotes recounted from Schopenhauer's life have entered into philosophical legend as candid images of an apparently unpleasant personality. These add a human dimension to a portrait of the philosopher, typifying Schopenhauer's negative philosophical outlook and unsociability toward the greater part of humanity.

After his parents moved from Danzig to Hamburg in 1793, Schopenhauer was apprenticed to a merchant to learn his father's trade. He appeased his family at first by agreeing to follow in his father's footsteps and abandon his intentions to follow a scholarly career. In exchange, he was offered a summer's travel in England, the Netherlands, France, Switzerland, and Austria. Previously, between 1797 and 1799, Schopenhauer had lived in France with his father on an extended business visit to Paris and Le Havre, where he perfected his French and gained an appreciation for French culture, theatre and literature. The elegance of Schopenhauer's German philosophical prose, its musical qualities, clarity and skilful use of metaphor, are generally attributed to the time he spent during his youth in England and France. There he absorbed distinctively non-Germanic models of expression that characterize his mature literary style, avoiding the ponderous, digressive and mannered writing of his contemporaries.[3]

The first insight we have into Schopenhauer's moral sensibility and philosophical awakening at this period is offered in an autobiographical remark included in his so-called "Cholerabuch", where he recalls:

> When I was seventeen, without any proper schooling, I was affected by the *misery and wretchedness* of life, as was the Buddha, when in his youth he caught sight of sickness, old age, pain, and death … The result for me was that this world could not be the work of an all-bountiful, infinitely good being, but rather of a devil who summoned into existence creatures in order to gloat over their anguish and agony … [I concluded] [a]bove all, [that] suffering is certainly the purpose of life, just as if it were the work of a devil, but this purpose is not the final one, it is itself the means of grace, and therefore as such … is contrived by ourselves for our true and ultimate good.
>
> (HN: 4, para. 36)

We recognize here, perhaps with the distortions that sometimes affect distant memories of formative events in one's early life, a story that as Schopenhauer says is reminiscent of the awakening to the suffering of others by the historical Buddha. When he was still a prince, leaving the shelter of his wealthy family's protection where at first he knew only happiness, kindness and pleasure, young Siddhartha was exposed to the misery that existed outside the manor walls and experienced a sudden overwhelming compassion for the poverty, pain and suffering of others.[4] Schopenhauer, in the year that his father died, seems to have undergone a similar jolting awareness of the plight of humankind. He draws an explicit comparison between his discovery of widespread suffering and the moment of the Buddha's disillusionment with the superficial joys of what until then had been an artificially insulated life.

What Schopenhauer adds to the account that does not seem to be part of the Buddhist legend is the attribution of the world's misery to a devil or evil force. He evokes the philosophical problem of theodicy, of understanding God's divine justice in a universe where natural evil prevails. Schopenhauer's remarks anticipate almost verbatim Nietzsche's later autobiographical comments in the opening sections of *On the Genealogy of Morality*, in which he grapples with a similar problem. It is worthwhile to compare Schopenhauer's remarks with what Nietzsche has to say about his early impressions of the source of evil. Nietzsche's contributions to philosophy after publishing *The Birth of Tragedy*, as we shall see, were dedicated to reversing Schopenhauer's denial of the will to life, which Nietzsche refers to derogatorily as a kind of "European Buddhism". Nietzsche, like Schopenhauer, was equally stirred in his youth to philosophical reflection by his encounters with the fact of evil, but, unlike Schopenhauer, the early Nietzsche attributes rampant evil directly to God:

> In fact, the problem of the origin of evil haunts me as a thirteen-year-old lad: at an age when one has "half child's play, half God in one's heart," I devoted my first literary child's play to it, my first philosophic writing exercise – and as to my "solution" to the problem back then, well, I gave the honor to God, as is fitting, and made him the *father* of evil.[5]

In his moral philosophy, many years later, Schopenhauer makes the feeling of compassion for the suffering of others the foundation of his ethics. The morality of compassion in Schopenhauer is contrary to Kant and in stark opposition to what would eventually become Nietzsche's uncompromising advocacy of the will to power. Schopenhauer, like the historical Buddha, sees suffering in all life, and finally identifies life with suffering. To live is to suffer, and to suffer is to experience the insatiability of individual empirical willing or will to life. Schopenhauer concludes that the soul's only attainable salvation from suffering is to renounce and to whatever extent possible deny and suppress the will to life in the interests of knowledge, to which willing is diametrically opposed.

Two years after his father's death, in 1807, Schopenhauer considered himself at last to be free of his promise to enter business, and embarked on the scholarly career he had always desired. He entered the gymnasium at Gotha, was expelled for writing satirical verses about a local social figure, and completed his preliminary studies for the university degree at a second gymnasium in Weimar. He began university studies in medicine at Göttingen, where he also attended philosophy lectures, and was advised by his teacher Gottlob Ernst Schulze to limit his reading primarily to Plato and Kant. This was a suggestion Schopenhauer faithfully followed, a decision that was to colour deeply every aspect of the future development of his philosophy. From 1811 to 1813 Schopenhauer relocated to Berlin, where he attended philosophy lectures by Johann Gottlieb Fichte, Friedrich D. E. Schleiermacher and Friedrich August Wolf. He fled Berlin in May 1813, when he feared that Napoleon Bonaparte was about to attack the city, and took refuge in Rudolstadt, Thuringen. At the end of this period Schopenhauer wrote his dissertation, awarded *in absentia* from the University of Jena in October 1813, on topics in the history and philosophy of epistemology. The thesis was subsequently published in the same year as *Über die vierfache Wurzel des Satzes vom zureichenden Grunde* [*On the Fourfold Root of the Principle of Sufficient Reason*].

After bitter disagreement with his aspiring socialite mother in Weimar, Schopenhauer broke off relations with her and moved to Dresden, where he lived from 1814 to 1818. His mother's literary salon, for as long as Schopenhauer could tolerate it, had afforded him the valuable opportunity to meet Wolfgang Johann von Goethe and other important thinkers, writers and artists. Schopenhauer corresponded for a time with Goethe, and Goethe's theory of colours in his *Farbenlehre* inspired Schopenhauer to write one of his earliest short books, *Über das Sehn und die Farben: Eine Abhandlung* [*On Vision and Colors: An Essay*]. Mother and son were frequently at odds over Johanna's administration of Schopenhauer's paternal inheritance, a responsibility with which she had been charged after 1809. It is in connection with these early business transactions that we discover another episode illustrative of Schopenhauer's implacable will and dogged abrasiveness. Along with other surviving members of his family, Schopenhauer was engaged in a prolonged lawsuit over some of his father's unrepaid investments. After a few years his mother and sister gave up and settled for a tiny fraction of the amount they were owed, but Schopenhauer persisted with unbending determination, and eventually triumphed, receiving the entire sum for which he had sued.

It was also during this time that Schopenhauer undertook some of his most important philosophical research. He wrote and published his aforementioned short treatise, *On Vision and Colors*, in 1816, and completed the manuscript for his great treatise, *Die Welt als Wille und Vorstellung* [*The World as Will and Representation*], published in 1918 with a 1919 copyright date. In 1820 Schopenhauer returned to Berlin and was accepted as Privatdozent, enabling him to offer fee-paid lectures in philosophy. The University of Berlin was also the home of G. W. F. Hegel. Schopenhauer vehemently disagreed with

Hegel's philosophy and was undisguisedly contemptuous of Hegel's ideas and of the man personally. Hegel was already a well-established, widely discussed and respected philosopher with an enthusiastically admiring local audience of students, and an enviable and, to Schopenhauer's mind, unbearably inflated, international reputation.

Schopenhauer's invectives against prominent contemporaries provide both an amusing and pathetic sideline to the course of his philosophical career. He takes no prisoners in his very first mention of Hegel, when, in the Preface to the Second Edition of his main treatise, he refers to "Hegel, that intellectual Caliban" (WWR 1: xxi). Later, in a similar moment of vituperative spleen, he writes that: "the times have become . . . degraded and crude through the stupefying influence of Hegel's sham wisdom" (WWR 1: 223). Nor is this an extreme case of the polemical potshots he is willing to take against the major figures of German idealism. In Chapter 24, "On Physiognomy", in his later *Parerga and Paralipomena*, his collection of aphorisms and short essays, he goes so far as to maintain:

> I would, therefore, like to advise my discriminating countrymen that, when they again feel inclined to trumpet abroad for thirty years a commonplace head as a great mind, they will not choose for the purpose such a publican's physiognomy as Hegel's, on whose countenance nature had written in her most legible handwriting the words "commonplace fellow", so familiar to her.   (PP 2: 640–41)

Schopenhauer's resentment of Hegel is epitomized by an infamous debacle. During his brief appointment at the University of Berlin, Schopenhauer was so convinced of the superiority of his work that he scheduled his lectures for precisely the same time as Hegel's. Schopenhauer seems to have assumed that the students in Berlin would appreciate the value of his ideas so much more than Hegel's that they would flock en masse from Hegel's lecture classroom to his own, providing a striking demonstration of the power of his philosophy over Hegel's. What must have been his humiliation, then, to learn that at first only a few curious students and soon no one at all was sufficiently interested in what he had to say to fill a single seat. The students, forced to choose between the two philosophers speaking at the same time, voted with their feet for Hegel against Schopenhauer, migrating to Schopenhauer's prestigious rival, and further fuelling his lifelong personal animosity toward Hegel's thought. Dependent as he was on students paying fees to attend his lectures, Schopenhauer had to cancel his course, and the incident effectively ended his hopes for a professional university career.

The situation was aggravated by the fact that Hegel and, to a lesser extent, Fichte and Schelling, gained widespread international recognition for theories that Schopenhauer considered to be shallow and confused. All the while, Schopenhauer's own philosophy during the greater part of his life was neglected, and the works in which he believed he had communicated the most profound and previously unknown truths of metaphysics were almost entirely ignored. The disappointment he encountered in Berlin was not the cause of Schopenhauer's bitterness towards Hegel. It was occasioned instead by a prior sense of outrage that Hegel's philosophy should have achieved worldwide fame despite Schopenhauer's conviction of its philosophical misdirection and obscurantism. For this reason Schopenhauer refers to himself somewhat self-indulgently as the philosopher in the iron mask. The lectureship fiasco seems to have reinforced his prior inclination to despise popular philosophical opinion, which had overlooked his revolutionary discoveries in favour of what he considered to be a palpably inferior philosophy.[6]

During this time Schopenhauer became entangled in yet another scandal. He lived in rented rooms in Berlin, where he was accustomed to working on philosophy in the morning and early afternoon, writing at his desk in full concentration and intolerant of disturbances. Schopenhauer was so preoccupied with the topic that in his later collection of aphorisms and short essays, the *Parerga and Paralipomena*, he includes a set of remarks "On Din and Noise", in which he complains of the "knocking, hammering, and banging [that] has been throughout my life a daily torment to me" (PP 2: 642). A seamstress and neighbour of Schopenhauer's in the apartment building was engaged in conversation in the anteroom one day when Schopenhauer was trying to work. He repeatedly asked her to quieten down, but she continued to annoy him until Schopenhauer, not exactly following the Buddha's enlightened path of compassion, took hold of her physically, kicked and beat her with his fists, and physically removed her from the room. She sued Schopenhauer in court and won her case, upon which Schopenhauer was required as penalty to pay her a yearly stipend. When after several years she died and Schopenhauer was relieved of further obligations, he reportedly wrote in his ledger book (some accounts say it was on the letter in which he received the news) "*Obit anus, abit onus*", meaning "The old woman (or ass, in the anatomical rather than zoological sense, the Latin being nicely ambiguous in this regard) is dead, the debt is cancelled" – a sign of his poetic wit, perhaps, but also an indication of his lack of remorse over the incident. It might further be construed as a window onto his cantankerous personality as someone capable of taking such an action in the first place. His later response when the court-ordered duty to the woman had ended was merely a sense of gratitude that he no longer needed to pay her, suggesting that he never doubted that his mistreatment of her was deserved.[7]

In August 1831 Schopenhauer fled Berlin to escape the cholera epidemic that was sweeping the city, a scourge to which Hegel among others fell victim. Schopenhauer lived in Mannheim for about a year, and then settled in Frankfurt am Main. Here he spent the remaining 28 years of his life, extending and refining his philosophy. During this time he notably wrote his 1839 Royal Norwegian Society of Sciences prize-winning essay, *Über die Freiheit des menschlichen Willens* [*On the Freedom of the Will*], and in 1840, *Über die Grundlage der Moral* [*On the Basis of Morality*]. The latter essay was submitted for a Royal Danish Society of Scientific Studies competition. In the event, Schopenhauer's paper did not win the Danish prize, even though it was the only submission entered. Schopenhauer devoted his energies during his last period to searching out confirmations and applications of the ideas he had formulated earlier in life. He published these as addenda to the second and third editions of *The World as Will and Representation* in 1844 and 1859, to the second edition of *The Fourfold Root* in 1847, and to the voluminous and absorbing, although largely unstructured, *Parerga und Paralipomena*, published in 1851.

Schopenhauer died peacefully in Frankfurt one year later in 1860, apparently as a result of pulmonary-respiratory failure, at the age of 72. It was only in the last several years of his life that he began to receive the recognition from the philosophical community that he had always sought, but of which toward the end he seems finally to have despaired.

Schopenhauer's life in many ways exemplifies his thought. To a great extent, he suppressed desire and individual willing in favour of scientific and philosophical knowledge and the appreciation of fine art. He developed his talents as polymath and devoted himself to many different kinds of in-depth study related to his distinction between the world as Will and representation. We can see the inner force of will and salty apprehension of the true state of the world etched on his face, particularly in his eyes, as depicted in portraiture. The 1815 oil painting of the youthful Schopenhauer by Ludwig Sigismund Ruhl (reproduced on the cover of this book) shows a handsome intelligent confident young man in a lacy white collar and greatcoat of the period. He appears the sort of early-nineteenth-century romantic figure who could have portrayed Goethe's tragic hero in *The Sorrows of Young Werther*, contemplating life as he loads his pistol and pours a final glass of wine, mourning a failed love affair. Schopenhauer himself suffered through several such tragedies of unrequited love, notably in 1807 and 1821. We then turn to admire Elisabet Ney's 1859 plaster study and marble bust of Schopenhauer as an older man, presented almost in the manner of the bust of a Roman senator, completed just one year before his death. Or, from roughly the same period, we might consider Angilbert Göbel's 1857–59 canvas "Portrait of the Philosopher Arthur Schopenhauer". The great curmudgeon is depicted sporting a bemused almost mischievous scowl, wisely seeing through the superficial vanity of the world, his face framed by massive muttonchop sideburns and an unruly shock of white hair surrounding his bald, expansive and sourly thoughtful forehead. We recognize the same frowning elder statesman of philosophy captured in sepia daguerreotypes from around 1852 to 1859, seated at a table and holding a watch, or standing with his hand tucked in his vest, now collected and displayed in the Schopenhauer Archives at the City and University Library in Frankfurt. It is tempting to see in this progression of portraits Schopenhauer's mounting disillusion with the world and its reluctance to accept or even give fair hearing to the main principles of his philosophy. It was a situation about which he first became increasingly embittered and eventually resigned.[8]

CHAPTER ONE

Schopenhauer's idealism

Accordingly, true philosophy must at all costs be *idealistic*; indeed, it must be so merely to be honest ... It is quite appropriate to the empirical standpoint of all the other sciences to assume the objective world as positively and actually existing; it is not appropriate to the standpoint of philosophy, which has to go back to what is primary and original. *Consciousness* alone is immediately given, hence the basis of philosophy is limited to the facts of consciousness; in other words, philosophy is essentially *idealistic*.   (WWR 2: 4–5)

A world in thought

To open the first pages of Schopenhauer's treatise *The World as Will and Representation* is to encounter an outrageous view of reality. We may easily be stunned into a sense of incredulity. Can Schopenhauer really be saying such things? Does he literally mean that the world of physical objects exists only in the mind?

Schopenhauer tells us in no uncertain terms that the world we experience in sensation exists entirely in thought, that everyone on reflection already knows this and that the world begins with the awakening to consciousness of each individual mind and ends with each thinking being's death. The implications of this radical commitment to the physical world's mind-dependence are as astonishing as they are intriguing. To understand Schopenhauer's metaphysics and epistemology with all their implications requires that we first try to make sense of his extreme idealism.

Introducing his philosophical system, Schopenhauer begins the book with the startling pronouncement:

> The world is my representation: this is a truth valid with reference to every living and knowing being, although man alone can bring it into reflective, abstract consciousness. If he really does so, philosophical discernment has dawned on him. It then becomes clear and certain to him that he does not know a sun and an earth, but only an eye that sees a sun, a hand that feels an earth; that the world around him is there only as representation, in other words, only in reference to another thing, namely that which represents, and this is himself. (WWR 1: 3)

With admirable if disconcerting aplomb, Schopenhauer calls attention to a proposition that he insists we all already know at some level. He claims that even non-rational animals and all living perceivers possess such knowledge, even if they are incapable of becoming aware of its truth or reasoning about it abstractly. He asserts that the world is *my* representation, a thesis he significantly puts in first-person formulation. What I am supposed to know without further proof is that the world is my representation, meaning that it is something that belongs to me and resides within my mind as a feature of my personal subjectivity.

Remarkably, Schopenhauer claims that the same knowledge is available to every thinking subject. How can this be? If the world is not only my personal representation, but is identical to each thinking subject's distinct representation, existing in each individual's thoughts, then it appears that the physical world cannot be one single and unitary thing. Instead, there must then be as many different distinct physical worlds as there are thinking subjects that represent the world, in each of whose thoughts the world is somewhat differently represented. Idealism is the thesis that the world consists of ideas, and thus exists within the mind as dependent on thought. Schopenhauer embraces idealism in this sense, while still insisting that the subjectivity implied by the world as representation is not philosophically objectionable. But how can it not be? The problem of multiplying the existence of as many worlds as there are perceivers is only one of the difficulties facing idealism. It is notably a problem, moreover, that does not arise for opposing theories of metaphysical realism. The standard view concerning the nature of reality (sometimes patronizingly designated "naive"), realism, is that there is a unitary external physical world consisting of diverse objects and states of affairs existing objectively outside the mind. In metaphysical realism, the world exists independently of thought as something about which different perceiving subjects can have different ideas that are represented subjectively in their thoughts in different ways. This Schopenhauer flatly denies. His commitment to idealism is unequivocal:

Therefore no truth is more certain, more independent of all others, and less in need of proof than this, namely that everything that exists for knowledge, and hence the whole of this world, is only object in relation to the subject, perception of the perceiver, in a word, representation. Naturally this holds good of the present as well as of the past and future, of what is remotest as well as of what is nearest; for it holds good of time and space themselves, in which alone all these distinctions arise. Everything that in any way belongs and can belong to the world is inevitably associated with this being-conditioned by the subject, and it exists only for the subject. The world is representation. (WWR 1: 3)

In the second edition, he says much the same. He qualifies the assertion that all thinkers recognize the truth of first-person idealism once they understand it, but remarks that not everyone immediately understands what it means to say that the world is their personal subjective representation. We, too, might not yet fully understand exactly what Schopenhauer means when he states:

"The world is my representation" is, like the axioms of Euclid, a proposition which everyone must recognize as true as soon as he understands it, although it is not a proposition that everyone understands as soon as he hears it. To have brought this proposition to consciousness and to have connected it with the problem of the relation of the ideal to the real, in other words, of the world in the head to the world outside the head, constitutes, together with the problem of moral freedom, the distinctive characteristic of the philosophy of the moderns. (WWR 2: 3)

It is unclear at first what could possibly entitle Schopenhauer to speak in the singular of "the" world or "this" world. If the world is representation and more particularly "my" representation, and if there are many representing subjects, then it would appear that there must be as many different worlds as there are perceivers. The fragmentation of the world into many distinct subjectively existing worlds is nevertheless at odds with common sense and Schopenhauer's own pronouncements.

The trouble is that Schopenhauer is no mad solipsist. He is not so deluded as to imagine that he is personally the only representing subject. If that were his position then his idealism would at worst be implausible, but not logically inconsistent. He affirms the existence of many living knowing thinkers, including but not limited to what are ordinarily taken to be the other minds of numerous other human beings. He holds that if each thinking subject could express thoughts in language, then each could equally say, and justifiably admit as a certain truth, that, in his first-person way of putting things, "The world is *my* representation". Since there appears at least superficially within our representations of the world to be more than one "I", more than one thinking subject, there is presumably more than one representation. How, then, if the world is identical to each subject's representation, can there be only one world?

We are consequently deep in philosophical difficultities before we have even completed the first paragraph of Schopenhauer's treatise. There are two main problems to be addressed in understanding Schopenhauer's idealism. Each concerns a different direction in time, backward to the past or forward to the future, and the existence of the world before or after the existence of a representing subject. We must try to make sense of Schopenhauer's contentions that the world as representation:

- begins to exist only when a first representing subject has a first representing experience, even though there is good reason to believe that there must have existed a past and prior physical world in order to produce and sustain the first representing subject
- ceases to exist when any individual representing subject dies or in another way becomes totally cognitively inactive, even though there is good reason to believe that in the normal course of things other representing subjects for whom the world as representation continues to exist survive the death of any individual representing subject.

We shall need to clarify several aspects of Schopenhauer's theory and its background in Kant's metaphysics before we can return to answer these problems.

We know that representing subjects are born at different times, that they become conscious at different times and that some die while others remain alive. Moreover, we believe that the world existed at a time before there were any conscious beings. Schopenhauer acknowledges that there were planets and stars and such non-thinking entities as rocks and trees before there were even the simplest thinking subjects. We can equally project a future time when all consciousness might be extinguished, in which no thinking world-representing subjects survive. In such a scenario, we naturally expect there still to exist a non-thinking world of planets and stars, rocks and trees, that by hypothesis are not represented by any existent thinking subject, but in which living things and representing subjects might later again eventually evolve.

Are these convictions simply mistaken? Is it Schopenhauer's mission to disabuse us of a comforting but ultimately incorrect naive realism? The answer is complex. Schopenhauer makes conciliatory concessions to our common-sense conception of the world as one and as existing in some sense before and after the birth and death of any individual perceiver. He likewise hopes to do justice to generally accepted beliefs about the historical emergence and possible future annihilation of all perceiving subjects. He considers no inconsistency to hold between these assumptions and the principles of radical idealism. He believes in spite of these intuitive truths that the physical world is mind-dependent representation, that it exists subjectively in each thinking subject's first-person thoughts, and that it originates and perishes respectively with each thinking subject's first and last moments of consciousness.[1]

Idealism and Kant's thing-in-itself

What appears to save Schopenhauer's idealism from outright logical inconsistency is his dual-aspect metaphysics. The world for Schopenhauer is not only representation, but Kantian thing-in-itself. The mind-independence of thing-in-itself makes it possible for Schopenhauer to argue that thing-in-itself, existing outside the mind, is a single unified world that is differently represented to different minds. The world itself as thing-in-itself is not fragmented into as many different worlds as there are representing subjects in a plurality of mind-dependent subjective realities. Thing-in-itself, according to Schopenhauer, is not subject to a principle of individuation or *principium individuationis*. The world as thing-in-itself cannot be differentiated into individual parts or moments existing in different minds as different thought sequences. It exists outside the mind as just one thing.

Schopenhauer accepts a version of Kant's distinction between the world as it is represented in thought, which he refers to as appearance (*Erscheinung*) or representation (*Vorstellung*), much as Kant speaks of *phenomena* (*Phänomene*), and as it exists independently of thought, which, like Kant, he speaks of as thing-in-itself or as it is in itself (*Ding an sich*). Schopenhauer argues that we cannot describe what the world is like as thing-in-itself outside all thinking, but only as it is represented to or within our thoughts. Whatever we may try to say about the world as we know it in experience will necessarily involve our thinking and hence our way of thinking about reality, thus bringing the world under the concepts and categories of mind. If we think that there must be something more to the world than the way in which it appears to particular minds, then we may consider the world as thing-in-itself. There is next to nothing we can say about thing-in-itself, according to Kant, except that it exists and transcends the world of sense appearance. This is the significance of Kant's referring to thing-in-itself as *noumenal*. By this he means that it is intelligible only to mind as something thinkable or conceivable, and is otherwise representationally unknowable. Schopenhauer avoids the terms "noumenon", "noumena", and "noumenal" in his own neo-Kantian metaphysics, although he retains Kant's other terminology by referring to mind-independent reality as thing-in-itself (WWR 1: 474–7). The importance of Schopenhauer's refusal to employ Kant's word "noumenon" and its cognates is that Schopenhauer, who regards Kant's distinction between phenomena and thing-in-itself as one of the most important discoveries ever to have been made in the history of philosophy, believes that he has achieved a groundbreaking advance over Kant's metaphysics by penetrating into the hidden nature of thing-in-itself as Will.

Unwavering in his challenges to other prevailing forms of idealism in the philosophy of Hegel, Fichte and Schelling, Schopenhauer is a thinker of an entirely different stamp. As unwilling as he is to be associated with the other representatives of the nineteenth century's greatest philosophical lights, Schopenhauer is nevertheless not only a post-Kantian but, in his own estimation, the only genuine post-Kantian. He believes that he is the only philosopher who has remained faithful to the true spirit of Kant's most valuable metaphysical discovery in the *Critique of Pure Reason*. He argues that he alone has properly understood Kant's essential distinction between the phenomenal world of appearance and thing-in-itself as the mind-independent world existing outside all representation. He further believes that, having better grasped Kant's fundamental metaphysical and epistemological division, separating the world within and outside the mind, he has further extended and improved upon Kant's principles. He offers insight into the true nature of thing-in-itself, which Kant despaired of explaining, but about which Kant, according to Schopenhauer, managed in unguarded moments to say a great deal more than he was logically entitled to say.

Unlike Kant, Schopenhauer does not consider thing-in-itself to be merely conceivable and otherwise absolutely inscrutable. He agrees that thing-in-itself is representationally unknowable, but he maintains that it is possible to uncover its nature in an unconventional way, by properly analysing the content of ordinary episodes of willing. He argues that the world in reality or as thing-in-itself is a blind urging or directionless, unmotivated and uncaused, subjectless and objectless desire, which he refers to as "Will". The world as thing-in-itself for Schopenhauer is in essential self-conflict. Thing-in-itself as Will is a kind of disembodied hidden force or energy, one that is not physical, measurable or describable, however, and that has no causal efficacy. The world as Will transcends the world of experience for Schopenhauer, and hence is not subject to explanation under the fourfold root of the principle of sufficient reason. We cannot even correctly say whether there is a distinct thing-in-itself in a plurality of things-in-themselves corresponding to each represented object. The reason is that the *principium individuationis* does not apply to thing-in-itself or world as Will, but only to aspects of the world as it is represented within thought in its phenomenal aspect. Despite these limitations, Schopenhauer holds that world as Will manifests itself to representing subjects in innumerable objectifications in the world of sense experience. Thing-in-itself expresses its character through its phenomenal objectifications , which we can come to know by learning to recognize the signs of its hidden inner nature.

If the world were only representation, then the existence of many different subjects would have the immediate paradoxical conclusion that there are as many worlds as there are representing subjects. The world in reality and in the only sense in which it could be discussed would then be purely subjective. The fact that thing-in-itself, unlike the world as representation, cannot be divided into multiple worlds existing only subjectively in each perceiving subject's thoughts, seems to be all that Schopenhauer needs to avoid the unwanted conclusion that there are as many different worlds as perceivers representing the world (WWR 1: 7–8).

Kant's refutation of idealism

By its very nature, Kant's *Ding an sich* is descriptively unknowable. In distinguishing the world as representation from thing-in-itself, Schopenhauer makes thing-in-itself representationally unknowable, as a matter of definition. Knowledge of the world is limited to the phenomena of appearance in the mind's conception.

For Kant, unlike Schopenhauer, there exists a physical reality as well as thing-in-itself outside of consciousness. We get a sense of the differences in Kant's and Schopenhauer's metaphysics, and of how radical Schopenhauer's idealism is, by comparing it with Kant's more moderate form. In the section of the *Critique of Pure Reason* on "The Refutation of Idealism", Kant distinguishes his critical idealism from George Berkeley's "dogmatic" idealism. The argument appears in the Transcendental Doctrine of Elements, as part of the Transcendental Logic, in the First Division on Transcendental Analytic. Kant does not propose to prove the existence of thing-in-itself, but only at this stage to establish that there must exist something in the physical world outside of consciousness. Although Schopenhauer accepts Kant's distinction between appearance and thing-in-itself, he rejects Kant's proof for the existence of thing-in-itself. Schopenhauer's division of the world as representation and the world as thing-in-itself is logically incompatible with

Kant's critical idealism in so far as Kant's refutation of (Berkeleyan) idealism is committed to the existence of a physical reality outside of thought. Kant's "refutation of idealism" provides a useful segue to Schopenhauer's objections to Kant's proof for the existence of thing-in-itself, calling attention to what Schopenhauer considers to be deep confusions in Kant's metaphysics.

Kant defends the following thesis: *"The mere, but empirically determined, consciousness of my own existence proves the existence of objects in space outside me"* (CPR: B275). The importance of proving the external existence of spatial objects in the overall plan of Kant's *Critique* is that it provides the basis for distinguishing critical idealism from problematic dogmatic or material idealism. By showing, if the argument is successful, that space and spatial entities exist outside of consciousness, Kant effectively refutes both types of material idealism. He thereby clears the way for the development of his own brand of critical idealism as distinct from Descartes's "material" idealism and Berkeley's "dogmatic" idealism. Kant's proof that real physical objects exist outside of consciousness is supposed to demonstrate the external existence of something permanent in perception, starting from the fact that a subject can be conscious of his existence as determined in time. He presents the following inference:

> I am conscious of my own existence as determined in time. All determination of time presupposes something *permanent* in perception. This permanent cannot, however, be something in me, since it is only through this permanent that my existence in time can itself be determined. Thus perception of this permanent is possible only through a *thing* outside me and not through the mere *representation* of a thing outside me; and consequently the determination of my existence in time is possible only through the existence of actual things which I perceive outside me. (CPR: B275–6)

Kant assumes that a subject experiences a stream of consciousness with all its contents as determined in time. He argues that the occurrence of consciousness could no more be determined in time by something within thought as a part of consciousness than we could determine our location along a river if we were to carry the distance-marking signposts along with us in the boat. The reference point for the occurrence of thought must accordingly be something other than thought – a thing outside of consciousness, external to thought – if moments of thought are themselves to be determined in time.

Schopenhauer agrees with Kant's main conclusions in the section on Transcendental Aesthetic in the *Critique*. He shares Kant's view that space and time are pure forms of intuition (perception), in that they cannot be derived from experience, but must be brought by the mind to experience in order for the world to be perceived as consisting of distinct spatiotemporally individuated objects. Kant asks what must be true transcendentally in order for the world to be experienced in this way. He maintains that space and time are either derived by the mind from experience or else the mind is pre-equipped with prior spatiotemporal concepts or categories. The mind cannot derive space and time from experience because, if the mind did not already possess and was not already able to apply these forms of perceived objects, it would be confronted with a formless chaos of sense impressions that in the absence of an innate concept of time could not even be characterized as changing colour or shape from moment to moment. Space and time, if Kant is right, are not acquired through or abstracted from experience, but presupposed by the possibility of experiencing the world as divided into distinct objects and events. If the mind were not already equipped with space and time, then it would never be able to experience the world in a sufficiently well-ordered way so as to be able empirically to acquire or extract spatio-temporal concepts from the content of sensation in what Kant refers to as the sensory manifold.

A physical entity outside of consciousness is not yet thing-in-itself, since it exists in space and time. According to Kant, space and time, as pure forms of perceptual intuition, belong to thought rather than to the world outside of thought. They are innate mind-dependent features of sense perception, even if they are not contained within the stream of conscious experiences. The existence of thing-in-itself is another matter. Kant hopes to prove that there must be thing-in-itself by means of another argument. Thing-in-itself in any case is not supposed to be a *physical* entity existing outside of thought; it is rather the presuppositional transcendental ground of all empirical phenomena, including all perceivable physical properties of the physical world.[2]

By arguing that there must exist something outside all consciousness in order for the events of consciousness to be determined in time, Kant adopts a tripartite metaphysics that contradicts Schopenhauer's dualistic concep-tion of the world as representation and thing-in-itself. If Kant is right, then there are three categories of existence-relevant factors superimposed on the distinction between noumena and phenomena and. There are, first of all, the phenomenal appearances of things experienced within consciousness that Schopenhauer calls representations; secondly, there are physical existences occurring outside of consciousness by which the events of consciousness are fixed in time, but which are still mind-dependent because they presuppose space and time as pure forms of intuition as well as other Kantian concepts and categories of the understanding; and finally, thirdly, there is thing-in-itself.

Schopenhauer's idealism as a result is more radical, more Berkeleyan, than Kant's critical idealism. For Schopenhauer, unlike Kant, does not countenance the existence of any occurrently unrepresented physical entity outside the occurrent consciousness of an individual thinking subject. Where Schopenhauer and Kant agree is that if there were no representing minds whatsoever, then there would be no space or time or anything existent except for thing-in-itself. Kant's refutation of Berkeleyan idealism assumes the existence of an individual consciousness that is self-aware in the sense of being conscious of its own events of consciousness taking place in time. From this basis, Kant proposes to prove the existence of something physical in space and time external to immediate ongoing conscious thought. The extra-conscious physical reality of which Kant speaks is nevertheless presumably an entity or event of which some thinker could in principle be conscious. The spatiotemporal, causal and other categorical properties of any such physical object would not be mind-independent, for Kant, as the Transcendental Aesthetic is intended to show. Schopenhauer's idealism opposes Kant's concession to common sense. His commitment to a more radical idealism locates all physical phenomena within the world of each individual representing thinker's consciousness. Schopenhauer thereby incurs the burden of reconciling idealism with the fact that there are many different consciously representing subjects, together with the view that the world precedes the birth and continues after the death of any individual representing subject.[3]

Schopenhauer's criticism of Kant's proof

We must now consider Kant's argument for the existence of thing-in-itself. Schopenhauer accepts a modified form of Kant's concept of an experience-transcending reality. Where he sharply disagrees is with Kant's efforts to provide the necessary proof, and with Kant's categorization of thing-in-itself as noumenal. In "Criticism of the Kantian Philosophy", the Appendix to the first volume of *The World as Will and Representation*, Schopenhauer outlines his dissatisfaction with many aspects of Kant's thought, including especially his reasoning concerning the metaphysics of thing-in-itself.

In the *Critique of Pure Reason* Kant maintains that since there are appearances, representations that are given to experience as the starting-point for philosophical reflections, there must be something that appears. Whatever it is that appears cannot itself be appearance, but can only be something outside appearance that constitutes the transcendental ground without which the existence of the appearances of objects in relation to subjects within thought would not be thinkable, and in that sense would not be logically possible.[4]

The Transcendental Aesthetic decrees that not all properties of appearances can belong to the appearances themselves. At least some properties of appearances belong to the thinking subject as forms of intuition and concepts and categories of the understanding. The refutation of Berkeleyan idealism in support of critical idealism is supposed to prove that not all of existence can possibly belong to any particular individual consciousness. There must then exist something beyond the appearances of things that is altogether outside the mind and its conscious thoughts. The transcendental ground of phenomena ostensibly discovered by Kant through this application of transcendental reasoning is supposed to be thing-in-itself. He argues that thing-in-itself is thinkable only in the most abstract terms, but is not descriptively knowable. In Schopenhauer's terminology, thing-in-itself is non-representable.

It is tempting to think of Kant's thing-in-itself as grammatically implied by the concept of appearance. If there is appearance, as there unquestionably is for thinking subjects such as ourselves, then presumably there must be something other than appearance that appears. Kant refers to that which manifests itself in appearances as thing-in-itself. The inference is not obviously sound, but raises the critical question of whether it is appropriate in the first place to speak of sense experiences as *appearances*. Why not assume with the naive realist that we subjectively perceive in different ways and from different perspectives all there is to the world of concrete existence? Perhaps what we encounter in any sensation is not an appearance of the world but more simply and directly the world. Here it must be said on Kant's behalf that he is on relatively firm ground by virtue of having argued that space, time, causation, quantity, quality, relation and modality cannot belong to appearances themselves, but must be pure forms of intuition or categories of the understanding.

The Transcendental Aesthetic and the Transcendental Analytic are supposed to break the hold of naive realism on the philosophical imagination. Kant's argument suggests that we cannot look to the content of perceptions alone as the source of all that is needed in order to explain fully the properties of perceptions and perceived objects. Kant, like other critics of unreflective empiricism, can also argue that we know there are appearances because we find even in ordinary perceptions sensory illusions of various sorts. Things appear differently at different times under different conditions to different subjects, so that their perceptually describable properties do not always concur. To consider only one familiar but suggestive example, a table top appears trapezoidal from a certain angle, while from another angle it appears rectangular. If we do not adopt this common mode of referring to the differing appearances of things, then we may have no alternative but to hold implausibly that the table top is in fact at the same time both trapezoidal and rectangular, at least to different perceivers. Admitting this much, however, already commits us to the existence of appearances in the form of the admission that the table appears differently to different perceivers from different angles or under different conditions. Otherwise we must implausibly conclude that from the standpoint of a single perceiver the table top changes its shape through no other cause than the perceiver's viewing it successively at different times from different angles, or that the table top is successively replaced by differently shaped surfaces as the perceiver changes viewing angles.

If it seems reasonable to believe that there are appearances of things then, Kant maintains, there must be something that appears. The two ideas of appearance and something that appears seem to go inseparably together. An appearance by definition cannot also be that of which it is an appearance; in Kant's language, it can only be the transcendental ground of appearance, which he denotes as thing-in-itself. Schopenhauer agrees with Kant that thing-in-itself must exist as distinct from the world as phenomena. In "Criticism of the Kantian Philosophy" (WWR 1: Appendix), Schopenhauer first indicates the extent to which his distinction between world as representation and thing-in-itself is indebted to Kant's transcendental metaphysics. He offers these heartfelt words of praise: *"Kant's greatest merit is the distinction of the phenomenon from the thing-in-itself*, based on the proof that between things and us there always stands the *intellect*, and that on this account they cannot be known according to what they may be in themselves" (WWR 1: 417). His reasons for rejecting Kant's argument for the existence of thing-in-itself help us to understand the differences between their respective forms of idealism. With the words "It is true that Kant did not arrive at the knowledge that the phenomenon is the world as representation and that the thing-in-itself is the will", Schopenhauer anticipates the criticism he is about to offer. "[Kant] did not deduce the thing-in-itself in the right way," he continues, "as I shall soon show, but by means of an inconsistency; and he had to pay the penalty for this in the frequent and irresistible attacks on this principal part of his teaching" (WWR 1: 421–2).

Schopenhauer's main objection to Kant's method of trying to prove the existence of thing-in-itself is that it is opposed to the principles of Kant's idealism. This is the "inconsistency" in Kant's proof of which Schopenhauer complains: "However, the way in which Kant introduces the *thing-in-itself* stands in undeniable contradiction to the fundamental, emphatic, and idealistic view so clearly expressed in the first edition of the *Critique of Pure Reason*" (WWR 1: 435). The contradiction in Kant's efforts to deduce the existence of thing-in-itself occurs in the second or B-edition of Kant's

Critique (B67–8). Schopenhauer now explicitly relates his objection to Kant's inconsistency in his proof of thing-in-itself to Kant's efforts to distance himself from Berkeley in the refutation of idealism. "Without doubt this is mainly why, in the second edition," Schopenhauer writes, "[Kant] suppressed the principal idealistic passage previously referred to, and declared himself directly opposed to Berkeley's idealism. By doing this, however, he only introduced inconsistencies into his work, without being able to remedy its main defect" (WWR 1: 435–6). The B-deduction of thing-in-itself in Kant's *Critique*, as Schopenhauer interprets it, is vastly inferior to the A-deduction, amounting to what Schopenhauer regards as a betrayal of a more philosophically respectable Berkeleyan idealism.

The fact is that Berkeley would surely have taken the greatest exception to both Kant's and Schopenhauer's concept of thing-in-itself. He would as much reject the possibility of a transcendental reality outside the mind as he did Locke's theory of primary qualities and the *je ne sais quois*, the "something I know not what", that Locke posits as an unthinking material substratum supporting the sensible qualities of things. He would say the same with respect to comparable ideas in Galileo or Robert Boyle.[5] Berkeley guarantees objectivity for his brand of idealism only by relying on the existence of God, who is supposed archetypally to perceive all sensible things at all times that finite human thinking subjects only ectypally, or finitely, perspectivally and discontinuously, perceive. Berkeley's effort to bring God into metaphysics is completely unacceptable to Kant. Kant's own religious convictions are ambiguous at best, but he would never have permitted Berkeley's appeal to the divine as a basis for philosophical explanation, just as he would never have accepted Berkeley's proposals to prove God's existence.[6] As an avowed atheist, Schopenhauer is more strenuously opposed to solving metaphysical problems by any Berkeleyan *deus ex machina*. We can accordingly characterize Berkeley's idealism in Schopenhauerian terms as an uncompromising commitment exclusively to what Schopenhauer describes as the world as representation, together with an additional category for finite minds and God as a divine infinite mind.

The nature of Kant's error, as Schopenhauer diagnoses the inconsistency in his proof of thing-in-itself, is its reliance on an *a priori* but at the same time subjective principle of causality. Schopenhauer finds it unacceptable to try to deduce the existence of something that by definition is supposed to exist entirely outside of thought from any *a priori*, and hence mind-dependent, category of the understanding. This, Schopenhauer believes, is confused. It is a contradiction that by itself does not invalidate the existence of thing-in-itself. It is only a question of arriving at a proper proof (WWR 1: 436).

Schopenhauer interprets Kant as trying to demonstrate the existence of thing-in-itself as the *cause* of appearance. Since causation is a category of the understanding in Kant's critical idealism, and one, moreover, that presupposes space and time as pure forms of intuition, it cannot constitute a proper basis for proving the existence of thing-in-itself standing entirely outside the mind independently of all subjectivity. We cannot consistently prove the existence of mind-independent thing-in-itself on the basis of anything that is irreducibly mind-dependent. Kant's proof of thing-in-itself is thus tainted in Schopenhauer's view. He begins instead with certain facts of consciousness and deduces thing-in-itself as something that is presupposed by and hence entirely independent of any act of consciousness. He rejects Kant's method of proving the existence of thing-in-itself when he sees that the argument trades on the mind's concept of causation, and thus on something mind-dependent. Kant's argument is incoherent from Schopenhauer's standpoint, because the existence of causal connections are themselves owing only to thought, and by Kant's idealist metaphysics they do not exist in the world outside the mind's concepts and categories.

Whether or not Schopenhauer accurately construes Kant's proof for the existence of thing-in-itself as assuming that there must exist a *causal* connection between phenenomal appearance and that which appears or of which it is the appearance, it is clear that his interpretation makes Kant's argument guilty of a serious defect. More importantly, if it is true that Kant bases his demonstration of thing-in-itself on the presupposition of a causal connection between perceptual appearances and that which appears, then Kant's concept of thing-in-itself and not just his attempt to prove its existence is woefully muddled. Thing-in-itself is supposed to be altogether removed from the concepts and categories of thought, so that thing-in-itself cannot coherently be supposed to cause anything whatsoever to occur. In particular, thing-in-itself cannot coherently be imagined causally to bring about the phenomenal appearances it objectifies. The problem in that case is deeper than even Schopenhauer describes. It is not only Kant's argument in support of the existence of thing-in-itself that is then flawed, but rather Kant's concept of thing-in-itself as transcendental reality that is still capable of causing perceivable appearances. The causal inefficacy of thing-in-itself makes its existence incapable of being proved as that which appears to mind. It cannot be the cause of perceptual appearances. Thing-in-itself is supposed to exist entirely beyond the spatiotemporal world as representation, transcending the only realm in which causation applies. The crucial point in Schopenhauer's criticism is the reminder that thing-in-itself cannot cause or be caused, change or bring about change, and that thing-in-itself is categorically incapable of causing anything to happen.[7]

Schopenhauer, with Kant, acknowledges a similar tripartite division of metaphysical categories entailed by Kant's theory. The two sets of categories imply a disparity between Schopenhauer's interpretation of Kant's doctrine of thing-in-itself, and the problem of relating Kant's refutation of Berkeleyan idealism to his effort at proving the existence of thing-in-itself. That a tripartite distinction of any sort seems to be required in Kant's philosophy where Schopenhauer accepts only a dualism of metaphysical aspects in the world as representation and thing-in-itself makes a Schopenhauerian criticism of Kant's critical idealism inevitable. The fact that there is a tripartite division in Kant where there should only be an aspect dualism is a clear sign for Schopenhauer that something has gone wrong in Kant's endeavour to prove the existence of thing-in-itself. He argues:

> In accordance with what has been said, the object of the categories with Kant is not exactly the thing-in-itself, but yet is very closely akin to it. It is the *object-in-itself*, an object requiring no subject, an individual thing, and yet not in time and space, because not perceptible; it is object of thinking, and yet not abstract concept. Accordingly, Kant makes a triple distinction: (1) the representation; (2) the object of the representation; (3) the thing-in-itself. The first is the concern of sensibility, which for him includes, simultaneously with sensation, also the pure forms of perception, namely space and time. The second is the concern of the understanding, that adds it in *thought* through its twelve categories. The third lies beyond all possibility of knowledge ... The distinction between the representation and the object of the representation is, however, unfounded.
>
> (WWR 1: 444)

It is obvious why Schopenhauer cannot abide any hint of a distinction between representation and its object. A representation for his radical idealism just is whatever object is represented, in the same way that the world as representation is indistinguishable from whatever objects are represented as among the contents of thought. Schopenhauer accordingly argues that Kant's proposal to abstract thing-in-itself from appearance amounts only and at most to a concept of object-in-itself.

There is not much difference in English or German between "object" and "thing". In many contexts the two words are used synonymously. In the context of Kant's or Schopenhauer's idealism, however, there is an important technical distinction. The concept of thing-in-itself or *Ding an sich* is that of mind-independent reality as it exists entirely outside of thought, with no relation to any thinking subject. The concept of an object-in-itself or *Gegenstand an sich*, a term that both Kant and Schopenhauer use only in highly restricted ways in a few special contexts, is not, as Schopenhauer observes, the same as thing-in-itself. The reason is that an object, even an object-in-itself, is defined only in relation to a thinking subject, and, unlike thing-in-itself, is always an object for a subject.[8] In the second volume of *The World as Will and Representation*, Schopenhauer makes this point unmistakably clear:

> It is also to be noted here that even Kant, at any rate so long as he remained consistent, cannot have thought of any *objects* among his things-in-themselves. For this follows already from the fact that he proved space as well as time to be a mere form of our intuition or perception, which in consequence does not belong to the things-in-themselves. What is not in space or in time cannot be *object*; therefore the being or existence of *things-in-themselves* can no longer be *objective*, but only of quite a different kind, namely a metaphysical being or existence. Consequently, there is already to be found in that Kantian principle also the proposition that the *objective* world exists only as *representation*. (WWR 2: 7)

Schopenhauer criticizes Kant's argument for the existence of thing-in-itself as producing nothing more than a proof of an object-in-itself. He characterizes the concept of an object-in-itself as "requiring no subject". The problem is that an object-in-itself would need to be an object for no particular thinking subject, while still remaining an object of thought and thinking. The idea of an object-in-itself ought, therefore, to be dismissed as a blatant inconsistency, an impossibility or contradiction in terms. The phrase might at best denote an abstraction from the concept of a subject perceiving an object in which the theorist tries as a thought experiment mentally to subtract away the idea of the subject from the idea of the object. Schopenhauer rightly remarks that object-in-itself does not constitute a genuine category as distinct from the represented object of a thinking subject. The object of representation as object-in-itself simply collapses into representation, because the idea of an object-in-itself is logically incoherent, and there is no difference generally between representation and object of representation.

Interpresuppositional subject and object

Schopenhauer rejects Kant's metaphysics of object-in-itself. He argues that the division between subject and object does not imply their possibly existing independently of one another. Subject and object are conceptually distinguishable only in abstraction, for Schopenhauer, and are otherwise ontically inseparable. As a result, we can also say that subject and object are interimplicative or interpresuppositional.

There can be no subject without an object, and no object without a subject; the one implies or presupposes the other. To be a subject is nothing more nor less than to represent an object in thought, whether perceptually, in memory or in some other way. Similarly, there can be no object as distinct from thing-in-itself without its being actively represented in a representing subject's thought. It is part of the concept of a subject that it represent an object, just as it is part of the concept of an object that it be represented by a subject. Another way of expressing the same conclusion is to say that a subject is always a subject of or in relation to an object, and that an object is always an object for or in relation to a subject. Representation, in turn, is always a relation between a subject and an object. The two relata needed for representation always go together in Schopenhauer's metaphysics, and are never found apart from one another; they form a single complex (WWR 1: 5).

The interpresuppositionality of subject and object provides the basis for Schopenhauer's objections to Kant's proof for the existence of thing-in-itself. It supports his critique of materialism and purely subjective idealism, and deepens our understanding of Schopenhauer's version of transcendental idealism. A single subject perceiving a single object is all that is minimally needed for the world as representation to exist. When a single subject perishes, therefore, Schopenhauer believes, the entire world of objects, the world as representation, must immediately disappear, in spite of the fact that in some sense we know, even if in thought we cannot represent the fact, that there continue to exist other actively representing subjects.

The fact that we can only represent the bodies and motions of other thinking subjects is part of what Schopenhauer means when he remarks that the subject does not reside in space and time, and is no part of the world as representation. Schopenhauer does not accept Descartes's distinction between material and spiritual substances. He regards any attempt at such a division as a violation of the interpresuppositionality of subject and object. He believes that it is impermissible to separate subject and object in metaphysics, as though the one could exist without the other, as mind–body Cartesian substance dualists have proposed. Schopenhauer is a materialist with respect to the metaphysics of mind and body. He identifies the phenomenal mind that is popularly regarded as the soul or personality of the thinking subject as nothing other than the brain. Additionally, he believes that there is a core of pure willing for each willing subject that is beyond the world as representation and hence outside the spatiotemporal world of objects. The pure willing subject for Schopenhauer lacks all personality, and has no memory or expectations. It is nothing like what we ordinarily think of as an individual soul, for it is outside the principles of individuation and sufficient reason. The pure willing subject is Will, which Schopenhauer identifies with thing-in-itself. All the particularity of individual psychology in

27

Schopenhauer's materialist philosophy of mind is reduced to and explainable in terms of the phenomenal properties of brain.

Kant's critical idealism, like Schopenhauer's, implies that if there were no thinking subjects, then there could be no world of spatiotemporal objects. Schopenhauer's transcendental idealism is more extreme than Kant's. It entails that if even a single representing subject dies or becomes incapable of representing, enters a coma or deep sleep, then the physical phenomenal world of objects must also immediately cease to exist.[9] Such an implication, to say the least, does not accord well with common sense. The inference appears inescapable to Schopenhauer because no individual representing subject can directly represent the representing states of any other representing subject. A representing subject, as a psychological entity, or its representing states, cannot be represented as such. At most, only the bodies and body movements of subjects can be perceived as external spatiotemporal phenomena. A subject's representational states pass into oblivion when the subject becomes permanently incapable of representing.

From the limited perspective of the individual thinking subject it is certainly true that if the soul does not survive death then the world disappears at the moment of death. Schopenhauer's point is that the only representing states of which we are directly aware are our own, so that when we become representationally incapacitated the only world as representation that we can possibly know must as suddenly disappear. The world as representation ceases to exist when the individual representing subject ceases to represent. Schopenhauer maintains that no one can reasonably deny this implication of idealism once it is understood, presumably because the proposition amounts to a tautology. At the same time Schopenhauer, paradoxically, recognizes that there exist other subjects for whom the world continues to be represented and in whose thoughts the world as representation exists even after any particular representing subject ceases to represent and the world as representation for that subject ceases to exist.

Schopenhauer does not suppose that there would be no world if there were no cognitive beings like ourselves. He maintains only that there would be no world as representation. If thinking subjects and all of the perceiving animal kingdom were to disappear from the universe, there would still be a world as thing-in-itself. It would presumably be the same world that we might otherwise like to say existed as thing-in-itself before the emergence and after the demise of consciousness. Without thinking subjects to represent the world, there can be no world as representation. There could then also be no objects, since subject–object interpresuppositionality implies that we cannot have one without the other. The imaginary elimination of representing subjects highlights another aspect of Schopenhauer's idealism. If there are no thinking subjects, then there can be no individuation of the world into objects separated by space and time. This is because the *principium individuationis* applies only to the world as representation. Space and time themselves Schopenhauer situates at what he calls the "boundary" (*Grenze*) between subject and object as Kantian pure forms of intuition. The physical dimensions of space and time, the objects into which the world as representation divides, and the *principium individuationis*, all fit together into one conceptual package in Schopenhauer's idealism. The reason is clear when we reflect that within the world as representation all objects are individuated one from another ultimately by virtue of their occupation of distinct spaces and times.[10]

Space and time for Schopenhauer are part of the mind-dependent empirical world cognitively represented in thought. Space and time do not limit or otherwise belong to thing-in-itself, which, existing outside the forms of perception and categories of mind, has no beginning or end. Thing-in-itself as such provides no foundation by which to clock or chronicle the passage in time of any event in the world as representation. This is why Schopenhauer must reject Kant's refutation of idealism as proving the existence of a physical reality outside any given first-person consciousness; nor, for the same reason, as we have seen in considering Schopenhauer's objection to Kant's argument for the existence of thing-in-itself, is thing-in-itself subject to any type of causation. It is neither actively nor passively involved in any causal relation, and can neither act nor be acted on by any other entity.

Schopenhauer on materialism and purely subjective idealism

In addition to distinguishing his transcendental idealism from Kant's critical idealism, Schopenhauer's thesis of the intersuppositionality of subject and object enables him to mount powerful criticisms against materialism and Fichte's purely subjective idealism. He thereby distinguishes his philosophy from a widely accepted kind of realism and an alternative type of idealism that he rejects, both of which theories contradict subject–object interpresuppositionality.

Materialism tries to advance a system of metaphysics based exclusively on the objects of representations, without considering the subject as anything other than just another object detached from all subjectivity. Fichte's purely subjective idealism, at the opposite extreme from materialism, proposes to reduce the material objects of experience to subjectivity detached from any object. Schopenhauer's diagnosis of the poverty of both materialism and purely subjective idealism eliminates these diametrically opposed theories, and leaves his own transcendental idealism standing as the only moderate alternative. If Schopenhauer is right about the interpresuppositionality of subject and object, then there is no subject without object and no object without subject. It then becomes a serious defect for any philosophy to try to latch onto just one part of interpresuppositional subject–object as the exclusive basis for an adequate metaphysics, as though the other half of the partnership did not also need to exist.[11]

Schopenhauer observes that his metaphysics does not fall into either of these opposed categories. He is a materialist with respect to the nature of the phenomenal thinking subject or soul, identifying thinker with brain, but not in his overall metaphysics. In the global metaphysical picture, he is partly materialist, equating matter with causation, and partly transcendentalist, with respect to that aspect of reality understood as Kantian thing-in-itself. He avoids both materialist and subjective idealist traps by beginning with neither object nor subject exclusively, but instead with representations as the primary data given to philosophy's reflections, interpresuppositionally involving both subjects and objects (WWR 1: 25). Materialism seizes upon the objects of representation and tries to make the representing subject just another material object among all the others it represents. Fichtean subjective idealism latches onto the opposite extreme, arguing that the subject is the only reality, and offering to reduce the existence of material physical objects to the mind's subjectivity.

Schopenhauer prefers his method of distinguishing subject and object within representations. He maintains that this is the only proper way of proceeding, one that sets his metaphysics apart "wholly and entirely from every philosophy ever attempted" (WWR 1: 25). "All previous systems started either from the object or from the subject," he declares, "and therefore sought to explain the one from the other, and this according to the principle of sufficient reason. We, on the other hand, deny the relation between object and subject to the dominion of this principle, and leave to it only the object" (WWR 1: 25–6). Schopenhauer sees misplaced emphasis on the object to the neglect of thinking subjects as the source of error in every purely materialist metaphysics:

The difficulties mentioned here only casually confront natural science in its own province. Regarded as philosophy, it would be materialism; but, as we have seen, it carries death in its heart even at its birth, because it passes over the subject and the forms of knowledge that are presupposed just as much with the forms of knowledge that are presupposed just as much with the crudest matter from which it would like to start, as with the organism at which it wants to arrive. For "No object without subject" is the principle that

30

renders all materialism for ever impossible. Suns and planets with no eye to see them and no understanding to know them can of course be spoken of in words, but for the representation these words are a *sideroxylon*, an iron-wood. (WWR 1: 29–30)

An iron-wood or *Eisenholz*, also referred to here in Greek transliteration as *sideroxylon*, is a common term for a concept that is internally inconsistent. It describes an impossible entity that is simultaneously uniformly made of both iron and wood. At the opposite pole, Schopenhauer finds equal grounds for objecting to pure subjectivism, because it ignores the complementary existence of represented objects presupposed by the existence of a subject as to any form of reductive materialism. "Opposed to the system we have discussed," Schopenhauer explains, "which starts from the object to make the subject result from it, is the system that starts from the subject and tries to produce the object therefrom" (WWR 1: 31).

Schopenhauer finds equal fault with pure materialism and Fichte's subjective idealism (WWR 1: 32–4). He believes that his transcendental idealism avoids both of these mistakes. It does not begin with either the subject or object, considered in themselves, but with representations, in which there are only inseparably represented objects for representing subjects. He congratulates himself on alone having rightly understood the interpresuppositionality of subject and object in the world as representation (WWR 1: 34). This, in Schopenhauer's estimation, is what is truly distinctive about his theory of transcendental idealism.

The importance of Schopenhauer's criticism of both pure materialism and Fichtean subjective idealism is not merely that it sets his own theory of transcendental idealism apart from its competitors. The interpresuppositionality of subject and object in Schopenhauer's metaphysics, and the objections to materialism and subjective idealism that it supports, drive his enquiry to look beyond representation for clues concerning the "inner nature of the world". We cannot expect thing-in-itself to be exclusively either matter or Fichtean subject, if subject and object presuppose one another and are distinct only in abstraction and otherwise ontically inseparable. It is through the failure of pure materialism and subjective idealism that Schopenhauer is driven to look behind representations in order to search for thing-in-itself as the underlying hidden reality transcending the subject's representation of objects. Thing-in-itself cannot be subject or object if representation is decomposable into both of these complementary components. It must rather be somehow altogether different from anything to be found within the world as representation. The difference between appearance and that which appears as objects appearing to a subject cannot be explained, therefore, by any reduction of subject to object or object to subject.[12]

World as representation for other subjects

We turn now to consider the second main problem in Schopenhauer's transcendental idealism. It is the challenge of accounting for the beginning and end of the world as representation with the birth or awakening to consciousness and death of the individual representing subject, and the idea that the world must have existed before and will continue to exist after the individual's birth and death.

What is paradoxical about Schopenhauer's idealism is that we are generally predisposed to imagine that the world we know in experience existed before we were born and will continue to exist for others even when we are dead. According to Schopenhauer, despite the common-sense acceptance of realism about the represented world, no such conception is logically coherent. The world as representation is represented in every case by an individual representing subject. Schopenhauer adopts a kind of epistemic methodological solipsism at just these interfaces between representing subject and objects represented in his metaphysics of death.

When a subject dies, the world as representation ceases to be represented by the only representing subject a representing subject can representationally know. If the world as representation ceases to be represented by the only subject whose existence the individual thinker can representationally know, then the world of represented objects presupposing the existence of a representing subject must immediately cease to exist. What continues to exist, no matter who lives or dies or whether or how or for how long they represent the world in thoughts, is the world as thing-in-itself. This is what is real, the transcendental ground, in Kantian terminology, of the empirical world. It is that which appears to consciousness only as representation, a panoply of constantly changing phenomena. When each representing subject dies, the world as representation ceases to exist. At most we can imagine in the abstract the world as thing-in-itself continuing to exist in the representational time and space of other surviving representing subjects. Significantly, however, we cannot adequately represent the world existing outside of our own representations.

Merely to think of the world as thing-in-itself being represented by other representing subjects does not make the proposition true or philosophically defensible. Schopenhauer leaves no doubt as to his thought in the matter, when he says that the world as representation is the world as experienced by the individual representing subject. It follows that when any individual thinking subject ceases to represent, the world as representation, consisting of objects for a subject, in the same instant and for the same reason, ceases to exist.

Schopenhauer speaks freely of his transcendental idealist metaphysics as one which "everyone knows" and "everyone agrees about". He dares to make idealism, the most controversial part of his philosophy, appear as something obvious, undeniable. It is supposed to be known indisputably even to philosophically untrained persons when they are being reflective and honest with themselves about the nature of the represented world and its dependence on their existence as representing subjects. What could be more obvious, Schopenhauer asks, than to see that the world as representation begins and ends with the awakening to consciousness and cognitive death of every individual representing subject? If we find the view implausible and extreme, he will argue that this is only because we have entangled ourselves unnecessarily in conceptual confusions. If we think things through correctly, we shall see that the world as representation begins with the opening act of our own personal consciousness, and ends when the curtain falls on all our representings at the moment of death.

What we can say about the phenomenal world is limited in just the way Schopenhauer describes. If we try to go beyond the world as representation by accepting the idea that the world as we know it in representation could exist before we have risen to consciousness or after we have died, then we must be confusing the world as representation, which presupposes the existence of the only subject we can know as subject, with the world as thing-in-itself that exists independently of all thinking subjects. If we keep these metaphysical categories straight, and consider the problem carefully and consistently, then, as Schopenhauer says, we should all agree without further hesitation in accepting the idealist thesis that the world is *my* representation. It is the world as representation, the world of perceptual experience, that we think of as the actual world of spatiotemporally individuated physical objects. Within that world, we each have knowledge only of the content of our own individual representations, and not, except inferentially, of the existence of any other representing subjects.

How, in that case, we may still want to ask, is it possible for more than one representing subject to participate together in action? Working cooperatively seems to presuppose that there is a shared world held in common by many persons. The world remains the same, or so we like to think, through overlapping lifetimes of births and deaths, with new people being born at different times while others die. How can the world as representation itself spring into being and cease to exist so many different times for so many different thinking representing subjects? How can the world come to be through a subject's representation, and then be extinguished in a single stroke when just one representing subject ceases to think? How can this happen over and over again with the birth and death of each individual representing subject? The answer can perhaps best be found in placing the right emphasis on the idea of *representation*. The world we know in experience as a series of representations begins and ends with the terminating beginning

33

and endpoints of each individual's conscious life. It is within that narrow compass that the only mental events that count as representations in considering these questions can possibly occur.

The world as representation exists only subjectively, idealistically, within the thoughts of each individual subject. Without a representing consciousness, there is no representing and hence no world as representation. This proposition is merely another way of expressing Schopenhauer's interpresuppositionality of subject and object. It is the same thesis by which he concludes that there can be no object without a subject for whom it constitutes an object, and similarly and reciprocally that there can be no subject in the absence of any represented objects for a subject to represent. If we agree that subject and object always go together, then we must learn to live with the idealist implications that the world of nature, the physical universe and all spatiotemporal reality, begins and ends with the birth and death of each representing subject.

When the first-person representing subject dies, when *I* die, Schopenhauer unequivocally maintains not merely that the world as representation no longer exists *for me*, whatever that might mean, but that it simply ceases to exist for once and for all. There is then no past, present or future time, and hence no possibility of the world as representation returning to existence on any later occasion. Moreover, strange as it may seem if we have not thought these things through as Schopenhauer has, the world as representation comes to exist as though out of nothing and vanishes completely with the birth and death of each thinking subject, over and over again, for as long as any subject *imagines* rather than *represents* the prenatal and postmortem existence of other representing subjects.[13]

Objectivity and the world as representation

The perceived world is objective, despite being *my* representation, because it is subject to the fourfold root of the principle of sufficient reason. Schopenhauer does homage to the common-sense view of the objectivity of the world while not backing away from the full implications of his radical idealism.

The law of causality applies to represented objects, which are experienced as independent of subjective volitional control. The objects we encounter in the world as representation and the lawlike succession of events in which the objects participate or by which they are governed are not subject to individual willing. I cannot stop a ball from rolling downhill simply by an act of will, or make it roll uphill by force of mind. Although the world as representation may exist only subjectively in my thoughts, I can know that it objectively obeys laws that are independent of my will. Schopenhauer accordingly identifies matter and physical reality with causality. He declares that: "the perceived world in space and time, proclaiming itself as nothing but causality, is perfectly real, and is absolutely what it appears to be; it appears wholly and without reserve as representation, hanging together according to the law of causality. This is its empirical reality" (WWR 1: 14–15).

Causality, on the other hand, exists only in and for the understanding of the representing subject. The world as representation is conditioned by space and time as pure forms of intuition, without which there can be no represented world. Schopenhauer defends the subjectively conditioned physical world against naive realism or "dogmatism". "Not for this reason only," he insists, "but also because in general no object without subject can be conceived without involving contradiction, we must absolutely deny to the dogmatist the reality of the external world, when he declares this to be its independence of the subject" (WWR 1: 15). Although the world of objects and the causal relations by which they are interconnected according to the principle of sufficient reason are part of the individual subject's world as representation, Schopenhauer argues that the world is not illusory, but has the only sort of reality of which it is capable, by virtue of conforming to lawlike regularities that are not of the subject's making. Thus, Schopenhauer holds that:

> The whole world of objects is and remains representation, and is for this reason wholly and for ever conditioned by the subject; in other words, it has transcendental ideality. But it is not on that account falsehood or illusion; it presents itself as what it is, as representation, and indeed as a series of representations, whose common bond is the principle of sufficient reason.   (WWR 1: 15).

The world as representation is in the appropriate sense objectively real, despite being conditioned by whatever is presupposed by the thinking subject's mode of representing.

As to the existence of objects in the world prior to the historical emergence of representing subjects, Schopenhauer makes an interesting concession to common sense. The reality of the world as representation subject to the lawlike regularities of the fourfold root implies that in a certain sense there existed objects before the existence at least of any thinking subjects such as ourselves. The reason is obvious when we consider that the objects and events we encounter have a history. If they are governed by causal regularities, then they must have been caused by events involving pre-existent entities that we as individual subjects have not necessarily experienced. Schopenhauer nevertheless remains steadfast in his commitment to the principles of his idealism. He offers the crucial qualification whereby the world as representation can be understood to exist prior to the first thought and to continue to exist after the last thought of any individual representing subject, even though the world of spatiotemporal physical objects is supposed to exist in and be conditioned by the requirements of each subject's representations. The solution to the problem of the causes and past history of the representing subject is now advanced:

> Thus animals existed before men, fishes before land animals, planets before fishes, and the inorganic before that which is organic; consequently the original mass had to go through a long series of changes before the first eye could be opened. And yet the existence of this whole world remains for ever dependent on that first eye that opened, were it even that of an insect. For such an eye necessarily brings about knowledge for which and in which alone the whole world is, and without which it is not even conceivable. The world is entirely representation, and as such requires the knowing subject as the supporter of its existence. That long course of time itself, filled with innumerable changes, through which matter rose from form to form, till finally there came into existence the first knowing animal, the whole of this time itself is alone thinkable in the identity of a consciousness. This world is the succession of the representations of this consciousness, the form of its knowing, and apart from this loses all meaning, and is nothing at all. Thus we see, on the one hand, the existence of the whole world necessarily dependent on the first knowing being, however imperfect it be; on the other hand, this first knowing animal just as necessarily [is] wholly dependent on a long chain of causes and effects which has preceded it, and in which it itself appears as a small link. (WWR 1: 30)

Schopenhauer steps away from the extreme position that the entire world as representation suddenly springs into existence when the first representing subject, even if it is only an insect, opens its eye upon the world. Indeed, we must wonder how there could be a world upon which an insect could open the first eye, how there could be an eye, and so on, if the world did not in some sense exist before the eye's opening.

Schopenhauer is not entirely clear about the way in which the prior existence of non-human animals and the inorganic world that supports the existence alike of human and non-human animals is supposed to be reconciled with the transcendental idealist thesis that the world is each representing subject's personal representation.[14] The idea can nevertheless be recovered from Schopenhauer's enigmatic pronouncement about the beginnings of the world before the opening of the first eye springing forth at that very moment from the consciousness of the first representing subject. Schopenhauer invokes a classic Greek myth to help explain the concept of the past history of the world opening up from the first moment of representational consciousness of each representing subject. He writes:

> Anyone who likes mythological interpretations may regard the birth of Chronos (Χρόνος), the youngest of the Titans, as the description of the moment here expressed, when time appears, although it is beginningless. As he castrates his father, the crude productions of heaven and earth cease, and the races of gods and men now occupy the scene. (WWR 1: 31).

The idea is comparable to the Big Bang theory in scientific cosmology. Past time, like the perceptual form of space and time itself, is created along with the complete prior history of the world at the boundary between subject and object in the exact moment when the individual representing subject opens the first eye. The world erupts into existence, according to Schopenhauer, obeying the law of causality as an objective reality under the principle of sufficient reason, in the very instant that an individual representing subject first represents the world. Included in this explosion of all of reality into consciousness is whatever might be required by the law of causality in order to be able to explain the existence of inorganic nature from which the first insect with its first eye emerges. There is a world that objectively exists before the creation of the first representing subject, and that will continue to exist as long as there exists any representing subject. The existence of the representational world of objects depends for its present, past and future, and for the objective causal and other explanatory laws by which it is governed, on the existence of each individual representing subject. All space and time, and whatever events of a historical past according to the law of causality are needed for the existence of biological entities sufficiently complex to be capable of representing the empirical world, are implied by the objectivity of events in the world as representation, by virtue of falling under the principle of sufficient reason.

Schopenhauer's transcendental idealism is in no way diminished by this admission. Like Kant, Schopenhauer distinguishes between what we can think about the world in the absence of overt contradiction within the contents of our thoughts, and what we can intelligibly represent as a possible state of affairs. Thus, it is only for us abstract thinking human beings that there exists a past and future. Non-human animals, as we ordinarily assume, exist only in the present, with no understanding of the fact that there is a history to the world or the possibility of its continuing beyond the moment of their deaths. For, as Schopenhauer also reasonably says, non-human animals have no idea of death or expectation of their own deaths (WWR 2: 5).

There is thus an answer, but not an obviously satisfactory answer, to the two problems we have posed for Schopenhauer's idealism. Schopenhauer recognizes that he must somehow account for the historical backdrop of the physical world without which we cannot make sense of the development of the material substances that over time produce the intelligent thinking subjects capable of representing the world and thereby bringing the world as representation into existence. Transcendental idealism embodies an interesting asymmetry. When we think about the past we recognize the necessary existence of something before our own empirical existences that contributes to the emergence in time of representing subjects such as ourselves. There must be something in the past that produces the first representing subject and enables it to open its first eye on the subject-conditioned world as representation. The past itself, moreover, like all moments of time, according to the Kantian Transcendental Aesthetic, is not and does not in any way qualify thing-in-itself, but belongs to the individual thinking subject as a pure form of intuition. Anticipating the demise of the last representing subject at the last moment of time at some point in the future, Schopenhauer draws a more startling conclusion. He argues in that case that the world of spatiotemporal physical objects decisively comes to an end, upon which there is no more world as representation, but only thing-in-itself.

This striking anomaly illustrates something important about Schopenhauer's idealism. The bursting forth of the world as representation from the first representing thought of the first representing subject requires a history. If the world as representation embodies causal laws, then there must at least be a past that is created along with the inception of all time and space through the agency of the individual representing subject's pure forms of intuition. The world before the opening of the first eye must exist in order for the eye to exist. This is true even if the events of the past leading to the evolution of representing subjects are only something we can imagine as necessitated by the objective law of causality. We imaginatively project the principle of sufficient reason backward from any moment within a representing subject's consciousness in order to recover the sense of past events causally responsible for the present. At the end of time, when there are no more representing subjects, there seems to be no comparable need to project into the future the continuance of any spatiotemporal physical entities or events. We do so only qualifiedly in thinking about the continuation of the world beyond our individual deaths when we suppose that there will still remain other representing subjects. We are free to imagine that the physical world will continue when there are no more subjects to represent. Yet there is no forward-looking necessity to any such occurrences under the law of causality to account for the existence of any facts concerning representing subjects who by hypothesis will no longer exist within *my* representation. What then exists is only thing-in-itself, transcending space and time, beyond individuation and explanation.

Is it enough for Schopenhauer to allow that a past and future before and after the first and last representing subject is thinkable but not representable? We certainly cannot explain the emergence of representing subjects by reasoning from a merely imagined past history of inorganic development. There are no physical objects, no space or time, no causation and none of the other applications of lawlike necessity predicated by the principle of sufficient reason in the absence of a real physical world. Nor is it clearly understandable how a first eye could open and thereby create the world as representation if before that event there are no spatiotemporal entities or events in time and space. As a thought experiment for Schopenhauer's idealism we might ask what would have happened to the pre-representational world if representing subjects had not evolved. We should quickly see that the question does not make sense. There are no objects or events, no progression of material reality in time, and, in a word, no happenings, in lieu of representing subjects.

Schopenhauer has the courage to embrace the assumption of transcendental idealism. He maintains that the world we experience can only be understood as what he refers to as the world as representation. It is the world whose objects and events and properties, space and time, individuation, causality and all forms of explanation, presuppose the existence of a representing subject. The implications of this idealist proposition for the subject-conditional existence of the empirical world make Schopenhauer's philosophy unique even when compared to the most daring conclusions of classical German idealism.[15]

Empirical knowledge of the world as representation: from natural science to transcendental metaphysics

We also find *physics*, in the widest sense of the word, concerned with the explanation of phenomena in the world; but it lies already in the nature of the explanations themselves that they cannot be sufficient. *Physics* is unable to stand on its own feet, but needs a *metaphysics* on which to support itself, whatever fine airs it may assume towards the latter.   (WWR 2: 172)

Scientific explanation

It is only after Schopenhauer has explained the basic principles of his transcendental idealism that he turns, first, to the question of empirical knowledge of the world as representation, and secondly to thing-in-itself in the transcendental metaphysics of the world as Will. This order of topics is appropriate to Schopenhauer's exposition, given his thesis that the only correct philosophical methodology is to begin, not with either the object, in the manner of pure materialists, nor with the subject, as in Fichte's purely subjective idealism, but with representations that are theoretically analysable into interpresuppositional ontically inseparable subject and object. Schopen-hauer is now prepared to begin a detailed investigation of the empirical world as representation, to be followed by an analysis of thing-in-itself as Will.

The world as representation for Schopenhauer is the realm where the *principium individuationis* and fourfold root of the principle of sufficient reason apply. It is also where epistemic criteria of empirical knowledge concerning the world of appearance that are falsely assumed by materialists and naive realists to constitute the only truths about the world find their proper place. A vital part of Schopenhauer's theory of knowledge is devoted to natural science, including physics, astronomy, biology, chemistry, psychology and other scientific disciplines. Schopenhauer regards all of natural science as providing a correct understanding of the empirical world. Natural science is as important to Schopenhauer's complete picture of the world as representation and the interpresuppositionality of subject and object as his transcendental metaphysics of the world as thing-in-itself (WWR 2: 120–29).

The fourfold root of the principle of sufficient reason

The essential background to Schopenhauer's philosophy of natural science is his theory of the fourfold root of the principle of sufficient reason. This is the topic of his doctoral dissertation, published as a separate treatise under this title in 1813. *The Fourfold Root* is probably Schopenhauer's most admired work by philosophers who otherwise have no sympathy for his transcendental idealism and metaphysics of thing-in-itself as Will.[1]

Schopenhauer assumes a familiarity with his earlier study in all his later work. Thus, in the "Preface to the First Edition" of *The World as Will and Representation*, he advises:

> that the introduction be read before the book itself, although this is not a part of the book, but appeared five years previously under the title *On the Fourfold Root of the Principle of Sufficient Reason: A Philosophical Essay*. Without an acquaintance with this introduction and propaedeutic, it is quite impossible to understand the present work properly, and the subject-matter of that essay is always presupposed here as if it were included in the book.   (WWR 1: xiv)

Although Schopenhauer expects the reader to be familiar with his earlier study, he does not say why. Perhaps it is because he believes that we can only comprehend the dual nature of the world as Will and representation by beginning with the world as representation. We have already found it expedient to make use of Schopenhauer's concept of the principle of sufficient reason and its division into four types of explanations in discussing his idealism and the distinction between the world as representation and thing-in-itself. As such we are unavoidably participating in the non-linear exposition of his system that he maintains must be followed. Methodologically, we begin with perceptual and scientific knowledge of the empirical world. It is the requirements for explaining natural phenomena in any possible category in turn that are critically examined in *The Fourfold Root*.

Placing undue emphasis on the objects that constitute the world as representation might seem to contradict Schopenhauer's claim that it is a mistake in metaphysics to focus exclusively on the subject or object. There is nevertheless a fine line of difference. For while Schopenhauer argues that metaphysics errs by beginning with any object to the exclusion of the subject, he maintains that philosophy should rather begin with representations and hence with representational knowledge analysable into interpresuppositional subject and object. The natural sciences are not an appropriate way to introduce the dual metaphysics of appearance and thing-in-itself, because they do as a matter of fact treat the empirical order in reductively material-ist or naive realist fashion as a realm of independently existing objects. We shall need to look more closely at what Schopenhauer says concerning the role of the fourfold root of the principle of sufficient reason in his system before we can fully grasp why he believes that his early treatment of these subjects is a necessary preliminary to understanding his idealist metaphys-ics of the world as Will and representation.

Four kinds of why-explanation

The first division of Schopenhauer's philosophy concerns the perceptual knowledge of objects in the world as representation. The second division concerns insight into the subject in the doctrine of thing-in-itself or world as Will. To begin, we consider Schopenhauer's theory of the empirical world represented to thought in perception and studied in the natural sciences. This is the experienceable world and everything that can be found therein as an object of representational knowledge. It is the world we encounter in sensation, consisting of objects individuated from other objects. These are the ways in which the world appears to thought that can be explained by appeal to laws and lawlike regularities in several categories. It is the world that, in lieu of accepting the existence of Kantian thing-in-itself, we may falsely think of as the only reality, in the manner of a metaphysical materi-alism or naive realism.

Schopenhauer does not dispute the importance of this empirical aspect of the world, or world as representation. He considers it to be the proper sphere of application for the natural sciences, and as such a valuable source of knowledge. With Kant, however, Schopenhauer denies that the phenomenal order is the only aspect of the world, whose other unseen face is mind-independent representationally unknowable thing-in-itself. Limiting atten-tion only to the world as representation, to the principles of individuation and sufficient reason, Schopenhauer is able to place the natural sciences in perspective. Within the confines of the world as representation, Schopenhauer believes that the principles of natural science hold absolute sway, that they explain all that can be representationally known about the natural world. There are four ways in which we can explain things, four kinds of facts about things that we can explain, in four modes of explanation. We can explain naturally occurring phenomena in the world as representation in terms of the laws of logic, mathematics, causation and motivation. What remains after everything that can be explained has been accounted for under one or more laws subsumed by the fourfold root is the hidden dimension of the world known to Kant only as thing-in-itself. In that part of his philosophy concerning only the world as representation, where every natural occurrence in principle admits of a sufficient explanation, Schopenhauer gives empirical science its due. We can expect to be able to explain everything that happens in the world of experience, up to the very limits of the world where representation ends, and beyond which there remains only thing-in-itself.

The principle of sufficient reason is thus the epistemic foundation of Schopenhauer's scientific philosophy of the world as representation (WWR 1: xiv; FFR: xxvi). Its importance is indicated by the fact that in 1847 he substantially revised it for republication in a second edition while preserving its central themes, when without his knowledge or approval the text had gone out of print for several years. There are frequent references to his dissertation throughout Schopenhauer's writings, implying that over the years his early reflections on epistemology never diminished in his opinion as the foundation for his philosophical system.

"Nothing is without a ground or reason why it is"[2] (FFR: 6) summarizes Schopenhauer's principle of sufficient reason. He classifies every aspect of the world as representation under four main categories. The concept of sufficient reason does not originate with Schopenhauer, but can be traced back under that terminology to at least the seventeenth century. Schopenhauer finds historical anticipations of the principle of sufficient reason in Plato and Aristotle, and traces its modern formulations in particular to Leibniz and Christian Wolff in the seventeenth and eighteenth centuries. Schopenhauer credits none of these thinkers with an adequate grasp of the principle, and accuses them with some justice of such elementary philosophical errors as confusing reasons with causes (FFR: 9–33). The doctrine in Schopenhauer's hands offers a vantage point from which it is possible to levy powerful criticisms against Spinoza's pantheological monism, as well as Descartes's proofs for the existence of God. He disputes especially Descartes's version of the so-called ontological argument, which had been thoroughly discredited in Schopenhauer's opinion by the refutation of Anselm's *Proslogion* in the section of Kant's *Critique* on "The Ideal of Pure Reason" (FFR: 14–16, 20, 59–62).[3]

The four roots, or four types of why-explanations of phenomena in the world as representation, are further elaborated by Schopenhauer in the following terms:

1. Causal laws that satisfy the sufficient reason of becoming.
2. Logical laws that satisfy the sufficient reason of knowing.
3. Mathematical laws that cover the sufficient reason of being, of space and time, conceived as pure forms of intuition after Kant's analysis of the Transcendental Aesthetic, as the basis, respectively, for geometry and arithmetic.
4. Moral laws that satisfy the sufficient reason of acting, concerning the empirical will or will to life and its motivations (FFR: 39–42).[4]

The categories roughly correspond to Aristotle's traditional "four causes", although there are important differences.[5] The four types of laws are supposed to cover exhaustively the ways in which objects and events in the world as representation can be explained. Each root of the principle of sufficient reason provides the basis for a distinct kind of science concerned with a distinct aspect of natural or social phenomena. Schopenhauer holds that explanations become confused or frustrated in their purpose when they are cross-directed towards another science's distinctive root of the principle, as when a moral or motivational science attempts to give mechanical- or efficient-causal explanations, or the reverse (FFR: 230–31).

The Fourfold Root demarcates everything that can be known and explained by reference to broadly scientific principles. There is a sense of completeness in Schopenhauer's list of four explanation types. It would be reassuring, but unfortunately Schopenhauer does not provide the required argument, to establish two essentially related claims: (i) That there are no fewer than these four categories of explanation – that none of the four types of explanation Schopenhauer mentions can be reduced to any of the others, but that all are independently necessary; and (ii), that there are no more than these four categories of explanation – that there are no other kinds of facts to be explained that do not fall under just these four categories of explanation, but that all four are jointly sufficient for all scientific explanatory needs concerning all phenomena.

With respect to requirement (i), we might wonder whether Schopenhauer can offer good reasons to show that mathematical explanations cannot be reduced to logical explanations. There is a school of philosophical logic and philosophy of mathematics in the late-nineteenth and early-twentieth centuries that took very seriously the idea that all of mathematics could be reduced to logic. *Logicism* is generally thought to have been refuted in its original optimistic or naive formulations, although these developments obviously postdate Schopenhauer's discussion of the principle of sufficient reason. There are nevertheless more sophisticated if in some ways less ambitious logicist programmes at work even today in the philosophy of mathematical logic. If any of these methods were to succeed, they might suggest the possibility of collapsing two of Schopenhauer's roots of the principle of sufficient reason into a single, perhaps appropriately designated *formal* root, combining logical and mathematical laws into a single category of logical-mathematical explanation.

Aristotle's famous four causes (*aitia*) makes an instructive comparison with Schopenhauer's like-numbered fourfold root of the principle of sufficient reason. In his treatise the *Physics*, Aristotle similarly distinguishes between what he designates as (i) formal, (ii) material, (iii) efficient and (iv) final causes. He illustrates the distinctions by the example of the explanations that might be given for the existence of a statue. To fully understand the statue, we must appeal to (i) the statue's form or shape and type, (ii) the material substance of which it is made, (iii) the physical motions by which it was produced from its raw material, including perhaps the striking blows of a hammer on a chisel with a certain force and at certain angles against the wood or stone and (iv) the reasons or purposes for which the statue was fashioned, which could include the desire to express artistic ideas, to honour the person or god depicted, or simply to earn a commission and gain renown (*Physics* 194b17–195a27).

Aristotle's four causes correspond roughly but imperfectly to Schopenhauer's fourfold root. Schopenhauer arrives at the same number of "causes" as Aristotle only because in effect he divides one of Aristotle's categories in two, and combines two of Aristotle's categories into one. He divides Aristotle's formal cause into logical and mathematical explanations rather than combining these into a single mode of explanation. He collapses Aristotle's material and efficient causes into a single category or mode of explanation, which he describes simply as causation. His justification for combining these categories of explanation is the theory that matter is nothing other than action in space and time, equated with the motion of substances described by Aristotle as efficient or mechanical causation.

We should ask whether Schopenhauer is justified in making either of these revisions, not out of reverence for Aristotle, but as a way of gaining a better understanding of why Schopenhauer divides up the field of scientific explanation for the world as representation just in the way he does. Where logical and mathematical explanations are concerned, Schopenhauer does not make reference to Aristotle or self-consciously deviate from Aristotle's four causes, but seems to be thinking things through for himself and arriving at his own set of explanation types. Although he might acknowledge that both logic and mathematics are in some sense formal, it is probable that even so, and even if he had been apprised of the logicist movement that gained momentum only later in the nineteenth century, Schopenhauer would still have wanted to distinguish between logical and mathematical explanations. The reason is that Schopenhauer interprets logical explanation as providing a basis for judgement in another judgement (FFR: 157–8). Such an account makes logical explanation a very general category, since the judgements in terms of which a judgement is explained might be of various kinds, including more specifically those that appeal to judgements about mechanical causal, mathematical, and moral or motivational factors. They are in any case not limited or essentially related to the mathematical.

The explanation of any given phenomenon need not fall only under one category of explanation in the fourfold root. Schopenhauer maintains, on the contrary, just as Aristotle does, that many if not most phenomena must be fully explained in terms of more than one of the four categories of explanation, and in some if not many cases by appealing to all four explanation types. Schopenhauer nonetheless requires that logical explanations as such, partly because of their greater generality, must be different from mathematical explanations. The latter make specific appeal to the propositions of arithmetic and geometry concerning the numerical and spatial properties of things. A logical explanation can but need not also be mathematical, which for Schopenhauer is enough to recognize these explanation types as distinct categories.

If we find it curious that Aristotle does not include a fifth category of logical causes, it might be because he regards logic as providing the form of explanation rather than a category of explanation on a par with formal, material, efficient and final causes. To the extent that such an approach seems to offer a more natural division of explanations, we may conclude that Schopenhauer's way of parsing the fourfold root of the principle of sufficient reason should be faulted as containing too many categories, and perhaps as confusing the concept of (logical) explanation generally with one of the several particular types or categories of explanation available to science for phenomena in the world as representation.

With respect to requirement (ii), whether Schopenhauer's four-part division of explanation types includes enough categories to cover all phenomena, we might again return to Aristotle by asking if Schopenhauer is right to collapse material and efficient or mechanical explanation into a single root. The justification for this from Schopenhauer's standpoint is that he regards matter as nothing other than (efficient) causality. If Schopenhauer's reduction of matter to causality is not defensible, then he does not seem to make adequate provision for all the kinds of explanation needed to account for every occurrence in the world as representation. Even if Schopenhauer's theory of matter as causality is accepted, it might still be objected that the fourfold root is not sufficiently fine-grained to recognize the difference between matter as objectified causality and the mechanical or efficient causal interactions by which complex material entities are created, modified or destroyed.

Returning to Aristotle's statue, we might say that Schopenhauer should recognize a difference in principle between explanations that focus on the material properties of substances in addition to the physical forces and mechanical actions through which material substances are physically modified. We may then find it worthwhile to distinguish between an explanation to be given of the existence of the statue as consisting of marble rather than mercury or granite, and explanations of how it comes to have the particular geometrical form it has as the effect of the mechanical processes to which its matter is subjected by the sculptor. We may prefer this choice of explanation categories, even if theoretically the metaphysics of matter, as Schopenhauer believes, turns out to be fully explainable in terms of efficient causation.

Schopenhauer argues that anything in the world as representation, anything that presents itself to thought, can in principle be understood. There always exists a sufficient reason, which, with enough patience, good luck and the right methodology, we should be able to find. Equally, Schopenhauer claims that whatever can be explained by laws falling under the fourfold root can only belong to the world as representation. The application of the principle thus turns out to be precisely coextensive with the limits of the phenomenal world. Schopenhauer exploits this fact to establish a sharp theoretical distinction between the world as representation and thing-in-itself. Whatever can be explained by the four types of laws belongs to the world as representation, and whatever cannot be explained in any of these ways is thing-in-itself. The fourfold root as such is important not only to Schopenhauer's epistemology, but more crucially as a criterion for the most fundamental distinction of his metaphysics.[6]

The principle of sufficient reason carves a sharp delimitation between empirical and transcendental reality. This implication rightly entitles the fourfold root to the place of theoretical prominence Schopenhauer accords it. To see the world as divided into representation and thing-in-itself, we need precisely this sort of basis for distinguishing its two fundamental aspects provided by Schopenhauer's application of the doctrine of sufficient reason. When we have explained everything it is possible to explain, or at least abstractly marked out those objects and events that might be explained as falling under the principle of sufficient reason, then what remains left over as unexplained and unexplainable is Kantian–Schopenhauerian thing-in-itself.

47

Intuitive versus abstract knowledge

Schopenhauer's epistemology distinguishes intuitive and abstract knowledge. Intuitive knowledge is perceptual, and vision has an especially important role. We read in Schopenhauer's 1816 essay *On Vision and Colors*, "All intuitive perception is intellectual, for without the *understanding* [*Verstand*] we could never achieve intuitive perception, observation [*Wahrnehmung*], the apprehension of *objects*" (VC: 10).

Although Schopenhauer regards the capacity for abstract knowledge as distinctive of humanity, he regards intuitive knowledge as in every way superior to abstract theoretical knowledge. He argues, indeed, that all theoretical knowledge is at bottom only abstracted from perception, in terms of which a theory of any type must ultimately be validated, and without which theoretical knowledge lacks a legitimating foundation. A bright person, according to Schopenhauer, is one who can directly perceive that things go together or that causality is at work in a certain way. The fool is someone who either cannot grasp such interconnections, or is capable only of doing so in practical circumstances at a greatly reduced speed, by pedantic inference from theory. Such a person is lacking a full comprehension of the situation when compared with the more perceptive among us, whom Schopenhauer describes as more intelligent.

The distinction between intuitive and abstract knowledge is important to Schopenhauer for a number of reasons. First, their hierarchical relationship, in which abstract knowledge is dependent on intuitive knowledge, leads Schopenhauer to describe human understanding as a continuation, extension and perfection of the sort of intuitive grasp of facts and situations that are found even among members of the non-human animal kingdom. We discover a natural progression from the awareness of the world as representation found among animals and the development from it through greater intellectual powers of abstraction. The fact that Schopenhauer requires philosophy to begin with perceptual experience, and hence with the world as representation, is a reflection of his commitment to the priority of intuitive over abstract knowledge, as it constitutes the basis for a hierarchy of epistemic categories in his philosophy. The superiority of intuitive to abstract knowledge also turns out to be essential to Schopenhauer's central argument for the proposition that thing-in-itself is Will. This vital conclusion cannot be supported as an item of abstract knowledge for Schopenhauer, but only as something we can know immediately in a certain way, through feeling, rather than as a logically inferred consequence of abstract theory.

Where logic and mathematics are concerned, Schopenhauer holds that it is only intuition or sense perception that leads to knowledge, through which all axioms and deductions of theorems are ultimately justified. He maintains that the rules of a logical system are not needed for correct reasoning. He argues that formal principles can actually obstruct logical inference in practice. They are accepted only in so far as they agree with intuition, and they would be rejected or modified if or to whatever extent they turn out to disagree with intuition, rather than the other way around. He thinks of abstract knowledge as at best a convenience for the codification, expression and communication of whatever knowledge is properly gained and justified intuitively through perception (FFR: 197–206).[7]

Schopenhauer argues that "The main difference among all our representations is that between the intuitive and the abstract" (WWR 1: 6). He explains the distinction in the face of the prevailing assumption that all knowledge is abstract or theoretical, a position he is concerned to overturn. He accordingly classifies all knowledge as representation, but singles out abstract knowledge as just one subcategory among the two basic kinds of representations available to thought. He does not limit knowledge, or even abstract knowledge, in principle, to human beings, but cautiously observes that among the beings with whom we have acquaintance, only human knowers are capable of abstract knowledge. "The latter constitutes only one class of representations, namely concepts; and on earth these are the property of man alone" (WWR 1: 6). He associates reason with abstract knowledge, limited again among representing subjects in our experience to the human species. Finally, he indicates his intention to begin by investigating the nature of intuitive representations, which he interprets primarily in terms of vision, while recognizing the need to extend reference to any sort of perception.

Given his emphasis on intuition over abstract theoretical knowledge, it is natural that Schopenhauer should proceed in this order. He offers evidence from many different kinds of considerations, including signs and ways of thinking and speaking about intelligence. He interprets the manner in which persons including theorists at the highest reaches of abstraction react to the occasional conflicts that arise between intuitive and abstract representations as a clue to the priority of intuition over abstract theoretical knowledge (WWR 1: 22). Adding more substance to his account of the concept of intelligence, he explains intuitive representation more fully as the perception of causal regularities. He identifies the perception of causal interconnectedness as the essence of intelligence in these terms. It is through the perceptual grasp rather than theoretical understanting of causality that intelligence is able to design and build machines to accomplish certain tasks. It is the same quality of intelligence in the form of the intuitive understanding of causal connections by which Schopenhauer believes persons appropriately so gifted are able to motivate and manipulate other persons to obtain their cooperation in the pursuit of their aims, and to avoid actions taken against themselves by anticipating what is being planned and how another's intentions might be used to their disadvantage.

There is agreement at least with ordinary ways of speaking in what Schopenhauer says. We generally regard persons as stupid, however uncivil it may be to say so in the wrong circumstances or to the wrong audience, when they are unable to perceive or otherwise immediately grasp causal connections in the situations they confront. The point is not to understand stupidity, but to reveal its opposite qualities as the essential elements of intelligence. We say of persons who are particularly slow on the uptake that they do not recognize that others may have disguised reasons for acting as they do. Such innocents are easily taken in by schemes and plots in which agents are acting in concert against their interests. Schopenhauer regards these characterizations as further evidence of his thesis that intuitive knowledge is the indispensable basis and ultimate justification for secondarily useful abstract theoretical knowledge. Even if it is not the only criterion for stupidity, it is undoubtedly true that persons who lack a basic grasp of causal interconnections either in general or in cases where we would expect most individuals to be able to see cause and effect are typically regarded as possessing less than average intelligence.[8]

Intuition and abstract reasoning in logic and mathematics

Schopenhauer's reference to the understanding (*Verstand*) and its opposition to reason (*Vernunft*) is significant in his theory of knowledge as representation. Understanding is the fruit of intuitive representation or perceptual grasp of states of affairs among the world's appearances, and does not require logical inference or appeal to abstract principles. This is why Schopenhauer says that "Reason can always only *know*; perception remains free from its influence, and belongs to the understanding alone" (WWR 1: 25).

Logic and mathematics provide an important application of Schopenhauer's distinction between intuitive and abstract knowledge. It is a classical assumption of rationalist philosophers that in justifying knowledge, reason and logical inference ought to have precedence over empirical observations. Schopenhauer challenges this concept, as does Kant, on whom Schopenhauer partly relies. Logic and mathematics as formal disciplines are often taken as paradigms of reason in its most abstract, purest form. The truths of logic and mathematics are supposed to be impeccably certain, setting a high benchmark for exactitude and certainty in all areas of knowledge. As such, logic and mathematics are often thought to belong to a very different category than the deliverances of empirical perceptions. The objection is that sensation in comparison can be vague, unreliable, subject to illusion, contingent rather than necessary, and at best less certain than the tautologies and deductively valid inferences of logic and the theorems of mathematics.

Schopenhauer, contrary to rationalist preference for pure reasoning in the formal sciences, is committed to the priority of intuitive over abstract representation, of perceptual over theoretical knowledge, and of the understanding over reason. Accordingly, he relegates logic and mathematics to subjects of secondary importance. He interprets them as products of rational theory whose principles can only be discovered and justified by intuitive representation, whose rules are subject to revision or rejection to whatever extent they come into conflict with perception and intuitive knowledge gained by sense perception. He draws a number of instructive comparisons between logic and philosophy and other supposedly foundational sub-disciplines with respect to their theoretical superstructures. He argues that logic, mathematics and abstract theory generally can never be of practical use, but are at most convenient ways of codifying and communicating the relevant principles of knowledge.

The fact, if true, that logic in and of itself has no practical worth reinforces Schopenhauer's position that reason takes a second seat to perception. Intuitive representation in that case has epistemic as well as anthropological priority over all types of abstract representation and theoretical knowledge. If these assertions hold good for logic and mathematics, how much more should they not also do so for any other branch of abstract enquiry? Schopenhauer begins by asking about the utility of logical rules. He argues that the rules of logical inference are of no use whatsoever in reasoning, because no one, including professional logicians, actually consults them in drawing logical inferences. Logicians and mathematicians are prepared in principle to reject whatever rules are currently in place if they contradict what intuitive representation in a particular case reveals as a correct or incorrect deduction. The rules are expendable in light of recalcitrant intuitive knowledge, in terms of which the only principles that might be offered are justified in the first instance as abstractions from particular episodes of reasoning that the subject recognizes as intuitively correct without recourse to theory.

Appealing to the distinction between theory and practice, Schopenhauer concludes that the rules of logic can at most have theoretical importance, and cannot possibly have any practical use. "[I]t is not necessary to load the memory with these rules", he writes, "for logic can never be of practical use, but only of theoretical interest for philosophy" (WWR 1: 44–5). He compares the role of logic in philosophy to that of other supposed theoretical foundations to practical activities. He makes the same point with respect to the irrelevance of abstract harmony and music theory for the appreciation of music, for theoretical ethics in moral conduct, and theoretical aesthetics in the production of artworks. "For although it might be said that logic is related to rational thinking as thorough-bass is to music," he continues:

> and also as ethics is to virtue, if we take it less precisely, or as aesthetics is to art, it must be borne in mind that no one ever became an artist by studying aesthetics, that a noble character was never formed by a study of ethics, that men composed correctly and beautifully long before Rameau, and that we do not need to be masters of thorough-bass in order to detect discords.   (WWR 1: 45)

He concludes that whereas theoretical knowledge in each of these areas can be useful in communicating the results of intuitive knowledge, it plays no part whatsoever in the successful practice of music, ethics, art or, finally, logic.

It is hard to dispute Schopenhauer's argument at least with respect to these analogies. Surely he is right to say that music was competently composed long before anyone sat down to formulate the rules for correct composition. It might even be said that to the extent that composers follow such rules mechanically rather than pursuing their own artistic sensibility they are more likely to produce only wooden and musically less interesting work. The same is true of the relation between ethics and virtue, aesthetics and the plastic arts. One does not become a virtuous person simply by learning a code of moral rules, nor a great artist simply by memorizing and then trying to practise what purport to be rules for making great art. Whether or not Schopenhauer is right about logic also fitting this pattern may be open to dispute. He argues that logic is even less useful to philosophy and as a system of rules of reasoning than moral or aesthetic rules:

> Aesthetics and ethics also, though in a much less degree, may have some use in practice, though a mainly negative one, and hence they too cannot be denied all practical value; but of logic not even this much can be conceded. It is merely knowing in the abstract what everyone knows in the concrete. Therefore we no more need to call in the aid of logical rules in order to construct a correct argument, than to do so to guard against agreeing with a false one. Even the most learned logician lays these rules altogether aside in his actual thinking.   (WWR 1: 45)

The difference between rules for ethics and art and logical rules is that the abstract knowledge codified as principles in these respective disciplines is more immediate than the practical activities themselves. Where moral and aesthetic rules are concerned, there is a definite substantive content that remains directly associated with, even when it is abstracted for theoretical purposes from, the respective practice. Logical rules, in contrast, are as far removed as possible from the practice of reasoning, because logical rules, due to their purely formal nature, are of necessity abstracted from any specific content.

Whereas in sciences other than logic the truth of a particular case is always tested by the rule, in logic the rule must always and can only be tested by the particular case. Schopenhauer remarks that: "Even the most practised logician, if he notices that in a particular case he concludes otherwise than as stated by the rule, will always look for a mistake in the rule rather than in the conclusion he actually draws" (WWR 1: 46). As a result, he maintains that to try to make practical use of logic would be comparable to people reading a book on mechanics in order to move the parts of their bodies, or studying physiology in order to induce their digestive systems to function. If Schopenhauer is correct, then not only are logical rules not needed in order to reason properly, but they can be a definite encumbrance to reasoning. This proposition, if true, casts even greater doubt on the utility of generalizing purely formal rules from the competent exercise of reason as an abstract system of theoretical principles.

The value of logic as a formal discipline, negligible or even detrimental to the practical conduct of reasoning, is nevertheless interpreted as having theoretical importance to philosophy in understanding the nature of reason. Logic in this sense provides an abstract theory of what inferential thinking is and how it works. We do not need the rules of logic in order to reason correctly, any more than we need music theory rules to whistle a tune. We can nevertheless better theoretically understand what music is from the principles of music theory, and, Schopenhauer maintains, we can similarly better understand the nature of reasoning at a theoretical level by arriving at a correct set of logical rules (WWR 1: 46).

Pursuing this motif of the relative priority of perception and intuitive representation as opposed to theory and abstract representation, Schopenhauer maintains that the conclusions of mathematics are equally perceptual in origin and ultimate justification. Mathematics in Schopenhauer's day, through the nineteenth and early twentieth centuries, was divided into classical arithmetic and geometry, including algebra and calculus. Kant's proto-intuitionistic philosophy of mathematics relates mathematical concepts intuitively to sense perception, and in particular to the pure forms of intuition of space and time. Arithmetic is associated by Kant with the experience of sequential order in time, as when we count off a series of numbers successively one after another. Geometry is associated in an even more obvious way with perceptions of space and of objects in spatial relations, including the shapes and volumes of things and distances from one place to another in space.

Schopenhauer insists that some thinkers can only believe mathematical theorems when their conclusions are verified by intuition. It is only when the implications of a mathematical proof agree with what we can see and feel or otherwise experience in sensation that we can confirm that the mathematical deduction is correct (WWR 1: 55). Schopenhauer does not insist that intuition is the only mode of mathematical understanding, but he acknowledges that some thinkers are more inclined to regard abstract mathematical demonstrations as convincing. He admits that such persons look to mathematical inferences not as the ultimate source of mathematical truth, which would be to confuse reason with understanding, but, as with all abstract theory, merely for purposes of codification, communication and application. There are different intellectual personality types, according to Schopenhauer, for which reactions to mathematical demonstration is a litmus test as to whether they are more intuitively or more theoretically oriented. In neither case does Schopenhauer consider that there is a legitimate role for mathematical demonstrations by which they are required for the discovery or verification of mathematical truths.[9]

Schopenhauer regards proofs in logic and mathematics as powerless in and of themselves to establish new results. He reduces all proof to Aristotelian syllogistic form, and he regards all syllogisms as a mode of presenting the conclusions in a chain of reasoning that receives its final validation only from the direct evidence of intuitive representation. A logical or mathematical truth, once discovered and established by pre-theoretical non-abstract reasoning, can always afterwards be expressed theoretically in the abstract deductive form of a syllogism. The syllogistic proof of an intuitively justified mathematical discovery then provides a compact unit for the sake of recalling, sharing and applying the information it contains (WWR 1: 65). The implication of Schopenhauer's treatment of logical and mathematical inferences, and of the role of intuitive representation in the most abstract sciences, is that even where knowledge seems to be furthest removed from perception, it is still direct intuitive representation rather than abstract theoretical representation that is decisive in determining truth. The moral is that mathematics as a systematic formal discipline by itself has no practical utility, and that it is the immediate intuitive grasp of mathematical relations, rather than abstract rules of mathematics, on which mathematical judgement is properly grounded (WWR 1: 68–9).

As a final observation about the distinctive nature of mathematics, Schopenhauer reminds us that mathematical truths are *a priori* (WWR 1: 76). How can this be true if the ultimate justification for mathematics is intuitive representation? We are supposed to satisfy ourselves about the truth of basic mathematical theorems visually, as when we compare a Euclidean theorem with the confirmation we obtain by examining a corresponding diagram. It is when we see that what the theorem states agrees with the appropriate picture of concrete spatial geometrical relations that we recognize its truth. If the picture or other intuitive representational evidence did not offer positive testimony in support of a mathematical proposition, then Schopenhauer holds we would not reject the intuition, but should instead begin seriously to question the theorem.

We should recall that for Schopenhauer not all intuitive representations concern logically contingent *a posteriori* empirical relations. There can be intuitive representations for any of the four categories of explanation falling under the fourfold root of the principle of sufficient reason. Thus, we can as easily have intuitive representations of logical and mathematical laws as of causal and moral or motivational laws. What makes Schopenhauer an empiricist in epistemology, at least in so far as it concerns the world as representation, is the fact that he does not elevate the knowledge-conferring status of pure reason above intuition, but insists in every case that intuitive representations take precedence over abstract representations. Where the *a priori* rather than *a posteriori* character of mathematical laws is concerned, Schopenhauer avails himself of Kant's proto-intuitionist philosophy of mathematics, in which space and time as *a priori* pure forms of intuition provide a perceptual basis for the necessary truths of geometry and arithmetic.

Principium individuationis, physics and idealist metaphysics of space and time

There is an exact coincidence in Schopenhauer's idealism between the perceived world, the field of explanation in which the fourfold root of the principle of sufficient reason applies, and phenomenal objects and events in the world as representation, distinguished from one another in space and time by the *principium individuationis*.

Schopenhauer considers the world of discrete physical objects as an objectification of thing-in-itself. The world as representation contains many individuals, represented objects for representing subjects, that are separated by space and time. It is only there and in this way that we come to know them under the principle of sufficient reason. Schopenhauer maintains that "In outer as well as in inner teleology of nature, what we must think of as means and end is everywhere only *the phenomenon of the unity of the one will so far in agreement with itself*, which has broken up into space and time for our mode of cognition" (WWR 1: 161). Thing-in-itself is not literally broken up into the individuated entities experienced in perception, but is objectified in the world as representation for perceiving subjects as a multiplicity of individuated objects. The *principium individuationis* consequently holds only within intuitive representation for representing subjects as experiencing a spatiotemporal division of represented objects.

The division of the world as repesentation into a plurality of different things is accomplished by the subject's perceptual forms of space and time. This is the effect of the *principium individuationis*, through whose *a priori* spatiotemporal distinctions represented objects are distinguished one from another as occurring at different times or different places in space. Schopenhauer explains:

> We know that *plurality* in general is necessarily conditioned by time and space, and only in these is conceivable, and in this respect we call them the *principium individuationis*. But we have recognized time and space as forms of the principle of sufficient reason, and in this principle all our knowledge *a priori* is expressed. As explained above, however, this *a priori* knowledge, as such, applies only to the knowableness of things, not to the things themselves, i.e., it is only our form of knowledge, not a property of the thing-in-itself. The thing-in-itself, as such, is free from all forms of knowledge, even the most universal, namely that of being object for the subject; in other words, it is something entirely different from the representation. Now if this thing-in-itself, as I believe I have sufficiently proved and made clear, is the *will*, then, considered as such and apart from its phenomenon, it lies outside time and space, and accordingly knows no plurality, and consequently is *one*.   (WWR 1: 127–8)

The *principium individuationis* distinguishes between the world as representation and thing-in-itself in yet another way. The spatiotemporal individuation of represented objects, made possible by space and time as pure forms of intuition in the minds of representing subjects, divides the world as representation from thing-in-itself.

Schopenhauer notes that if the *principium individuationis* applies only and exclusively to the world as representation, then thing-in-itself is one. It further follows, as Schopenhauer later maintains, that if thing-in-itself is Will, then the world as Will, despite its many subjectively different objectifications in the world as representation in the minds of different representing subjects, is also and for the same reason one. It might be objected that if the *principium individuationis* does not apply to thing-in-itself, but only and exclusively to the world as representation, then thing-in-itself, whether or not it is also characterized as Will, should be neither one nor many, neither an individual nor a plurality of individuals. Schopenhauer evidently does not understand the *principium individuationis* in this way, but concludes from the inapplicability of the principle to thing-in-itself that thing-in-itself, by virtue of being indivisible into many things, must therefore be one.

The conclusion that thing-in-itself is one enables Schopenhauer to address the problem previously considered concerning the identity of the world as representation in the thoughts of many distinct representing subjects. If thing-in-itself is one, then it can be variously represented in the thoughts of many different subjects. The situation philosophically is much the same from the standpoint of identity requirements and epistemic principles as what a materialist or naive realist typically says with respect to the relation between the objectively existing mind-independent world and the multiple perceptual perspectives on the world available to a plurality of perceivers. There is no necessity in either case, provided, as Schopenhauer is now prepared to argue, that thing-in-itself is one, to conclude on the basis of Schopenhauer's radical idealism that the world itself is a many-fragmented thing existing only within the representations of many different representing subjects.

Schopenhauer's circle and the sceptic's demand for proof

Schopenhauer formulates the principle of sufficient reason with full generality, holding that every true judgement has a sufficient ground or reason (FFR: 6, 33). This suggests a philosophical problem of self-application and self-justification, and also, perhaps, of potentially infinite regress. Does the principle of sufficient reason itself have a ground or sufficient reason? Schopenhauer dismisses the question as circular in the sense that the difficulty could not intelligibly arise unless it were already assumed that the principle is true.

In *The Fourfold Root*, a form of the problem appears explicitly in a statement of what might be called "Schopenhauer's circle". There Schopenhauer argues:

> The principle of sufficient reason is just the expression of this necessity of a reason or ground for every judgement. Now whoever requires a proof for this reason, already assumes thereby that it is true; in fact he bases his demand on this very assumption. He therefore finds himself in that circle of demanding a proof for the right to demand a proof. (FFR: 33)

The attempt to justify the principle of sufficient reason raises a number of questions. Can the principle of sufficient reason itself constitute an exception to the principle of sufficient reason? If the principle of sufficient reason is not supported by a sufficient reason, how can it possibly be true, as Schopenhauer requires, that *every* true judgement has a sufficient reason? Is it ultimately circular merely to question the truth of the principle of sufficient reason? If it is circular to raise doubts about the principle, does the circularity argument itself constitute a sufficient reason in support of the principle of sufficient reason in any of its four categories of explanations? What, on Schopenhauer's view, prevents sufficient reasons, justifications or why-explanations from "going in a circle" or producing a circular truth-dependence interrelation in the first place? Why, if they do so, would that be a problem? Is the concept of sufficient reason necessarily committed to an unacknowledged epistemic foundationalism that precludes any (broadly) mutually sustaining "circular" coherentist explanations? How could such a structural justificatory limitation possibly derive from the principle of sufficient reason alone?

Schopenhauer's argument entails that it is circular to require a proof for the principle of sufficient reason, because to do so is already to assume that the principle is true. If it were not the case that "Nothing is without a ground or reason why it is rather than is not",[10] Schopenhauer urges, then there would be no basis for demanding a proof of the principle that everything admits of proof. To question whether the principle is true is to undermine the demand for proof generally, and hence in particular for any proof of the principle of sufficient reason. On the absurd assumption that a proof of the principle could be given, the demonstration would immediately produce a vicious circle, since a presentation of proof can only be motivated by a demand that is utterly groundless unless it is presupposed from the outset that the principle is sound. What, then, of the circularity argument itself? What is its logical status, and what are its methodological implications for Schopenhauer's system?

D. W. Hamlyn draws some interesting trans-systematic connections between Aristotle's dialectical demonstrations of the principle of contradiction and Schopenhauer's circle involving the principle of sufficient reason. He writes:

> Schopenhauer did not think that it was possible to provide an argument for the principle [of sufficient reason] ... Nor did he ever attempt to set out such a proof and *The Fourfold Root* should not be interpreted as doing so. Schopenhauer thinks that the principle is in fact presupposed in any argument or proof; hence to ask for a proof of the principle itself involves a circle, in that the principle is

presupposed in the very demand ... It might be suggested that this very fact gives rise to the possibility of a proof of sorts – a proof that is dialectical in the sense implied in what Aristotle says with regard to the principle of contradiction. Aristotle suggests that in the case of the principle of contradiction anyone who denies it can be shown to presuppose it; the sceptic is, so to speak, refuted out of his own mouth.[11]

Hamlyn then raises the difficult question as to whether Schopenhauer's argument can be interpreted as a kind of Aristotelian dialectical proof of the sufficient reason principle. He links the Aristotelian form of argument to Kantian transcendental reasoning when he observes:

Aristotle's treatment of the principle of contradiction involves in effect a version of what Kant was to call, although in a special application to possible experience, a transcendental argument – an argument to the effect that something must be so because the very possibility of something else presupposes it. Could Schopenhauer have allowed a transcendental argument for the principle of sufficient reason?[12]

Even if it is historically problematic to identify Aristotelian dialectical demonstrations with Kantian transcendental justifications, the logic of Schopenhauer's circularity argument can be illuminated without invoking the comparison. Schopenhauer recalls Aristotle's strategy in defending the law of contradiction, and includes both non-contradiction and sufficient reason as particular instances in the same general category of principles for which proof neither can nor need be given (FFR: 32). "On the contrary," he explains, "Aristotle's remark applies to all those proofs ... namely where he says: 'They seek a reason for that which has no reason; for the principle of demonstration is not a demonstration'" (FFR: 32).[13] Parenthetically, in this context, Schopenhauer portrays Kant's purpose in offering transcendental arguments not as attempts at proof of *validity*, but instead of apriority, and mentions Kant's method as an exception to the style of argument subject to Aristotle's criticism.[14]

If Hamlyn's hypothesis is correct, and Schopenhauer means to advance the circularity argument as an exercise in Aristotelian dialectical or Kantian transcendental proof, then the circle is not supposed to justify the principle of sufficient reason as valid or true, but only as *a priori*. Perhaps Schopenhauer intends to treat all of Aristotle's dialectical and Kant's transcendental arguments as proofs of apriority rather than validity or truth. Alternatively, he might be understood as recognizing distinct roles for these kinds of arguments, distinguishing among inferences within the category, some of which are while others are not offered as demonstrations of a principle's truth.

Schopenhauer provides no textual support for the hypothesis that Aristotle or Kant regarded dialectical or transcendental proofs as anything other than proofs of validity or truth. He quotes Aristotle in the *Metaphysics* as saying that "They seek a reason for that which has no reason; for the principle of demonstration is not a demonstration" (*Metaphysics* III, 6; *Posterior Analytics* I, 3). What Aristotle says here, however, does not obviously substantiate Schopenhauer's point. He needs to say that the law of (non-) contradiction is *unsupported* by reason, not that the principle of demonstration (which Schopenhauer without further ado equates with the principle of sufficient reason) does not *admit of* demonstration. Aristotle merely asserts reasonably enough that the principle of demonstration *is* not (itself) a demonstration.[15]

Schopenhauer's appeal to Kant's transcendental style of reasoning is similarly ambiguous. He claims that Kant's transcendental proofs, at least of the necessity of the law of causality, are not directed towards establishing the truth or validity of causal law, but only its apriority (FFR: 32). We should not accept this classification without taking note of some important implications concerning which Schopenhauer is silent. Judgements in Kant's philosophy are not *a priori simpliciter*, but *a priori* true or *a priori* false.[16] Transcendental arguments construed as proofs of apriority in anything like a Kantian framework must then demonstrate that a judgement is *a priori* true or *a priori* false. This fact contradicts Schopenhauer's effort to drive a wedge between demonstrations of truth or validity and Kantian proofs of apriority. The proof of apriority is at once proof either of a judgement's validity or truth, if the judgement is *a priori* true, or of the validity or truth of its negation, if the judgement is *a priori* false.

There is no greater or more fundamental philosophical distinction between arguments proving validity or apriority than there is between arguments proving validity or truth and arguments proving invalidity or falsehood. Furthermore, Schopenhauer explicitly accepts the principle of sufficient reason as true. He does not banish it to a semantic no-man's-land of truth-valueless constructions, but time and again refers to its validity or truth (FFR: xxviii, 32–3, 156–7). If the principle is true, and if there is a sufficient reason why every true judgement is true rather than false, then how can there not be a sufficient reason that justifies the principle of sufficient reason?

There is thus a relatively straightforward way to challenge Schopenhauer's circle. All we need do is ask whether it is true that an absurdity or circularity is involved in the demand for proof of the sufficient reason principle itself. The circle is supposed to show that scepticism about the principle of sufficient reason is irrational or unintelligible. We must therefore try to think like a sceptic to determine whether the position is incoherent. Suppose we doubt the principle, and want solid proof before we are willing to accept it. Does it follow that in making this demand we are already implicitly committed to the principle? No such conclusion can validly be inferred, provided that we are being selectively sceptical. We may recognize that many propositions, principles and theories are capable of proof, but this does not oblige us to regard every true judgement as having a sufficient reason. In the same way we can remain sceptical as to whether every event has a cause in lieu of a decisive demonstration, which in another way questions the truth of the principle of sufficient reason in its efficient causal root. We enquire, in part as an expression of unsettled doubts as to whether in fact every true judgement is supported by a sufficient reason, seeking to determine whether or not the principle is true.

Schopenhauer assumes that if we demand proof in this instance, then we automatically suppose that a positive proof is forthcoming. We thereby presuppose the truth of the principle for which we disingenuously require evidence. In one sense of "demand" this may well be so. The sense in which we are entitled to demand such proof is the sense in which we demand proof of any proposition put forward by proponents committed to its truth. If someone asserts the truth of Goldbach's conjecture in elementary number theory, that every even number greater than 2 is the sum of two primes, then we may naturally require that the thesis be proved before we accept it. Yet surely in making this demand we do not assume or presuppose that the conjecture is true; we call for proof precisely because we are not satisfied that the proposition is true.

Not every demand or kind of demand presupposes even the logical possibility of its own applicability. This is particularly so when the demand for proof is issued from a sceptical standpoint about the proposition's truth. It may nevertheless be imagined for a special category of principles, including notably the principle of sufficient reason, the law of non-contradiction in Aristotle's dialectical argument, and Kant's transcendental conclusions in the exposition of his critical idealism, that scepticism is always circular, absurd or self-defeating. Demanding proof of any of these, even from the standpoint of an honest although possibly unreflective scepticism, is to presuppose that the principles are true. If scepticism about the principles themselves is unintelligible unless the principles are true or implicitly held true, then to doubt them is irrational. How, on the other hand, can we determine that there is such a category of principles, that the principle of sufficient reason belongs to such a category, and that these preliminaries do not constitute a proof for the truth (or apriority) of a principle that is supposed to be unprovable?

We are confronted by several interconnected paradoxes of method. What might Schopenhauer say about this situation? It appears that in order to uphold the circle, Schopenhauer must implausibly argue that the principle of sufficient reason is presupposed in every demand for proof. To ask for reason or evidence for *any* assertion made by anyone under any circumstances is then tacitly to declare adherence to the principle that *every* occurrence or true judgement has a sufficient reason. The generality required to carry Schopenhauer's conclusion is not found in and cannot be obtained from the fact that every certified proof presupposes the principle. For this is evidently compatible with a qualified acceptance of sufficient reason, according to which some judgements are capable of proof, at least those for which successful proofs have been given, as well as a cautious scepticism about whether or not every true judgement can be explained by a sufficient reason in terms of which the judgement is proved. If the principle belongs to a special category of propositions that cannot intelligibly be doubted without being presupposed, then even the sceptic is unknowingly committed to its truth in full generality. Hamlyn attempts to preserve the circle in this way, when he contends in the passage referred to above: "Schopenhauer thinks that the principle is in fact presupposed in any argument or proof; hence to ask for a proof of the principle itself involves a circle, in that the principle is presupposed in the very demand".[17]

Even if Schopenhauer's principle of sufficient reason is presupposed in any argument or proof, blatantly begging the philosophically interesting question here, and generating a vicious circle of its own, it still does not follow that the sceptical demand for proof of the principle presupposes that the principle is true. The *demand* for proof is not itself an argument or proof. If the demand is not satisfied, that only contributes to scepticism about the principle's full generality. Schopenhauer seems to believe that the right to demand proof can only be licensed by the principle of sufficient reason. He claims that without supposing every true judgement capable of proof the sceptic logically is not permitted to doubt whether any particular true judgement, including the principle of sufficient reason itself, is capable of sufficient reason or proof. If, indeed, the principle of sufficient reason is false, then the sceptic's demand for proof is not unintelligible, merely unsatisfiable.[18]

Schopenhauer's scientific method

The principle of sufficient reason supports a two-part application of scientific method in Schopenhauer's philosophy. All occurrences in the world as representation are capable of explanation, a reason why they occur rather than fail to occur. Schopenhauer superimposes a taxonomy of tasks for scientific explanation that is compatible with but not obviously necessitated by his epistemology. He first distinguishes between descriptive and causal explanatory tasks.

"Finally," Schopenhauer observes, "if we look at the wide province of natural science, which is divided into many fields, we can first of all distinguish two main divisions. It is either a description of forms and shapes, which I call *Morphology*; or an explanation of changes, which I call *Etiology*" (WWR 1: 96). Although Schopenhauer considers morphology as the study of "permanent forms", it is not clear that he need restrict the investigation of types of objects belonging to a particular branch of science in terms of their geometrical shapes. He subsequently expands the concept of natural history to include the equivalent of a descriptive inventory of all the objects appropriate to a science's specific subject matter. He clarifies the two components in his division of scientific method:

> The former considers the permanent forms, the latter the changing matter, according to the laws of its transition from one form into another. Morphology is what we call natural history in its whole range, though not in the literal sense of the word. As botany and zoology especially, it teaches us about the various, permanent, organic, and thus definitely determined forms in spite of the incessant change of individuals; and these forms constitute a great part of the content of the perceptive representation. (WWR 1: 96)

"In natural history", he continues, "they are classified, separated, united, and arranged according to natural and artificial systems, and brought under concepts that render possible a survey and knowledge of them all" (*ibid.*).

The idea is that for a natural science to proceed systematically the scientist must first identify the range of objects that fall under its purview. Then specific explanations of the relevant phenomena must be articulated under the fourfold root of the principle of sufficient reason. Science must explain why such things exist and how they are interrelated, and devise ways to predict their behaviour on the basis of the causal relations in which they participate. In Chapter 12, "On the Doctrine of Science", in the second volume and later edition of *The World as Will and Representation*, Schopenhauer expands on his original two-part division of the tasks of natural science. He explains the work of scientific method as a four-part project of collecting data, forming abstractions that bring together under appropriate heads the properties of the objects with which a given science is concerned, examining and analysing the data and abstract concepts for the purpose of "fully comprehending" them, and, finally, with this preparation in hand, organizing the analysed abstractions into proofs constructed as syllogisms.

Thus, in this somewhat more complete but still naive characterization of scientific method, Schopenhauer properly links together the two alternative purposes of intuitive and abstract representation. The work of natural science is offered as a systematic progression of specific objectives to be undertaken in a definite order (WWR 2: 120). Intuitive representation enters into a programme of scientific explanation in so far as it requires perception, judgement and intuitive classification. These factors are needed especially in the recognition of causal connections and the similarities between individual objects and aggregates of objects. It is by virtue of such properties and causal interrelations that the objects of scientific study are classified together under a single abstraction. The collection of data in the form of perceived instances organized under abstractions makes it possible to construct theories designed to explain the objects and events in question. Such principles of explanation are at last structured into deductive syllogisms for purposes of codification, communication and application.

The limitations of this caricature of natural science are transparent. Anyone familiar with the way scientific research is actually conducted will appreciate the crudeness of Schopenhauer's description. The naivety of his philosophy of science is reminiscent of Francis Bacon's oversimplification of the new method of investigating nature in *Novum Organon*. Bacon argues that if we simply collect data about the world, the information will more or less organize itself into specific categories ready for abstraction and hypothesis.[19] Schopenhauer is almost as myopic as Bacon about the extratheoretical collection of relevant data and its virtually automatic organization into abstract concepts and categories. He does not even consider the need for hypothesis and testing in the confirmation or disconfirmation of hypotheses, as an essential part of scientific enquiry. While Bacon, in the seventeenth century at the very dawn of modern natural science, might be more easily excused for misdescribing the difficulties confronting scientific theorizing, Schopenhauer, more than two hundred years after the time of Galileo, Descartes and Newton, in the context of early-nineteenth-century natural science, has less justification for failing to recognize the real complications. The fact that Schopenhauer limits theoretical scientific explanations to those that can be formulated as syllogisms is another indication of his antiquated view of scientific method.

Despite these shortcomings, Schopenhauer's philosophy of science offers a valuable perspective on empirical observation and theory. The natural world can be understood at least in part and at some level through perception, conceptualization, theorization and explanation. We should recall that Schopenhauer began his university studies in medicine, and as such has more than an average philosophical acquaintance with the methods and principles of empirical science as it existed in his day. Although Schopenhauer does not properly recognize the roles of hypothesis and hypothesis testing, his requirements for explanation, even if too narrowly construed in terms of classical syllogisms as the only systematization of logical inference available at the time, at least provides a framework for hypothesis construction.

Schopenhauer's concepts of intuitive and abstract forms of knowledge are interrelated in his philosophy of science. He connects the two types of knowledge as complementary moments in the scientific enterprise. His ideal of scientific method begins with intuitive representation, observation, perception and experience of the natural world of objects and events, and concludes with abstract ideas, laws and principles formulated in logical inferences for purposes of explanation. The principles of science, as Schopenhauer also holds in the case of the rules of logic, music, art and morality, can be presented syllogistically. They are not formulated for the sake of arriving at correct judgements about the nature of reality, but for convenience in codifying, communicating and applying the intuitively justified conclusions of scientific theory.

An important example of the interpenetration of empirical observation and transcendental metaphysics in Schopenhauer's philosophy of science is seen in his ontological reduction of matter to causality. Schopenhauer relies on the telescoping of matter into causality in endorsing a fourfold rather than fivefold root of the principle of sufficient reason. "Now in just the same way", he says:

> he who has recognized that form of the principle of sufficient reason which governs the content of those forms (of time and space), their perceptibility, i.e., matter, and hence the law of causality, has thereby recognized the entire essence and nature of matter as such; for matter is absolutely nothing but causality, as anyone sees immediately the moment he reflects on it.   (WWR 1: 8)

The principle by which Schopenhauer proposes to reduce matter to causality is to consider how matter figures into the scientific explanation of physical substances. The analysis of matter as causality is not the discovery of an open-ended enquiry on Schopenhauer's part. As a transcendental idealist, he cannot countenance the external existence of mind-independent matter. For Schopenhauer, as for Kant, causality is a category of the understanding. It is as much a property of the representing subject as space and time are perceptual forms or pure forms of intuition. If we think of causation as a relation among spatiotemporal objects or events, then we cannot separate causality from the mind's forms. "Thus [the] being [of matter] is its acting", Schopenhauer adds; "it is not possible to conceive for it any other being. Only as something acting does it fill space and time; its action on the immediate object (which is itself matter) conditions the perception in which alone it exists" (WWR 1: 8–9). Matter is nothing real in and of itself. It is only known and only knowable, as in the equations of mathematical physics, in terms of its physical activity, which we can interpret in more contemporary terms by reference to energy and force fields. Schopenhauer's reduction of matter to causality depends in part on epistemic considerations. He argues that the only way we can come to know about the existence or properties of matter is through whatever effects we discover are brought about in events by observing the changes they produce (WWR 1: 9).

There can be no special category for matter in Schopenhauer's metaphysics. Material substance, like the rest of the world as representation, is always an object for a subject. Matter is not thing-in-itself, and consequently cannot coherently be supposed to exist independently of thought. It exists only as representation within the representational thoughts of an individual representing subject. Matter, like space and time, is ideal. It nevertheless appears at least superficially to be something solid and enduring. We naturally think of it as beginning in time before and outliving the individual subject within space and time. We believe it to be indifferent to perceivers coming and going, observing the world of matter as something that exists independently of thought from their particular perspectives.

Schopenhauer must effectively challenge this common-sense conception in order to uphold his radical scepticism. He tries to do so by turning the concept of matter in science against itself. Scientific explanations of material substances are directly concerned only with what matter does, its activity and power to bring about change. That is to say, with its causality. Causality, however, Schopenhauer asserts on Kantian grounds, is a subjective, ideational concept of the understanding. It is a product of thinking, and without thinking subjects there can be no causation. There is no causality for thing-in-itself, because causal relations take place in space and time, which thing-in-itself transcends. Where thing-in-itself is concerned, there are no objects or subjects, no interpresuppositional subject–object, and hence no space or time in which the active powers to which matter reduces in Schopenhauer's metaphysics can be engaged. If causality is nothing independently real, but belongs only to the subject, and if matter is causality, then, as an idealist like Schopenhauer sympathetic to Berkeley's idealism is compelled to argue, matter is nothing independent of thought. Rather, like all other aspects of the world as representation, matter, and physical reality generally, belong ideationally only to the thought processes of the representing subject (WN: 85–97; FFR: 46–50, 56).

Limits of empirical knowledge

At its best, empirical science can do nothing to uncover the hidden nature of the world. Natural science can explain any and every aspect of the world as representation under the principle of sufficient reason. Science can do nothing at all, on the other hand, to explain what lies beyond the world as representation in or concerning the existence or character of thing-in-itself.

Schopenhauer builds on his prior reduction of matter to causality to dramatize the limits of empirical science in explaining the world as representation. The epistemic boundary of the fourfold root is the same as the metaphysical boundary of the *principium individuationis*, and hence of the world as representation. What lies on the opposite side, beyond the reach of natural science, is scientifically unknowable thing-in-itself. A proper etiological understanding of the causal mechanisms of physical phenomena shows how little of metaphysical interest can be accomplished in scientific explanation. Natural science, in its preoccupation with causal interrelations, can only explain how objects and events within the world as representation are arranged in regular succession, temporal order and spatial proximity or propinquity, as David Hume observes concerning the origin of the idea of causation in *A Treatise of Human Nature*.[20]

Natural science cannot possibly hope to penetrate beyond the limits of representation to reveal anything of substance concerning the hidden nature of reality, which Kant and Schopenhauer refer to as thing-in-itself. The scientific study of the world of nature, the representational order of things, merely whets the metaphysician's appetite for something more. What is kindled thereby is a desire for the kind of insight that is strictly needed in order to understand fully the nature of reality that empirical science can only partially disclose. If we thirst for greater insight into what is real, then we shall begin to long for transcendence of the world as representation. We shall then be moved to look beyond the principle of individuation and the four types of explanation to which scientific explanation is inherently confined in order to consider the nature of thing-in-itself.

"On the other hand," Schopenhauer states:

> etiology teaches us that, according to the law of cause and effect, this definite condition of matter produces that other condition, and with this it has explained it, and has done its part. At bottom, however, it does nothing more than show the orderly arrangement according to which the states or conditions appear in space and time, and teach for all cases what phenomenon must necessarily appear at this time and in this place. (WWR 1: 97)

The kinds of explanation available within natural science point toward something beyond the world as representation. They do so by virtue of the fact that scientific explanations involve a universal form and a lawlike necessity that are not validly derived from passive perceptual experience of the world encountered only as representation.

"This is called a *natural force*", Schopenhauer explains, speaking of whatever hidden factors support empirical phenomena in the natural world as representation, that "lies outside the province of etiological explanation, which calls the unalterable constancy with which the manifestation of such a force appears whenever its known conditions are present, a *law of nature*" (WWR 1: 97). When we undertake etiological scientific enquiry, trying to determine the nomic causal interrelations among occurrences, representational knowledge can only take us so far. We soon run into limits beyond which we cannot expect empirical confirmation for the explanations we would like to be able to give. We cannot peer beyond the constant regularities that constitute causal connections between event types, because to do so would require lifting what Schopenhauer speaks of as the *veil of Maya*, invoking the Vedic myth of the cloaking of reality behind a tissue of illusion. There is nothing for us empirically to discover beyond the constant conjunction of events, as Hume observes. Confronted with the brute facts of constant regularity in successions of event types, we are driven to posit natural forces and natural laws. These summarize the conclusions of our intuitive representations in abstract form, but they offer nothing to explain why in the first place such constant conjunctions of event types occur.

Mechanics is the natural science that most perfectly identifies the abstract principles of mathematical physics. Schopenhauer remarks that even in this branch of science, dedicated to discovering the regularities that govern the motions of projectiles and planets, falling bodies and inclined planes, the impact and repulsion of physical entities in collision, and the like, etiology is capable of nothing more than abstracting regularities from observed phenomena without offering the slightest explanation as to how or why such regularities occur. The same is true to an even greater degree, according to Schopenhauer, with respect to the less rigorously developed sciences of biology or physiology (WWR 1: 97).

He summarizes the purpose of mechanics and other exact sciences as establishing purely etiological interconnections among physical entities. As such, there is no more for the natural sciences to do than to collect information about regular recurrences among events. These are conveniently expressed as the effects of natural forces and summarized as natural laws, concerning which natural science can never hope to offer a deeper or more penetrating explanation. The natural sciences, pressed as far as they can go in trying to explain the world, run up against the invisible barrier that divides the world as representation from thing-in-itself. The explanatory limitations of empirical science in this way suggest the existence of a reality beyond appearance that transcends the empirical spatiotemporal physical order, and that is considered only superficially and etiologically even in the greatest advances of mathematical physics (WWR 1: 97–8).

Where natural science fails, we can only proceed by turning to the principles of transcendental metaphysics. It is in this context that Schopenhauer proposes to explain thing-in-itself as that which grounds, objectifies and manifests itself in the represented objects that appear within the thoughts of representing subjects. Having confronted the limitations of the world as representation by pursuing causal explanation under the fourfold root of the principle of sufficient reason, and longing for further insight into the hidden workings of things, we are moved to seek answers beyond the limits of the phenomenal world as representation. Schopenhauer, accordingly, invokes thing-in-itself as that which in Kantian terms appears and is known only through the perception of its appearances in the phenomenal world, which it transcends.

Transition from natural science in the world as representation to metaphysics of the world as thing-in-itself

We are now prepared with Schopenhauer to proceed from empirical scientific investigations of the world as representation and a philosophical appreciation of the limits of the only possible methodologies of natural science to a yearning for deeper insight into what lies beyond. We undertake in this way a transition from representational phenomena to nonrepresentational Kantian thing-in-itself. When we have exhausted the possibilities of natural science and understood that its etiological explanations under the principle of sufficient reason cannot account for the hidden workings of natural forces or for how or why the causal regularities they collect together as natural laws obtain, then we are ready to take the next step from natural science to transcendental metaphysics.

In Chapter 17, "On Man's Need for Metaphysics", in the second edition of *The World as Will and Representation*, Schopenhauer introduces the concept of metaphysics as a speculative enterprise concerning the hidden nature that transcends the world as representation. He describes the project of metaphysics as taking thought beyond the limits of representation (WWR 2: 164). The transition from natural science to the metaphysics of thing-in-itself is a continuation of the effort to demarcate the limits of empirical knowledge and pure reason, in which Schopenhauer acknowledges his intellectual debt to Kant:

> I admit entirely Kant's doctrine that the world of experience is mere phenomenon, and that knowledge *a priori* is valid only in reference thereto; but I add that, precisely as phenomenal appearance, it is the manifestation of that which appears, and with him I call that which appears the thing-in-itself. Therefore, this thing-in-itself must express its inner nature and character in the world of experience; consequently it must be possible to interpret these from it, and indeed from the material, not from the mere form, of experience. Accordingly, philosophy is nothing but the correct and universal understanding of experience itself, the true interpretation of its meaning and content. This is the metaphysical, in other words, that which is merely clothed in the phenomenon and veiled in its forms, that which is related to the phenomenon as the thought or idea is to the words. (WWR 2: 183–4)

We need metaphysics because, once we understand the inherent limitations of natural science, we understand that it can never satisfy the desire for knowledge that draws us to science in the first place. We want to know that even our natural scientific explanations are based upon something more fundamental than appearance, on something that is true and unalterably real, as the metaphysical underpinning of science.

The entire first book of *The World as Will and Representation* is devoted exclusively to the world as representation. There we are offered an inside look at the workings of natural science, its scope and limitations. In principle we can discover a sufficient reason why everything exists, why everything in the world of experience is as it is. There are no inexplicable phenomena as long as we recognize that they are only phenomena. We must understand that our explanations under the fourfold root can only take us so far. They serve us well up to, but cannot help us to go beyond, the division between the world as representation to which scientific explanations are necessarily limited, and thing-in-itself. That is where Schopenhauer promises to pursue his enquiry next. He offers insight into the world beyond representation, beyond the principles of individuation and sufficient reason, and the explanations of natural phenomena afforded by the most complete empirical science, to the non-representational insights of transcendental metaphysics.

CHAPTER THREE

Willing and the world as Will

Here we already see that we can never get at the inner nature of things *from without*. However much we may investigate, we obtain nothing but images and names. We are like a man who goes around a castle, looking in vain for an entrance, and sometimes sketching the façades. Yet this is the path that all philosophers before me have followed.   (WWR 1: 99)

Thing-in-itself

We now stand ready with Schopenhauer to cross over from the world as representation to thing-in-itself. Schopenhauer observes that no previous philosophers had been able to make progress with respect to understanding thing-in-itself, but have had to satisfy themselves with only negative characterizations of it as unknowable. They have thought of it only as something other than the world of phenomena, as noumena, in Kant's critical idealist terminology, or that which lies beyond the veil of Maya.

What shall we find on the other side? In one sense, we should have learned from Schopenhauer's discussion of explanation in the world as representation that such a question as it would usually be understood is misplaced. We are not literally travelling across a borderline where we can exercise our ordinary methods of gathering information and verifying knowledge in the transcendental world just as in the empirical. Schopenhauer states that we cannot hope to acquire representational knowledge of thing-in-itself. The most we can expect in transcendental metaphysics is insight, intuitive grasp or inchoate understanding of thing-in-itself. He maintains that we can non-representationally know the nature of thing-in-itself as Will. We must try to understand what he means by this and why he thinks it is true, as it is key to all the other conclusions in his idealist philosophy. Schopenhauer relates his discussion of thing-in-itself to Kant's noumenal reality in these terms:

> [T]o use Kant's language, time, space, and causality do not belong to the thing-in-itself, but only to its appearance or phenomenon, of which they are the form. In my language, this means that the objective world, the world as representation, is not the only side of the world, but merely its external side, so to speak, and that the world has an entirely different side which is its innermost being, its kernel, the thing-in-itself. This we shall consider in the following book, calling it "will" after the most immediate of its objectifications. But the world as representation, with which alone we are dealing here, certainly begins only with the opening of the first eye, and without this medium of knowledge it cannot be, and hence before this it did not exist. But without that eye, in other words, outside of knowledge, there was no before, no time. For this reason, time has no beginning, but all beginning is in time.   (WWR 1: 30–31)

Again, Schopenhauer mentions the first eye opening as the defining moment of the world as representation. The beginnings of things, their past history, are projected backwards from within rather than originating at the inception of time. Space and time come into existence with the first representation, which presupposes the perception of a representing subject through which the represented object also comes into being. This is not yet thing-in-itself, which is something altogether different from the world as representation, and consequently beyond all space, time and causality.

Schopenhauer does not speak of thing-in-itself as Kantian noumenon. The terminological differences between Kant and Schopenhauer on this point are important, because they indicate the extent to which Schopenhauer believes he has surpassed Kant's critical idealism. Kant's term "noumenon" means literally that which is known only to the mind as something conceivable. It is at most a kind of X or blank space in Kant's metaphysics, because for Kant we can know nothing more about it. Schopenhauer proposes to fill in the blank with an explication of thing-in-itself as Will. He argues that in an unexpected way we can move beyond Kant's distinction between the world as it is represented to thought and thing-in-itself to gain a correct understanding of reality beyond the world as representation.[1]

Schopenhauer proposes to take a giant step beyond the unknowability of transcendent reality. While remaining truer, he believes, to the main lines of Kant's philosophy than any of his contemporaries, he argues that the world as thing-in-itself is Will. By this choice of term he proposes to convey his insight that the world in reality, independent of its representation in thought, is blind urging, undirected desire, or objectless and hence subject-less, uncaused, unmotivated striving. Schopenhauer intends these pro-nouncements quite literally. Ultimately, his doctrine of thing-in-itself as Will identifies thing-in-itself as existing within the subject at the core of all phenomenal willing. In a certain sense, thing-in-itself is identical with the individual subject when considered as pure willing. Thing-in-itself in Schopenhauer's transcendental metaphysics turns out, remarkably enough, to be identical with the fundamental pure willing that underlies each individual willing, knowing, representing subject.

World as Will

It may be worthwhile, before entering into Schopenhauer's reasons for identifying thing-in-itself with Will, to reflect on the strangeness of his con-clusion. Without trying to do justice to the implications of Schopenhauer's concept of the world as Will, we can begin to appreciate the revolutionary force of suggesting, even metaphorically or analogically, that the world in reality, independently of the way it is represented to thought as a dynamic spatiotemporal order of causally interrelated physical events and the empiri-cally perceivable properties of empirically perceivable entities, is Will.

We are familiar with willing in the ordinary sense through everyday first-person acts of volition. In willing to do something, we decide upon a course of action, and then as a rule make an effort to carry out the intention in practice. The idea is that in such instances we are engaged in the pursuit of a desire that impels us to motion. We must be careful not to confuse the properties of psychological willing as we experience it phenomenologically or introspectively with whatever Schopenhauer means by the non-represen-tational nature of thing-in-itself as Will. We glimpse what Schopenhauer has in mind by this identification if we begin with a commonplace episode of volition and try to think away from it the prominent features that may otherwise seem to be essential to ordinary willing. These are the cause and motivation for willing, the willing subject and with it necessarily the object. If we can accomplish this conceptual feat, subtracting these factors from phenomenal willing, we shall be left only with what is absolutely essential to an everyday act of will. This is pure willing, willing itself or as it is in itself, which Schopenhauer refers to as Will. Pure willing or Will in Schopenhauer's transcendental metaphysics satisfies the conceptual requirements of thing-in-itself, implying that thing-in-itself is Will.

Schopenhauer describes his revelation of thing-in-itself from behind the veil of Maya as a way of gaining entrance to a fortress. Rather than battering futilely against its ramparts, Schopenhauer seeks to enter by subterfuge. If we confine ourselves to empirical investigations, we shall inevitably remain outside the impenetrable fortress walls, excluded from entry. We can circle the fortress repeatedly without finding a way in, just as Schopenhauer says of conventional theorists who try to gain access to the reality of things, to thing-in-itself, as though it was merely another subject for empirical study. These deluded metaphysicians, as he thinks of them, limit themselves to the external surfaces explainable only as features of the world as representation to be known as intuitive or abstract theoretical representations. From Schopenhauer's account of the limits of empirical knowledge, we recognize that such methods can never take us beyond the boundary that divides the world as representation from thing-in-itself. A superficial metaphysics can never lead us to an understanding of the mind-independent world of reality beyond its mere appearances as objects in relation to a subject.

What we need in order to enter the fortress is a strategy like the one the ancient Greeks are supposed to have devised to break the ten-year seige at the battle of Troy. We need a way of sneaking into the fortress whose walls we cannot otherwise breach. Schopenhauer in effect describes individual willing as a kind of Trojan horse by which, through stealth, we can penetrate the otherwise invincible curtain of the world as representation to reach thing-in-itself on the other side. No matter what we study or how we try to study thing-in-itself by the limited means available to science or conventional metaphysics, we can only theorize the existence of explanatory connections linking represented objects or events with one another. The Trojan horse that we can think of metaphorically as Schopenhauer's proposal for entering the fortress is none other than individual will in the sense of a volitional act as we know it phenomenologically in empirical psychology. The fact that we rational beings are capable of willing as well as knowing is exploited by Schopenhauer as the point of entry he seeks. There understanding can cross over from the world as representation to insight into the transcendental metaphysics of thing-in-itself, which in the process he discovers to be pure willing or Will.

First argument for thing-in-itself as Will

Schopenhauer offers what appear to be two distinct arguments, or perhaps a single argument that lends itself to two different interpretations. The inferences appear in the first and second volumes of *The World as Will and Representation*. The chronology of their separate publication suggests that in the intervening 26 years between the first and second editions of the text

Schopenhauer may have changed his mind. He may have rethought the topic, or at least the exact presentation of the reasoning he intended, possibly reconsidering what would provide the most acceptable basis for his conclusion.

The first argument trades on what Schopenhauer describes merely as an analogy between individual empirical willing and his interpretation of thing-in-itself as Will. He begins where he left off in considering the explanatory limitations of empirical science in the world as representation under the fourfold root of the principle of sufficient reason: "what now prompts us to make enquiries", he writes:

> is that we are not satisfied with knowing that we have representations, that they are such and such, and that they are connected according to this or that law, whose general expression is always the principle of sufficient reason. We want to know the significance of those representations; we ask whether this world is nothing more than representation. In that case, it would inevitably pass by us like an empty dream, or a ghostly vision not worth our consideration.
>
> (WWR 1: 98–9)

Far from satisfying us, the most intimate familiarity with represented objects gained through science only makes us wonder more urgently whether there is anything more to reality transcending the bounds of sense. That which we seek, if it exists at all, must take its principles from beyond the limits of perception (WWR 1: 99).

Schopenhauer projects a quest for greater metaphysical understanding. He describes a psychological perspective on the attitude that leads enquiry from the limitations of the world as representation to the discovery of something more. Why are we so inclined? Schopenhauer's conjecture is that, in the active contemplation of empirical phenomena, we eventually come to the conclusion that if there is only appearance, then the physical world of experience is essentially of no greater significance than an "empty dream" or "ghostly vision" that passes by like a magic lantern show. He seems to believe that we would be justifiably disappointed if the world should turn out to be no more than such a parade of representations, with nothing more substantial behind it. We are in any case properly motivated at least by sheer curiosity to want to determine whether there is not another aspect of reality that is not exhausted by the ways in which the world appears to perception in empirical knowledge and scientific explanation. Schopenhauer's interest in Plato's philosophy makes it natural to compare his remarks about the limitations of the phenomenal world with what Socrates says in the *Republic* concerning prisoners in the famous allegory of the cave. These unfortunates are chained in such a way that they can never directly experience ordinary physical things, but see only images made by a backlit fire that casts shadows from the puppets and other moving objects displayed behind them along a gallery.[2]

The person who is dissatisfied with limited knowledge of the empirical world recognizes that the answers to questions about the hidden workings of nature can only be found beyond the world of representation. The search for greater understanding must consequently be directed toward something other than the superficial representations of ephemeral things in the phenomenal world of perception. Schopenhauer refers to this as the "inner" or hidden nature of the manifestations that appear to the senses. He argues that each knowing subject has the answer to the problem of thing-in-itself within first-person knowledge.

He begins by distinguishing between internal and external self-knowledge, as two kinds of knowledge of the human body. External knowledge is gained through perception. It is the representation of the body in sensation, the features of it we can see, hear, feel, smell, and taste, just as we can of any other physical entity in the world as representation. The internal knowledge we have of our own bodies is acquired through first-person experience of willing and acts of will in action, directing the movements of the body from within through volitional decision and resolve. Schopenhauer asks, "What is this world of perception besides being my representation? Is that of which I am conscious only as representation just the same as my own body, of which I am doubly conscious, on the one hand as *representation*, on the other as *will*?" (WWR 1: 18). Later, he maintains that the dual nature of our bodies, and corresponding to it our dual knowledge of its nature, suggests the same two ways of coming to know or understand the world at large. If the world as a whole has both an inner and external side, if we can know about its external representational side through perception, then, as we become aware of the limitations of exploring and theorizing about the phenomenal world, we may increasingly feel the need to turn from natural science to transcendental metaphysics. It is only there that we can consider the inner knowledge of our bodies in acts of will as a key to the inner hidden nature of the world. By analogy, if inner knowledge of the body's actions reveals individual will, as the hidden side of its parts and qualities known externally by perception, then insight into or understanding of the hidden inner nature of the world as thing-in-itself can similarly be referred to as Will. Schopenhauer explains:

> He would then also call the inner, to him incomprehensible, nature of those manifestations and actions of his body a force, a quality, or a character, just as he pleased, but he would have no further insight into it. All this, however, is not the case; on the contrary, the answer

to the riddle is given to the subject of knowledge appearing as individual, and this answer is given in the word *Will*. This and this alone gives him the key to his own phenomenon, reveals to him the significance and shows him the inner mechanism of his being, his actions, his movements. To the subject of knowing, who appears as an individual only through his identity with the body, this body is given in two entirely different ways.   (WWR 1: 100)

The inner awareness of our bodies consists of direct experience of acts of will through which we exercise control over our body movements. It is this non-representational "knowledge" of the body that we obtain through the inward direction and control of its motion when we choose to do something and then carry out the intent in voluntary activity.

The analogy crucial to Schopenhauer's first argument for thing-in-itself as Will identifies thing-in-itself as the hidden inner side of the world as representation, the non-representational understanding of which in both cases provides insight into whatever it is that transcends perceptual experience of external appearance. Inner awareness of the individual will is a kind of Trojan horse through which Schopenhauer proposes to disclose the nature of thing-in-itself. The analogy implies that the world of representation is to thing-in-itself as our external bodies experienced in sensation are to the inner workings of our individual wills. We do not yet necessarily know whether there is anything more to the world than we experience perceptually in its representations and can explain scientifically within the limits of the principle of sufficient reason. At this stage we are only asking out of dissatisfaction with the limits of superficial investigation of the world as representation whether or not there might not be something more, something deeper and hidden behind the veil of Maya.

There is nothing we are more immediately familiar with or know more intimately than our own bodies. If there are only two ways in which we can know our bodies – through perceptual representation of the body's external appearance and inner understanding of the activity of will – then it seems reasonable to consider these same two modes of knowledge with respect to the world. The world is evidently divided into external and internal aspects, appearance or representation and thing-in-itself. Perhaps, then, the same inner faculty that produces one kind of knowledge of the body can also be used to reveal the hidden inner nature of thing-in-itself. If we have just these two and no other ways of knowing about our bodies, if we are so fortunately placed as to have external and inner knowledge here in the microcosm of reality in which the representing, knowing and willing subject is embodied, then we might be justified in pursuing these same two modes of knowing to the macrocosm of the entire world. The workings of the individual will are hidden and representationally unknowable to ourselves and others. We do not see or otherwise perceive the will in the bodies of other representing subjects. Nor, for that matter, do we perceive or represent to ourselves our own personal first-person individual acts of willing. We are directly aware of our own willing in another, non-representational, way, through the very act of willing our bodies to move and living through the motions that result as we exercise inward control of our bodies' movements. Thing-in-itself, by analogy, as the inner nature of the world as representation at large, is best understood as something like the individual will actively functioning as the hidden principle of motion in the inner nature of the individual subject's representational body. It is for this reason, in his first analogical argument, that Schopenhauer concludes that thing-in-itself is appropriately designated as Will.

Schopenhauer leans heavily on the consideration that, in addition to external knowledge by perception and inner awareness of the activity of will, there is, in familiarity with our own bodies, no other known or even conceivable mode of knowledge. Although he does not quite present things in this way, it is natural to add that were it not for the fact that we happen to be volitional as well as cognitive agents, willing as well as knowing beings, we would not even have a dual-mode capacity for knowing about and understanding the hidden inner nature of the world as representation and as thing-in-itself. When we reflect on the epistemology supported by the kinds of knowing subjects we are, in intuitive and abstract representation and in awareness of willing and the wilful ("will-ful") active direction and control of our body movements, we should ask whether we can make sense of anything over and above these two ways of "knowing". It strengthens Schopenhauer's inference to consider that these are the only two possibilities conceivable to us, given our nature as thinking subjects. Schopenhauer asks, in effect, what else could there be?

> The double knowledge which we have of the nature and action of our own body, and which is given in two completely different ways, has now been clearly brought out. Accordingly, we shall use it further as a key to the inner being of every phenomenon in nature. We shall judge all objects which are not our own body, and therefore are given to our consciousness not in the double way, but only as representations, according to the analogy of this body. We shall therefore assume that as, on the one hand, they are representation, just like our body, and are in this respect homogeneous with it, so on the other hand, if we set aside their existence as the subject's representation, what still remains over must be, according to its inner nature, the same as what in ourselves we call *will*. For what other kind of existence or reality could we attribute to the rest of the

WILLING AND THE WORLD AS WILL

material world? From what source could we take the elements out of which we construct such a world? Besides the will and the representation, there is absolutely nothing known or conceivable for us.

(WWR 1: 104–5)

In the same way that individual willing expresses itself in the body's actions, so thing-in-itself as Will expresses itself in the world as representation. The analogy turns out to be essential to every further implication of Schopenhauer's philosophy built around the central distinction between world as representation and thing-in-itself as Will. He concludes, as a result, among other things, that there is a character of the world considered as the expression of Will, in the same way that each subject has a moral psychological character. Individual character is reflected in action as the expression of phenomenal willing. What is identified by analogy as the character of the world as Will has startling ramifications for ethics, politics, aesthetics and religious salvation, as well as the metaphysics of natural laws studied in physics and the biological sciences (WWR 1: 107).

Schopenhauer recalls his previous distinction between intuitive and abstract knowledge. We cannot have abstract knowledge of thing-in-itself, but only an intuitive understanding derived from direct experience of our own individual willing as we direct and control the motions of our bodies in action. Schopenhauer has already warned us that the failure to grasp these kinds of intuitive relations indicates a lack of high intelligence, and that it is a mistake to substitute for such knowledge an appeal to abstract principles expressed in the form of a syllogism. Such demonstrations can at best only come afterwards, when thought has arrived at an intuitive insight into the relevant relations. We have already seen that Schopenhauer denies logic any practical utility, arguing that it is useful only for codifying, communicating and applying relations that have been independently intuited. The same is now said to be true in the case of intuitively grasping the fundamental metaphysical insight that thing-in-itself is Will. By analogy with our dual external and internal knowledge of our bodies, Schopenhauer maintains that we can directly and concretely come to *feel* that thing-in-itself is Will.

We misunderstand the purpose of his analogy if we suppose that the argument is meant to be assimilated as an item of abstract theoretical knowledge. Schopenhauer proposes instead to guide thought to the same intuitive grasp of truth that led to his revelation of thing-in-itself as Will. We know the body externally through perception in representational knowledge, and internally from the effects of will on the body's actions. Schopenhauer claims that everyone in principle has both types of knowledge at their fingertips, if only it is pointed out to them. "From all these considerations", he advises:

79

the reader has now gained in the abstract, and hence in clear and certain terms, a knowledge which everyone possesses directly in the concrete, namely as feeling. This is the knowledge that the inner nature of his own phenomenon, which manifests itself to him as representation both through his actions and through the permanent substratum of these his body, is his *will*.   (WWR 1: 109)

Schopenhauer's purpose in working out an abstract analogical argument for the identification of thing-in-itself with Will is to bring to immediate awareness something that everyone already "knows". He believes that everyone possesses at least an implicit feeling that thing-in-itself is Will, and that the world has the same internal–external duality as the body. The body as a physical entity and wilful agent on this analogy is the microcosm of the world at large, respectively, as representation and Will. Acting in a certain way, we reveal in outward body language our inner character, which we know more immediately from inner first-person volitional control of the body's external movements. Schopenhauer relates the inner–outer dichotomy in body knowledge to a parallel inner–outer dichotomy in the world taken as a whole. There is a similar feeling concerning the relation between external knowledge of the world as representation and the inner non-representational "knowledge" or understanding, insight or feeling of thing-in-itself as something willing or will-like, which he refers to here by analogy in his first argument as Will (WWR 1: 109).

Schopenhauer indicates the analogical inference by which he proposes to identify thing-in-itself as Will. He announces his intention to borrow the terminology of willing from what he describes as the "most complete" of thing-in-itself's phenomena, which he attributes to individual acts of willing:

Now, if this *thing-in-itself* (we will retain the Kantian expression as a standing formula) – which as such is never object, since all object is its mere appearance or phenomenon, and not it itself – is to be thought of objectively, then we must borrow its name and concept from an object, from something in some way objectively given, and therefore from one of its phenomena. But in order to serve as a point of explanation, this can be none other than the most complete of all its phenomena, i.e., the most distinct, the most developed, the most directly enlightened by knowledge; but this is precisely man's *will*.   (WWR 1: 110)

The analogy in Schopenhauer's first argument identifying thing-in-itself as Will raises several questions. There are conceptual problems affecting both parts of the comparison on which it depends. First, the perceptual knowledge of the body is not merely analogous to, but is precisely the same perceptual mode of cognition as that involved in knowledge of the world as representation in its entirety. Perceptual knowledge of the body is not merely analogous to knowledge of the world as representation as a whole, and hence not a basis for analogical inference, but is rather a focus of perceptual knowledge directed specifically to the individual knowing subject's body. Secondly, the business end of the analogy concerning the relation between the will as the body's inner principle and the Will as thing-in-itself for the greater "body" of the world as representation is weak and conjectural.

What must be true in order for the analogy to hold? How are we supposed to know that inner knowledge of the body in acts of will corresponds analogically to thing-in-itself as inner principle of the world, and is therefore interpretable as Will? The will as we experience it introspectively or phenomenologically is temporal if not spatial, directed toward specific intended objects, motivated, purposive and individuated as the willing of a particular subject. In particular, it is the willing of the knowing subject reflecting on the analogy and considering its content in order to obtain understanding of the hidden inner nature of thing-in-itself. Why should a theorist conclude, as a result of Schopenhauer's analogy, that thing-in-itself is Will, given that there are also significant disanalogies between the individual will and thing-in-itself? What could possibly sustain the analogy if Schopenhauer does not simply beg the crucial question? He seems to assume rather than prove that thing-in-itself is sufficiently will-like to merit referring to it as Will. He believes from the outset that thing-in-itself is an active principle that moves the world from behind the scenes in something like the way that the individual will exercises control over the body whose motions it directs. The assumption is logically incompatible with Schopenhauer's insistence that thing-in-itself has no causal efficacy, as he complains in criticizing Kant's proof for the existence of thing-in-itself.[3]

The individual willing subject exercises control over body movements by possessing certain properties of agency that Schopenhauer denies can ever hold true of thing-in-itself. The individual will, unlike thing-in-itself, is motivated to act. It directs its actions toward intended objects, and so may be caused to will by external events, while acting from within in turn to cause the body to move. In view of these significant disanalogies, we cannot judge whether or not the main part of the analogy holds without having prior knowledge of thing-in-itself as Will, which is the very thing the analogy is supposed to prove. If the most fundamental truths of metaphysics depend only on a subjective "feeling" that thing-in-itself is one thing – if that is any way to do philosophy – then why might not a critic reply that he or she feels that thing-in-itself is God or matter or time or abstract form or something entirely different? If it is reasonable to think of Schopenhauer's early argument as an analogical inference, then it provides at best doubtful grounds for his principal metaphysical thesis that thing-in-itself is Will.

Second argument for thing-in-itself as Will

The argument in the first edition of *The World as Will and Representation* is not Schopenhauer's final word on the relation between individual will and thing-in-itself as Will. In Chapter 18, "On the Possibility of Knowing the Thing-in-Itself", in the second volume, he offers another style of proof. As before, Schopenhauer clarifies his purpose as going beyond Kant's negative conclusion that thing-in-itself is noumenal. He repeats that the effort to explicate the nature of thing-in-itself is what is most important and distinctive about his philosophy. "In 1836," he reports:

> under the title *Ueber den Willen in der Nature* (second edition, 1854), I already published the really essential supplement to this book, which contains the most characteristic and important step of my philosophy, namely the transition from the phenomenon to the thing-in-itself, given up by Kant as impossible. (WWR 2: 191)

It is remarkable for Schopenhauer to refer in this context to his later 1836 work, rather than the first 1819 edition of *The World as Will and Representation*. For there, as we have seen, Schopenhauer presents a cogent if inconclusive analogical argument for the proposition that thing-in-itself is Will.

Although the introduction of *On the Will in Nature* contains a brief summary of Schopenhauer's earlier statement of the conclusion, it does not convey any new breakthrough arguments in support of the theory. Like most of the second edition of *The World as Will and Representation* and the *Parerga and Paralipomena*, *On the Will in Nature* is an album of afterthoughts gathered as further evidence in support of Schopenhauer's primary metaphysical discovery that thing-in-itself is Will. The book assembles findings in the natural sciences in particular that Schopenhauer interprets as upholding the proposition that the character of Will is exemplified in the world as representation. The purpose of the book is clearly indicated in its subtitle: *A Discussion of the Corroborations from the Empirical Sciences that the Author's Philosophy has Received Since its First Appearance*. This does not sound like an advertisement for an entirely new contribution to Schopenhauer's idealism, but describes a supplementary verification of results he believes he has already established.[4]

Returning to the second edition of *The World as Will and Representation*, Schopenhauer sets the stage there for what appears to be a similar but notably non-analogical argument for the identification of thing-in-itself as Will. He emphasizes the limitations of approaching knowledge through representation alone, which he argues would constitute no advance over Kant (WWR 1: 4). The problem is that if we try to limit metaphysics to phenomena, then we have no choice but to collapse the real into the ideal. This is idealism of a more Berkeleyan sort, albeit a Berkeley manqué, without the objectivity of the archetypal existence of sensible things guaranteed by God's infinite knowledge. Kant, in the *Critique*, refutes Berkeleyan idealism by arguing that there must exist spatiotemporal entities outside of consciousness in order for thinking subjects to be conscious of their own existence in time. This, Schopenhauer remarks, could not possibly carry Kant beyond the limits of Berkeley's idealism, because Kant regards space and time themselves as pure forms of intuition. Hence, space and time are every bit as subjectively ideal as the contents of representation considered only, as Berkeley would classify them in his terminology, as congeries of ideas. Schopenhauer reasons that thing-in-itself must be something altogether different:

> However, if, without questioning further, we stop altogether at the *world as representation*, then of course it is immaterial whether I declare objects to be representations in my head or phenomena that exhibit themselves in time and space, since time and space themselves are only in my head. In this sense, then, an identity of the ideal and the real might still be affirmed; yet since Kant, this would be to say nothing new. Moreover, the inner nature of things and of the phenomenal world would obviously not be exhausted in this way, but with it we should still always be only on the *ideal* side. The *real* side must be something *toto genere* different from the *world as representation*, namely that which things are *in themselves*; and it is this complete diversity between the ideal and the real that Kant has demonstrated most thoroughly. (WWR 2: 193)

It is futile to attempt making contact with reality through even the most complete and detailed knowledge of the world as representation. We are then like the person Schopenhauer describes as trying to gain entrance to a fortress by repeatedly circling its walls and drawing pictures of the fortifications as they appear from the outside. "In consequence of all this," Schopenhauer writes:

> on the path of *objective knowledge*, thus starting from the *representation*, we shall never get beyond the representation, i.e., the

phenomenon. We shall therefore remain at the outside of things; we shall never be able to penetrate into their inner nature, and investigate what they are in themselves. So far I agree with Kant.

(WWR 2: 195)

Where Schopenhauer hopes to carry his own transcendental idealism an important step further than Kant's critical idealism is by explicating his intuitive insight into the hidden inner nature of thing-in-itself beyond the limits of representation (WWR 1: 82). What is noteworthy about Schopenhauer's later argument in the book's second edition is that in it the relation between the knowing subject's individual will and thing-in-itself as Will is not offered merely as an analogy among similar things, but as a strict numerical identity. The shift is subtle between these two versions of Schopenhauer's argument, when he continues the original line of thought:

> But now, as the counterpoise to this truth, I have stressed that other truth that we are not merely the *knowing subject*, but that *we ourselves* are also among those realities or entities we require to know, that *we ourselves are the thing-in-itself*. Consequently, a way *from within* stands open to us to that real inner nature of things to which we cannot penetrate *from without*. It is, so to speak, a subterranean passage, a secret alliance, which, as if by treachery, places us all at once in the fortress that could not be taken by attack from without. Precisely as such, the *thing-in-itself* can come into consciousness only quite directly, namely by *it itself being conscious of itself*; to try to know it objectively is to desire something contradictory. (WWR 2: 195)

The change of perspective from the first to the second argument is significant. Schopenhauer now maintains that we falsely believe ourselves to be excluded from the fortress. The walls that seem to separate us from thing-in-itself are only an illusion. The truth is rather that all along we are already inside the gates, if only we recognize the fact that we are ourselves thing-in-itself, or that thing-in-itself is identical with the pure willing within us, identically at the core of every thinking, representing, willing subject. We can then understand that we are already "all at once" within the fortress whose walls we previously thought would require some sort of frontal "attack" to break through, a tactic that Schopenhauer in company with Kant acknowledges in any case could never possibly succeed.

Schopenhauer warns that we mistakenly impose the wrong cognitive model on insight into thing-in-itself as Will if we try to think of thing-in-itself as the individual will known by means of introspection. Inner perception involves a subject–object dichotomy. It remains a type of phenomenological representation in which willing and the individual will confronts the subject psychologically, through its own acts of willing, taken as object. That, for obvious reasons, given what Schopenhauer has said about the impossibility of gaining access to thing-in-itself via knowledge of the world as representation, cannot provide the basis for a correct understanding of thing-in-itself. Inner perception of individual willing is nevertheless the starting-point for what Schopenhauer describes as a more complete method whereby thing-in-itself is identified with Will. It is the intervention of this further intermediate process that justifies preserving the typographical distinction we have observed throughout between "will" and "Will" (WWR 2: 196–7).

Thing-in-itself is a mystery even when we have identified it with Will and recognized that the pure willing within each of us is thing-in-itself. If we put all knowledge on the side of the world as representation, on the side of explainable phenomena falling under the *principium individuationis* and fourfold root of the principle of sufficient reason, then there is nothing more to be said about thing-in-itself. We cannot subsume thing-in-itself in any of the categories of knowledge and explanation we are accustomed to apply in the world as representation. At best, we may come to an insight through what Schopenhauer refers to as an intuitive inner feeling as opposed to outward or external understanding. We cannot explain thing-in-itself, but only arrive intuitively at the insight that thing-in-itself is Will. The alternative is to admit that phenomena have a transcendental ground about which nothing substantive whatsoever can be known. Schopenhauer believes that we can attain non-representational insight into thing-in-itself in spite of these obstacles. He characterizes thing-in-itself by this choice of term after what he claims is the highest degree of thing-in-itself's objectification manifested in the world as representation, within our own inner lives, where it occurs as the foundational uncaused, unmotivated, objectless and subjectless willing that underlies the will to life. It is the pure or raw willing that occurs whenever in real time we will this or that.

The account of thing-in-itself in Schopenhauer's transcendental metaphysics is more complicated than Schopenhauer sometimes makes it appear. It is not that each act of will in the ordinary sense, as when we desire a drink of water, is identical with thing-in-itself. Rather, it is within the desire for a drink of water that pure willing or Will as thing-in-itself can be intuited at the deepest core of ordinary episodes of phenomenologically experienced willing. We can locate Will by thinking away all of the external trappings of phenomenal willing to expose its pure naked form. Reflection then reveals that pure willing satisfies the theoretical requirements of the Kantian thing-in-itself. The pure willing or Will that underlies ordinary willing is not a mere analogue or something similar or corresponding to thing-in-itself, but is identical instead to thing-in-itself; it is the thing-in-itself itself. Pure willing is non-representational, non-individualizable and, as a further sign of its transcendence of the world as representation, it is not subject in any way to the fourfold root of the principle of sufficient reason.

We must ask, how can this be? How can individual willing in each individual willing subject fail to be individualizable? Why should we not be able to identify my willing to have a drink of water, as opposed to yours, and why should it not be individualizable precisely as my desire and no one else's? How can there not be a sufficient causal and motivational explanation of my willing to drink water, with logical and mathematical dimensions as well, if under the circumstances I am thirsty, I have not imbibed any liquids for a long time, my physiology is in such and such a state, I am not physically prevented or otherwise inhibited from drinking, and the like? If all aspects of my individual willing are individualizable and explainable in the manner of other representational phenomena, even if they are in this case psychological, how can my individual willing possibly be directly related to what is supposed to be non-representational thing-in-itself?

The pure willing or Will underlying any individual act of will is intuited by means of a thought experiment. Consider any act of will, such as desiring a drink of water. Schopenhauer instructs us to ask a specific series of questions. We start out with introspective representational recognition of willing to drink, and ask *why* we will to drink. The answer could be this or that, depending on the circumstances. A representing willing subject could have any number of reasons for wanting to drink some water. Perhaps the reason is to quench one's thirst, to wash down an accidentally swallowed bug, to keep an oboe reed lubricated, to walk past the water fountain and try to attract the attention of an interesting person, or any number of other possibilities. The exact reason does not matter so much as the fact that as an event in the world as representation the psychological act of willing to drink water implies that there exists some kind of motivation for the act of will. This much is already assumed by the assumption that all occurrences in the world of representation can be explained by appropriate, including motivational, laws, under the fourfold root of the principle of sufficient reason. Suppose in a given case that the reason is because of thirst. Then we can ask regressively: why does one will to quench one's thirst? If the answer is that we will to quench our thirst because we will something else again, to survive, or to be happy, or the like, then we can continue to ask: why do we will these things? If Schopenhauer is right, then there is always a good motivational reason to explain why we will each of these things at each step in turn, in a complete account of the motivation for a willing subject's willing to drink.[5]

Schopenhauer further claims that the regress of motivations can proceed indefinitely. Eventually, and often quite quickly, we reach a point where we may decide to ask a slightly different question. Clearly, moreover, nothing prevents us from asking this kind of question right away without further ado. We can ask: why does one (simply) will? We will to drink because we are thirsty. We may be thirsty for any number of complex reasons. But why do we will? Why is it that we will anything, as opposed to not willing at all or willing only this or that? Schopenhauer insists that this apparently legitimate question has no correct answer. The fact that one wills can be deduced from the fact that one wills this or that: to have a drink of water, or to own a houseboat, or to become the Prime Minister of Cameroon. When one wills this or that, one always does so for a reason aimed at a particular object and with a particular motivation. Since motivational explanation is one root of the principle of sufficient reason, it follows for Schopenhauer that a subject's willing this or that is an explainable phenomenon, like other psychological events.

There is, by contrast, no correct answer to the general question why we will, as opposed to why we will this or that. Pure willing or Will as such is beyond the scope of explanation. If we reach back far enough, to the point where it no longer makes sense to enquire into the motivations generally for willing anything whatsoever, as opposed to willing this or that, then Schopenhauer holds we have passed beyond the power of the fourfold root, at which point we shall have crossed over to thing-in-itself. It is precisely there and then that our reflections are met with the recognition of unmotivated, uncaused willing that lies deep within us, at the heart of every act of ordinary willing. Pure, undirected, objectless, unmotivated and uncaused willing is not the willing of any particular object by any particular willing subject for any particular reason. As such, it is unindividualizable and inexplicable; it is pure willing, plain and simple. If we know how to look for it, we can find it at the core of any act of ordinary willing, when we dig deep enough and think away the objects and reasons for willing in order to arrive at willing in its purest form. It is because pure willing or Will is unmotivated, undirected toward any objects, unindividualizable and inexplicable by any of the modes of explanation available under the fourfold root, that Schopenhauer regards it as satisfying the theoretical requirements of Kantian thing-in-itself.

The nature of thing-in-itself is thus found in the only place it could possibly be located, deep within every act of willing. The pure unmotivated willing that transcends my willing to drink water and your willing to drink wine, or my willing to acquire a houseboat and your willing to acquire a law degree, is indistinguishable. There is no difference between my unmotivated willing and yours, in so far as it is simply willing. If we begin with individual willing, and recognize that at the core of any act of willing this or that there must always be pure willing for which no motivational explanation is available, then we shall have discovered that thing-in-itself is Will. There is pure willing or Will underlying every particular act of will for every willing subject. Pure willing, moreover, must satisfy the requirements for thing-in-itself. Schopenhauer's argument can be divided into the following steps:

1. The only conceivable sources of insight into thing-in-itself are perceptual knowledge and inner acquaintance with individual willing, corresponding to the only two conceivable ways in which we can come to know our own bodies.
2. Perceptual knowledge is limited to representations, and cannot possibly offer knowledge or understanding of thing-in-itself; it must therefore be excluded.
3. This leaves only inner acquaintance with individual willing as the only possible source of insight into thing-in-itself.
4. Beginning with individual willing, we can abstract or think away from it all object, direction, causation and motivation, mentally substracting these features from individual willing.
5. What remains is pure willing or Will, which satisfies the requirements of thing-in-itself as beyond the *principium individuationis* and fourfold root of the principle of sufficient reason.
6. Hence, thing-in-itself is Will, taking its name from the highest and most complete and immediate grade of thing-in-itself's objectification in acts of individual willing.

Schopenhauer says repeatedly throughout his philosophical writings that thing-in-itself is pure, uncaused, unmotivated, objectless and subjectless willing, which he also describes as undirected striving or blind urging. If we cannot imagine willing without its being directed toward a particular object by a particular subject and without some motivation for its occurrence, it is undoubtedly because we are stuck in the mould of thinking only about willing this or that, rather than pure willing.

Will, as Schopenhauer interprets it in this context, is non-representational, inexplicable thing-in-itself. It is Kant's *Ding an sich*, whose nature for Kant is utterly unknowable beyond the mind's merely conceiving of its existence. It exists within all of us at the bottommost foundation of every individual act of willing in every exercise of individual will. It is not just that familiarity with phenomenal willing suggests that thing-in-itself might be similar or analogical, something wilful. Schopenhauer argues that Will as pure uncaused, unmotivated, objectless and subjectless willing is identical with thing-in-itself as the transcendental ground of every act of ordinary willing, and ultimately of the entire world as representation.

The Trojan horse metaphor mentioned in connection with Schopenhauer's first, analogical, argument to show that thing-in-itself is Will is consequently inappropriate for the later argument. We cannot say, as Schopenhauer unhesitatingly does in the first edition of *The World as Will and Representation*, that individual acts of willing enable us by stealth to enter the fortress walls that divide the phenomenal world as representation from thing-in-itself. To speak more accurately, whenever and wherever an act of individual empirical willing this or that occurs there also is to be found, within or without the city's defences, thing-in-itself as pure willing or Will. Considered only as such it exists for no reason, it is directed toward no particular or general object, and belongs as an act of thought to no particular willing subject. Schopenhauer unsurprisingly drops references to circling the castle walls in the second edition of *The World as Will and Representation*, and speaks instead in terms of our already being inside the fortress, of having been there all along. We need only come to recognize that every act of phenomenal willing already contains pure willing as thing-in-itself at its core, transcending all representation within individual psychology, and hence of the world as representation at large.

We may wonder whether Schopenhauer speaks literally when he describes thing-in-itself in the first-person as "my" will. This parallels his idealist designations of the empirical world as "my" representation, relative in the first-person to each individual subject. Thing-in-itself, on the other hand, by definition, is supposed to be non-individual and altogether non-individualizable. It can no more be my will in particular than any other individual thinking subject's will. It must rather be understood as pure willing, as the Will that underlies all phenomenal acts of willing on the part of individual willing subjects. Schopenhauer nevertheless writes unqualifiedly:

> The inner reluctance with which everyone accepts the world as his mere representation warns him that this consideration, quite apart from its truth, is nevertheless one-sided, and so is occasioned by some arbitrary abstraction. On the other hand, he can never withdraw from this acceptance. However, the one-sidedness of this consideration will be made good in the following book through a truth that is not so immediately certain as that from which we start here. Only deeper investigation, more difficult abstraction, the separation of what is different, and the combination of what is identical can lead us to this truth. This truth, which must be very serious and grave if not terrible to everyone, is that a man also can say and must say: "The world is my will".   (WWR 1: 4)

In adopting a first-person way of relating thing-in-itself to Will, Schopenhauer means to emphasize the fact that thing-in-itself transcends each individual subject's phenomenal acts of willing. We begin, in his methodology, with each willing subject's personal acts of will. When the enquiry is complete, we transcend all personality and individuality, gaining intuitive insight into the hidden inner nature of thing-in-itself. We must, as Schopenhauer remarks, undertake a "deeper investigation". If we have accurately described his mode of transcendental reasoning, then the more penetrating procedure he requires is to think away or abstract from willing as inner knowledge of the body all objects of and motivations for individual willing (WWR 1: 164–5).

With a grain of salt, we can accept Schopenhauer's otherwise paradoxical first-person statement that the world is "my" will. The pronouncement is true enough, provided that the Will is understood to transcend each representing subject's individual acts of will. Thing-in-itself, in that case, uncaused, unmotivated and objectless, also transcends all particular phenomenal psychological acts of personalized individual willing, and hence all particular subjects. It is subjectless because it is blind, undirected, or objectless, and because there is no subject without an object. Schopenhauer's conclusion is not that thing-in-itself is identical with my individual will or any of my individual acts of willing. It is rather that each willing subject engaged in abstraction – thinking away the particularity of their individual acts of willing – can reveal thing-in-itself as pure willing through first-person individual acts of willing. Will as thing-in-itself universally transcends each individual thinking subject's first-person acquaintance with personal acts of will.[6]

Why does Schopenhauer fasten onto acts of individual willing rather than other equally "inner" psychological processes? Why does he not begin with reason or passion and think away their individuality, causation, motivation and the like, until he arrives at pure reason or pure passion stripped down to satisfy the requirements of thing-in-itself? The answer is that we cannot perform the same abstraction with reason or passion as with willing in order to arrive at something that in its pure form is beyond the principles of individuation and sufficient reason. Reason, for example, because of its nature, even in its purest most abstract form, can never stand outside the logical root of the principle of sufficient reason. It is for the same reason that perception can never be so purified as to stand outside the causal root, and no doubt the logical and mathematical roots as well, if perception by definition is always of something that occurs in space and time.

What, then, of passion? Can we not purify an individual experience of passion to strip it of all its individuality? Can we not abstract from it all of the same kinds of accidental qualities that Schopenhauer thinks away in abstracting pure willing from phenomenal acts of will to arrive at Will as thing-in-itself? Why could we not similarly arrive at pure passion as thing-in-itself? Passion, needless to say, is something passive. As such, it is the very opposite of willing, which Schopenhauer regards as an active force directing and controlling the body's movements. This is what makes the consideration of abstract passion so intriguing as the most extreme alternative to the conclusions Schopenhauer wants to draw concerning Will as thing-in-itself. If pure passion, or Passion, is not a suitable candidate for thing-in-itself because it does not offer insight into the hidden forces that transcend phenomenal appearance, then perhaps we should begin to be more sceptical about the possibility of ever achieving such understanding of the relation between thing-in-itself and the world as representation. If we are not quite at that stage, it is only because we do not yet know whether or not Passion is an acceptable rival to Will as thing-in-itself.

A moment's reflection shows that Passion does not seriously compete with Will in Schopenhauer's uncovering of thing-in-itself. The concept of passion, and hence of Passion, is inherently of something done to a subject, whereas an action is something a willing subject does. We suffer passions as a result of different sorts of interactions with the world. This makes the concept of passion, individual or abstracted as much as possible from all individuality, necessarily causal. Willing, in contrast, in its most pure abstract form, need not be causal because willing as such need neither be caused nor causally efficacious. If, on the contrary, we try to subtract from passion the fact that the experience has been brought about or visited upon a subject, something that has been caused to happen, often against the subject's will, then we have either contradicted ourselves or are no longer talking about passion in the proper sense of the word. The passive nature of passion is necessarily of something caused or inflicted. This, in turn, makes it altogether unsuitable for abstraction beyond the principle of sufficient reason, disqualifying it as something other than Will to stand as a possible counter-Schopenhauerian thing-in-itself.

If we try to think away from an act of phenomenal willing its cause, motivation, object and therefore its subject, do we have reason to suppose that there will be anything left at all? Is the situation not like that of peeling all the layers from an onion only to discover at the end that there is nothing more inside at the centre because an onion consists entirely of its layers? Schopenhauer would have us believe that pure willing, Will as thing-in-itself, is at the core of every episode of ordinary willing, of willing this or that. The conclusion can be upheld if we suppose that the same four factors of cause, motivation, object and subject attach to phenomenal psychological occurrences other than willing. Pure willing remains left over as distinctive of a phenomenal act of will in the process of subtracting these factors, for otherwise there can be no way of distinguishing phenomenal willing from phenomenal believing, doubting, suffering passion, being in pain or the like. We can think away from these mental states the same four factors, but what is left behind then, unlike the end result of the process beginning with phenomenal willing, as in the case of passion or perceiving, has no pretence of qualifying as thing-in-itself. Only pure willing seems to meet the test, satisfying the requirements for Kantian thing-in-itself by virtue of falling outside the principles of individuation and sufficient reason.

Character of Will as thing-in-itself in the world as representation and as revealed in the laws of natural science

An important implication of Schopenhauer's identification of thing-in-itself as Will is that Will objectifies or manifests its inner character externally in the world as representation. Schopenhauer upholds the inference by acknowledging the same relation in the observable character of individual will in an agent's body.

We sometimes say that a person's character is revealed in his or her actions. Although we may not be able to experience immediately the will that directs an individual's deeds, we imagine that whatever thoughts are moving them to act are reflected either directly or through a distorting lens in their observable behaviour. We additionally do not expect simply to be able to read off an individual's character from any particular example of behaviour, since we know that many people are capable of disguising their real intentions and personality, at least for certain periods of time, and of dissimulating their intentions in interactions with others. Still, we generally believe that if we had access to a wide variety of a person's behaviours in many different circumstances, both among others and when they are by themselves, then we would have many essential clues to their true underlying character.[7]

Schopenhauer argues that thinking subjects reveal their inner characters in their external appearance, both in body and behaviour. He argues that the same is true of the world as representation considered as a whole with respect to its character reflected in all its representable features known to empirical science. When we study the natural properties of the physical universe, we are in effect inferentially learning as much as we can about the inner character of thing-in-itself. We discover the character of Will as it is revealed by its objectifications manifested in the world as representation. The process is much the same as that by which we judge the character of an individual willing subject as revealed by their appearance and actions. The human being considered epistemically from dual aspects through knowledge of external body and internal wilful action is a microcosm of the relation between the hidden inner character of Will or thing-in-itself that is externally expressed through its objectifications in the world as representation.

The transcendental metaphysics of thing-in-itself as Will reveals its character. It is indirectly perceivable in every scientifically knowable aspect of the world as representation. Although of necessity we cannot represent thing-in-itself, or explain it or individuate it into distinctive entities, parts or moments, we find suggestive clues and partial confirmation of the character of thing-in-itself as Will by scientifically studying its phenomenal objectifications. The method is the same as that by which we seize on information about an individual subject's will as manifested externally in their body and behaviour. There is a character of the world as representation that reflects its manifestation of thing-in-itself as Will, just as there is a character of each individual willing subject that is reflected in actions construed as external expressions of inner acts of will.

Considering the most familiar aspects of the world as representation known to empirical science, Schopenhauer calls attention especially to those features that are not fully or satisfactorily explained by the morphology and etiology of the natural sciences. The principle of sufficient reason guarantees explanations of any observable events exhibiting lawlike regularities. As Schopenhauer frequently remarks, we cannot delve more deeply than this to gain a more profound understanding of how or why the particular causal laws of nature obtain or why natural processes function as they do. Where empirical methods fail us, traditional Kantian transcendental metaphysics can only attach the name of thing-in-itself to whatever lies behind and beyond phenomena as something conceivable, the noumenon, while offering nothing contentful by way of insight into its hidden inner nature. Schopenhauer believes he has outpaced Kant's vacuous concept of thing-in-itself by identifying thing-in-itself as pure willing or Will. He approaches the problem of the nature of the world as representation and the hidden nature of thing-in-itself from two complementary directions, in much the same way that one thinking subject can try to get to know another person's character.

Schopenhauer finds signs of the character of thing-in-itself in such physical phenomena as gravity, electricity, magnetism, chemical attraction and repulsion, vegetable physiology, phototropism and photosynthesis, comparative anatomy and so-called animal magnetism. He discusses some of these occurrences in relation to his metaphysics of thing-in-itself as Will in *The World as Will and Representation*, and supplements them in his catalogue of corroborative scientific testimony in *On the Will in Nature*. He collates the discoveries of empirical science looking for indications that the world is Will and for information concerning its inner non-representational character. The world as Will projects itself imperfectly and in distorted but still discernible ways through its objectifications in the empirical world as representation.

The knowledge of nature in both intuitive and abstract representation takes us only so far. It helps us to identify distinguishable features of the world, to be organized and systematically arranged, classified under covering laws and considered as causally related one to another. Schopenhauer begins with what he considers to be the lowest grades of the Will's objectification in the physical forces of gravity and attraction. "As we proceed", he writes:

> we shall see that this [natural force] belongs not to the inner nature
> of the will, but merely to its most distinct phenomenon as animal
> and human being. Therefore, if I say that the force which attracts a
> stone to the earth is of its nature, in itself, and apart from all repre-
> sentation, will, then no one will attach to this proposition the absurd
> meaning that the stone moves itself according to a known motive,
> because it is thus that the will appears in man.   (WWR 1: 105)

We are puzzled by the reality behind the laws of nature. At best, the principles of mathematical physics do not reveal the forces of nature in their deeper essence, but only explicate how they work superficially in relating phenomena to phenomena. What is concealed by such laws, according to Schopenhauer, is the fact that the forces described in natural science are expressions of the inner character of the world as representation, of thing-in-itself as Will.

It is tempting to interpret such assertions metaphorically. The Will is supposed to be blind urging, undirected desire and the inner principle of motion of the world as representation. The same seems to be true at least by analogy with respect to the individual will as the inner principle of motion for the willing subject's body. If we consider the world as representation in its entirety as a body, like the human body, with thing-in-itself as Will, like the human will, then just as we can will to move a finger or toe, we can picture the Will underlying all physical phenomena in the world as representation as directing and controlling all natural events under its unthinking blind objectless "direction" and "control" as transcendental thing-in-itself. What is less easy to understand is how in that case Will as thing-in-itself can objectify itself in many different ways in the world as representation without willing this or that or anything in particular. Thing-in-itself as Will is supposed to be blind, objectless, subjectless, undirected and unmotivated. The will as the body's inner principle is able to control the movement of limbs because the subject chooses to do something specific, such as to move a body part in a certain way. The analogy breaks down if we try to think of thing-in-itself as Will objectifying, expressing or manifesting itself in the world as representation at large if it cannot also have specific intentions and specific purposes to fulfil by bringing about specific changes in phenomena. The problem is that Schopenhauer rightly disallows the possibility of thing-in-itself having any sort of causal efficacy, or being involved in any cause–effect relation. Will as thing-in-itself transcends and is altogether outside any mode of explanation under the fourfold root of the principle of sufficient reason, including, especially, causation.

Schopenhauer recognizes Will as the innermost transcendent nature of reality objectified in the world as representation and manifested among other ways as natural forces. The scientific investigation of the world as representation only partly satisfies the desire for knowledge that motivates philosophical enquiry. When we have exhausted the explanations of natural phenomena that can be given in terms of efficient causation, and by means of logical, mathematical and motivational laws, when we have attained as much superficial knowledge as we can of objects and events in the world as representation, then we long to go beyond empirical representations to the transcendental metaphysics of thing-in-itself. Although we cannot expect to arrive at explanations in the usual sense, or of the sort that apply to representational phenomena, recognizing that thing-in-itself is Will provides insight into the transcendental metaphysics of such natural forces as gravity and electromagnetism, principles of growth, nutrition and procreation in living things and crystals, processes of animal and vegetable generation, sexual energy, procreation rites and societal practices, cultural movements, political intrigues and war. Schopenhauer claims to detect the objectification of Will in mechanics, astronomy, biology, physiology, chemistry, psychology and all other natural and social sciences (WWR 1: 110).

Quest for transcendental knowledge

If we question more closely the value of investigations of the world that carry enquiry beyond phenomena to thing-in-itself, we may wonder whether such metaphysical insights are truly satisfying. We should briefly take stock of the reasoning by which Schopenhauer has brought us to this point.

We learn about the world through perception, but we are dissatisfied with the superficial explanations to which we are limited by the principle of sufficient reason. We can do no more than knit together phenomenal objects and events into relations and regularities under lawlike principles, but we can never discover what natural forces are or why they exist. Nor can we learn why objects and events are ruled by particular natural laws other than to refer again to the regularities that happen to prevail within the empirical order of phenomena. Schopenhauer says that we are driven by natural curiosity in that case to look beyond the world as representation, to ask whether there is not after all something more to the world than a tissue of appearances.

Suppose, then, that we agree with Schopenhauer that there is more to the world than representation, that there is also thing-in-itself, and that thing-in-itself is Will. Since we cannot know anything more about thing-in-itself other than the fact that it is Will, how does it help to satisfy our cravings for a deeper understanding of the hidden nature of the world behind the veil of Maya? Can we not still ask why there is thing-in-itself and why it is Will? Schopenhauer will no doubt answer that there must be thing-in-itself because there are representations and there must be something that is represented, something that is objectified for representing subjects in the world as representation. Of course, he will not agree with Kant, as he interprets his argument, that thing-in-itself *causes* its representations. As to why thing-in-itself is Will, we have two versions of Schopenhauer's answer. He offers analogical reasoning concerning individual willing as inner knowledge of the body, as the only conceivable source of knowledge other than perceptual knowledge of the body's external representational properties, and of Will or pure willing as what remains of phenomenal willing when its motivations and objects, and hence all particularity, are stripped away in thought by a process of abstraction.

Do appeals to thing-in-itself as Will truly satisfy our desire to know more about the world, to progress beyond the superficial veneer of phenomenal representations, to know that the world is also thing-in-itself and that thing-in-itself is Will? If we believe Schopenhauer's proposition that the hidden factor in gravity, electromagnetism, plant and crystal growth and the like is Will as thing-in-itself, and that these are among the many ways in which Will objectifies itself in the world as representation, does it really answer our desire for a deeper more profound understanding of the hidden inner workings of the phenomenal world? What is objectification, and what is it for Will as thing-in-itself to be objectified in the world as representation, if there is no causal or other explanatory connection between Will and representation? Does transcendental idealism do anything more than attach a label to that which we would like to understand? Schopenhauer anticipates the thrust of this objection and tries to blunt its force:

> I should be misunderstood by anyone who thought that ultimately it was all the same whether we expressed this essence-in-itself of all phenomena by the word will or by any other word. This would be the case if this thing-in-itself were something whose existence we merely *inferred*, and thus knew only indirectly and merely in the abstract. Then certainly we could call it what we liked; the name would stand merely as the symbol of an unknown quantity. But the word *will*, which, like a magic word, is to reveal to us the innermost essence of everything in nature, by no means expresses an unknown

quantity, something reached by inferences and syllogisms, but something known absolutely and immediately, and that so well that we know and understand what will is better than anything else, be it what it may. Hitherto, the concept of *will* has been subsumed under the concept of *force*; I, on the other hand, do exactly the reverse, and intend every force in nature to be conceived as will.

(WWR 1: 111)

The concept of Will, as Schopenhauer understands it, is supposed to have the effect of a magic incantation that reveals to us the inner nature of the world as representation. Does it really have this potential? Whereas other theorists have tried to interpret phenomenal psychological will as a kind of energy, Schopenhauer declares his intention to reverse this order, maintaining on the contrary that natural forces are among the manifestations of Will. This is an interesting statement of the priority Schopenhauer attaches to Will in understanding the transcendental ground of natural phenomena. By itself, however, it does not necessarily satisfy the desire for a more profound metaphysical understanding of the phenomenal world.

We observe physical events in the world as representation in which forces of attraction hold between physical objects, from planetary motion to such mundane occurrences as an apple falling to earth as it drops from a tree. We study the laws of gravity as Newton formulated them and, let us suppose, we accept Schopenhauer's philosophical interpretation of natural laws as summary statements of the regularities that obtain among empirical events. Now we want to progress another step in understanding the hidden nature of gravity and whatever physical phenomena are subject generally to the laws of physics. We have the magic word "Will", as Schopenhauer says, and we are told that beyond the limits of the world as representation there is thing-in-itself, and that thing-in-itself is Will. We know that Will is blind, objectless, subjectless, unmotivated, uncaused and undirected pure willing. It is whatever is left over when we have taken an individual act of willing as we experience it in our own volitional direction and control of body movements, as the inner knowledge of body, and then subtract away from it object, subject, motivation and cause. It is pure willing, then, willing in its most refined essence, or Will as thing-in-itself.

This is not an insignificant conclusion. Nor, as Schopenhauer says, is "Will" merely a word for noumenal thing-in-itself. Whatever Kant's noumenon is supposed to be, it does not add anything of substance to the deeper insight we hope to attain of the natural forces such as gravity that govern physical phenomena. We understand that there is more to the world than the ways in which it is represented to thought. We expect that what transcends phenomenal appearance is not just thing-in-itself under any

97

arbitrary name we might care to give it as a kind of blank space in transcendental metaphysics. We may also agree with Schopenhauer that thing-in-itself identified more specifically as Will constitutes an advance in our understanding of the world's hidden inner nature. The Will is already intuited in direct acquaintance within our own experience of wilful actions, shorn of all their particularity, direction, motivation and causation. It is in this way that we understand thing-in-itself as pure willing or Will abstracted from its purest imaginable form. If Schopenhauer is right that thing-in-itself is Will, then his conclusions concerning gravity and other natural forces as objectifications of Will offer something that is more profound in understanding the world as representation than we can hope to find within the empirical sciences or conventional non-Schopenhauerian metaphysics.

If thing-in-itself is Will, then there is no hope of attaining any further understanding of natural phenomena than to know that thing-in-itself as Will transcends all aspects of the world as representation. Thing-in-itself neither needs nor can possibly have any further transcendental ground, nor does it provide any further occasion for speculation or desire for deeper or greater understanding. We cannot sensibly ask why thing-in-itself is Will. There is no further question beyond the fact that pure willing underlying individual acts of will meets all the theoretical requirements of transcendental thing-in-itself by virtue of being unindividualizable, unmotivated, uncaused, objectless and subjectless. For, in that case, Will as thing-in-itself is also inexplicable. When we have reached thing-in-itself, we have struck metaphysical bedrock, just as in the world of representation we hit explanatory bottom when we have ordered all occurrent phenomena under all the possible relations and lawlike regularities permitted by the principle of sufficient reason. It is the same pure willing that we find at the heart of any individual act of phenomenal will, after which there is nowhere else to seek further metaphysical understanding. We discover the answers within ourselves, when we recognize that thing-in-itself in any first-person experience of volitional activity in the inner knowledge of our bodies is the microcosm of which the entire world as representation is the macrocosm.[8]

Platonic Ideas as grades of the Will's objectification

Schopenhauer finds a place for Platonic Ideas in his philosophy as grades of the Will's objectification. Will is objectified in distinct grades, depending on the degree of individuality or differentiation among similar objects instantiating an Idea. The Ideas for Schopenhauer as a result are not abstract entities existing in a Platonic heaven or museum of archetypes, but instead are all of the possible grades of the Will's objectification. They are the many ways in which Will can transcendentally ground the phenomenal appearances of thing-in-itself as objects for subjects.

Schopenhauer identifies Platonic Ideas with distinct grades of the Will's objectification, when he writes, "Now I say that these *grades of the objectification of the will* are nothing but *Plato's Ideas*. I mention this here for the moment, so that in future I can use the word *Idea* in this sense" (WWR 1: 129). He is committed to this account of Platonic Ideas analysed as grades of the Will's objectification as the only historically correct interpretation of Plato's theory. "Therefore with me the word ['Idea'] is always to be understood in its genuine and original meaning", he adds:

> given to it by Plato; and in using it we must assuredly not think of those abstract productions of scholastic dogmatizing reason, to describe which Kant used the word wrongly as well as illegitimately, although Plato had already taken possession of it, and used it most appropriately. (WWR 1: 129–30)

He concludes, "Therefore, by *Idea* I understand every definite and fixed *grade of the will's objectification*, in so far as it is thing-in-itself and is therefore foreign to plurality. These grades are certainly related to individual things as their eternal forms, or as their prototypes" (WWR 1: 130).

Where Plato identifies a Form or Idea as a real abstract entity in Platonic heaven, such as the archetype Dog, in which all individual dogs and kinds of dogs participate or which they imitate or instantiate, Schopenhauer refers to a specific grade of the Will's objectification, different in degree from any other, corresponding to the general concept of Dog. He conceives of Platonic Ideas as organized into a hierarchy, in which human beings occupy the highest rank. The justification for this honour is supposed to be that human beings exemplify the highest grade of the Will's objectification by virtue of possessing the greatest individuality. Schopenhauer's ordering of Platonic Ideas as grades of the Will's objectification is reminiscent of pre-Darwinian conceptions of the animal kingdom arranged in a strictly linear rather than branching order, beginning with the simplest most primitive lifeforms and proceeding upward teleologically to humankind as the glory of creation. He writes:

> Although in man, as (Platonic) Idea, the will finds its most distinct and perfect objectification, this alone could not express its true being. In order to appear in its proper significance, the Idea of man would need to manifest itself, not alone and torn apart, but accompanied by all the grades downwards through all the forms of animals, through

the plant kingdom to the inorganic. They all supplement one another for the complete objectification of the will. They are as much presupposed by the Idea of man as the blossoms of the tree presuppose its leaves, branches, trunk, and root. They form a pyramid, of which the highest point is man.   (WWR 1: 153)

The Ideas for Schopenhauer might in principle be set down as belonging alternatively to the world as representation or to thing-in-itself identified as Will. Unlike Plato, Schopenhauer believes in the existence not of two worlds, but of a single world with two aspects. As a result, Schopenhauer has a problem about where and how to situate the Platonic Ideas that does not touch Plato's original theory.

There is no prospect for Schopenhauer to consign Platonic Ideas to thing-in-itself, because there are differences between the Ideas that make them individual. Since there are many grades of the Will's objectification, there are many distinct Ideas that are different and hence individualizable from one another *as* Ideas. The Idea of Dog, for example, is not the same Idea as the Idea of Horse or Cat. Platonic Ideas, as a result, cannot belong to the world as Will, and so cannot call thing-in-itself home in Schopenhauer's transcendental idealism. Nor does it appear at first that Platonic Ideas can be appropriately situated in Schopenhauer's world as representation. Ideas are not supposed to be spatiotemporal; they are usually assumed, at least in Plato's theory as it is standardly interpreted, as the abstract entities that individual things in the world of appearance only imperfectly "imitate" or "strive", metaphorically speaking, to become, or in which they "participate". Since these are the only two aspects of Schopenhauer's one and only world, there is no third metaphysical realm or category to which he can plausibly assign the Platonic Ideas, no place to which they can reasonably be said to belong.[9]

Schopenhauer agrees with Plato in classifying Ideas as aspatiotemporal, unsusceptible to alteration or change of any kind, and existing eternally rather than involved in any process of becoming. "Accordingly," Schopenhauer says, speaking from the standpoint of widely received scholarship on Plato's metaphysics, "what follows ... has already impressed itself as a matter of course on every student of Plato ... Those different grades of the will's objectification, expressed in innumerable individuals, exist as the unattained patterns of these, or as the eternal forms of things" (WWR 1: 129). Significantly, Schopenhauer then adds: "Not themselves entering into time and space, the medium of individuals, they remain fixed, subject to no change, always being, never having become. The particular things, however, arise and pass away; they are always becoming and never are" (WWR 1: 129). His solution is to situate Platonic Ideas as grades of the Will's objectification in the objectified world as representation where they are in some sense perceivable. This is an odd way to think of the Platonic Ideas that have always been assumed to occupy a world distinct from all ephemeral phenomena. Schopenhauer nevertheless insists that degrees of the Will's objectification are as abstract as mathematical properties, which in a limited way can also be perceived.[10]

Relation of Platonic Ideas to Kantian thing-in-itself

The concept of a Platonic Idea and the Kantian thing-in-itself may appear at first to be diametrically opposed. There are numerous Platonic Ideas, we are told, but for Schopenhauer there is only one thing-in-itself. Identified by Schopenhauer as Will, thing-in-itself is not subject to the principle of individuation; hence, there cannot be a plurality of things-in-themselves as there are of Platonic Ideas. Platonic Ideas, moreover, are supposed to belong to the world as representation, explainable by the laws subsumed under the principle of sufficient reason. The Ideas, as distinct grades of the Will's objectification, can therefore hardly be the same as Will. Finally, Schopenhauer maintains that thing-in-itself is not an object of perceptual knowledge, whereas a passive apprehension of the Platonic Ideas in sensation is the goal and substance of abstract general knowledge, and the first indispensable step of aesthetic appreciation and artistic creativity.

Despite these discrepancies, Schopenhauer assimilates Platonic Ideas as grades of the Will's objectification to the Kantian thing-in-itself as Will in one crucial respect. He does not simply identify Platonic Ideas with thing-in-itself, some of whose theoretical differences he acknowledges. Instead, he proposes by way of shedding light both on Plato's Ideas and Kant's thing-in-itself that the two concepts are distinct ways of addressing the same philosophical problem from different but related perspectives. He sets the stage for a comparison of Plato and Kant, taking preliminary steps toward a synthesis of the history of two great streams of thought in Western philosophy, brought together for the first time in Schopenhauer's theory of transcendental idealism.

The basis for the analogy, which Schopenhauer describes as holding between thing-in-itself and the Platonic Ideas, is something that has frequently been recognized as essential to Plato's theory of Ideas. It is the one–many relation, whereby a Platonic Idea, a one, is instantiated by many different individuals that exemplify the Idea. This instantiation, Schopenhauer states, is reminiscent of a similar one–many relation, whereby the Kantian thing-in-itself, as a unitary transcendent reality, is objectified in the world as representation as many different perceivable entities. Plato's theory of Ideas and Kant's thing-in-itself are aimed in different ways at the same goal of articulating a metaphysics relating a one–many relation between a transcendent unitary reality and its plurality of instantiations or objectifications in the phenomenal world. Schopenhauer accordingly discerns in Plato and Kant a common effort to account for the appearances of many individual things in relation to a unitary appearance-transcending reality. Many objects of experience in both cases are brought into correspondence with a one. The many individuals inhabiting the empirical world are related respectively to a singular Platonic Idea or Kantian thing-in-itself. Schopenhauer believes that only his theory of Will as thing-in-itself and Platonic Ideas as grades of the Will's objectification, combining the best features of Plato's and Kant's metaphysics, satisfies the need to correlate a unified transcendent reality with a plurality of individual objects in the world as representation.

Schopenhauer synthesizes Plato's Ideas and Kant's thing-in-itself in a series of steps. First, he calls attention to the one–many relation in Kant's transcendental metaphysics whereby thing-in-itself corresponds to its many representational objectifications. "Just as a magic lantern shows many different pictures," he reasons:

> but it is only one and the same flame that makes them all visible, so in all the many different phenomena which together fill the world or supplant one another as successive events, it is only the *one will* that appears, and everything is its visibility, its objectivity; it remains unmoved in the midst of this change. It alone is the thing-in-itself; every object is phenomenon, to speak Kant's language, or appearance.　　　　　　　　　　　　　　　　　　　　　　(WWR 1: 153).

Schopenhauer is prepared on this basis to establish a significant commonality between the Platonic Ideas and Kantian thing-in-itself. He refrains from simply identifying the two philosophical concepts, but argues that they are two similar but still different ways of attaining the same purpose. They both venture to account for the plurality and diversity of individual objects in the world as representation in terms of the relation of many kinds of objects to something simple and unitary that transcends individuality in the phenomenal world. Schopenhauer interprets the leading concepts of the two great philosophical traditions as dovetailing in his own theory of thing-in-itself as Will and Platonic Ideas as grades of the Will's objectification.

> Now if for us the will is the *thing-in-itself*, and the *Idea* is the immediate objectivity of that will at a definite grade, then we find Kant's thing-in-itself and Plato's Idea, for him the only ὄντως ὄν

["truly being"] – those two great and obscure paradoxes of the two
greatest philosophers of the West – to be, not exactly identical, but
yet very closely related, and distinguished by only a single modification. The two great paradoxes, just because, in spite of all inner
harmony and relationship, they sound so very different by reason
of the extraordinarily different individualities of their authors, are
even the best commentary on each other, for they are like two
entirely different paths leading to one goal.   (WWR 1: 170)

He suggests that even stylistic differences between Plato and Kant illumi-
nate more substantive similarities in their metaphysics. We need only look
beyond the superficial incongruities in Plato and Kant to see that they are
attempting in different ways to achieve the same end. They each propose in
comparable ways to explain the plurality and diversity of objects for subjects
in the phenomenal world. They do so, moreover, in comparable ways, by
relating perceived entities as a many to something transcendent that is not
merely another object among the totality of representations.

We must not lose track of the distinctions between Platonic Ideas and Kantian thing-in-itself, even as Schopenhauer interprets these metaphysical
concepts in his transcendental idealism. He argues, however, that it is possible
"to bring Kant's expression even closer to Plato's", by saying "that time, space,
and causality are that arrangement of our intellect by virtue of which the *one*
being of each kind that alone really exists, manifests itself to us as a plurality
of homogeneous beings, always being originated anew and passing away in
endless succession" (WWR 1: 173). It is vital to recall that for Kant, and more
explicitly for Schopenhauer, there can be no multiplicity of things-in-
themselves of different kinds. There is only indivisible non-individualizable
thing-in-itself as the one and only unitary reality transcending the world as
representation.

Schopenhauer is willing provisionally to overlook differences between
Plato and Kant for the sake of emphasizing what he sees as a philosophically
more interesting underlying commonality. Having emphasized the similarities, Schopenhauer now owns up to some of the most telling differences
between Plato's Ideas and Kant's thing-in-itself. He mentions the fact that
thing-in-itself is supposed to be outside all forms of knowledge, which he
equates with either intuitive or abstract representation, as the Platonic Ideas
are generally said to be. He regards this fundamental epistemic distinction
as one of the principal divisions between Platonic Ideas and Kantian thing-
in-itself:

It follows from our observations so far that, in spite of all the inner
agreement between Kant and Plato, and of the identity of the aim

that was in the mind of each, or of the world-view that inspired and led them to philosophize, Idea and thing-in-itself are not for us absolutely one and the same. On the contrary, for us the Idea is only the immediate, and therefore adequate, objectivity of the thing-in-itself, which itself, however, is the *will* – the will in so far as it is not yet objectified, had not yet become representation. For, precisely according to Kant, the thing-in-itself is supposed to be free from all the forms that adhere to knowledge as such.   (WWR 1: 174)

He further specifies what he now proclaims as the only difference between Platonic Ideas and thing-in-itself. The two cannot be identical because, on Schopenhauer's interpretation of Platonic Ideas as grades of the Will's objectification, Ideas by definition are in effect cognitive objects for a thinking subject.

There is more than a subtle note of understatement in Schopenhauer's characterization of this distinction. To say that Platonic Ideas and Kantian thing-in-itself are different only by virtue of the Platonic Ideas being perceivable objects for subjects is comparable perhaps to saying that the only difference between the living and the dead is that the dead are not living. What greater difference could there be, it is tempting to ask, between Platonic Ideas and the Kantian thing-in-itself, than for Platonic Ideas not to be thing-in-itself by virtue of being a plurality of experienceable features of represented objects for a representing subject? It is peculiar that Schopenhauer should devote his efforts to trying to establish similarities between the Ideas (generally plural) and thing-in-itself (always singular) in view of such overwhelmingly significant metaphysical and epistemic differences.

Schopenhauer answers the objection by calling attention to another crucial basis of agreement. He maintains that, despite the real differences between Plato and Kant, their convergence on a matter of such fundamental importance places their deepest metaphysical insights essentially in harmony with respect to the question of the relation between individual objects for subjects and thing-in-itself as appearance-transcending reality. Between these, Schopenhauer insists, only Platonic Ideas intervene as the Will's direct objectivity, since they do not take any special form "peculiar to knowledge as such", other than that of "representation in general". This, Schopenhauer holds, makes the Platonic Ideas the "most adequate objectivity possible" of Will as thing-in-itself (WWR 1: 175).

If Schopenhauer is right that the Platonic Ideas are the only direct, immediate or most adequate objectivity of thing-in-itself or Will, then he is also presumably correct to conclude that the Ideas are just thing-in-itself under the form of representation. In a sense, it could be said that represented objects for representing subjects are also thing-in-itself under the form of representation, since they are the expression, objectification or manifestation of thing-in-itself as Will in the world as representation. The main difference between individuals and Platonic Ideas is the immediacy of Ideas, the fact that they are subsumed only by the form of representation as such, and not by any other form of knowledge. The same cannot be said of individual represented objects, which in their full dynamic complexity naturally fall under many different categories of knowledge. The Platonic Idea of Dog, for example, is not any particular dog. There is consequently nothing more to know about the Idea than its representational content concerning whatever it is that is general to the concept of Dog. By contrast, any chosen individual dog presents indefinitely many possibilities for learning about the dog's indefinitely many properties.

Schopenhauer does not say exactly why, but he clearly regards all such ramifications of knowledge as distancing individuals further from thing-in-itself than the corresponding Platonic Ideas. A Platonic Idea is so abstract, interpreted simply as a specific grade of the Will's objectification, according to Schopenhauer, so thin in terms of the knowledge it embodies, that it is virtually indistinguishable from thing-in-itself. It is, finally, distinguishable only in that it embodies a particular representational form, with none of the dense informational content of any chosen represented object exemplifying the Idea. Platonic Ideas are thus the next closest thing to thing-in-itself, except for the fact, as Schopenhauer remarks, that Ideas are perceivable features of objects in the spatiotemporal causal order, whereas thing-in-itself is not. "The particular things of all particular times and spaces", he states, "are nothing but the Ideas multiplied through the principle of sufficient reason (the form of knowledge of the individuals as such), and thus obscured in their pure objectivity" (WWR 1: 180).

The analogy is that between one among various Ideas and the plurality of its instantiations and the one and only thing-in-itself with respect to its many objectifications in the world as representation. As a further positive correlation, Schopenhauer notes that "When the Idea appears, subject and object can no longer be distinguished in it, because the Idea, the adequate objectivity of the will, the real world as representation, arises only when subject and object reciprocally fill and penetrate each other completely" (WWR 1: 180). The comparison with thing-in-itself is obvious, since for thing-in-itself there is no applicable distinction between interpresuppositional subject and object. An Idea again is so abstract and general that it is not itself represented despite residing in the world as representation as a specific grade of the Will's objectification (WWR 1: 180). Thus, there can be no difference between object and subject where thing-in-itself is concerned.

The point of recalling the non-objecthood and non-subjecthood of Will as thing-in-itself is to dramatize the virtual assimilation of thing-in-itself and

Platonic Idea. The Platonic Idea of Dog is independent of any particular dog, and thus of any particular representing subject for whom any particular dog might stand as a represented object. The situation in this limited regard is precisely the same as for thing-in-itself as Will, although, as Schopenhauer does not hesitate to remark, Ideas are themselves represented objects residing as grades of the Will's objectification in the perceivable objects constituting the world as representation. "As will", Schopenhauer continues:

> outside the representation and all its forms, it is one and the same in the contemplated object and in the individual who soars aloft in this contemplation, who becomes conscious of himself as pure subject. Therefore in themselves these two are not different; for in themselves they are the will that here knows itself. (WWR 1: 180)

"Plurality and difference", we are reminded, "exist only as the way in which this knowledge comes to the will, that is to say, only in the phenomenon, by virtue of its form, the principle of sufficient reason" (WWR 1: 180). It follows, for Schopenhauer, that individuality exists only in the world as representation, where subject–object interpresuppositionality obtains, where there are objects for subjects and subjects for objects. "Without the object," Schopenhauer concludes, "without the representation, I am not knowing subject, but mere, blind will; in just the same way, without me as subject of knowledge, the thing known is not object, but mere will, blind impulse" (WWR 1: 180). This reasoning recapitulates Schopenhauer's argument for the existence and hidden inner nature of thing-in-itself as Will. Take a subject–object complex and think away either the subject or the object, and there is nothing left but pure willing or "mere will" without the individuality of subject that otherwise situates a thinking psychological entity as both represented object and representing subject squarely in the world as representation. Schopenhauer should probably have taken the inference one step further and deduced that without the representation, without object, there is no "I". "In itself," he explains,

> that is to say outside the representation, this will is one and the same with mine; only in the world as representation, the form of which is always at least subject and object, are we separated out as known and knowing individual. As soon as knowledge, the world as representation, is abolished, nothing in general is left but mere will, blind impulse. (WWR 1: 180)

We are directed in this way back to Schopenhauer's primary justification for identifying thing-in-itself as Will. It is the phenomenological method of beginning with an episode of individual willing and thinking away from it all individuality. Here, as Schopenhauer says, the process involves abstracting the represented object from the representing subject. The thought experiment leaves us with no correlated subject existing as a psychological entity standing on its own within the world as representation. The procedure isolates the pure willing or Will that transcends the act of willing. Subtracting the object from the interpresuppositional subject–object in an individual act of phenomenal willing entails that pure willing, Will, satisfies the theoretical requirements of thing-in-itself by placing it outside the principles of individuation and sufficient reason. The blind impulse that remains when the object of willing is deleted in thought from a phenomenal act of will yields Schopenhauer's characterization of the hidden inner nature of the world through which he identifies thing-in-itself as Will.[11]

CHAPTER FOUR

Suffering, salvation, death, and renunciation of the will to life

By virtue of such necessity, man needs the animals for his support, the animals in their grades need one another, and also the plants, which again need soil, water, chemical elements and their combinations, the planet, the sun, rotation and motion round the sun, the obliquity of the ecliptic, and so on. At bottom, this springs from the fact that the will must live on itself, since nothing exists besides it, and it is a hungry will. Hence arise pursuit, hunting, anxiety, and suffering. (WWR 1: 154)

Insatiable Will

The Will, Schopenhauer maintains, is hungry. This is its manifest character, evidenced in all its objectifications. We see it all around us in the strife and suffering that pervade every aspect of life, and even in the non-living material world. There is nothing in existence besides Will as thing-in-itself and its objectifications in the world as representation. The hungry Will, as a result, can only feed on itself. The restless blind urging of Will, its pure wanting without wanting this or that, keeps the physical universe in motion without any purpose or plan. Will as thing-in-itself is the hidden inner force of gravity, electromagnetism, the principles of crystal growth, vegetation, nutrition, the reproductive urge, and all other natural phenomena. Will noncausally objectifies itself in these and countless other ways, but always as competition, discord and the opposition of predator and prey.

The only field of action where the Will can feed on itself is the world as representation. It is the arena where objectifications of Will face off against each other in harsh competition for resources and, ultimately, for the most precious commodities of space and time. There can never be release from

108

this relentless antagonism of Will feeding on itself, in which one objectification of the Will is pitted against all other objectifications, because pure willing must objectify itself in these ways. The fact that there is no prospect for attaining lasting peace or satisfaction of the Will's endless demands for gratification is the basis for Schopenhauer's notorious moral pessimism. There is no philosophical justification for expecting the misery in the world ever to be meaningfully alleviated, because the world in reality, thing-in-itself as Will, is never satisfied. The psychological objectification of Will in each will to life is correspondingly caught up in a never-ending cycle of suffering want, frustration in its brutal confrontations with others, and boredom and dissatisfaction when it temporarily attains its desires.

Thus, for Schopenhauer, as in the first of the Four Noble Truths of Buddhism, life is suffering and existence a sin. "For this reason," Schopenhauer explains:

> we wish to consider in *human existence* the inner and essential destiny of the will. Everyone will readily find the same thing once more in the life of the animal, only more feebly expressed in various degrees. He can also sufficiently convince himself in the suffering animal world how essentially *all life is suffering*.   (WWR 1: 310)

The inevitable suffering for all willing beings occurs because of the necessity of the Will's feeding on itself, setting itself in eternal opposition to itself through its objectifications in the world as representation. Schopenhauer describes the struggle that takes place between all living things as combat between distinct forms of existence fiercely engaged in dispute for the means of survival and advantage. He characterizes one source of suffering for willing creatures in these terms:

> Thus everywhere in nature we see contest, struggle, and the fluctuation of victory, and later on we shall recognize in this more distinctly that variance with itself essential to the will. Every grade of the will's objectification fights for the matter, the space, and the time of another. Persistent matter must constantly change the form, since, under the guidance of causality, mechanical, physical, chemical, and organic phenomena, eagerly striving to appear, snatch the matter from one another, for each wishes to reveal its own Idea. This contest can be followed through the whole of nature; indeed only through it does nature exist ...   (WWR 1: 146–7)

The battle is seen not only in the non-human animal kingdom but in human interactions of every kind. We can readily confirm what Schopenhauer means from even the most sheltered experience. Conflicts are rife in virtually universal forms of sibling rivalries, efforts to gain parental attention and affection, confrontations with schoolyard bullies, competition for grades, and later in life for jobs and assignments, contracts, preferences and advancement, and from what we know of lawsuits, wars and territorial disputes concerning everything of value for the sake of which we must struggle and compete throughout our lives. All the while, every willing being suffers the ups and downs of desire, frustration, the ennui of satiety and ever greater and unsatisfiable desires, with no promise of relief.

Schopenhauer first addresses the world of animals, whose struggles are more naked and unsublimated than those among members of our own species. "Yet this strife itself is only the revelation of that variance with itself that is essential to the will", he proclaims.

> This universal conflict is to be seen most clearly in the animal kingdom. Animals have the vegetable kingdom for their nourishment, and within the animal kingdom again every animal is the prey and food of some other. This means that the matter in which an animal's Idea manifests itself must stand aside for the manifestation of another Idea, since every animal can maintain its own existence only by the incessant elimination of another's.   (WWR 1: 147)

Every living thing feeds on other living things, or competes with them for the possession and use of the inorganic world of substances. There is no avoiding the endless aggression and vying for advantage that determines the place of each objectification of Will in the world's mammoth foodchain. As the poet Alfred Lord Tennyson describes the situation, nature is red in tooth and claw.[1] And not only nature, in Schopenhauer's view, but even and especially in the most advanced human cultures and civilizations. We are all a part of the struggle for existence, like it or not, as predator or prey. We are in that regard the inevitable hapless creatures of the world as Will. The inner character of thing-in-itself is revealed in the world as representation, where the reality of Will is objectified as the law of eat or be eaten. In the end, no matter what, it is the fate of all things ultimately to be eaten, at least by bacteria or worms, or consumed by fire or another destructive element, as yet another objectification of the hungry Will.

"Thus the will-to-live generally feasts on itself," Schopenhauer continues:

> and is in different forms its own nourishment, till finally the human race, because it subdues all the others, regards nature as manufactured for its own use. Yet ... this same human race reveals in itself with terrible clearness that conflict, that variance of the will with

itself, and we get *homo homini lupus* ["Man is a wolf for man" (Plautus, *Asinaria*)]. However, we shall again recognize the same contest, the same subjugation, just as well at the low grades of the will's objectivity. (WWR 1: 147)

What sustains each individual subject in the struggle for existence against all other objectifications of thing-in-itself as Will, according to Schopenhauer, is the Will's most immediate objectification known only inwardly in the guise of individual willing, which Schopenhauer interprets in all of its activities as the will to life.

Will to life

Schopenhauer's concept of the will to life is an expansion made for emphasis, a redundancy, in fact, for what he otherwise speaks of more economically as simply the individual empirical will or willing. To will in any sense at all for Schopenhauer as a phenomenological occurrence or psychological episode, whether consciously or merely dispositionally, is to will life or something required or thought to be required for life. As such, all phenomenal willing is in every instance an activity of the will to life.

Interpreting the will to life in this way, Schopenhauer explains:

> The will, considered purely in itself, is devoid of knowledge, and is only a blind, irresistible urge, as we see it appear in inorganic and vegetable nature and in their laws, and also in the vegetative part of our own life. Through the addition of the world as representation, developed for its service, the will obtains knowledge of its own willing and what it wills, namely that this is nothing but this world, life, precisely as it exists. (WWR 1: 275)

Will as thing-in-itself is blind urging, as Schopenhauer frequently remarks. "We have therefore called the phenomenal world the mirror, the objectivity, of the will", he repeats, "and as what the will wills is always life, just because this is nothing but the presentation of that willing for the representation, it is immaterial and a mere pleonasm if, instead of simply saying 'the will,' we say 'the will-to-live'" (WWR 1: 275). Will to life is, as Schopenhauer likes to say, the most immediate objectification of Will. It is that from which, in its purest form in our inner experience of willing, thing-in-itself takes its name in Schopenhauer's metaphysics. We learn that every living thing embodies and is driven internally in all its actions by a will to life. The activity of every living thing, according to its inner principle as objectification of Will, is to engage relentlessly in life or death struggles with every other living thing that equally embodies and is equally driven by the will to life, whose needs and wants cannot be satisfied except at the expense of all other willing subjects and all other non-willing physical substances.

Anticipating his subsequent detailed examination of the problem of death, Schopenhauer argues that the will to life is guaranteed existence (WWR 1: 275). Schopenhauer believes that will to life as a phenomenal objectification of Will cannot fail to exist as part of a more complete world that in turn is sure to sustain it, at least until it is consumed by another objectification of the hungry Will. Why should this be true? Why could it not be the case that the individual willing subject is the only existent entity, the only objectification of Will? Why should it not be the case that all other aspects of the world be understood as mere illusion? Although Schopenhauer does not consider a further explanation, it appears from the main principles of his idealism that the external world is real in the only conceivable sense because it is governed by natural laws under the principle of sufficient reason. As long as there is will to life, individual phenomenal willing, there is subject. Where there is subject, in turn, we know, for Schopenhauer, there is interpresuppositional object, a world of objects. There is always in that case a world as representation that is equally the objectification of thing-in-itself interpreted as Will to nourish the representing subject, as long as it exists. Since the Will is a hungry Will, we can be assured that we are objectified along with whatever we need to sustain us. For the Will feeds upon itself, each of its objectifications feeding on all others. We can also unfortunately be assured that we will be there to be eaten by whatever it is that will eventually eat us.

This is not to say that we cannot perish, although Schopenhauer will soon argue that death for related reasons is unreal. "It is true that we see the individual come into being and pass away", he admits:

> but the individual is only phenomenon, exists only for knowledge involved in the principle of sufficient reason, in the *principium individuationis*. Naturally, for this knowledge, the individual receives his life as a gift, rises out of nothing, and then suffers the loss of this gift through death, and returns to nothing.   (WWR 1: 275)

How, then, can will to life be guaranteed to exist? It is only because, from the standpoint of the world as Will and representation, death is not an event through which a representing subject can endure or that it can representationally experience.

The beginning and end of the will to life as a result are equally unreal. Schopenhauer argues that birth and death are the endpoints of life, and are held in balance as mutual conditions (WWR 1: 275). Birth and death are the poles of an essential duality that exists only in the phenomenal world as representation and as necessary complements of the Will's objectification. The Will must objectify itself in this among other ways, according to Schopenhauer, because it must manifest itself in as many different ways as possible. If we ask why there is birth and why there is death, it is because the world is Will and objectifies itself according to its hidden inner principle, which we can only discover through its objectifications as clues to its character. Schopenhauer again invokes an Asian myth for the duality of birth and death. He observes that Brahma, the most sinful and lowest god of the Trimurti, symbolizes generation, origination, and Vishnu stands for preservation, while Shiva is generally represented in religious artworks not only as wearing a necklace of skulls appearing as the counterpart of death, but also the lingam, a stylized representation of the male generative organ, symbolizing continuing life (WWR 1: 275–6). A single god that embodies both creation and destruction, birth and death, is thus the perfect emblem for the termini of the Will's objectification in the phenomenal will to life.

Much as subject and object are interpresuppositional for Schopenhauer, so he maintains that birth and death are interimplicative aspects of the will to life. He explains that even non-living objectifications of Will are in competition, caught up like the rest of creation in a struggle for momentary dominance, at the very least for the occupation of space and time. The natural forces of gravity, attraction and repulsion typify the violence and upheaval in the constant processes that are at work in the universe to physically replace one thing with another (WWR 1: 161). Beginning with living organisms and the competition among individuals within species for the means of subsistence, and finding parallel struggles even among inorganic things involving natural forces, Schopenhauer describes all the Will's objectifications as in competition with one another for exclusive occupation of the perceptual forms of space and time. "The scene of action and the object of this conflict is matter that they strive to wrest from one another," he writes, "as well as space and time, the union of which through the form of causality is really matter" (WWR 1: 161).

Thing-in-itself, the insatiably hungry Will that feeds upon itself in the world of represented objects for representing subjects, leaves in its path a wake of carnage and misery. With his eyes attuned to the suffering in the world, Schopenhauer can see little else. He finds only temporary islands of reprieve from the general pattern of pain, unfulfilled but tormenting desires and bitter disappointments, as the only reward for when we do happen to succeed temporarily in obtaining whatever it is we tell ourselves we need. At the end, taunting us at every step, is the spectre of death as something that threatens to take away whatever it is we might otherwise have achieved.

We dread death, despite its being nothing real, as the closure of both representing subject and represented object, and hence of the entire world as representation. The only release from the fear of dying lies in attaining that rare form of philosophical wisdom that Schopenhauer offers as a corollary to his idealism in emulating certain types of religious saints who renounce the will to life.[2]

Suffering and ascetic salvation

The cause of suffering is not accidental, according to Schopenhauer, but the world's most essential feature. We might imagine that suffering happens to some persons who are unlucky or who make ill-advised choices. There is no need for persons to suffer if they choose wisely in life, if they are lucky in being born with good health and sound genes, raised in a supportive and sufficiently affluent family and community, and then proceed to judge intelligently how to conduct themselves, following life's path with skill and good humour wherever it leads.

This, we might think, is all that one needs to avoid unnecessary suffering. As moral optimists, while recognizing that misfortune is always possible, we may look about to see numerous people who seem to be living just such happy and satisfying personal lives. If there are also dangers, diseases and reversals of happiness, on the whole we may assume that these are not necessarily the lot of every person, and that a good life within its natural limits is possible in principle for all. At the end of such a life, there may further be the possibility of an eternal reward and the soul's salvation in an afterlife, in which the trials and tribulations of the present existence will be left behind and our spirits will remain active and content in a higher plane of existence removed from all strife.

Schopenhauer admits none of this. He interprets all of life as a parade of uninterrupted suffering from which there is no possibility of relief in this world or in a life after death. His pessimism consists in the fact that he regards thing-in-itself, the reality that lies hidden beneath the world as representation in which our struggles occur, as Will in perpetual self-conflict. Its objectifications in competitions of every kind, ultimately for matter understood as causality, space and time, in one way or another pit every represented object against every other. From plants seizing precious space to root in stony terrain, water, light and soil, predator and prey, nourishment, attraction of a mate and the raising of offspring, sibling rivalries, dog-eat-dog business struggles and the battle of the sexes, to world wars and the planetary push and pull of gravitational forces across vast distances of space, the world as representation for Schopenhauer is pervaded by conflict. It is a monstrous coliseum in which every existent entity, living or non-living, tries, like a gladiator, to defeat every other existent entity. It must be so, moreover, if Schopenhauer is right, because the world in reality, thing-in-itself, reveals its character in the world as conflict, and is eternal and unchanging in its self-opposition. The world as Will endlessly consumes itself in the only way it can, according to Schopenhauer, objectifying itself in the world as representation where every entity always tries to consume every other.

Schopenhauer describes a pathetic cycle of desire, want and lack, satiety, surfeit and boredom as the inevitable pattern of human suffering even for the most fortunate willing subjects caught up in the life of desire. In all of philosophical literature there is no more uncompromisingly negative perspective than Schopenhauer offers on the prospects of existence. He exploits the mythological imagery of many different cultures as illustrating subconscious insights into human nature and the human condition. "Thus the subject of willing", he concludes, "is constantly lying on the revolving wheel of Ixion, is always drawing water in the sieve of the Danaids, and is the eternally thirsting Tantalus" (WWR 1: 196). Without necessarily knowing why they did so, the ancient myth-makers intuitively devised tales that resonated powerfully with their audiences because they were in touch with something deeply revealing about the limits and problems of life. Schopenhauer sees black comedy, but mostly tragedy, in human existence and everywhere throughout the world as representation.

Whether he is right in viewing the world so pessimistically, it is clear that Schopenhauer has fully anticipated the objection to be raised from the standpoint of those who see the world more positively. Schopenhauer will say that optimists have simply not lived long enough nor looked deeply enough into the sufferings that surround them on every side, if only they would open their eyes. What is misinterpreted as the bright future or highest potential for the world and for human life, Schopenhauer maintains, is at best only a momentary respite from an overall pattern of one objectification of the insatiably hungry Will devouring another. If the true nature of thing-in-itself, the world as Will, is to cannibalize itself by proxy through its objectifications in the world as representation, then there must be give and take. There must be times of eating for some and of being eaten for others. Eventually, however, all things in one form or other must suffer the same destructive fate. The cycle ends only when the world as representation ends, with the death or permanent inability to represent of any representing subject.

An optimist, lacking the proper metaphysical foundation for understanding the world as representation, adopts an unbalanced attitude based on exclusive concern with the fate of those who, for a time, are privileged to be eating rather than eaten, and mistaking these limited one-sided occurrences as typical of life. What optimists fail to appreciate is that for every objectification of Will that is temporarily thriving, there are countless others that must pay the price. If human life in a particular historical period is good for many persons, the pleasure that occurs requires the desolation of many other objectifications of Will that are sacrificed in the process. It involves, among other things, the depletion of natural resources or pollution of the environment to the disadvantage of future generations. For every successful happy individual there must be many more individuals who are used and consumed. Indeed, the suffering and exploited must always heavily outnumber those who benefit by taking necessities away from others, living or non-living. In the end, more importantly, the satisfaction of desires produces its own intense dissatisfaction. Malaise followed by death, and often poverty, humiliation and debility are waiting even for those who appear in the course of life to have succeeded temporarily in gratifying their individual will to life.

The sober realistic view of life is therefore unqualifiedly pessimistic in Schopenhauer's philosophy. Not only is life suffering, but there is no hope for things to change for the better. The world as representation is necessarily the objectification of an avaricious Will. Schopenhauer carefully defines the distinction between happiness and suffering. Happiness is the satisfaction of the goals of individual willing, and suffering is its obstruction (WWR 1: 309). The definition enables Schopenhauer to advance his thesis of universal suffering as the inevitable companion of individual willing, interpreted as the immediate objectification of thing-in-itself as Will. The image is disheartening in the extreme. Schopenhauer understands the role of individual willing commonsensically as one of setting certain goals, experiencing desires that are lived through, causing suffering when they are not satisfied, and then giving rise to new desires, new agonies of will as soon as the previous wants are attained, in a never-ending cycle. It is the striving of will that Schopenhauer identifies as the source of all suffering. If we did not will, we would not suffer. Since the reality of the world as thing-in-itself is Will, and individual willing is its most immediate objectification in the world as representation, there is no avoiding suffering. To will is to strive, and to strive is to suffer, even and especially when the will temporarily succeeds in achieving that for which it strives. The reality of the world, thing-in-itself as Will, reveals its inner character in the world as representation through its most immediate objectification in the form of individual willing. The pain of the world is due entirely to will, and ultimately to Will.

"Now absolutely every human life", Schopenhauer writes:

> continues to flow on between willing and attainment. Of its nature the wish is pain; attainment quickly begets satiety. The goal was only

apparent; possession takes away its charm. The wish, the need, appears again on the scene under a new form; if it does not, then dreariness, emptiness, and boredom follow, the struggle against which is just as painful as is that against want.   (WWR 1: 314)

Schopenhauer, accordingly, seeks salvation from the suffering that accompanies every activity of will, attaining indifference to the will to life through knowledge. Willing and knowing stand opposed, since willing obstructs knowing, and knowing alone offers relief from the sufferings attendant on willing. "What might otherwise be called the finest part of life", Schopenhauer now essays, "its purest joy, just because it lifts us out of real existence, and transforms us into disinterested spectators of it, is pure knowledge which remains foreign to all willing" (WWR 1: 314).

Knowledge and will exist in limited proportions in every individual. For gifted persons of extraordinary capacity, the suffering that willing otherwise produces can at least be partially overcome through knowing. Knowing and willing are in so basic an opposition that we can overcome the will and its occasions for suffering only by cultivating knowledge. We, as human beings generally, can transcend the will to life by pursuing knowledge along either of two paths, although not every individual necessarily possesses the required ability or discipline, by living the life of an ascetic saint or aesthetic genius. The renunciation of the will to life is deliberately chosen by the saint for the sake of attaining salvation. The aesthetic genius transcends the strivings of will by a kind of enraptured perceptual knowledge of the Platonic Ideas passively received as existing in beautiful and sublime objects of nature and great works of art, when the will to life is suppressed. The life of the saint and that of the artist are involved in radically different ways with the attainment of a kind of knowledge that lifts the individual out of the cycle of willing. Denying and transcending the will to life enables the true and constitutionally committed seeker of knowledge at least to a certain extent to avoid the pangs of suffering induced by every act of will.

The alternative, if in the end there is no hope of salvation from the sufferings of will, is what Schopenhauer sees around him every day in the unrelieved misery of human existence. Persons who seem superficially well off, who are healthy and wealthy, and the beneficiaries of what otherwise look to be all the blessings life has to offer, are in reality also suffering the cycle of desire, frustration, greater desire, satiety and boredom, even in the very best of circumstances. We only need consider our own lives to discover confirmation of what Schopenhauer describes. The pattern of desire and its fulfilment, followed by ever more ambitious desires, greater want and greater suffering, followed again in turn by moments of dissatisfaction with the fulfilment of desire, is all too familiar to any reflective person. If the true character of thing-in-itself is to be discerned in the world as representation, then it is hard to dismiss Schopenhauer's diagnosis of the woes of existence. The misery of the world is then an unavoidable manifestation of thing-in-itself. It is the insatiably hungry Will feeding on itself through the individual wilful acts of aggression and competition among its objectifications in the world as representation that makes all the world as representation a kind of living hell.

Schopenhauer offers a mournful picture of the plight of human life. He considers the Will as thing-in-itself manifesting its blind urging in objectified form in the daily facts of our existence:

> The ceaseless efforts to banish suffering achieve nothing more than a change in its form. This is essentially want, lack, care for the maintenance of life. If, which is very difficult, we have succeeded in removing pain in this form, it at once appears on the scene in a thousand others, varying according to age and circumstances, such as sexual impulse, passionate love, jealousy, envy, hatred, anxiety, ambition, avarice, sickness, and so on. Finally, if it cannot find entry in any other shape, it comes in the sad, grey garment of weariness, satiety, and boredom, against which many different attempts are made. Even if we ultimately succeed in driving these away, it will hardly be done without letting pain in once again in one of the previous forms, and thus starting the dance once more at the beginning; for every human life is tossed backwards and forwards between pain and boredom. (WWR 1: 315)

The inevitable result for all individual willing subjects, whose nature is the most immediate objectification of thing-in-itself as Will, is to be condemned to suffer. Suffering is unavoidable, although the less intelligent among us may seem from time to time to live in blissful denial of the truth.

We may try ineffectually to distract ourselves with shallow momentary pleasures that only disguise the true state of human existence. Only the more saintly and artistically gifted among us can find relief from the sufferings of will by transcending desire through self-renunciation in ascetic discipline or loss of self in moments of aesthetic contemplation. Aesthetic genius attains the saint's indifference to life and death in another form in a mystic absorption of personality and momentary dissolution of any immediate sense of the subject–object distinction. The two ways of avoiding suffering, ascetic and aesthetic, amount to at least a temporary suspension of the will to life, in an indifference to life and death. Here we shall be concerned only with Schopenhauer's remarks about ascetic sainthood, reserving the topic of his aesthetics and philosophy of art for Chapter 5.

The ascetic saint renounces all pleasures in life and seeks to mortify the flesh in order to suppress its desires. In extreme cases, ascetic saints reject even the most basic life-sustaining necessities to the point of self-immolation, sacrificing their lives in denial of the will to life. While Schopenhauer is no Christian, he admires the lives of Christian saints, as he does the ascetic practices of Buddhism and Hinduism. He is interested in positive analogies between the concepts of asceticism found in extreme forms of these religious traditions. He claims to see a common unspoken recognition of the same effort to avoid the sufferings of will by denying the will to life. The very fact that many religions promise their believers a heavenly afterlife is taken by Schopenhauer as evidence that they recognize that life here on earth, as it would be anywhere in the world as representation, is imbued with suffering that we can only bear if we imagine that we shall eventually escape it to a better place. Schopenhauer is concerned to distinguish his philosophy from similar religions and ethical systems that have also approved a course of life aimed at alleviating suffering.

Stoic philosophy is made a particular target of Schopenhauer's criticism. He clarifies his view of salvation by distinguishing it from similar philosophical positions associated with classical Greek and Roman Stoicism and Epicureanism. He argues that Stoicism and Epicureanism are logically incoherent moral doctrines that hold out the prospect of achieving indifference to the world for the sake of pleasure in the absence of pain. This, Schopenhauer believes, is both practically impossible and philosophically misconceived. He finds more merit in the image of Christ of Nazareth as a symbol of suffering, the man of sorrows or *Schmerzenman*, scourged and crucified. "Compared with [the Stoic]," Schopenhauer proclaims, denouncing a philosophy that subdues suffering for the sake of procuring happiness:

> how entirely different appear the overcomers of the world and voluntary penitents, who are revealed to us, and are actually produced, by the wisdom of India; how different even the Saviour of Christianity, that excellent form full of the depth of life, of the greatest poetical truth and highest significance, who stands before us with perfect virtue, holiness, and sublimity, yet in a state of supreme suffering.   (WWR 1: 91)

The saints of every great world religion are edifying models of the intuitively grasped need to renounce the will to life. Religious asceticism dimly glimpses but still confirms the true nature of the world and the conditions of human life that Schopenhauer believes he for the first time has properly understood. He is concerned especially to draw on religious doctrines and rituals as support for his theoretical conclusions, to show that they are not merely idle speculation. He maintains that his pessimistic moral philosophy embodies a view of the world that religious saints and sages of many cultures have recognized without the more rigorous trappings of abstract metaphysical principles (WWR 1: 383). He claims to be the first to elaborate systematically ideas that many religious thinkers intuitively grasped but were unable to articulate concerning the sufferings we endure as a result of the powerful demands of the will to life (WWR 2: 164).

The fact that religions of self-denial and self-sacrifice have not merely paid lip service to the renunciation of the will to life, but have practised extreme forms of asceticism, has great significance for Schopenhauer. The life of self-imposed suffering and denial of the will speaks more eloquently than any abstract theory to the fact that the world is Will, that its objectification in the phenomenal world of experience is the will to life, and that wherever there is will there is suffering. It further supports Schopenhauer's conclusion that the proper course for enlightened thinking is to renounce the will to life through denial of desires for the sake of knowledge, and in every way to overcome the demands of will. It is no accident, from Schopenhauer's standpoint, that ancient Indian religious traditions distinguish between the passing world of appearance and the real world obscured from our eyes by the veil of Maya, and as a corollary emphasize the value of conquering the will to life, denying desire and every pleasure for the sake of the higher virtues of contemplation and understanding. These proto-metaphysical, proto-ethical religious insights are mirrored in Schopenhauer's abstract philosophical formulations, which he believes harmonize powerfully with the proto-philosophical teachings of ancient Asian religions and Christianity, and corrupted incoherently in Graeco-Roman Stoic and Epicurean philosophy (WWR 1: 386).

The unworldliness of Christianity at its finest is in accord with Schopenhauer's path of salvation from the sufferings of the will to life through its renunciation (WWR 1: 386–7). He seems to favour medieval monastic Christianity, with its practice of self-flagellation, hair-shirts, penance and vows of poverty and silence as ways of overcoming the flesh. For the sake of the comparison he wants to develop, he ignores, but can hardly be ignorant of, the fact that in many documented instances the ascetic practices and visions of saints in this period were as much a route to heightened sensuality and pride, and to a kind of unconventional eroticism, as attempts to surmount the will to life. He may presumably be prepared to distinguish, as many Christian apologists have tried to do, between those who merely profess to be following the road to righteousness for ulterior motives of their own, and those who, more in keeping with higher moral principles, observe all the right practices for all the right reasons (WWR 1: 388–9).

The proper religious and philosophical attitude, in so far as religion and philosophy converge, and the shortcomings and hypocrisy of so many of whose practitioners Schopenhauer overlooks for the sake of their deeper message, is to have compassion for every suffering being. We are to try to relieve the sufferings of others, and in the meantime to deny the nagging urges of the will to life by suppressing our desires. We should recognize that the world in which we live is in some sense unreal, that it is not the end and purpose of our lives to gratify our wants by the pursuit of pleasures and material goods. The vicious cycle of desire, frustration, satiation and heightened cravings, as Schopenhauer says and as the ascetic religious sages of great religions seem to have understood, only sustains and prolongs the suffering that walks with will, from which salvation can only be gained by renouncing the will to life.

The opposition between will and wisdom pervades Schopenhauer's recommendation of religious–philosophical asceticism. We cannot pursue knowledge effectively and sometimes not at all when we are caught up in efforts to satisfy the requirements of will. We need quiet and contemplation in order to attain knowledge. When we have genuine knowledge, moreover, our desires are subdued (WWR 1: 397). The way to salvation is therefore through the denial of the will to life. "True salvation," he argues:

> deliverance from life and suffering, cannot even be imagined without complete denial of the will. Till then, everyone is nothing but this will itself, whose phenomenon is an evanescent existence, an always vain and constantly frustrated striving, and the world full of suffering as we have described it.   (WWR 1: 397)

Such knowledge, if we can attain it, is a form of metaphysical nihilism. Schopenhauer believes that the world of experience is nothing. The world as representation is an illusion, so that each person can say that the world is "my" representation.

The implication of Schopenhauer's transcendental idealism is the denial of the world as representation, in the recognition that the phenomenal world is unreal. Schopenhauer agrees with Socrates and Plato in denying the reality and ultimate value of the world of appearance. Hence, it is nothing worthwhile for the thinking person to be absorbed in, concerned about, or to forge deep attachments toward. "We freely acknowledge", he writes, "that what remains after the complete abolition of the will is, for all who are still full of the will, assuredly nothing. But also conversely, to those in whom the will has turned and denied itself, this very real world of ours with all its suns and galaxies, is – nothing" (WWR 1: 412).

The profound insight of Christianity is its recognition of suffering and the importance of salvation (WWR 2: 170). There is no call to be saved if the world in principle is a friendly place where human satisfaction and happiness can finally be attained. The need for salvation is pervasive, and what it is we need to be saved from is ourselves. It is the will to life, an objectification of the hungry Will, that is responsible for all the suffering that results from the fact that every objectification of Will in the world as representation is set against every other. The Will's insatiable appetite gives rise to the will to the individual life's complex cycle of desire, frustrations and ever greater desires, followed by the dissatisfaction of not attaining its wants, or by the momentary satiety and the accompanying disappointment in how little and how briefly the will to life can be made content. As products of the Will's most direct and immediate objectifications, we need salvation from the individual willing and will to life that characterizes our species in all but its most exceptional members.

Death and immortality

Schopenhauer's philosophy often gives the impression of having been composed expressly for the purpose of reconciling the phenomenal will to the inevitability of death. All the apparatus of his main treatise, the fundamental distinction between the world as Will and representation, the concept of thing-in-itself as beyond the *principium individuationis*, and fourfold root of the principle of sufficient reason, can be understood as contributing to a moral, metaphysical and mystical religious recognition that death is nothing real and hence nothing to fear.

If Schopenhauer is correct, he proves that death is not an event, and hence altogether unreal. Death is not an event in the world as representation, but is rather an endpoint or limit of the world as representation, and in particular in the first-person formulation as *my* representation. The world as representation begins and ends with the consciousness of the individual representing subject. At the moment of death, all representation comes to an immediate abrupt end, after which there remains only thing-in-itself. An individual's death is not something that occurs in or as any part of the world as representation. Nor can death possibly be in or a part of the world as thing-in-itself or Will. There are no events or individuated occurrences, nothing happening in space or time, for thing-in-itself, and in particular there is no progressive transition from life to death or from consciousness to unconsciousness. If with Schopenhauer we assume that there exists only the world as representation and as thing-in-itself interpreted as Will, then there is no place on either side of the great divide for death, no possibility for the existence or reality of death.

Death is nothing whatsoever. It is unreal, and yet it is the purpose and fulfilment of life. Like the Stoics and Epicureans, Schopenhauer argues that death is nothing to fear. Nor, although it offers release from the sufferings of the will to life, does death provide a meaningful form of salvation. Schopenhauer attributes an implicit understanding of the unreality of death to persons who are able to face each day of life without abandoning themselves to despair, and to soldiers and other persons with dangerous occupations who confront the challenges of each moment with courage. Such persons act in practice just as though they understood in theory that death is nothing real. At the moment of death, when consciousness runs up against its limit in the last instant of life, at the final moment of consciousness, Schopenhauer maintains that the world as representation, "my" representation, as each person can say, ceases to exist. The only world an individual subject can possibly know ceases to exist as immediately and completely, and in the only conceivable way, as any existent thing can ever be destroyed, at the moment of death. There is nothing whatsoever left over when death limits representation, except for thing-in-itself (WWR 1: 280).

Schopenhauer's Kantian and Platonic metaphysics is tempered by its uniquely Buddhistic and Hinduistic, rather than Jewish, Christian or Islamic, concept of the soul's salvation. The immortality of the soul is understood by Schopenhauer as the indestructibility of Will as thing-in-itself, the pure willing that transcends or underlies the empirical individual willing that Schopenhauer refers to as the will to life. As thinking subjects we are immortal only in the attenuated sense that Will willing purely within us can never be destroyed. When the world as representation in its entirety, including the representing subject's body, ceases to exist with the passing of the representing subject's last moment of conciousness, Will as thing-in-itself at the core of each thinking subject alone remains (WWR 2: 215). There is therefore something in each of us that is immortal. The part of us that survives death is not, according to Schopenhauer, as some sects of Judaism, Christianity and Islam have taught, the personality or self or soul of the thinking subject. It is rather the impersonal Will within, the indestructible thing-in-itself, transcending space, time and causality, that is in no way part of the world as representation or subject to any sort of change.

The individual will as an objectification of thing-in-itself, of the world as Will, has a dual nature. It is at once the ephemeral subject of life and death, and the expression in the world as representation of thing-in-itself. "There is something in us, however," Schopenhauer observes, "which tells us that this is not so, that this is not the end of things, that death is not an absolute annihilation" (WWR 1: 324). The thought at first makes it seem as though

Schopenhauer is holding out the possibility for personal survival after death. If death is not absolute annihilation, then some part of a living person must persist through the event of death. This Schopenhauer admits, but only in a limited sense that precludes the possibility of an afterlife for the empirical self.[3] This is not the comforting sense of survival by which a particular person with specific memories and expectations continues after the body's death, promised by popular religions and mind–body dualisms in the philosophy of Plato and Descartes. Schopenhauer offers only the metaphysical indestructibility of Will as thing-in-itself in the pure willing of any willing subject. The non-finality of death is no more than the persistence of Will as thing-in-itself that "endures" (WWR 1: 282–3). That death is not total annihilation for Schopenhauer is true enough; yet death remains the total annihilation of the self, soul, or subject in the psychological sense of the individual will to life or particular empirical personality.[4]

Thus, Schopenhauer rejects the Socratic doctrine of immortality. The soul, as Socrates describes it in Plato's dialogues, if it is to be capable of thought, can neither belong to the world of Becoming nor to the world of Being consisting of timeless eternal abstract Ideas. The soul, furthermore, with its personality intact, has no mode of conveyance by which it can be transported from the ephemeral world of Becoming to the eternal changeless and timeless world of Being. Schopenhauer, unlike Plato, does not hold that the individual's personality survives death. The sense of immortality that Schopenhauer allows involves the identification of pure willing at the core of every individual empirical act of will with thing-in-itself as Will. Immortality does not carry the individual over into a promised land. The only part of the willing subject to survive death in Schopenhauer's metaphysics is its core of pure willing or Will. It is only that which is left over after subtracting every individuating factor from the phenomenal will to life that Schopenhauer identifies with thing-in-itself. Thing-in-itself survives each individual death, but it was never alive in the empirical biological sense in the first place. It is the transcendent reality that exists independently of all thought, outside individuality, space, time, causation and rational explanation.

Although we thinking subjects cannot be annihilated by the destruction of our bodies, it is not what we ordinarily think of as "we" that survives. Schopenhauer denies that any of our memories, expectations or aspirations can persist through a moment of death and survive intact, crossing over to the other side in an afterlife. The part of us that survives, the Will that Schopenhauer identifies with thing-in-itself, is impersonal, indistinguishable and non-individual. The Will that survives death outlasts its own spatio-temporal objectifications, but does not do so in time or space, which cease to exist at the exact instant that the individual representing subject closes its representing eye for the last time on the world as representation. The part of me that survives death, therefore, Schopenhauer believes, the Will that transcends my individual willing, is no different from but exactly the same as the pure willing part of you that survives death.

What is immortal in each of us is at most a kind of generic world-soul that is not personally individualized, that does not entertain any succession of thoughts, but is simply the Kantian thing-in-itself identified by Schopenhauer as Will. It has no psychological episodes as we ordinarily think of them occurring in time. It has no memories of a past embodied life or expectations or ongoing experiences following the body's death. We as thinkers share in thing-in-itself as the immortal part of our willing and representing psychologies with every other thinker. If the Will surviving death is in any sense a part of us, it is equally the same part of every other representing subject, and not only of human psychological subjects, but of every willing thinker, beginning with the simplest and most primitive lifeforms capable of perceiving. The immortality in which we share has nothing about it that is individual or empirical. It is not like going to heaven and playing a lyre, feasting on ambrosia, or meeting and conversing with God or with those who have already gone before us into death. It is not like anything at all, because it is only the existence of thing-in-itself outside space and time without the interpresuppositional subject–object objectification in psychology that constitutes the world as representation, and only as long as the individual representing subject remains conscious (WWR 2: 199–200).

Matters of life and death

Schopenhauer interprets death as the aim and purpose of life. He maintains that the triumph of death is inevitable, and that existence is a constant dying. Death for Schopenhauer is the denial of the individual will to life, and birth and death as events in the phenomenal world are alike unreal, although death is not complete annihilation. Suicide, although not morally objectionable, is philosophically pointless because it only reaffirms the will to life in desperate form. The paradoxes in Schopenhauer's reflections on the nature of death must be understood in order to appreciate what he means by the empirical will in its relation to Will as thing-in-itself (WWR 1: 275–382 and *passim*).

What is death? How should philosophy try to explain the significance of the extinction of individual consciousness? Schopenhauer's pessimism consists in his affirmation of all phenomena as manifestations of Will in essential self-conflict. The importance of the concept of death for his philosophy is indicated even in his unpublished Berlin Manuscripts of 1818–1830 on *Adversaria* §175, where he writes: "We abhor *death*, and as nature does not lie and the fear of death is the voice of nature, there must yet be some reason for this" (HN 3: 623). The purpose of Schopenhauer's reflections on death is to clarify its meaning in relation to his theory of the individual will to life, to reach a philosophically sound understanding of what death is and what it is not, of whether death is anything to fear or in any case what a philosophical attitude toward individual death ought to be, both metaphysically and morally.

Schopenhauer regards the attitude of hopeful expectancy that embraces life as a deluded involvement with the most superficial aspects of the phenomenal world. He celebrates death as a welcome release from the individual will's condemnation to ineffectual suffering, of constantly willing what we need or think we need, struggling in competition with others who want many of the same things and who actively oppose us in the fulfilment of our desires. It is the suffering of always desiring more, and having to cope with the melancholy that inevitably follows acquiring what we first desire. Schopenhauer not only paints a pessimistic picture of the prospects of life as an objectification of the insatiably hungry Will, but criticizes what he considers to be a philosophically unfounded moral optimism as failing to understand the nature and limits of individual will to life in the world as representation (WWR 2: 584).

As a consequence also of his idealist metaphysics of time, Schopenhauer argues that existence is a constant dying, a process of the individual empirical will moving inexorably toward death as its final purpose. Dwelling as an objectification of Will in the world as representation, an individual human psyche is caught up in the flow of time whereby the present is continually streaming into the past. Schopenhauer seems to conceive of the past as a kind of repository of death, of no longer existent events, from which he concludes that life, like sand in an hourglass, trickles through the narrow bottleneck of the present moment into the dead past. Existence as a consequence is both a constant process of dying and a momentary postponement of ongoing death (WWR 1: 311).

In the second edition and second volume of *The World as Will and Representation*, Schopenhauer quotes Byron's *Euthanasia* with approval. He regards the sentiment it expresses as congenial to his own outlook on the nature of life and death, when Byron proclaims:

> Count o'er the joys thine hours have seen,
> Count o'er thy days from anguish free
> And know, whatever thou has been,
> 'Tis something better not to be.[5]

At its best, according to Schopenhauer, life is delayed dying. Life is nothing positive, but merely a temporary reprieve from death, toward which life from the moment of conception is irrepressibly impelled. Considered in itself, there is no value to life. Like the Asian sages he admires, Schopenhauer agrees that life transpires in a comparatively unreal world of appearance, in the world as representation. We can take heart only in the mercifully brief time during which we are required to live. Suffering is unavoidable because the will to life objectifies the internal self-conflict of Will as thing-in-itself. There is nothing to look forward to as the meaning or final reward or consummation of life except its termination in death. Schopenhauer considers only a dismal prospect of life leading finally to death, and of the fleeting duration of life as its one redeeming virtue in ending at last the suffering of each individual will to life.[6]

We learn about death by analogy. We see others die and draw the inference that death must also visit each of us. The further belief that death is the cessation of consciousness and irreversible destruction of the self, or the hopeful expectation of an afterlife in which the soul survives bodily death, are reactions to the awareness of death in faulty philosophical reasoning and religious faith. The awareness and anticipation of death distinguishes human beings from non-human animals. "The animal learns to know death only when he dies," Schopenhauer says, adopting a common-sense view of animal versus human nature:

> but man consciously draws every hour near his death; and at times this makes life a precarious business, even to the man who has not already recognized this character of constant annihilation in the whole of life itself. Mainly on this account, man has philosophies and religions ... (WWR 1: 37)

We might object that in such passages Schopenhauer seems to lack a sympathetic understanding of animal psychology. The close observation of animal behaviour may suggest a recognition of potential death in the way in which some non-human animals seem to act deliberately to preserve their safety, as though at some level they understood the concept of danger and the possibility of dying. Similar interpretations in field studies by naturalists suggest that the responses of higher non-human animals to the death of other animals, especially their parents, offspring and siblings, may also evince a primitive awareness of death. Schopenhauer, of course, in that case can fall back, as many philosophers do, on the fact that animals have no language by which to articulate their anticipations of death in order to maintain that they have no corresponding concepts, or argue that we simply anthropomorphize animal instincts for self-preservation when we try to ascribe human-like attitudes toward death to non-human animals. These would nevertheless be difficult positions for Schopenhauer to uphold, given the emphasis in his epistemology on intuition over abstract reasoning, along with his moral compassion for the sufferings of non-human animals.

Awareness of death appears to be neither a necessary nor sufficient condition for self-consciousness, let alone for human self-consciousness. Schopenhauer nevertheless strikes a resonant chord when he associates philosophy and religion as distinctively human concerns motivated at least indirectly by a preoccupation with the fact of death. He is surely right that even if non-human animals have a limited awareness of death, they evidently do not know about or live in anticipation of their own deaths in the same way or to the same extent as human beings. The innocence of non-human animals in the face of death stands in stark contrast with human understanding of the inevitability of death and all its ramifications for the way human beings pursue the will to life.

Schopenhauer explains the awareness of death as a combined outcome of reason and self-consciousness. He interprets the expectation of death as the origin not only of philosophy and religious belief, but more specifically of what he defines as the characteristic need for metaphysics (WWR 2: 160). He describes death as an essential precondition without which there would be no philosophy. In "On Death and Its Relation to the Indestructibility of Our Inner Nature", a supplement to the fourth book of *The World as Will and Representation*, Schopenhauer appeals to Socrates' pronouncements about death as the wellspring of all philosophical thinking: "Death is the real inspiring genius or Musagetes of philosophy," Schopenhauer remarks, "and for this reason Socrates [in Plato's dialogue, the *Phaedo*] defined philosophy as θανάτου μελέτη [preparation for death]. Indeed, without death there would hardly have been any philosophizing" (WWR 2: 463).

Awareness of death is a strange kind of knowledge. The mind cannot express its apprehension of death, according to Schopenhauer, because all its concepts derive from the objectification of Will in appearance as the individual will to life, of which death is the antithesis. He characterizes the knowledge of death dialectically as an imagined interrogation of the will to life in which the will is hypothetically questioned concerning its desire to continue suffering. The conflict experienced by individual will can only be conceived as ending when the empirical self is destroyed. The mind tries unsuccessfully to represent death as the negation of its knowledge and experience of life, as an altogether aspatiotemporal, objectless and subjectless oblivion. All consciousness and the individual will at once then cease to exist, and the world as representation that the subject had lived through as an objectification of Will as thing-in-itself is destroyed. There is nothing left of the world that had existed in thought when the individual dies; nothing, that is, in Schopenhauer's transcendental idealism, but thing-in-itself, the Will that transcends all space, time and causality, irreparably removed from all individuality and all possibility of explanation. There is then as there had been all along in reality only thing-in-itself, and everything else appears to be no more than a compelling dream. The epistemic limitations of the world as representation prevent us from adequately explaining the metaphysics of death, except, Schopenhauer indicates, as the negation of experience and knowledge of the represented world (WWR 2: 609).

Although of necessity we can have no positive representational knowledge of death, nature conveys a concept of death in its beckoning toward a release from the sufferings of will. The desire to sustain life, according to Schopenhauer, is confused. The idea of death confronts each person not as the representation of an event or state of being, but more abstractly as the possibility of a definitive end to the individual will's perpetual suffering. There is a conflict in the mind's effort to represent death when the suffering of the individual will induces it to improve its condition by willing its own destruction. The contemplation of suicide, too, Schopenhauer hints but does not explicitly argue, is part of the suffering endured by intelligent willing subjects as part of the awareness of approaching death compounded by the insistent demands of the will to life.

Schopenhauer in many places seems perversely to relish the inevitability of death. He repeats the commonplace that every moment of life brings us one step closer to the abyss. He observes that despite this fact we cannot avoid taking an avid interest in life when death is not immediately at our door, knowing all the while that in the end death must prevail. Here, as in other morbid passages, he dwells at length on the problem of death:

> Every breath we draw wards off the death that constantly impinges on us. In this way, we struggle with it every second, and again at longer intervals through every meal we eat, every sleep we take, every time we warm ourselves, and so on. Ultimately death must triumph, for by birth it has already become our lot, and it plays with its prey only for a while before swallowing it up. However, we continue our life with great interest and much solicitude as long as possible, just as we blow out a soap-bubble as long and as large as possible, although with the perfect certainty that it will burst.
>
> (WWR 1: 311)

While Schopenhauer regards death as the purpose of life, he insists that death is illusory. The distinction between the world as Will and representation, and the theory of the individual empirical will as part of the world as representation, implies that life and death are alike unreal (WWR 1: 275).

Schopenhauer, in effect, paints a verbal *vanitas* still life, like a Dutch canvas with a grimacing skull, pocket watch and an overturned wine glass, to put existence in perspective and remind us that death awaits every willing subject at the end of even the happiest life. He holds, as have other thinkers of pessimistic outlook, that few persons would voluntarily choose to live their lives over again, but that most gratefully look forward to death as a release from life's sufferings (WWR 1: 324–5).

Schopenhauer's stance is in part an extrapolation from the ability of suffering to "sanctify" the individual. The idea is one that many philosophers and religious thinkers have described, in which suffering causes the individual to withdraw from false attachment to the urgings of the phenomenal will. If suffering can produce such detachment, the same result can no doubt be achieved to an even greater degree by contemplating death. A similar concept of separation from the will to life through prolonged suffering or philosophical reflection on death is described by William James in *The Varieties of Religious Experience* as *anhedonia*, a symptom of what he calls "the sick soul".[7] Extensive suffering eventually makes the will lose interest in life, an outcome that Schopenhauer believes is even more enhanced by a full awareness of the inevitability of death (WWR 2: 636–7).

There is a strange reciprocity between life and death in Schopenhauer's pessimism. All life tends towards death, and could not be otherwise in light of being swept along in the phenomenal flux of time. Life and death are unreal in so far as they are merely objectifications of thing-in-itself within the world as representation. The opposition between individual wills by which thing-in-itself, the world as hungry Will, feeds on itself, unavoidably causes suffering to every willing subject, culminating in death.[8] He maintains that unavoidable suffering makes life so miserable that only the fear of death as the great unknown restrains most individuals from self-destruction; while if life as a whole were enjoyable, the idea of death as its culmination would be intolerable. In his zero-sum philosophical bookkeeping, Schopenhauer concludes that we can find extraphilosophical comfort in the fact that death is sometimes welcomed as a deliverance from suffering (WWR 2: 578–9).

This is not a rosy outlook on life, death or the human condition. Schopenhauer does not affirm life as a positive value, but holds that death and birth alike are merely phenomenal endpoints limiting both ends of the world as representation. The philosopher or mystic who understands the unreality of death has no reason to fear it, while knowledge of the unreality of life removes any philosophical justification for the reluctance of non-philosophers to accept death as a merciful release from suffering. "However," Schopenhauer adds:

he will be least afraid of becoming nothing in death who has recognized that he is already nothing now, and who consequently no longer takes any interest in his individual phenomenon, since in him knowledge has, so to speak, burnt up and consumed the will, so that there is no longer any will, any keen desire for individual existence, left in him. (WWR 2: 609)

As a final consideration relevant to Schopenhauer's general treatment of death, we should recall that for Schopenhauer death is known only analogically through representation of the deaths of others, and in particular of the end of animation and destruction and decay of their bodies. Does this not indicate the extent to which we believe in the existence of other minds, despite not having direct access to or inner acquaintance with the willing and representing psychologies of other thinking subjects?

What shall we then say of Schopenhauer's argument that the world as representation ends when the individual representing subject dies or ceases consciously to represent? We are supposedly not entitled to know that other representing subjects will survive our death. We have knowledge only of their bodies and actions as represented objects for the one and only representing subject, which is each of us considered in the first-person, such that each of us can truthfully say that the world is "my" representation. If this representational knowledge of the existence of other minds is not sufficient for us to know that the world as representation continues after our individual deaths, why are we so moved and alarmed by what is also merely representational knowledge of the death of representing subjects other than ourselves? Why do we not simply assume that death will at worst visit other persons and never ourselves?

Schopenhauer does in fact reach the conclusion that death is unreal for the individual representing subject. His reasons are consistent with the proposition that we know of death only by inferring the probability of its occurring also to each of us, given our representational knowledge of what befalls the bodies of others. He maintains that death is nothing real because we cannot live through or experience death representationally in our own case or as the cessation of consciousness of any other thinking subject. We have no direct access to the thinking processes of others in the first place, but can only know about them indirectly through body language and verbal behaviour. The same limitations of representational knowledge that require us to infer the existence of other minds equally require us to infer only analogically that there is such a thing as death. Thus, we are prepared to agree that death for each individual representing subject is not a real event nor an occurrence that can be visited upon each subject as something each in turn must eventually endure. Schopenhauer in this spirit can sympathetically echo the words of the great ancient Stoic philosopher Epicurus, in his *Letter to Menoeceus*, that "Death, the most terrifying of ills, is therefore nothing to us, for when we are death is not come, and, when death is come, we are not".[9]

Suicide no solution to the problem of willing

In confronting incurable pain or unbearable humiliation or ruin, a person considering suicide in ignorance of Schopenhauer's metaphysics of Will as thing-in-itself is caught up in the contradiction of trying to annihilate the individual will to life, while also affirming the will to life by acting to remove pain through the irreversible elimination of consciousness (WWR 1: 313).

Suicide, like death from any other cause, brings down the curtain on individual willing and on all the world as representation. What remains is only thing-in-itself. Suicide is therefore no exit from suffering in the sense a potential suicide may hope to achieve. Schopenhauer identifies individual character with will to life as the source of all suffering. There is no escape from individual willing to be found in the individual's willing to end his or her life. To do so is only to express another aspect of the suicide's character and individual will to life, from which the suicide cannot escape by the act of self-destruction. Schopenhauer depicts individual willing as a kind of prison from which suicide provides no way out. If we are to avoid the suffering brought about by the phenomenal will, the solution is not to end life, but to enter on one of the two paths of ascetic self-denial or aesthetic self-absorption that offer release from the torments of willing by renouncing, transcending or otherwise overcoming will to life for the sake of knowledge. He explains:

> Death (the repetition of the comparison must be excused) is like the setting of the sun, which is only apparently engulfed by the night, but actually, itself the source of all light, burns without intermission, brings new days to new worlds, and is always rising and always setting. Beginning and end concern only the individual by means of time, of the form of this phenomenon for the representation. Outside time lie only the will, Kant's thing-in-itself, and its adequate objectivity, namely Plato's Idea. Suicide, therefore, affords no escape; what everyone *wills* in his innermost being, that must he *be*; and what everyone *is*, is just what he *wills*.   (WWR 1: 366)

"To be or not to be, that is the question" for Shakespeare's Prince Hamlet. Schopenhauer sees in the dramatist's perspective the desperation of human suffering that drives some weary souls to contemplate ending their lives.

Schopenhauer interprets the famous soliloquy in terms afforded by his pessimistic moral philosophy. The most important remaining lines of Hamlet's speech are worth quoting as illustrating the kinds of attitudes toward suicide that Schopenhauer wants to emphasize:

> Whether 'tis nobler in the mind to suffer
> The slings and arrows of outrageous fortune,
> Or to take arms against a sea of troubles,
> And by opposing end them? To die: to sleep;
> No more; and by a sleep to say we end
> The heart-ache and the thousand natural shocks
> That flesh is heir to, 'tis a consummation
> Devoutly to be wish'd. To die, to sleep;
> To sleep: perchance to dream: ay, there's the rub;
> For in that sleep of death what dreams may come
> When we have shuffled off this mortal coil,
> Must give us pause. There's the respect
> That makes calamity of so long life;
> ...
> But that the dread of something after death,
> The undiscover'd country from whose bourn
> No traveller returns, puzzles the will,
> And makes us rather bear those ills we have,
> Than fly to others that we know not of?
> Thus conscience doth make cowards of us all;
> And thus the native hue of resolution
> Is sicklied o'er with the pale cast of thought,
> And enterprises of great pith and moment
> With this regard their currents turn away,
> And lose the name of action.   (*Hamlet*, III.i.64–77, 86–96)

The resistance that drags Hamlet back from the precipice is not just the will to life asserting itself in spite of his sufferings. It is rather the tacit recognition that there is more to the world than its phenomenal appearances marked by pain and misery, and that to end life does not resolve the deep and interesting problems of existence. Taking one's life as a result does not provide release. It does not save us from ourselves, from the individual character within each of us, unless or until we find a way of overcoming the will. Schopenhauer further analyses the drama from the standpoint of his transcendental idealism:

> The essential purport of the world-famous monologue in *Hamlet* is, in condensed form, that our state is so wretched that complete

non-existence would be decidedly preferable to it. Now if suicide actually offered us this, so that the alternative "to be or not to be" lay before us in the full sense of the words, it could be chosen unconditionally as a highly desirable termination ("a consummation devoutly to be wish'd" [*Hamlet*, Act III, scene I]). There is something in us, however, which tells us that this is not so, that this is not the end of things, that death is not an absolute annihilation.

(WWR 1: 324)

He identifies a subtle contradiction in the act of suicide that prevents it from constituting any sort of philosophical solution to the problem of suffering and salvation. The contradiction is that in order to avoid suffering we must somehow overcome the will to life. Suicide, however, is nothing of the kind, but rather a drastic avowal of the will to life. The suicide hopes to avoid further suffering by taking his or her life. In this act, no transcendence of the will to life can possibly occur, because the desire to avoid suffering *qua* desire is just another expression of the will to life. Schopenhauer accordingly concludes that "far from being denial of the will, suicide is a phenomenon of the will's strong affirmation" (WWR 1: 398).

If Schopenhauer is right that Will is thing-in-itself, then nothing anyone does or fails to do, chooses or chooses not to do, can make any difference to the individual's essential nature before or after death. In that case, there can be no sound Schopenhauerian objection to philosophical suicide, provided that the willing subject is not deluded about what self-induced death can accomplish. We cannot answer philosophical questions or resolve moral metaphysical problems by committing suicide. Schopenhauer's reflections stand in sharp contrast to what Albert Camus a century later maintains in "An Absurd Reasoning" in *The Myth of Sisyphus and Other Essays*, when he writes that "There is but one truly serious philosophical problem, and that is suicide. Judging whether life is or is not worth living amounts to answering the fundamental question of philosophy."[10]

Schopenhauer is sometimes wrongly interpreted as holding that suicide is metaphysically futile because there can be no escape from Will as thing-in-itself. Frederick Copleston, for example, in *Arthur Schopenhauer: Philosopher of Pessimism*, states that: "Individual consciousness is indeed destroyed [in the act of suicide], i.e. phenomenal existence, but man's inner nature, identical with Will, persists and can never be destroyed".[11] This is true enough for Schopenhauer, as far as it goes, but it is by no means the basis for his objection to suicide as affording no solution to the philosophical problems of life and death. As we have seen, Schopenhauer believes that there can be no real annihilation of the true as opposed to the apparent phenomenal nature of the individual will to life. He develops the position eloquently in "On the Doctrine of the Indestructibility of Our True Nature by Death" in *The World as Will and Representation*, and again in his essay "On Suicide" in *Parerga and Paralipomena*.[12] Suicide affords no departure from phenomenal willing, because the concept of escape implies the personal survival or persistence of the individual soul from a worse to a better state, which Schopenhauer regards as impossible.

The soul or psychological subject of individual willing, which Schopenhauer identifies materialistically with the brain, perishes along with the death of the body. Something philosophically more interesting is suggested by Schopenhauer's enigmatic remark that "what everyone *wills* in his innermost being, that must he *be*; and what everyone *is*, is just what he *wills*" (WWR 1: 366). He seems to accept the proposition that the content of individual willing defines each individual will as a unique entity. It is what he elsewhere refers to as the moral character of each willing subject. This is part of Schopenhauer's proto-existentialism that many commentators have attributed to his philosophy. It is not only the doom and gloom of modern alienation, the mental atmosphere of the insane asylum and concentration camp, but the individual human body and the conditions of its existence as an outward expression of the thinking subject. Where individual will to life is concerned, we are what we desire and choose for ourselves, as classical existentialism holds – it is that toward which we are impelled as the objectification of our innermost character (WWR 2: 240).

Schopenhauer at first appears to position himself for an enthusiastic philosophical defence of suicide. If to live is to suffer, and if life and death are unreal anyway, why permit oneself to suffer needlessly? Why wait impatiently for death to come if we can hasten its arrival? If life has death as its aim and purpose, if life is only an ephemeral headlong descent toward death swept along in the torrents of time, and if death is nothing to be feared, then why should not every enlightened consciousness destroy itself immediately in order to escape the sufferings of individual will and achieve life's purpose more quickly and deliberately? Death is a blessing for those who have come to see existence as ineluctable suffering in the phenomenal world, where the brevity of life, contrary to popular will-dominated opinion, is its best feature. Once we get the picture, why not make life even briefer?

Schopenhauer vehemently rejects any universal philosophical endorsement of suicide. He regards self-murder as it is usually practised as an unworthy affirmation of the will to life by those who wish to escape pain rather than seek non-discursive awareness of the Will through suffering. There is no salvation from individual willing to be found in individually willed annihilation. We should rather endure suffering until death arrives on its own to free us. Socrates says much the same in Plato's *Phaedo* 61e2–62e7, interpreting self-destruction as an attachment to earthly desire by which the soul is made impure. But why? Is Schopenhauer's position necessitated by or even logically consistent with the concept of death he has elaborated? Or is Schopenhauer, having offered a powerful motivation for self-destruction, merely trying awkwardly now within the framework of his pessimistic and avowedly nihilistic philosophical system to accommodate the squeamishness of traditional morality, or, indeed, his own personal revulsion, concerning the act of suicide?

Schopenhauer falls far short of Kant's repudiation of suicide as a violation of the categorical imperative, when in a famous passage of the *Foundations of the Metaphysics of Morals*, Kant considers:

> A man who is reduced to despair by a series of evils feels a weariness with life but is still in possession of his reason sufficiently to ask whether it would not be contrary to his duty to himself to take his own life. Now he asks whether the maxim of his action could become a universal law of nature. His maxim, however, is: For love of myself, I make it my principle to shorten my life when by a longer duration it threatens more evil than satisfaction. But it is questionable whether this principle of self-love could become a universal law of nature. One immediately sees a contradiction in a system of nature whose law would be to destroy life by the feeling whose special office is to impel the improvement of life. In this case it would not exist as nature; hence that maxim cannot obtain as a law of nature, and thus it wholly contradicts the supreme principle of all duty.[13]

Kant reasons that suicide for the sake of self-love is self-contradictory. The categorical imperative in its main formulation requires that we ought always to act in such a way that we can will the maxim of our action to be universal for every rational being. Here the "can" that enforces moral judgement should be understood as logical possibility. We test the morality of an action by asking whether it is logically possible for the maxim that justifies an act to be accepted by every rational being. If our willing such universal acceptance is logically possible, if we can without contradiction will such a thing, then the categorical imperative entails that we are obliged by duty to follow the maxim. If as reasoning moral agents our willing universal acceptance of the maxim is not logically possible, if and only if willing the universal acceptance of the maxim implies a contradiction, however loosely construed by Kant, so that we cannot will that the principle be universalized, then the categorical imperative entails that we are forbidden to follow the maxim in any of its consequences. Self-love, according to Kant, runs into a contradiction when it tries to will that all rational beings should commit suicide when "by a longer duration [life] threatens more evil than satisfaction", for it simultaneously seeks to improve and destroy.

This is not the place to dispute whether Kant's categorical imperative forbids or ought to forbid suicide. Arguably, the maxim Kant considers, to choose death merely when life offers more pain than pleasure, as opposed to, say, in order to avoid excruciating incurable chronic pain, is too weak to represent the kind of judgement a person actually contemplating suicide is likely to entertain. With respect to Kant's formalist moral injunctions against suicide as an implication of the categorical imperative, Schopenhauer is unimpressed with the claim that moral reason cannot consistently will the suicide's maxim to be universal law. He argues:

> Moreover, in the examples given by him as an introduction to that classification, Kant supports the duties of law first ... by the so-called duty to oneself, that of not ending one's life voluntarily when the evils outweigh the pleasures. Therefore this maxim is said to be not even *conceivable* as a universal law of nature. I say that, as the power of the State cannot intervene here, this very maxim shows itself unchecked as an *actually existing law of nature*. For it is quite certainly a universal rule that man actually resorts to suicide as soon as the immensely strong, inborn urge to the preservation of life is definitely overpowered by great suffering; daily experience shows us this ... At any rate, arguments against suicide of the kind put forward by Kant ... certainly have never yet restrained, even for one moment, anyone who is weary of life. Thus a natural law incontestably existing as a fact and daily operating is declared to be *simply unthinkable* without contradiction, in favor of the classification of duties from Kant's moral principle!   (BM: 93)

Schopenhauer offers an analogous argument against suicide, in which he describes the reasoning of the potential suicide as contradictory. In contrast with Kant, Schopenhauer locates the contradiction in the suicide's simultaneous denial and affirmation of the will to life. More importantly, unlike Kant, Schopenhauer, especially in his essay "On Suicide" in *Parerga and Paralipomena*, finds nothing morally objectionable in principle to suicide (PP 2: 306–11). The first reference to such a contradiction appears in the first volume of *The World as Will and Representation*, where Schopenhauer detects an inconsistency in the Stoic concept of the "blessed life", counselling suicide for those in dire straits. Schopenhauer now protests:

> we find a complete contradiction in our wishing to live without suffering, a contradiction that is therefore implied by the frequently

used phrase "blessed life." This will certainly be clear to the person who has fully grasped my discussion that follows. This contradiction is revealed in this ethic of pure reason itself by the fact that the Stoic is compelled to insert a recommendation of suicide in his guide to the blissful life (for this is what his ethics always remains).

(WWR 1: 90)

He identifies a different kind of contradiction than Kant in criticizing the usual rationale for suicide. In "On Suicide", Schopenhauer argues that:

We then of necessity hear [from "monotheistic" religious teachers] that suicide is the greatest cowardice, that it is possible only in madness, and such like absurdities; or else the wholly meaningless phrase that suicide is "wrong", whereas there is obviously nothing in the world over which every man has such an indisputable *right* as his own person and life. (PP 2: 306)[14]

Schopenhauer's objection to suicide, as many commentators have noticed, is metaphysical rather than moral.

If we reach the level of Schopenhauer's insight into the world as Will and representation, and if we see individual willing as inherently a life of suffering, then we cannot be satisfied with suicide as a philosophical solution to the predicament of life. The objection is that there is a kind of contradiction in the phenomenal will's wilfully seeking to exterminate itself as a way of escaping the wretchedness of willing.[15] Suicide ends life, true enough; but, as the result of a wilful decision in the service of the individual will to life, it cannot by its very nature altogether transcend willing.[16] The only logically coherent freedom to be sought from the sufferings of the will to life is not to will death and set about wilfully to destroy the self, but to continue to live while quieting the will, in an ascetic submissive attitude of sublime indifference toward both life and death (WWR 1: 399–400). Similarly, in the essay *On the Basis of Morality*, Schopenhauer argues:

What is usually laid down as duties to ourselves is first a line of argument against *suicide*, which is greatly steeped in prejudice and rests on the shallowest of reasons. Unlike the animal, man is a prey not merely to *bodily* sufferings, restricted to the present moment, but also to the incomparably greater *mental* afflictions that borrow from the future and the past. By way of compensation, nature has granted to man alone the privilege of being able to end his life when he wishes, before she herself terminates it, and accordingly of not living, like the animal, necessarily as long as he *can*, but only as long as he *will*. Now whether he in turn has to forgo that privilege on ethical grounds is a difficult question, which at any rate cannot be decided by the usual shallow arguments. The arguments against suicide, which Kant does not disdain ... I cannot conscientiously describe as other than paltry and not even worth an answer. We are forced to laugh when we think that such reflections could have wrested the dagger from the hands of Cato, Cleopatra, Cocceius Nerva ... If there really are genuine moral motives against suicide, then at all events they lie very deep and are not to be reached by the plummet of ordinary ethics. (BM: 59–60)

Suppose now that in contemplating suicide I simply will to end my life. As a disciple of Schopenhauer's metaphysics of Will as thing-in-itself and of the individual will to life as phenomenal objectification of Will, I will to end my life not as part of a witless plan to benefit myself, nor with the idea of destroying even the Will as thing-in-itself that I objectify in my individual will to life, but merely as a way of fulfilling my purpose, the goal or end of my life, by terminating my individual consciousness and returning to Will as thing-in-itself. This desire "in my innermost being", by hypothesis, according to Schopenhauer, partially constitutes who and what I am. This is something I cannot change or escape by ending my life, but something that I shall have become as long as my will remains active. I am (in a certain sense eternally and indestructibly) what I will, even if I will to cease willing. In that case, my moral character playing itself out in my actions in life is that of a suicide.

Schopenhauer nevertheless regards destruction of the self as a pointless and obstructive act that prevents us from attaining knowledge. It accomplishes nothing of value and answers no philosophical problems, and in the meantime it cuts short the amount of time we might have better used to gain knowledge through contemplation. He concludes:

Conversely, whoever is oppressed by the burdens of life, whoever loves life and affirms it, but abhors its torments, and in particular can no longer endure the hard lot that has fallen to just him, cannot hope for deliverance from death, and cannot save himself through suicide. Only by a false illusion does the cool shade of Orcus allure him as a haven of rest. The earth rolls on from day into night; the individual dies; but the sun itself burns without intermission, an eternal noon. Life is certain to the will-to-live; the form of life is the endless present; it matters not how individuals, the phenomena of the idea, arise and pass away in time, like fleeting dreams. Therefore suicide already appears to us to be a vain and therefore foolish action ... (WWR 1: 280–81)

The point of a philosophically enlightened suicide for a Schopenhauer-ian might nevertheless be the rationally justifiable desire to bring about an end to the suffering of continued willing. The purpose is then merely to eliminate personal consciousness and the phenomenal will to life that through empirical circumstances no longer wills to live. This is a Kantian-type contradiction only if Schopenhauer stubbornly requires that we continue to designate whatever the individual will wills as will to life when the content of what the individual will has come to will is rather the will-not-to-live. It appears more plausible in such a case to speak of the will to life having been replaced by a reluctant but possibly equally determined will to death. That such a decision might be reached on Schopenhauerian philosophical grounds, at some point in a philosopher's existence, moral questions aside, may therefore not be as metaphysically confused as Schopenhauer seems to think.[17]

It is tempting to interpret the disproportionate attention Schopenhauer devotes to the question of suicide in light of the possibility that his father is likely to have died at his own hand. Could Schopenhauer be trying to deal morally and metaphysically with the personal implications of a parent's decision to end his life, and concluding, as would not be difficult, that his father the tradesman was acting unphilosophically, failing adequately to grasp the meaning of existence?

Fatal renunciation of the will

Schopenhauer makes an interesting exception to his blanket objections against suicide. He finds philosophically praiseworthy the suicide of ascet-ics who in total renunciation of the will to life choose the extraordinary course of slow death by starvation. In *The World as Will and Representation*, he writes:

> Thus [the saint] resorts to fasting, and even to self-castigation and self-torture, in order that, by constant privation and suffering, he may more and more break down and kill the will that he recognizes and abhors as the source of his own suffering existence and of the world's. Finally, if death comes, which breaks up the phenomenon of this will, the essence of such will having long since expired through free denial of itself except for the feeble residue which appears as the vitality of this body, then it is most welcome, and is cheerfully accepted as a longed-for deliverance. It is not merely the phenomenon, as in the case of others, that comes to an end with

death, but the inner being itself that is abolished; this had a feeble existence merely in the phenomenon. This last slender bond is now severed; for him who ends thus, the world has at the same time ended.   (WWR 1: 382)

If we define suicide simply and unqualifiedly as any self-caused death, and distinguish it as such from wilful or intentional acts, then Schopenhauer is prepared to recognize as a philosophically justifiable and even morally praiseworthy kind of suicide the ascetic saint's death by starvation. He argues that we must separate from such incidents the religious fanaticism and superstition that frequently accompany the ascetic's choice to avoid nourishment resulting in death. What is essential for his praise of the ascetic's suicide is that the saint end life as a result of a supreme indifference to the will to life, an indifference to both life and death, that in the natural course of things can only bring about the ascetic saint's death (WWR 1: 400–401).

The theme is first explored in Schopenhauer's early *Manuscript Remains*, where he declares that "The highest degree of asceticism, the total denial of the temporal consciousness, is the *voluntary death through starvation*; of this only two instances have so far come to my knowledge". He continues, "From absolutely pure asceticism we cannot think of any other death than that through starvation, since the intention to avoid a long agony and affliction is already an affirmation of the world of the senses" (HN 1: 74–5). His approval of the ascetic's suicide by starvation is not entirely persuasive. If we try to imagine ourselves in that situation, we are likely to think of the overwhelming desire for nourishment that would accompany a prolonged deathfast. This is hardly the kind of occurrence that is likely to help anyone overcome the suffering of individual will. What Schopenhauer seems to have in mind, and what in this kind of case could only excite his admiration about the ascetic's decision, is a scenario in which the ascetic has so completely renounced the will to life before this point that starvation is accepted without succumbing to physical cravings. What is supposed to be noble about this kind of suicide for Schopenhauer is not the death that it occasions, but the subject's prior separation from all concern for the individual will to life. The ascetic who embarks on a course of death by starvation presumably does so as a manifestation of neither the will to life nor the will to death, but with an absolute indifference to any object of individual willing.[18]

Still, there is another qualification that the starving ascetic must satisfy. Schopenhauer contends that persons as self-conscious beings have an unconditional duty to place knowing above willing. The starving ascetic must first attain the highest degree of philosophical wisdom, for there can be no justified exception from such an epistemic obligation even for the saintly suicide (WWR 1: 399–400). Schopenhauer indicates that the height of knowledge required is achieved precisely as a result of this cruel manner of death. The knowledge that every subject is supposed to seek is facilitated by the ascetic's suppression of will. The denial of will in turn constitutes the profound indifference to life and death that makes suicide by starvation at first possible, and then inevitable. Schopenhauer depicts the saint's life as a renunciation of will for the sake of obtaining a more valuable state of understanding.[19]

The problems in Schopenhauer's philosophy of death are also revealed by these implications. If the philosophically appropriate response to suffering is to withdraw from the phenomenal will to life by entering into an ascetic attitude of indifference toward both life and death, then why should death be preferred? If we admire the starving ascetic, it is probably because we suppose that starving oneself to death requires an extraordinary act of will, rather than for Schopenhauer's explanation involving the total suppression of will. Suspending the will to life to the extent necessary to starve to death cannot occur as the result of a wilful decision. If the act is not deliberately chosen, then in what sense can it be meaningfully attributed to the saint's inner moral character? In what way does the "unwilful" suicide by starvation through a supposedly exalted indifference to the will to life redound creditably to the ascetic if the event is not the result of a conscious decision? The best that Schopenhauer can say is that the denial of will and its obliteration resulting from the ascetic's "unwilful" death through starvation is a good thing. Such a death is not good because it results from starvation, but only because it is generally better from the standpoint of Schopenhauer's pessimism for the world to contain less willing and therefore less suffering. The same might nevertheless be said of any death brought about by accident, disease or even murder.[20]

Here the deeper contradictions underlying Schopenhauer's theory of death begin to appear. If the goal of philosophy is to reconcile individual will to the misery of existence as the end and purpose of unreal life, then it appears impossible to explain why anyone should not prefer death to a life of even the most acute turmoil, suffering and pain. If the aim of life is death, and if death is unreal, then why should the philosopher not accelerate its arrival? The moral obligation of the individual will that has attained to an understanding of the world as Will and representation would seem to be to eliminate individual willing by any means at its disposal in order, by the destruction of consciousness, to return from its state of phenomenal misery to thing-in-itself. The philosopher is not to choose suicide as a bad-faith affirmation of the will to life in an abject effort to avoid suffering. Why, on the other hand, according to Schopenhauer, should a person not do so while enjoying good health, the love of family and friends, productive activity and all of life's pleasures, precisely in order to fulfil life's purpose by ending it for philosophical reasons immediately upon achieving realization of the appearance–reality distinction?

If suffering sanctifies, and if sanctification is a good thing, should it not then be wrong to avoid, let alone wilfully avoid, the vicissitudes of the will to life, no matter how unpleasant? Despite himself, Schopenhauer appears to rely on the repugnance the individual might naturally feel for life construed as unmitigated suffering in order to uphold death as preferable to the wilful continuation of life. Any sort of preference for anything whatsoever is already at least a sublimated expression of the will to life, even, paradoxically, when it embraces the idea of an ideal death. It is not the same as a transcendent attitude of indifference to both life and death. The difficulty in Schopenhauer's philosophy as a result is not the internal conflict of will that it deprecates, but the inconsistencies in Schopenhauer's pessimism as he tries in a more positive light to demystify the meaning of death.[21]

Optimism versus Schopenhauer's moral pessimism

It is useful at this stage to ask whether Schopenhauer's pessimism is strictly entailed by his metaphysics of the world as Will and representation, or whether his moral pessimism is detachable from the speculative theoretical foundations of his philosophy. Schopenhauer's generally sour outlook on life might be more a matter of his personality than a logical consequence of his transcendental idealism. We approach the problem by asking as a thought experiment whether it would be possible to build something entirely different, a moral optimism rather than pessimism, grafted onto Schopenhauer's distinction between thing-in-itself and the world of represented objects for representing subjects.

Suppose for the sake of argument that Schopenhauer had a happy rather than unhappy perspective on life, a personality prepared to see optimism rather than pessimism prevailing or at least possible through good luck and the right sort of prudent decision-making in the world as representation. Might he not then read back into the character of thing-in-itself objectified in the phenomenal world a beneficent and generous rather than malicious and insatiably voracious Will? Perhaps he would then also interpret the spirit of compassion manifested in his own moral thinking and in that of world religions such as Christianity, Hinduism and Buddhism, among others, to mention only those he discusses approvingly, as signs of thing-in-itself in a more positive light? Is this possible in the moral superstructure of Schopenhauer's transcendental idealism? Why should it not be equally possible for things to go in the opposite direction, toward universal optimism, for Schopenhauer, rather than abject pessimism?

We must remember that in Schopenhauer's metaphysics thing-in-itself is Will. The world in reality is pure willing, which cannot intrinsically have any particular benevolent or malevolent object, or, indeed, any object at all. The nature of Will is only (monstrously) to will. We are asking whether Schopenhauer's impression of the world as representation as a reflection of the character of thing-in-itself is not prejudiced by his own personal disappointments and negative outlook on life, for which there may be a psychological basis rather than a sound philosophical justification. Is it inevitable, given that thing-in-itself is Will, the most immediate, and in human beings the highest, grade of the Will's objectification, for the Will's manifestations in the world as representation always to be in eternal mutual conflict, internecine struggle, strife and competition?

Schopenhauer believes that pessimism is strictly entailed by transcendental idealism. His negative perspective on the world and the nature of human interactions especially as a result is, if anything, philosophically inspired and motivated by his epistemology and metaphysics, rather than the other way around. The reason is that Will must objectify itself in all possible ways and hence in particular as the phenomenal willing that we experience in the inner knowledge of the body through the volitional control of the body's actions. It is by means of an intuitive acquaintance with ourselves as will that we are led to conclude that thing-in-itself is Will. If we agree with Schopenhauer that willing necessarily produces suffering, then we may not be able to avoid the conclusion that the world as representation is inevitably the scene of suffering where conflicts must always occur between distinct objectifications of Will.

Schopenhauer's moral pessimism is thus predetermined by his metaphysics of thing-in-itself. There is no escape from the misery produced by willing even in suicide, but only through the kind of salvation available in the life of the ascetic saint or aesthetic genius, and in general through knowledge of the Platonic Ideas. We can only seek relief by renouncing and transcending the will to life for the sake of knowledge. It is in the denial or loss of self that comes about through sacrifice and mortification of the flesh or the immersion of individuality in the Platonic Ideas through the experience of beauty and the sublime in nature and art that we can master the will to life and achieve peace of mind.[22]

CHAPTER FIVE

Art and aesthetics of the beautiful and sublime

That the Idea comes to us more easily from the work of art than directly from nature and from reality, arises solely from the fact that the artist, who knew only the Idea and not reality, clearly repeated in his work only the Idea and not reality, separated it out from reality, and omitted all disturbing contingencies. The artist lets us peer into the world through his eyes. That he has these eyes, that he knows the essential in things which lies outside all relations, is the gift of genius and is inborn; but that he is able to lend us this gift, to let us see with his eyes, is acquired, and is the technical side of art.

(WWR 1: 195)

Philosophy of art

In Schopenhauer's aesthetics we discover a lighter side of his philosophy. Although his moral pessimism continues unabated as a recognition of the inevitable conflicts among the Will's objectifications, Schopenhauer is not as obsessively concerned with the facts of death and human misery when he turns to topics of aesthetic pleasure and enjoyment of the fine arts.

Whether Schopenhauer's metaphysics of Will as thing-in-itself is brilliant or delusional, the distinction between the world as Will and as representation supports a philosophy of art that is unique in the history of aesthetics. Schopenhauer's theory is worth studying for two reasons, even if we do not accept his metaphysics of Will and representation or his heterodox interpretation of Platonic Ideas. It is valuable for the light it sheds on Schopenhauer's philosophy as a whole, and for its own sake, because of the unifying principles by which Schopenhauer proposes to understand the nature of art and its relation to the will to life. Schopenhauer is well informed about many kinds of art, of which he possesses a detailed knowledge and the appreciation of a professional critic and connoisseur. His sometimes idiosyncratic judgements are offered with a remarkable sense of taste and from the standpoint of the more general philosophical framework of his transcendental idealism.

Nietzsche, in his 1874 essay "Schopenhauer as Educator", in the collection published as *Untimely Meditations*, states as one of the most valuable lessons of Schopenhauer's aesthetics:

> It is the fundamental idea of *culture*, insofar as it sets for each one of us but one task: *to promote the production of the philosopher, the artist and the saint within us and without us and thereby to work at the perfecting of nature.* For, as nature needs the philosopher, so does it need the artist, for the achievement of a metaphysical goal, that of its own self-enlightenment ...[1]

In this passage, Nietzsche epitomizes all the essential concepts of Schopenhauer's theory of art and artistic creativity. Schopenhauer asks: What is art? What is the relation between knowledge and desire in art? How are we to interpret the mission of art and the suffering of great artists? Why does artistic creativity alienate the most gifted artists from everyday life, and occasion the personal misunderstandings of which many artists complain in what has come to be called the romantic conception of art? How does the contemplation of great art manage to offer an anodyne sanctuary from the cares of the world? Does it amount to anything more than simply mere escapism? What role do perception and imagination play in artistic depictions of idealized natural forms?

Schopenhauer bids us regard the artist of genius not merely as a craftworker making decorative objects to amuse or entertain, but as what we would now consider to be a kind of existential hero, as well as victim, engaged in terrible struggles of passion and will. The picture seems appropriate to many artistic talents, and certainly to those artists Schopenhauer would include as worthy of the name genius, including Michelangelo, Beethoven, Dostoyevsky and Van Gogh, among many others. He sees great art as the outcome of a deep conflict and frustration of the will in what are often emotionally painful efforts of self-expression. He encourages us to expect a deeper philosophical explanation of genius than we find in their circumstantial psychological biographies. Schopenhauer's aesthetics exerted an enormous influence on a large and diverse number of thinkers and artists in philosophy and the arts, who grasped in his thought the principles for a personal philosophy of life along with its message for the arts.

With the distinction between the world as Will and representation as its metaphysical foundation, Schopenhauer's aesthetics can be understood as an elaboration of these basic themes:

- the concept of art
- the three-part activity of passively intuiting Platonic Ideas, completing and perfecting them in the imagination and expressing them in an artistic medium
- the distinction between lower and higher art forms corresponding to higher and lower Platonic Ideas interpreted as higher and lower grades of the objectivity of Will and reflected in distinct art forms
- music at the highest tier of art forms as the direct expression of Will, in opposition to the Socratic thesis of the iterative imitation of nature at second remove from reality in the case of all other art forms
- the distinction between the beautiful and the sublime in Schopenhauer's rethinking of Kant's analyses
- the suppression of the will to life in aesthetic contemplation as a precondition for intuiting the Platonic Ideas exemplified in the world as representation, and as a path of salvation through the quieting of will for aesthetic genius in the counterpart to saintly asceticism
- criteria of evaluation for distinguishing good or successful from bad or unsuccessful art in the intelligible expression of form and the antipathy of aesthetic genius and the charming
- the problem of ascetic aestheticism or aesthetic asceticism in Nietzsche's critique of Schopenhauer's philosophy of art.

Art in the world as Will and representation

Art, like everything else in Schopenhauer's metaphysics, is an objectification of Will. Artworks belong to the world as representation, and everything in the world as representation objectifies thing-in-itself. The artist must manage a delicate balancing act between surrendering individual will so as to passively receive the Platonic Ideas in experience, curbing the will as an obstacle to knowing, and then imaginatively completing the Ideas imperfectly represented in nature, and labouring to express them as intelligible forms in artworks by means of wilful coordinations of deliberate actions. Schopenhauer is aware of the tension in the artist's conflicting need for disassociation from and engagement of the phenomenal will, each in the right amount and at the appropriate stage of the creative process.

147

There is a parallel two-part division in Schopenhauer's philosophy of art with respect to the perception of Ideas and their artistic expression in completed form. The relation between the intuitive grasp of Platonic Ideas and their presentation in artworks is a special case of what Schopenhauer describes concerning all representational knowledge in which intuition is articulated in abstract theory for the convenience of codifying, communicating and applying its content. Intuitive knowledge is more important than abstraction for Schopenhauer, because it is the foundation of theory to which even the laws of logic must answer when disagreements arise between theory and intuitive understanding. The same is true with respect to the artist's passive reception of Platonic Ideas in nature and their complete expression in artworks. We recall that some of Schopenhauer's most vivid examples of the distinction between intuitive and abstract representation concern such artistic enterprises as the composition of pleasing music versus the elaboration of abstract theories of harmony, counterpoint and thorough-bass.

Schopenhauer emphasizes two challenges facing artists. In his later collection of philosophical remarks in the second volume of the *Parerga and Paralipomena*, he writes:

> By virtue of his objectivity the genius with *reflectiveness* perceives all that others do not see. This gives him as a poet the ability to describe nature so clearly, palpably, and vividly, or as a painter, to portray it. On the other hand, with the *execution* of the work, where the purpose is to communicate and present what is known, the *will* can, and indeed must, again be active, just because there exists a *purpose*. (PP 2: 418–19)

He identifies three separate stages in the creative aesthetic process. Artworks begin with the sensory reception of Platonic Ideas instantiated in the world of nature. Intuited Ideas are then completed and perfected in imaginative abstraction. Finally, the Ideas are given non-discursive representational expression in intelligible form for popular consumption in an artistic medium. Individual willing is switched off involuntarily for the aesthetic genius only during the first and possibly second of these stages, when Platonic Ideas are passively received in an act of perception and then completed and perfected by an act of imagination. Schopenhauer regards these first two stages as the most important part of aesthetic activity. It is in the course of these preliminaries to artistic production that an artist receives inspiration for the work of genius. The Idea and its imaginative completion as an abstract concept is primary; its expression in an artwork is only secondary and in some ways dispensable. The purpose of aesthetic genius is fulfilled for Schopenhauer when the first or second stage is reached. The expression of abstracted non-

148

representational Ideas in the concrete representational form of public art is an afterthought that does not add much if anything to what is of real value when genius arrives at an intuitive knowledge of a Platonic Idea.

As many artists report about their own methods and the ways in which they conceive of their endeavours, it is nevertheless the third stage that is often the most crucial for creative work. It is in the process of making something concrete that the ideas (or Platonic Ideas) that are eventually to be expressed in a finished artwork begin to take shape opportunistically through chance by refining unanticipated suggestions inherent in the materials, while beforehand the end-project is often provisional and ill defined. This, realistically, is when the artist in Schopenhauer's language attempts to sort out the Ideas that have accumulated in disinterested exposure to the world as representation. It is also when artists temporarily lose their egos and at the same time express themselves personally in creative activity. An artist's decisions about what to represent progresses gradually as the work unfolds through many stepwise decisions in the activity of producing an art object (WWR 1: 212; WWR 2: 370).

Schopenhauer can readily accommodate these facts. His purpose is to describe the artist's non-discursive expression of intuitive knowledge. From such a standpoint, it is understandable that the artist need not always or even typically be able to articulate the Ideas she or he is attempting to concretize in art. The non-discursive mode of aesthetic expression of intuitive knowledge of Platonic Ideas might even lead Schopenhauer to disregard entirely whatever an artist has to say about the psychological occurrences that accompany the making of art. It is a commonplace, after all, to which Schopenhauer can also ascribe, that artists are often the least reliable authorities to explain discursively their own artistic practices. Schopenhauer might add that he is trying to describe the activity of aesthetic genius of the highest ideal order. The most accomplished artists of the greatest genius fit his two-part (intuitive–abstract) three-stage (perception–completion/perfection–expression) model exactly, while, admittedly, artists of lesser genius, the majority in fact, or all artists in practice rather than theory, might need to refine their abstraction of Ideas by actually working with art instruments and materials in a preliminary way before the work is finished and the final concept is fully grasped. Artists are nevertheless capable of passively receiving and subconsciously abstracting Platonic Ideas in an aesthetic reverie or while working at the mechanical tasks of art, experiencing the changing shape of clay turning on a wheel, of musical passages tried out experimentally on a keyboard, or arrangements of pigment on canvas. The clarification, completion and perfection of Ideas can evolve along with the making of something that is at first unexpected, in the process whereby an Idea takes shape in an artist's work, with or without the artist's deliberate intent.

"At the lower grades of its objectivity," Schopenhauer remarks, beginning with natural science and progressing to the fine arts, "where it still acts without knowledge, natural science as etiology considers the laws of the changes of its phenomena, and as morphology considers what is permanent in them" (WWR 1: 184). "But now," he asks:

> what kind of knowledge is it that considers what continues to exist outside and independently of all relations, but which alone is really essential to the world, the true content of its phenomena, which is subject to no change, as is therefore known with equal truth for all time, in a word, the *Ideas* that are the immediate and adequate objectivity of the thing-in-itself, of the will? It is *art*, the work of genius. (WWR 1: 184)

Like science, art fixes on the Platonic Ideas by which the Will objectifies itself in the world as representation. Unlike science, art seeks no explanations of phenomena under the fourfold root of the principle of sufficient reason. "It repeats", instead:

> the eternal Ideas apprehended through pure contemplation, the essential and abiding element in all the phenomena of the world. According to the material in which it repeats, it is sculpture, painting, poetry, or music. Its only source is knowledge of the Ideas; its sole aim is communication of this knowledge. (WWR 1: 184–5)

The absence of explanation in art facilitates its unique mode of communicating intuitive knowledge. By eliminating inessentials and translating intuitive knowledge of the Platonic Ideas perceived in nature, art passes along a vision of the truth of things recovered from a special relationship to the world as representation and the Platonic Ideas embodied in represented objects as grades of the Will's objectification.

The principle of sufficient reason allows that every phenomenon has a scientific explanation. Since this includes whatever may be invoked in explaining a given occurrence, these factors are also capable of further explanation, and so on, indefinitely. Art, in contrast, standing outside the nexus of all explanation, avoids regress by presenting another phenomenon in the form of a specially chosen and prepared object, the artwork. An art object is meant to reflect a grasp of Platonic Ideas, and to convey for the benefit of others a sense of the Ideas received in the artist's experience (FFR: 41–2). Schopenhauer posits a collaboration between aesthetic contemplation entirely divorced from will in the experience of objective, purely passive perception, and the active play of imagination. He refuses to identify imagination with genius, but admits it as an essential ingredient. The role of imagination in aesthetic genius is to eliminate what is accidental in perceived forms in nature, and to add whatever is needed in order to complete nature's intentions as the artist perceives them. The conflict of natural forms cited by Schopenhauer as cause of the inevitable incompleteness and imperfection in the phenomenal world recapitulates the ground of his romantic moral pessimism in what he sees as the artist's tragic existence, driven to represent the unrepresentable, and hence frequently misunderstood by whoever encounters the artist's work.

Platonic Ideas as grades of the Will's objectification in higher and lower art forms

Schopenhauer distinguishes higher and lower art forms. These belong to a hierarchy corresponding to the higher and lower Platonic Ideas. The Ideas are themselves higher or lower grades of the Will's objectification, as determined by their respective degrees of individuality among the instances of each Idea. Such an ordering of the fine arts is not only appropriate but strictly required by Schopenhauer's theory of Ideas. The connecting link needed to justify a hierarchical arrangement of art forms in Schopenhauer's theory, which Schopenhauer freely supplies, is the proposition that distinct art forms are specifically concerned with particular Ideas.

There are pure and mixed art forms. Music, painting, and poetry are pure. Opera is an obvious example of a mixed art that combines poetry or literature with music. All art forms can be ordered by virtue of the Platonic Ideas they feature and their relative grade of the Will's objectification. Architecture is the lowest art form, according to Schopenhauer, because, although it can also involve sculpture, painting and other forms of decoration, in its purest form it concerns the lowest, most primal grades of the Will's objectification in the world as representation. These include especially Gravity, Rigidity, Hardness and Mass, and in general those involving the control and distribution of natural forces in the creation of spaces intended for a variety of practical functions. Music exhibits the highest grade of the Will's objectification, or belongs to a separate category all by itself, in the sense that music in its pure form is altogether independent of the world as representation. Its existence is interpreted by Schopenhauer as an immediate direct objectification of Will, like the natural world itself, with no further representation or iterative imitation separating it from Will as thing-in-itself or mediating between the two.

If we begin with architecture as the lowest art form in Schopenhauer's hierarchy, corresponding to the lowest grade of the Will's objectification, we may then compare it with music at the opposite extreme. Schopenhauer offers two reasons for dividing these broad artwork categories so dramatically. Architecture, unlike music, is rarely if ever undertaken purely as a fine art, or as art for art's sake, and is therefore almost invariably related to purpose and the satisfaction of desire. This puts it in closer relation to phenomenal willing and the will to life, and farther away from thing-in-itself and the most highly individualized grades of the Will's objectifications. The highest grade Ideas are necessarily connected to human beauty in artistic representations of human form (WWR 1: 214). The distancing of architecture from music on the spectrum of art forms obliges Schopenhauer, in the second volume of *The World as Will and Representation*, to renounce Goethe's otherwise suggestive image of architecture as frozen music (WWR 2: 453–4).

With music at the top of or standing outside the ordering of arts, and architecture at the bottom, Schopenhauer arranges the remaining fine arts in between. They are ranked according to their relation to a specific degree of the Will's objectification corresponding to the Platonic Ideas with which each is associated. The scale begins with such universal physical forces as Gravity and proceeds up to Man, at the peak of the Ideas, reflecting the highly particularized nature of human beings. The complete hierarchy is easy to provide on the basis of this principle, interpolating poetry, literature, painting and sculpture on the basis of hints Schopenhauer sprinkles throughout his remarks on art. Sculpture, for obvious reasons, is closer to architecture than to music. Painting falls between sculpture and poetry and literature, with poetry occurring between music and literature. The hierarchy from higher to lower artforms in rough outline accordingly looks like this:

architecture → sculpture → painting → literature → poetry → music

(grades of the Will's objectification in art forms: low → high)

Schopenhauer locates landscape gardening between architecture and sculpture. He divides the category of painting more finely, so that landscape painting is placed above historical painting, and these in turn above still-lifes. Similarly with respect to epic and lyric poetry; dance; opera, and orchestral music; fountain or hydraulic and other sculpture; and all other art forms. The hierarchy supports Schopenhauer's theory of art as the objectification of Will by providing a classification from lower to higher art forms according to his conception of their dependence on and exemplification of respective grades of the Will's objectification.

Although Schopenhauer insists that the fine arts fall into a rank ordering from low to high, depending on their relation to similarly ordered Platonic

Ideas, he maintains that there is no bar to regarding anything whatsoever as beautiful. He illustrates the proposition that everything is beautiful by Dutch still-life painting, in which even the most everyday objects are elevated to the status of fine art by the artist's attention to their forms, colours, and individuality (WWR 1: 210). We can see how Schopenhauer's thesis that everything is potentially beautiful follows directly from his argument that everything in the world as representation is the manifestation of thing-in-itself. For everything embodies some grade or other of the Will's objectification, which is to say of some Platonic Idea or other. The stronger thesis that everything is actually beautiful might be derived from Schopenhauer's claim that a Platonic Idea simply by virtue of being such is automatically beautiful. Schopenhauer does not explicitly say this, nor does he provide any positive reason for thinking that it would be true, although the concept fits nicely into his metaphysics and aesthetics. Why not suppose on the contrary, then, that some Platonic Ideas are beautiful, some are plain or non-beautiful, and some unbeautiful or even ugly?

Schopenhauer in any case acknowledges degrees of beauty. While every represented object is beautiful, some things are more beautiful than others, depending on the exact way in which they embody their respective Platonic Ideas (WWR 1: 210). Some things express more highly ranked Platonic Ideas, construed as higher grades of the Will's objectification. Thus, a good representation of a flower is inherently more beautiful for Schopenhauer than a good representation of a stone. Other objects of nature and works of art are more clearly and distinctly concrete embodiments of whatever Platonic Ideas they are chosen to express. These factors, in Schopenhauer's view, also contribute in another way to an object's greater beauty.

It is in these terms and for these reasons that Schopenhauer acknowledges human beauty, the beauty of the Idea of humanity, and the human form, as the highest type of beauty in any art form. The exalted classification of human beauty fits Schopenhauer's overall theory of the stratification of art forms and particular types of representations within art forms. His hierarchy corresponds exactly with the grades of the Will's objectification in the phenomenal world. The fact that human beings as members of a species associated with a Platonic Idea exhibit the highest degree of individuality among the things we know guarantees that artworks devoted to human beauty embody the highest type of beauty. Schopenhauer demonstrates the superiority of human beauty over all other subcategories by the common-sense comparison of artworks of individual persons in portrait art with artworks of non-human animals. The latter may be interesting and beautiful to a limited degree, but Schopenhauer insists that the greater beauty will always belong to anything directly associated with human interests. As one way of characterizing the difference, he remarks that any competent painting of a given breed of horse or dog would serve as well as any other, while the same is obviously not true of human portraits, the individuality of which at each stage of life is always in evidence (WWR 1: 221).

Thus, Schopenhauer's nineteenth-century transcendental idealism confirms the ancient Greek ideal of the human form as paramount among artistic subjects. It is not merely that we as human beings are preoccupied with ourselves and with every aspect of the human body, nor that we take a certain erotic pleasure in realistic representations of youthful athletic human anatomy. Schopenhauer, on the contrary, argues that artworks displaying the sensuality of human nudity in any medium are unworthy as being too closely related to the will to life. The reason why Schopenhauer regards human beauty as the highest, greatest and most interesting of all types and degrees is that it exemplifies the highest Platonic Idea, the highest grade of the Will's objectification, given that human beings possess the greatest diversity and individuality among the members of any known species.

Music and nature as immediate objectifications of Will

The best known conclusion of Schopenhauer's aesthetic theory, familiar to many who know little else about his philosophy, is that music, like the natural world and unlike any other art form, is the direct expression of Will. Schopenhauer makes music an exception to the Socratic criticism of art as an iterative imitation at two removes from reality, an imitation of the world of appearance, which is itself in turn supposed to be an imitation of the eternal Forms or Ideas.[2] Painting, poetry, sculpture, architecture and the like, are all separated from reality in just this way. Good music, the only music Schopenhauer finds worthy of consideration as exemplary of the art form, is entirely on a par with the world of nature as the immediate representation of thing-in-itself, the world as Will objectified in the world as representation.

Schopenhauer begins his discussion of music as the immediate objectification of Will by first distinguishing in Socratic fashion between literature and the plastic arts as expressive in other ways of Platonic Ideas. Music, he maintains, alone among art forms, bypasses the Ideas, because it does not try to further represent anything that is already a representational object. A painting of a horse is a representation of the Idea of Horse, and as such communicates through its selection and emphasis of essential features the relevant Platonic Idea in a form that can be perceived and from which intuitive knowledge of the Idea can be indirectly recovered. Since a particular horse is already an objectification of the world as Will, a painting of a horse is a representation of a representation at two removes of objectification from the reality that is thing-in-itself.

The same is not true of music. Schopenhauer believes that music, like the world of nature itself, is a direct objectification of Will. Music belongs to a distinct aesthetic category of its own. Schopenhauer is explicit that this classification is intended to pay tribute to what should be obvious to any listener about the special character of music as a fine art. He describes all music worthy of the name as standing outside phenomenal representation, the principle of individuation and presumably also, therefore, although he does not mention it, the principle of sufficient reason. Arts other than music imitate in their production of represented objects other represented objects that are already to be found in the world as representation. The artist expresses intuited Platonic Ideas from which, when the art is good, an appreciative audience can grasp the twice-removed Ideas. This is precisely Socrates' complaint about the representational arts in Plato's *Republic*. The objection does not apply in the unique case of music, which Schopenhauer regards as the only exception to the Socratic rule (WWR 1: 257).

Music fails and falls disastrously short of its true potential when it seeks imitatively to express emotions. It succeeds when through its pure forms of melody and harmony, representationally unconnected to anything else in the phenomenal world, it simply objectifies Will. This alone is the proper province of music, that which makes it outstanding among all other art forms. Schopenhauer concludes:

> Therefore music does not express this or that particular and definite pleasure, this or that affliction, pain, sorrow, horror, gaiety, merriment, or peace of mind, but joy, pain, sorrow, horror, gaiety, merriment, peace of mind *themselves*, to a certain extent in the abstract, their essential nature, without any accessories, and so also without the motives for them. Nevertheless, we understand them perfectly in this extracted quintessence.   (WWR 1: 261)

The proof of Schopenhauer's assessment of music's special gift is found in enjoyment of the effect music has on the listener's imagination in trying to give substance to the feelings it evokes.

Schopenhauer seems to think that the only way to explain what is special about music, the undeniable impact it has on aesthetic sensibilities, is by attributing to it non-iteratively representational status as the immediate objectification of Will in the auditory world as representation. There its effect is to invite the listener to construct a world in the imagination corresponding to the moods and feelings it arouses. Schopenhauer is prepared to take the sentiment literally and at face value when people say, as they sometimes do, that music is a world in and of and unto itself. If for Schopenhauer architecture, in Goethe's simile, is not like frozen music, music is in any case precisely akin to the direct objectification of Will in such beautiful represented objects of nature as snowflakes and rivers and mountainsides, the vascular structures of plants, their leaves, roots and stems, honeycombs and seashells, among countless other examples.

Schopenhauer's distinction between the non-imitation of (good) music and the iterative imitation of all other arts raises interesting problems. Schopenhauer says that music has nothing to do with the phenomenal world, "positively ignores it", "passes over the Ideas", and, most remarkably, unlike the other arts, "could still exist even if there were no world at all" (WWR 1: 262). We should begin by noting Schopenhauer's normative loading of the term "music" to refer specifically to non-programmatic music that does not attempt to imitate the sounds of nature or particular types of emotion. He speaks only of music that meets his evaluative Socratic standard for good music by not being iteratively imitative. His theory of music involves something like the following chain of inferences: music is good music; good music is non-imitatively expressive; non-imitative expression is the immediate objectification of thing-in-itself as Will; therefore, music is the immediate objectification of Will. There is something bordering dangerously on circular reasoning in any such effort to champion what is unique about music as an art form, its metaphysics and its psychological effect on listeners.

When Schopenhauer speaks of art, not only in the case of music, he usually means the highest and most accomplished artworks, the products of genius. It is as though for Schopenhauer so-called artworks that do not fit his definition or measure up to his aesthetic standards simply do not count as art and are not to be mentioned in the same breath as recognized masterpieces. There is a difficulty here. Although it is incumbent on aesthetic philosophy to define the concept of art *and* to establish normative guidelines for the evaluation of artworks, the combination of these features in a normative definition that distinguishes (good) art from non-art threatens to trivialize the resulting theory both as conceptual analysis and as a basis for judging artworks in distinguishing successful from unsuccessful efforts. Art by definition, according to the theory's peculiar bias, is necessarily good, whereas the category of bad or unworthy art has no application. Such an approach potentially deprives the definition of significance. What might otherwise cast doubts on the theory's evaluative pronouncements of good art, artworks that might be deemed bad, are automatically excluded by virtue of not constituting genuine artworks in the first place. To make art good by definition is to make the distinction between good and bad art meaningless, an implication that seems especially hazardous in Schopenhauer's aesthetics of music.

An even greater difficulty in distinguishing music from other arts looms for Schopenhauer's doctrine that music "passes over" the Ideas of the phenomenal world. This seems to contradict the central proposition of Schopenhauer's aesthetics that genius creates art by passively receiving Platonic Ideas, projecting them through imagination into complete perfected abstract concepts, and then representing them in a concrete medium. If the description applies to (good) music, then, since for Schopenhauer the Platonic Ideas are imprinted on aesthetic genius in moments of will-suppressed perception, music like the other arts similarly has to do with the phenomenal world's Ideas. If the description does not apply, then Schopenhauer's theory of aesthetic genius and artistic creativity is refuted out of his own mouth by the counter-example he unwittingly provides. The problem is not resolved by acknowledging music as an exception, however embarrassing it might be for Schopenhauer's philosophy of art. If music does not involve Platonic Ideas, but is the direct expression of Will, then we have yet to understand the artist's role, and how it is that the composer of itera-tively non-imitative music is supposed to have direct access to Will. Why is music not found as naturally as daffodils and rhinoceros beetles? Why is it, like other art forms, something that exists only when created by human beings?

Schopenhauer also rejects the Leibnizian account of music as mathemati-cal in nature. Despite the internal arithmetic of the ratios of musical inter-vals in the formal harmony of chords, melody, discord and resolution, rhythms and polyrhythms, Schopenhauer insists that there is something more to music. Music can only be understood by coming to terms with its effect on our emotions, when it is not merely an effort representationally to imitate certain states of mind. As a consequence, he rejects the mathematical status of music as an explanation of its metaphysics: "we certainly have to look for more than that *exercitium arithmeticae occultum nescientis se numerare animi* [an unconscious exercise in arithmetic in which the mind does not know it is counting] which Leibniz took it to be" (WWR 1: 255–6).

Schopenhauer invokes intuition to uphold these conclusions; in effect, he relies on feeling. Intuitive knowledge is supposed to be superior to, while constituting the ultimate ground of justification for, abstract knowledge. Schopenhauer's only recourse in trying to understand the nature of some-thing as remarkable as music is to fall back on personal reactions to the effects that music has on his own emotions. This is the method he recommends in all special disciplines, including logic and mathematics. He recognizes that the approach is not likely to be accepted by sceptics, and he tries to antici-pate and blunt the edge of their criticisms. The personal nature of the enquiry stands out by comparison with Schopenhauer's efforts at abstract knowledge elsewhere in his treatise. Here, in contrast, he seems to say nothing more than that, after listening to music for many years and thinking about what kind of thing it is, he simply finds it compelling to conclude as a revelation of insight that music is the immediate objectification of thing-in-itself as Will (WWR 1: 256–7).

Schopenhauer admits that he has no way to prove that music is different from other art forms. He offers instead, almost as an article of faith, the hopeful expectation that a reader who has agreed with his previous findings will now go along also with the proposition that music is not itself the representation of any other representation, but is itself the direct objectification of Will. To sustain his conclusion, as we have seen, Schopenhauer needs to discount all programme music and other types of iteratively representational music as unworthy of the art form. What remains is merely the coherent description of music as the direct objectification of the Will, which he says is sufficient for him, and which he trusts will appeal to at least some sympathetic readers as providing the truth of the matter. This is surprisingly weak, although it is obviously not intended as an argument. Like any other theorist, Schopenhauer is entitled to express philosophical opinions to see whether they resonate with other thinkers on the basis of their informed experience and appreciation of music. If he is right, then we are supposed to recognize the appropriateness of classifying music in this way. Beyond this, Schopenhauer admits that he has no further resources with which to try to persuade a reluctant critic. Schopenhauer's strategy can be understood as more like an inference to the best explanatory hypothesis in accounting for the nature of music, within what he believes is an already rigorously justified metaphysics, epistemology and aesthetic theory of the non-musical arts.

This set of issues is related to another puzzle in Schopenhauer's philosophy of music. He notes that, unlike the other arts, music would exist ("to a certain extent") even if there were no phenomenal world. If music is the direct non-imitative objectification of Will, then some version of this extravagant claim must be true. At one level, it is perhaps easy enough to see what Schopenhauer is trying to say. Music is more abstract than the literary and plastic arts; it is more like mathematics. We might regard Schopenhauer as a kind of modern Pythagorean in characterizing music as independent of the phenomenal world. Yet he has already explicitly rejected the Leibnizian mathematical concept of music. The difficulties entailed by such a position are at once apparent. Take away the world as representation, and there are no artists, composers, performance musicians, instruments, sound vibrations or listeners. If music exists independently of the world of experience, it can only be because music in essence is a set of abstract relationships to be instantiated in any number of different ways.

The trouble is, first, that such relationships could equally be non-musically instantiated. This, indeed, is another implication of Pythagoreanism. The real nature or essence of music as an art form in that case clearly eludes Schopenhauer's theory. Nor does the thesis adequately distinguish music by virtue of its abstractness alone from modern abstract and minimalist plastic art, although perhaps we should not blame Schopenhauer for not foreseeing these developments. Secondly, and more importantly, it follows that Schopenhauer as a result has not adequately explained the relation between musical aesthetic genius, the existence of music as an art form, and musical compositions as expressions of artistic genius. Ideas are involved only in the other arts. They derive from phenomenal contact with the world as representation and are abstracted by imagination, completed and perfected, before being concretely expressed in the artist's choice of media. By hypothesis, Platonic Ideas play no essential part in the existence of music, even though music on this conception in some sense consists essentially of abstract relations. The limitations of interpreting music purely formally or mathematically without taking its effect on a listener's emotions as an essential aspect of the nature of musical expression is undoubtedly part of the reason why Schopenhauer repudiates Leibniz's soulless mathematical analysis of music as overlooking what music does and what it means to the appreciative subject. It is also probably part of the reason why Schopenhauer's aesthetics has enjoyed such widespread appeal among musicians and music lovers.

Beauty and the sublime, good and great art

Schopenhauer revisits the "Analytic of the Beautiful" and "Analytic of the Sublime" in Kant's *Critique of Judgement*.[3] In doing so, he recommends a different basis for the distinction and an alternative account of its significance in terms of his metaphysics of the world as Will and representation. The beautiful and the sublime are distinguished in non-Kantian ways by Schopenhauer as implications of the essential beauty of Ideas, and the attitude of will toward itself as representation and towards the world as Will in the aesthetics of the sublime.

By beauty, Schopenhauer means nothing other than the natural forms of Platonic Ideas. Ideas are beautiful by definition. Schopenhauer speaks without qualification of "Ideas, in which beauty, in the objective sense, consists" (WWR 1: 200). Later, in "Criticism of the Kantian Philosophy", his Appendix to the first volume of *The World as Will and Representation*, he describes "a pure perception free from reflection and from will, like that of the beautiful, the deepest comprehension of the true essence of things, in other words, of their Platonic Ideas" (WWR 1: 451). Clarity of expression of the

Ideas is both the aesthetic goal and basis for judgement of beauty. In a single stroke Schopenhauer cuts the Gordian knot that had perplexed young Socrates in Plato's dialogue the *Parmenides*, about whether or not there are Forms or Ideas of "ugly" and disgusting things, such as hair, mud and dirt.[4] Schopenhauer excludes such possibilities by fiat on the basis of his understanding of what is implied by the concept of a Platonic Idea and of beauty. He holds that even if there are such Ideas they are necessarily beautiful as natural forms, and that they appear loathsome if at all only in non-aesthetic relation to individual willing and the preoccupations of the will to life.[5]

The sublime in contrast is defined by the attitudes and emotional responses of phenomenal will toward the world as representation. Like Kant, Schopenhauer distinguishes between two categories of the sublime: the dynamical and mathematical. The dynamical sublime is experienced through imaginative contact with great and sometimes terrifying natural forces. It is the aesthetic feeling produced by standing above a deep ravine, mountain range or rushing waterfall. The mathematical sublime is the product of awe in contemplation of great distances in space and time, such as that induced by staring in wonder at the seemingly infinite immensity of stars in the night sky, or considering vast regressions of geologic time. In Kant's analytic of the sublime, the impression made on the senses by such phenomena suggest in turn the infinity of God. They lead the intellect toward religious contemplation of its own limitations in relation to the greatness of the deity.[6] Schopenhauer, as we should expect, does not follow Kant's analytic of the sublime in these directions. He nevertheless accepts Kant's terminology and his basic divisions of subcategories in an aesthetics of the sublime. "The impression of the sublime can arise in quite a different way by our imagining a mere magnitude in space and time, whose immensity reduces the individual to nought", he allows. "By retaining Kant's terms and his correct division, we can call the first kind the dynamically sublime, although we differ from him entirely in the explanation of the inner nature of that impression, and can concede no share in this either to moral reflections or to hypostases from scholastic philosophy" (WWR 1: 205).

Included in the dynamical sublime are standard textbook examples from Longinus to Edmund Burke and Kant. Great storms at sea, cataracts rushing through steep gorges and the like are all potentially life-threatening natural occurrences in which the individual will finds exhileration at the thought of its survival in hostile circumstances, and in which its relative insignificance in size and power are personalized.[7] Whereas beauty appears without effort in the clear reception of natural form, the Platonic Ideas embodied as distinct grades of the Will's objectification in the world as representation, the sublime additionally requires a specific feeling of satisfaction that results from the struggle and victory of will.[8] Schopenhauer explains the feeling of the sublime:

> [W]hat distinguishes the feeling of the sublime from that of the beautiful is that, with the beautiful, pure knowledge has gained the upper hand without a struggle, since the beauty of the object, in other words, that quality of it which facilitates knowledge of its Idea, has removed from consciousness, without resistance and hence imperceptibly, the will and knowledge of relations that slavishly serve this will ... The feeling of the sublime is distinguished from that of the beautiful only by the addition, namely the exaltation beyond the known hostile relation of the contemplated object to the will in general. Thus there result several degrees of the sublime, in fact transitions from the beautiful to the sublime, according as this addition is strong, clamorous, urgent, and near, or only feeble, remote, and merely suggested. (WWR 1: 202)

In company with most other aesthetic theorists, Schopenhauer acknowledges different degrees of the dynamical sublime. Their quality depends on the intensity of the perceived threat posed by violent natural events to the individual will to life, or on the effort of imagination required to come to terms with the magnitude of forces. The very fact that Schopenhauer has available to his aesthetic theory a predetermined account of individual willing and the individual's will to preserve life provides a unique basis from which he can more exactly interpret distinct qualitative divisions within the general catgory of the sublime. Schopenhauer's narration of the most impressive experiences of the sublime is as remarkable for its romantic *Sturm und Drang* poetry as for the philosophical observations it contains (WWR 1: 204–5).

The distinction between the beautiful and the sublime is drawn exclusively by reference to the subjective feeling encountered in the sublime as menacing the will to life. Schopenhauer argues that the only difference between beauty and the sublime is the feeling of threat to life in the case of the sublime. This conclusion, too, is inescapable, given Schopenhauer's prior commitment to the proposition that everything is beautiful. It follows that the sublime is a particular type of beauty; namely, it is that which is also experienced as a danger to the will to life. Schopenhauer believes that once again he has excelled Kant, this time in his aesthetic philosophy of the beautiful and the sublime as much as in his metaphysics of thing-in-itself. The advance is only made possible by Schopenhauer's emphasis on the will to life as the Will's most direct (psychological) objectification in the world as representation, and as that for the sake of which thing-in-itself is identified with Will. Schopenhauer's theory of the sublime has the further interesting implication that the beautiful and the sublime are not exclusive categories, but that the sublime is merely a special case of the beautiful. This is a welcome result for those who do not sense any inherent division between beauty and the sublime, for whom what is sublime can also be beautiful, and conversely.

Schopenhauer's concept of the sublime is subjective in its reliance on the feelings aroused especially by scenes in nature that inspire terror. The sublime is a state of mind produced by fear for the safety of the will to life in the perception of potential dangers. They include mountain crags and sea storms and the feeling of relative smallness and vulnerability of the will to life relative to the vastness of a desert wilderness or the starry heavens. There is no reason why such objects should not also be regarded as beautiful, just as Schopenhauer's theory entails. The night sky is beautiful as well as humbling, as are the desert and mountain range, and the plunging waterfall spilling into a terrifying gorge. It is, if Schopenhauer is right, all a matter of how we as representing subjects feel in the presence of such objects. Just as every object is actually beautiful for Schopenhauer, so every object is potentially sublime, depending on whether or not we happen to experience any sort of threat to our phenomenal will to life in its presence. It is possible, then, that the simplest, most innocent appearing objects could be sublime as well as beautiful, if they happen circumstantially to arouse a sense of fear. "The course of our remarks has made it necessary to insert here a discussion of the sublime", Schopenhauer states, "when the treatment of the beautiful has been only half completed, merely from one side, the subjective. For it is only a special modification of this subjective side which distinguishes the sublime from the beautiful" (WWR 1: 208).

It is clearly the dynamical rather than mathematical sublime that most impresses Schopenhauer. The theory of the sublime in its relation to the will is also accordingly quite different for Schopenhauer than for Kant. For Kant, the mathematical sublime, seen, for example, in the vastness of the starry heavens, suggests to imagination the infinite, which in turn is supposed to lead by subtle turns of contemplation eventually to the concept of God.[9] Schopenhauer's atheism will have none of this. He rightly observes that despite adopting Kant's distinction between the dynamical and mathematical sublime, his theory, making reference to the struggles and sufferings of will, is in all other respects unlike Kant's. It is in encounters with the untamed forces of nature that the will to life confronts its limitations, sensing something like the raw energy of the world as Will, while glorying in the superiority of its perception and knowledge over the world as representation. If the mind also happens to entertain thoughts of God as a result, that effect, for Schopenhauer, is purely accidental.

Aesthetic genius and will

Schopenhauer regards the ability to engage in purely disinterested perception, excluding all signs or stirrings of appetite, desire or will to life, as the mark of aesthetic genius. Experience of the world as representation without interference of will leads genius first to grasp the Platonic ideas underlying appearance, to their completion and perfection in imagination, and then in a wilful act of communication to depict the ideal in art. The ability objectively to perceive the world with no interference of will is rare, and Schopenhauer exploits the scarcity of this talent at the very source of artistic production to explain the infrequency of true aesthetic genius.

Schopenhauer divides the activity of will from the passivity of purely objective perception. "The *punctum saliens* of every beautiful work," he writes, "every great and profound thought, is an entirely objective perception. But such a perception is absolutely conditioned by a complete silencing of the will which leaves the person as pure subject of knowing. The aptitude for the prevalence of this state is simply genius" (WWR 2: 370). The idea that desire and individual willing or will to life, however conceived, should in some sense be separated from aesthetic contemplation in the experience of genius is a perennial thesis of aesthetic philosophy. Schopenhauer describes the pure extreme form of aesthetic genius as a kind of ideal, to which only a few attain, but that others may approximate, and that almost everyone is capable of experiencing in limited ways if they are able in any degree to experience the enjoyment of beauty or the sublime.

Aesthetic appreciation involves the passive intuition of Platonic Ideas. It is a kind of knowledge, which for Schopenhauer always stands in opposition to the phenomenal will to life. It follows that we can only experience beauty and the sublime by suspending the will and suppressing its demands on our time, attention, and energy for the sake of receiving knowledge of the Ideas. The ideal case, the most extreme and perfect form of aesthetic appreciation, is that of aesthetic genius, who in theory is capable of sufficiently quieting the will to intuit Platonic Ideas in objects and scenes of nature and great works of art.

Since the Ideas are imprinted on genius during episodes of will-suppressed perceptions of the phenomenal world, something more is required to make sense impressions into abstract Platonic Ideas. Genius also requires imagination, by which it generalizes perceived natural forms into typified abstractions. Aesthetic genius for Schopenhauer does not merely report on the Platonic Ideas received in moments of will-suppressed aesthetic contemplation, but completes and perfects the forms in imagination, and then finds ways to represent them in works of art according to its own sense of style. Genius, as such, requires a collaboration between the passive reception of

Platonic Ideas and the active role of imagination in completing and perfecting the forms nature reveals, to be represented in a work of art.

Willing obstructs the grasp of Platonic Ideas. The Ideas present themselves to genius only when and to the extent that willing is suppressed. The experience of natural form coloured by taint of will obscures the Ideas, and pollutes the well-spring of aesthetic contemplation that Schopenhauer holds is presupposed by great art. Aesthetic genius enters into moments of pure objectivity and total loss of individuality, an absolute denial of will, in which objects are experienced purely perceptually, without desire, belief or relation to the self. Considered as a means to an end, aesthetic contemplation and great artistry are an alternative to saintly asceticism in transcending the will to life and attaining salvation from the suffering that accompanies every act of willing (WWR 1: 186–7). It offers another way in which the suffering induced by the phenomenal will can be quieted, suppressed and transcended.

Schopenhauer describes the blessed aesthetic consciousness in these laudatory terms. "Finally, it is also that blessedness of will-less perception," he writes:

> which spreads so wonderful a charm over the past and the distant, and by a self-deception presents them to us in so flattering a light. For by conjuring up in our minds days long past spent in a distant place, it is only the objects recalled by our imagination, not the subject of will, that carried around its incurable sorrows with it just as much then as it does now. (WWR 1: 198)

It is not quite aesthetic escapism that Schopenhauer finds most valuable in the enjoyment of art, but something that is not far afield. He emphasizes the role of memory and aesthetic amnesia that occurs through the loss of self in the complete absorption in a work of art or scene of nature (WWR 1: 198–9).

Finally, the therapeutic effects of artistic dissociation from self and the individual will to life are seen in proper perspective. "We can withdraw from all suffering", Schopenhauer promises us:

> just as well through present as through distant objects, whenever we raise ourselves to a purely objective contemplation of them, and are thus able to produce the illusion that only those objects are present, not we ourselves. Then, as pure subject of knowing, delivered from the miserable self, we become entirely one with those objects, and foreign as our want is to them, it is at such moments just as foreign to us. Then the world as representation alone remains; the world as will has disappeared. (WWR 1: 198–9)

We are supposed to be able briefly to abandon our selves in aesthetic contemplation, losing sight for at least a while of the tormenting will to life. We thereby enter a will-transcending blessed state of consciousness that offers the temporary illusion of detaching represented object from the representing subject, merging subject unselfconsciously into object. The resulting altered state of subjective awareness is free of individual willing, finding temporary aesthetic release from all sufferings of will. Through aesthetic contemplation we may come as close as it is possible ever to experience the existence of represented objects as they are in and of themselves, without awareness of the willing subject.

We recall in this connection Schopenhauer's insistence that the Platonic Ideas as grades of the Will's objectification, passively intuited in will-less moments of pure aesthetic contemplation, are virtually thing-in-itself. This is a consequence of the near convergence he discerns in the metaphysics of Plato's Ideas and Kant's thing-in-itself. In art, through the imagination's completion of perceptually intuited Platonic Ideas, the intrusion of will to life in the world as representation is minimized, as the Ideas take over consciousness and displace the willing subject far into the background. When this occurs, the subject of aesthetic contemplation is rendered negligible in comparison with Platonic Ideas standing in close approximation to thing-in-itself, or, with these qualifications, as object-in-itself.

With his usual depth of penetration, Schopenhauer puts his finger on one of the principal benefits of art. It is probably fair to say that few persons would formulate the transcendence offered by great art in quite the way Schopenhauer does, with or without his technical philosophical vocabulary. Something in what he says should nevertheless ring true for those who have had transporting aesthetic encounters with artwork of genius or outstanding scenes of natural beauty or the sublime. Stand before Michelangelo's *Pieta* in St Peter's Basilica in the Vatican and you might find yourself completely captivated, unable to take your eyes away from its beauty. It is so small and yet so perfect, even when seen today from behind bullet-proof glass at a considerable distance. Regardless of your religious inclinations, you might discover yourself deeply moved by the form and universal appeal of the marble, of Jesus's mother, Mary, holding his broken body in her arms after being taken down from the cross on the day of his crucifixion. Schopenhauer would probably approve of this choice of artwork as illustrating his theory of aesthetic genius. It exemplifies his concept of how a viewer of great art can be lifted out of willing and the sense of self. Moreover, it depicts as a kind of universal theme the emotional suffering of Christ's mother, and the bitter physical suffering and death of a saintly ascetic, who, in another way, grappling intensely with the problems of existence, was misunderstood and reviled by those for whose salvation he is sacrificed.

Schopenhauer is impressed with the fact that many artists in their ordinary and professional lives do not always live up to the contemplative ideal of suppressing desire and the will to life. It appears, on the contrary, if Schopenhauer has correctly diagnosed the situation, that persons of aesthetic genius are frequently agitated, even more so than ordinary citizens, precisely because they are endlessly in search of new objects of knowledge, new ideas and Ideas to nourish their art. "This explains the animation, amounting to disquietude, in men of genius," he states:

> since the present can seldom satisfy them, because it does not fill their consciousness. This gives them that restless zealous nature, that constant search for new objects worthy of contemplation, and also that longing, hardly ever satisfied, for men of like nature and stature to whom they may open their hearts. (WWR 1: 186)

The life of genius in Schopenhauer's aesthetics can be understood as yet another manifestation of will impelling the knower and artist in a restless quest that precludes serenity and peace. If so, it does not change the fact that genius, no matter how driven to increase knowledge and create more and better art, still requires the suppression of will to receive Platonic Ideas in perception, even if before and after such moments genius is generally in motion, eager to learn and do more.

As in other aspects of his philosophy, Schopenhauer projects an extreme case, and then explains the situations we encounter in actual experience as approximations to the ideal. Here the ideal is the aesthetic genius, with respect to which all other persons are capable of aesthetic appreciation and enjoyment by virtue, not of complete, but at most of a partial and imperfect, suppression of the will to life. Having established the ideal of perfect knowledge obtained through total overcoming of the will, Schopenhauer next considers the intermediate range of lesser knowledge and correspondingly lesser aesthetic appreciation to which most persons who are not aesthetic geniuses are limited (WWR 1: 194–5). Finally, his evaluation of a wide range of degrees of ability to suspend and suppress the will for the sake of gaining knowledge enables him to characterize aesthetic genius at the far end of the scale. Schopenhauer's theory of aesthetic genius positions him admirably to account for the limited numbers of geniuses to be found in any discipline, especially in the arts, and to explain how it is that the greater number of persons, who are not geniuses in his sense, are nevertheless able at some level or other to appreciate the value of beauty and the sublime in nature and art.

Genius itself in any case is a matter of degree. There is a rank ordering of greater and lesser geniuses among and within the class of geniuses.

Schopenhauer suggests an aristocracy of talent when he writes: "The objectivity of knowledge, and above all of knowledge of perception, has innumerable degrees, depending on the energy of the intellect and its separation from the will. The highest degree is *genius* . . ." (WWR 2: 291). Aesthetic genius on this conception is elevated to an asymptotic status toward which many may aspire and approach, but which few if any actually attain. Here an important further distinction must be emphasized. Schopenhauer does not say that the aesthetic genius must always be able to transcend individuality in purely objective perception, but implies at most that aesthetic genius is capable of passive reception of Platonic Ideas in at least some situations. Others may be able to approximate the purely aesthetic state, but the highest degree in this progression marks its actual achievement, in the pure objectivity that only genius attains. In many passages, Schopenhauer exults in the rarity of genius (WWR 1: 234).

Aesthetic genius as suffering and salvation

The two non-cognitive channels through which Schopenhauer contends we can overcome individual willing are asceticism and aesthetic contemplation. Saintly self-denial and the overwhelming self-absorbing experience of beauty and the sublime offer the ascetic and aesthetic genius momentary encounters with something approximating Will as thing-in-itself, in the objective knowledge of Platonic Ideas. The world of beauty and the sublime offers relief from the sufferings of phenomenal will by suppressing its urges for the sake of knowledge (WWR 1: 267).

Schopenhauer compares respite from suffering obtained through aesthetic contemplation with saintly asceticism as another path of indifference to life and death that overcomes the will to life and with it the sufferings that attend every act of will:

> Meanwhile, he [the artist] himself is the will objectifying itself and remaining in constant suffering. That pure, true, and profound knowledge of the inner nature of the world now becomes for him an end in itself; at it he stops. Therefore it does not become for him a quieter of the will . . . in the case of the saint who has attained resignation; it does not deliver him from life for ever, but only for a few moments. For him it is not the way out of life, but only an occasional consolation in it, until his power, enhanced by this contemplation, finally becomes tired of the spectacle, and seizes the serious side of things.   (WWR 1: 267)

How can suffering and aesthetic contemplation offer a perspective on reality, of the world as Will? Suffering is non-representational, in the sense that it does not depict anything in the phenomenal world. When we suffer pain or frustrations of desire, the experience of suffering by itself, unlike perception, while phenomenal, is not obviously representational. To suffer can therefore be construed as experiencing non-representational reality as intimately as possible within the confines of empirical psychology.

What individual suffering reveals about reality is that it is a force necessarily at odds with itself, in essential self-conflict. If this were not so, reality could not move the world from within through its restless activity, but would be at peace. For Schopenhauer, Will objectifies itself most nakedly as individual suffering, because it is in these experiences that willing encounters the harshness of an uncontrollable personally unaccommodating external reality. The suffering of will in the world of appearance is also the basis of Schopenhauer's much-misunderstood romantic moral pessimism. It is a consequence of what he regards as the most profound truth of metaphysics that there can be no harmony of individual wills in the world as representation objectifying thing-in-itself as the hungry Will.

Acute suffering reveals the world as Will. Ecstasy and other emotions of like intensity do not have the same effect, because they necessarily involve the will's attachment to objects of desire. Schopenhauer believes that individual willing is an obstacle to attaining insight into thing-in-itself, when the will to life persists in seeking objects in the phenomenal world, such as alleviation of pain or victory over an adversary, that may temporarily satisfy its desires. The best understanding of the world as Will for Schopenhauer is therefore through suffering induced by deliberate efforts at suppressing the will to life. This is the ascetic path of disciplined self-denial, leading by degrees from deprivation of the will's longing for such bodily necessities as food, water, companionship and sleep, to the experience of a mystical–religious loss of individuality and dissolution of the subject–object dichotomy in a feeling of "oneness" with the unrepresented universe. If desire intrudes, the spell is broken, and individual will is no longer effectively suppressed, disengaging the ascetic's non-representational access to the thing-in-itself as Will.

With important differences, much the same is true of aesthetic contemplation. Aesthetic experience is like suffering in that it involves a brief but pregnant suppression of individual willing. In contemplating nature or great art, aesthetic genius stands so riveted in its encounter with beauty or the sublime that there occurs something like a mystical union of the subject with the object in a sensation that seems to dissolve the subject–object distinction. The desires of individual will are overruled by total absorption in the moment of aesthetic appreciation, and genius passively receives the Platonic Ideas instantiated as perceptible grades of the Will's objectifications.

In its efforts to grasp and communicate the Ideas, aesthetic genius, through will-suppressed moments of aesthetic rapture, in other ways and at other times suffers more acutely than ordinary persons. Like the prisoner released from Plato's cave, the genius, having caught sight of the Ideas as the nearest approximations to thing-in-itself, is compelled to share non-representational knowledge with those left behind in darkness.[10] To undertake such thankless labour is to be condemned to inevitable misunderstanding by those who have not experienced the revelation. It is also to incur additional suffering in acquiring specialized skills and applying every energy of mind and body to harness non-discursive representational media for the expression of non-representational concepts. It is in epiphanic moments of aesthetic contemplation that the self paradoxically is most free from itself, from the mental oscillations by which individual will as the direct phenomenological objectification of Will is otherwise tormented. To live is to will, and hence to suffer, and no one suffers more, for Schopenhauer, than the aesthetic genius. The artist suffers extraordinarily because genius experiences the greatest frustrations of creative activity in its compulsion to represent non-representational knowledge. It is at the same time the saving grace of aesthetic contemplation that it lifts the artist out of the suffering induced by the concerns of phenomenal will to life when willing is suppressed for the sake of gaining knowledge of the Platonic Ideas.

Genius, as Schopenhauer likes to say, does not let willing get the upper hand, but strives always to put knowing above willing. If suffering occurs through willing, and if aesthetic genius puts knowing above willing, why does genius suffer at all, let alone more so than the average mortal? The reason is that genius has a vocation of higher order in which will is enlisted in the service of knowledge. Aesthetic genius is engaged in a noble effort doomed to the frustration and disappointment of imperfect attainment in attempts to represent a non-representational reality. This is the ultimate ground of the peculiar suffering of genius. It is yet another distinguishing mark of genius, related to the compensations of ascetic saintliness, to be endowed with disinterested aesthetic contemplation as a temporary respite from the punishing strife of individual willing. Schopenhauer concludes that those who because of their acute aesthetic sensibilities must undergo the most exquisite sufferings of will mercifully are also those who are best equipped to find salvation in aesthetic transcendence.

If the purpose of art were merely to escape from the suffering caused by strivings of individual will, then aesthetic genius could simply submerge into phenomena, immerse itself in the world as representation, and spend as much time as possible extracting Platonic Ideas from its perceptions. Unreflective involvement in the phenomenal world of appearances is what most of humanity does anyway, disregarding thing-in-itself and thinking only of the evanescent world as representation. Schopenhauer remarks on this sort of aesthetic intellectual mediocrity sometimes with a pitying sigh, sometimes with a contemptuous sneer. He believes that genius can never be satisfied with such a vulgar solution having once grasped the fundamental distinction between reality and appearance. He considers exclusive concern with phenomena both naive and demeaning, an attitude fit only for human beings who have barely risen above the condition of beasts. He concludes that it is a mark of greater intellect to place less value on ephemeral appearance, while embracing the hard pessimistic truth that the world as Will is objectified as inescapable turmoil. The artist is first and foremost a knower, someone with a distinctive albeit non-representational imagination-enhanced knowledge of Platonic Ideas acquired through sensation. The mastery of technical skills whereby Ideas are expressed for the satisfaction of genius and the enlightenment of others is secondary for Schopenhauer. It is the knowledge and imaginative extension of Platonic Ideas that constitutes aesthetic genius, without which the most accomplished artist is a mere craftsperson.[11]

Appetite and the will to life in art

Schopenhauer says surprisingly little about the criteria by which good and bad artworks are to be judged. Part of the explanation for his reticence undoubtedly has to do with the fact that he has built so much normative content into the definition of art that for him the concept already excludes what other theorists might regard as bad, unsuccessful or unworthy art. Objects, however sensually pleasing, that do not meet the requirement of expressing the will-suppressed intuitive reception of Platonic Ideas, do not count as genuine artworks.

Still-life and historical paintings provide unexpected targets for Schopenhauer's criticism. On the whole he admires these genres, except when they represent objects that irresistibly arouse the appetite, and thereby engage the phenomenal will to life. He castigates its most admired exemplars as instances of what he calls "the charming", and, despite appreciation of the technical accomplishment of Dutch still lifes, dismisses them in particular as anti-aesthetic when they realistically depict edible foodstuffs. "I find in the province of art only two species of the charming," Schopenhauer remarks:

> and both are unworthy of it. The one species, a very low one, is found in the still life painting of the Dutch, when they err by depicting

edible objects. By their deceptive appearance these necessarily excite the appetite, and this is just a stimulation of the will which puts an end to any aesthetic contemplation of the object.

(WWR 1: 207–8)

The difficulty is that many Dutch still-life masters are so adept at realistically portraying delicious items, especially of prepared food, that the will is unavoidably summoned to desire, thus adulterating the purely aesthetic objective contemplation of art. Schopenhauer distinguishes between permissible still-life renderings of fruit and flowers from aesthetically forbidden portraits of gourmet table delicacies. "Painted fruit ... is admissible," he writes, "for it exhibits itself as a further development of the flower, and as a beautiful product of nature through form and color, without our being positively forced to think of its edibility" (WWR 1: 208). However, he adds, "unfortunately we often find, depicted with deceptive naturalness, prepared and served-up dishes, oysters, herrings, crabs, bread and butter, beer, wine, and so on, all of which is wholly objectionable" (WWR 1: 208).

Apparently, these paintings make Schopenhauer hungry. His will does not rest quiet and permit him to experience the purely passive perception that characterizes aesthetic genius. He raises analogous complaints about another aspect of the will in an aesthetic context, for the charming in historical paintings of nudes. "In historical painting and in sculpture," Schopenhauer maintains, "the charming consists in nude figures, the position, semi-drapery, and whole treatment of which are calculated to excite lustful feeling in the beholder. Purely aesthetic contemplation is at once abolished, and the purpose of art thus defeated" (WWR 1: 208). It is the same faux aesthetics in both cases, deriving from a misguided effort to charm the viewer, by awakening the will to carnal desire. "This mistake is wholly in keeping with what was just censured when speaking of the Dutch", he argues.

> In the case of all beauty and complete nakedness of form, the ancients are almost always free from this fault, since the artist himself created them with a purely objective spirit filled with ideal beauty, not in the spirit of subjective, base sensuality. The charming, therefore, is everywhere to be avoided in art.   (WWR 1: 208)

It is the base direction of desire that especially troubles Schopenhauer. What are to be avoided are not merely the ripples of will that disturb the calm of purely aesthetic contemplation, but desires directed toward eating and sex in particular.[12] Why else does he not complain that the exquisite still-life painting of tulips in a vase might excite the will to want to sniff their fragrance? Why, if that were made the basis of his reply, should olfactory pleasure be less base than gustatory? Schopenhauer's language is instructive here, because he projects a limit to what the will can reasonably be expected to resist. Evidently, the will, at least for those few with aesthetic genius, can remain disengaged during episodes of purely passive objective perception in contemplating still-life paintings of flowers and fruit, no matter how temptingly luscious and ripe. Display, however, before Schopenhauer's aesthetic genius, a canvas featuring a Delft plate of smoked eels or oysters, strawberries, sausages, a wedge of cheese and white wine in a green-stemmed goblet with a faint chill haze and translucent beads of shimmering condensation trickling down the side, and suddenly the will is *necessarily* excited to appetite, the previously objective observer *positively forced* to think of devouring these morsels. Similarly with respect to the portrayal of nudes in historical paintings.

Schopenhauer already believes that aesthetic genius is the gift of the precious few.[13] Perhaps he is correct to hold that no one now, in the past, or at any other time, is capable of contemplating a mouth-watering Dutch still life or certain less than classically ideal nudes, without being moved by the forces of will. Experience suggests that if you see enough of these one after the other in a short period of time, then at least toward the end they need have no such effect. Nevertheless, if aesthetes themselves rather than genres are to blame, then the correct consequence is not that there is something aesthetically objectionable about realistic portrayals of edibles in art or sensual nudes. Instead, Schopenhauer might conclude that the actual number of true aesthetic geniuses in his terminology shrinks from a very few to perhaps none at all.

In light of his remarks about the absolute compulsion of will in the experience of Dutch still lifes and nudes, it seems possible to draw only two unflattering hypotheses: (i) Schopenhauer regards himself as the final measure of aesthetic genius, and so elevates his own weakness of will in the presence of artistic renderings of foods and nudes to the status of an absolute limitation for all, blaming the genre itself rather than his own inability to objectify aesthetic beauty beyond the mundane call to appetite; (ii) Schopenhauer simply does not like Dutch still lifes of food or historical paintings of nudes, and, not articulating precisely his dissatisfaction with them, takes the occasion to berate them, despite glaring exceptions and inconsistencies, by twisting his metaphysics of representation and the will in such a way as implausibly to exclude them. On this interpretation, Schopenhauer does not try to derive aesthetic conclusions from more fundamental metaphysical categories, but tailors his metaphysics to fit largely unexamined aesthetic prejudices.

As uncharitable as such an attribution may be, from what we know of Schopenhauer's crotchety personality, at least as it has come down to us in philosophical folklore, it would not be difficult nor far-fetched to interpret his pronouncements against unclassical nudes and Dutch still lifes by either supposition. In rejecting the charming in art, Schopenhauer considers still lifes of food and historical paintings of nudes as his only examples, and makes *ad hoc* exceptions and adjustments in unexpected ways for flowers, fruit and classical nudes. This seems to provide nothing more than an inventory of personal aesthetic likes and dislikes, and as such does not present the philosophical basis for an aesthetic theory of objective perception bereft of any appetite or strivings of the will to life.

Why must aesthetic value and the charming collide? Is there no irresistible evocation of will in erotic dance or literature? Why are these not addressed? Presumably prepared foods, as much as fruit and flowers, partake of Platonic Ideas, which the artist might also receive in a moment of purely objective individual-transcending perception, and render afterward in a lifelike representational painting. How does Schopenhauer know that this is not what the Dutch still-life masters have tried to do? The impressive realism of Dutch still lifes is especially disturbing to Schopenhauer. This too raises the question whether his criticisms derive from more general aesthetic principles, or merely record his cranky aesthetic preferences. A Cezanne or Cubist still life might not meet with Schopenhauer's censure, since he seems most strongly opposed to the combination of photoreal Dutch skill with their sometime choice of the edible as subject matter. The same comparison could be made with respect to Tiepolo's, Picasso's or Modigliani's nudes. Technique and realistic finish alone cannot be the deciding factor, for then how could we explain that Courbet's impressionistic *Still Life with Apples and a Pomegranate* may recommend the fruit and pewter tankard to our appetite equally if not better than even the most vivid colour photographs of apples in grocery advertisements? Schopenhauer, it is clear, does not like paintings of enticing nudes and delectable foodstuffs; but is there any system, rhyme or reason to his rejections?

He has somewhat similar things to say about the misguided effort to incorporate realistic imitations of the world as representation in music. Painting and music are placed in widely separated categories, as an application of the thesis that music like the natural world itself is the immediate objectification of thing-in-itself. There is nevertheless a link between his remarks about Dutch still lifes of food and voluptuous nudes in historical painting with cannon shots and marching timpani in military programme music, which many agree in finding objectionable as a miscalculation on the part of the artist to charm by imitation. Unfortunately, Schopenhauer's rationale cannot be extrapolated to explain his denunciation of the charming in still lifes of comestibles and historical paintings of nudes. The argument holds only with respect to music as the immediate objectification of Will in the world as representation, and has no direct implications for other fine art media. Schopenhauer might be entitled logically to invoke his metaphysics of the world as Will and representation to criticize the decision to mimic the swishing sounds of a howling mountainside windstorm, or the distant drum-rumbling of thunder. Nothing comparable, however, serves to justify his objections to the charming in other arts that, unlike music, are not supposed to be immediate objectifications of Will.

An obvious incongruity in Schopenhauer's rejection of Dutch still lifes of food and historical paintings of nudes is that with equal justification he might have drawn the opposite conclusion. He might have reasoned that these art objects on the contrary are the most aesthetically praiseworthy and highly recommended foci of contemplation for the person of true aesthetic genius. The direct appeal to motivation of will in these artworks challenges aesthetic genius to the most pristinely disinterested observation under the most trying circumstances. The ordinary aesthete can no doubt objectively appreciate a still life with nothing edible depicted in it without arousal of will, if it does not especially tempt desire. The true test of aesthetic genius, by Schopenhauer's criterion, should in part be the ability to restrain the will to life and preserve purely objective contemplation in the face of the greatest temptations. Only aesthetic genius, specially gifted with the aesthetic virtues Schopenhauer repeatedly praises, could be expected to remain impassive on a hot day after several hours without nourishment in the purely objective contemplation of a Dutch still life of salted herrings and a foaming krug of ale.

Finally, it may be doubted whether it is possible to separate intuited knowledge from will to life. How can the most accomplished aesthetic genius perceive the world without "interference" by the empirical will? An act of will is required even to keep the eyelids open. To attend to and later remember sufficiently what is observed to be able to represent it afterward in art, to depict the Platonic Ideas grasped in experience of "purely" passive objective perception of the world, presumably requires the will's intervention. The basis for negative art criticism in Schopenhauer's theory is the confusion of or failure to represent Platonic Ideas clearly and distinctly, together with the antipathy of aesthetic experience and the charming. Ideas for Schopenhauer are necessarily beautiful, so that the artist need only exhibit them plainly and with bold definition, as in the best classical art, for their intrinsic beauty to appear. An artwork, moreover, is supposed to enable the art appreciator to enter into a will-suppressed state of contemplation similar to that in which the work of aesthetic genius is inspired. There is to be a temporary loss of self or individuality in experiencing as in producing good or successful art. The primary obstacle to a lofty aesthetic experience occurs when an artwork charms a viewer with representations that stir the will through appetite or desire.

Schopenhauer undoubtedly glimpses something important about the relation between perception and will in aesthetic appreciation, obstructed by the distractions of appetite and desire. The distinction might nevertheless be better drawn between aesthetic value, on the one hand, and the decidedly non-aesthetic value of an object or experience. The latter category of factors can certainly interfere with the former, and not only in the case of the derogatorily charming, although increasingly less so for those with more refined aesthetic sensibilities. It clouds our appreciation of beauty in nature to contemplate its commercial value or battlefield suitability, just as it can sour the experience of a fine art exhibit to overhear the inevitable museum boors chatting about whether a painting would be appropriate for their living room decor. These detract from even a qualifiedly "pure" aesthetic experience. Yet, in Schopenhauer's view, the will must not be permitted to enter even in deliberate efforts to exclude non-aesthetic elements any more than in ordinary manifestations of desire. What threatens to charm, moreover, is not the only lure of the phenomenal will to life.[14] The will can just as easily be coaxed into sullying a purely aesthetic experience by external inducements to fear, repulsion, scientific and philosophical curiosity, or the practical demands of memory and artistic appraisal or production techniques. An objection of the sort Schopenhauer wants to mount against certain types of artworks might therefore be more appropriately addressed to the weaknesses of particular aesthetic perceivers than to categories of artistic subject matter and styles.

Nietzsche's critique of Schopenhauer on the ascetic–aesthetic transcendence of the will to life

The separation of aesthetic contemplation and desire leads Nietzsche in *On the Genealogy of Morality* to speculate that Schopenhauer's theory of art and the Will–representation dichotomy may have arisen from an ascetic attitude to resist erotic desires. Like Schopenhauer, Nietzsche enquires philosophically into the relation between religion, ascetic ideals and aesthetic values.

In the Third Treatise of the *Genealogy*, Nietzsche asks: "What do ascetic ideals mean?"[15] He mentions Richard Wagner as a follower of Schopenhauer who tries to exemplify Schopenhauerian ascetic ideals in his music. He investigates the implications of a philosophical as opposed to religious avowal of ascetic ideals, which he thinks must ultimately depend on underlying aesthetic values. He looks into the philosophical meaning of asceticism, and suggests psychological motivations for the appreciation of fine art in Schopenhauer stemming from his denial of the will to life.[16]

The connection between ascetic and aesthetic values in Schopenhauer is that both are offered as ways of attaining release from the inner turmoil of will. Ascetic sainthood and aesthetic genius in different ways enable the adept to overcome the strivings of the phenomenal will to life. Nietzsche criticizes Schopenhauer for forging this connection between ascetic and aesthetic anti-values. He regards Schopenhauer as dishonouring beauty and art by converting them into a channel of disinterested escape from the struggles of will. He further objects to the subjectivity of aesthetic value that arises through an overemphasis on the role of thinkers who experience beauty and the sublime, because of what he regards as the pernicious influence of Kant on Schopenhauer's aesthetics:

> Schopenhauer used the Kantian formulation of the aesthetic problem for his own purpose – although he most certainly did not view it with Kantian eyes. Kant intended to honor art when, among the predicates of the beautiful, he privileged and placed in the foreground those that constitute the honor of knowledge: impersonality and universal validity. Whether this was not on the whole a mistake cannot be dealt with here, I wish only to underscore that Kant, like all philosophers, instead of envisaging the aesthetic problem starting from the experiences of the artist (the one who creates), thought about art and the beautiful from the viewpoint of the "spectator" and thus, without it being noticed, got the "spectator" himself into the concept "beautiful."[17]

The critique Nietzsche offers conforms predictably with his general moral preference for action over passive principles in philosophy. He believes that art like any other endeavour should say "yes" rather than "no" to life. He objects to the Kantian and Schopenhauerian emphasis on those who experience art rather than on those who make artworks, on the passive viewing of art rather than on active artistic creativity. He further criticizes the ascetic-aestheticism or aesthetic-asceticism in Schopenhauer's philosophy of art from the standpoint of its denial of the self and those aspects of the will to power associated with sexual desire that are frequently found in art. He calls attention to passages in Schopenhauer where the latter advocates the asexuality of genuine aesthetic experience as a remedy for the perturbations of mind that occur through stirrings of erotic will:

> There are few things about which Schopenhauer speaks so certainly as about the effect of aesthetic contemplation: he says of it that it counteracts precisely *sexual* "interestedness," much like lupulin and camphor, that is; he never grew tired of glorifying *this* breaking free

from the "will" as the greatest merit and use of the aesthetic condition. Indeed, one might be tempted to ask whether his basic conception of "will and representation," the thought that there can be a redemption from the "will" only through "representation," did not originate from a generalization of that sexual experience. (... one must never ignore the fact that it is the conception of a twenty-six-year-old young man; so that it participates not only in that which is specific to Schopenhauer but also in that which is specific to that that season of life.)[18]

We are expected to know that lupulin and camphor are substances reputed to have the property of suppressing sexual desire. Schopenhauer does not try to conceal this aspect of his theory of art, but, according to Nietzsche, proudly asserts that aesthetic contemplation has the function of inhibiting the stirrings of sexual interest, a kind of anti-aphrodisiac.

Nietzsche mentions Schopenhauer's youthful age when he first developed the principles of his philosophy. He hints that Schopenhauer in his early years is likely to have been especially prone to sexual inclinations, and may have sought to avoid such distractions and the sense of shame associated with them through aesthetic escapism. Schopenhauer, we know, regards involvement in the conflicts of empirical will as a torment and source of perpetual conflict, in which the attainment of one desire is soon satiated and then surpassed by greater desires. Nietzsche cites those parts of *The World as Will and Representation* in which Schopenhauer praises aesthetic experience as a momentary suppression of the will. Schopenhauer extols the virtues of art in releasing us from the lower desires of will, speaking in colourful mythological images:

> Let us hear, for example, one of the most explicit of the countless passages he wrote in honor of the aesthetic condition (World as Will and Representation I, 231), let us hear the tone, the suffering, the happiness, the gratitude with which such words were spoken. "This is the painless condition that Epicurus praised as the highest good and as the condition of the gods; we are, for that moment, freed from the base drive of the will, we celebrate the Sabbath of the prison-house work of willing, the wheel of Ixion stands still" ... What vehemence of words! What images of torture and of prolonged satiety! What an almost pathological temporal juxtaposition of "that moment" and the usual "wheel of Ixion," the "prison-house work of willing," the "base drive of the will"! But supposing that Schopenhauer were right a hundred times over for himself, what would this have contributed to our insight into the essence of the beautiful?[19]

It may appear strange to think of art as somehow antithetical to erotic interests. The two are often directly related in much of sculpture, painting, poetry, literature and even music. When Schopenhauer addresses these issues, he makes an exception for historical paintings of nudes and still-life paintings of food and drink, which he says are anti-aesthetic precisely because they arouse the carnal appetites. This may seem to be an arbitrary distinction in Schopenhauer, and to that extent it supports Nietzsche's interpretation of Schopenhauer's aesthetics as an attempt to advance a view of beauty that is meant to repress rather than excite and gratify erotic inclinations. Nietzsche renounces Schopenhauer's aesthetic theory because of its ascetic dimensions as yet another indication of Schopenhauer's denying the will to life or will to power, and hence as denying the self by saying "no" to life.

Schopenhauer's influence on aesthetics and the arts

The Schopenhauerians of the nineteenth and twentieth centuries, those through whom Schopenhauer's thought changed not only the theory but the practice of fine art, were almost cultish in their aesthetic worship of Will, and in their attitudes, imbibed from *The World as Will and Representation*, toward death and the suffering and salvation of artists in the pangs of aesthetic creativity. The romantic conception of aesthetic genius, the true artist as a figure of special suffering, misunderstood by inferior minds in the most painful struggles to complete and express Platonic Ideas, is an enduring legacy of Schopenhauer's thinking about art and the difficulties of working toward artistic perfection.

Through its diffusion into the history of post-nineteenth-century art, especially in idealism, symbolism, romanticism and certain phases of naturalism and gothic and neoclassical revivals, Schopenhauer's aesthetics provides the philosophical subtext for major artistic movements, as it does for particular psychological and philosophical developments. It is consequently no exaggeration to say that Schopenhauer's aesthetics is central to understanding the history of modern and contemporary art and philosophy of art. Schopenhauer discovers something immensely revealing about the relation between perception and will in aesthetic appreciation, and about the distractions of appetite and desire in the contemplation of beauty and the sublime. The distinction might be drawn without the trappings of Schopenhauer's metaphysics of the world as Will and representation in terms of aesthetic and extra-aesthetic or even anti-aesthetic aspects of experience. Schopenhauer recognizes that there is something special about music that makes it unique among the arts, even if he has not quite understood precisely what it is that makes music different. Many theorists share his intuition that music belongs in a special category, that it is an art more of time than space, directly in tune with the emotions, and with a life of its own, unlike the solid stationary plastic arts of painting, sculpture, architecture, or even (printed) poetry and literature. To have intuited this distinction and offered a powerful explanation of the nature of music in terms of the metaphysics of Will and representation is an impressive achievement, worthy of serious reflection, and suggestive of other approaches to the problems of music to be explored independently of Schopenhauer's transcendental idealism.

If we want to appreciate a great work of art, Schopenhauer may be on the right track to maintain that we must lose ourselves in the experience. We may understand an art object better by distancing ourselves at least for a few precious moments from petty business and social and personal concerns. Such stirrings of will cloud our appreciation of beauty in art, just as it obscures our experience of nature to consider a majestic rocky shoreline's commercial value. The clamouring of the will to life can detract us from the most rewarding aesthetic experience, even for those with more refined or better disciplined aesthetic sensibilities. To have a richly satisfying aesthetic experience, Schopenhauer seems justified in demanding that we allow nothing but the artist's presentation of natural forms to occupy our full attention. Equally, if we want to create or encourage great art, Schopenhauer, with qualifications, is undoubtedly right again that we must receive ideas (if not the Platonic Ideas), modify them to make them our own through imagination and master the practical artistic techniques whereby our thought in its most essential forms can be communicated to others in artistic production. Schopenhauer's model of aesthetic creativity synthesizes the distinction between thing-in-itself or the world as Will and as representation in the veil of Maya, and the Platonic Ideas as intuitively accessible in phenomenal experience of the world as representation. The theory advances insightful interpretations about the distinction between beauty and the sublime, defends criteria for good and great art, while explaining the status of the aesthetic genius and the relation of aesthetic genius to the community at large, along with the relief from suffering that results from the will to life and everyday cares of the world that is afforded by the highest aesthetic enjoyment of beauty and the sublime in nature and art.[20]

CHAPTER SIX

Transcendental freedom of Will

As the will itself is not phenomenon, not representation or object, but thing-in-itself, it is also not subordinate to the principle of sufficient reason, the form of all object. Thus it is not determined as consequent by a reason or concept or ground, and so it knows no necessity; in other words, it is *free*. The concept of freedom is therefore really a negative one, since its content is merely the denial of necessity, in other words, the denial of the relation of consequent to its ground according to the principle of sufficient reason ... Everything as phenomenon, as object, is absolutely necessary; *in itself* it is will, and this is perfectly free to all eternity.

(WWR 1: 287)

World and individual

The individual thinking subject, like the world as a whole, has both an inner and outer aspect. There is a parallelism in Schopenhauer's philosophy between, on the grand scale, the world as representation and thing-in-itself as Will, and, on the personal scale, the individual's body and phenomenal will to life. The will to life also has a dual nature. It consists primarily of psychological episodes occurring in real space and time, as an overlay on a transcendent core of unmotivated, uncaused, objectless and hence subject-less, unindividuated and inexplicable pure willing. Pure willing is identical in each willing subject with Will as the one and only thing-in-itself, that, unlike the body and mind, is indestructible and immortal.

The isomorphism of world and individual distinguishes in each case that which is perceptually intuited from its hidden inner nature. Schopenhauer considers both representations and that which is represented by the individual representing subject as objectifications of thing-in-itself. The dual knowledge of body is extended first by analogy, and then as the literal truth about the relation between world at large as representation and as thing-in-itself in Schopenhauer's arguments for identifying thing-in-itself as Will. Schopenhauer maintains on the basis of the microcosm–macrocosm parallelism between the individual body and will to life and the world as representation and Will that individual willing subjects and the world at large each have a distinctive character.

The fact that the world considered as a whole as well as each human being has character is owing to the fact that human beings exemplify the highest grade of the Will's objectification, due to their extraordinarily high degree of intratypical individuality. The differences between one human being and another are manifest in their unique personalities and varieties of ways of thinking and acting. Character in turn is reflected in external appearances, in the body and behaviour of persons generally, but more prominently in their physignomies, in the individuality of each subject's face, as different and distinctive as their signatures or fingerprints. It is this notion of individual character that provides the basis for Schopenhauer's metaphysics of freedom and morality. Ethics for Schopenhauer begins with the fact that each human agent has an unalterable underlying character that is expressed in body and behaviour over the course of a person's lifetime, and that constitutes the source of moral responsibility.[1]

Dependence of morality on freedom

Although the main lines of Schopenhauer's doctrine of freedom of the will and ethical philosophy are already contained in *The World as Will and Representation*, he develops these ideas at greater length in two long essays written in 1838 and 1840. The essays were submitted for competitions sponsored, respectively, by the Royal Norwegian Society of Sciences and Royal Danish Society of Scientific Studies. Schopenhauer's essay, *On the Freedom of the Will*, was successful in its bid for the Norwegian prize, which was awarded in 1839. He must have felt encouraged by this long-desired sign of public acceptance for his ideas, and thereafter submitted *On the Basis of Morality* to the Danish competition. The essay on ethics, remarkably, was rejected in 1840, even though it was the only essay received.

Annoyed, but undeterred as usual by lack of popular appreciation, and bolstered by having won the Norwegian prize, Schopenhauer published the two essays together in a single volume in 1841, titled *The Two Fundamental Problems of Ethics*. The fact that he found it appropriate to present these two texts within the covers of a single book justifies our also treating them together in two successive chapters. The topics are related intimately in Schopenhauer's thought, as in Kant's very different account of the metaphysical foundations of freedom and morality. It is only if we are in some sense free, as Kant and Schopenhauer maintain, in agreement also with many other thinkers in the history of philosophy, that the question of how we ought to behave, what we should and should not do, can be regarded as intelligible. Without freedom in some pertinent sense, we are no different than the rest of nature, to which we do not ordinarily ascribe moral responsibility nor stand in ethical judgement toward.

Schopenhauer builds his theory of freedom and morality on the foundations of an underlying epistemology of the principle of sufficient reason, metaphysics of identity in the *principium individuationis*, and distinction between thing-in-itself or world as Will and representation. He prepares the ground for an ethical superstructure by offering an account of the will to life and individual character. He portrays the character of the world as the Will's objectification, the hungry Will as thing-in-itself, sorrowfully objectified in the world as representation, whose internal self-conflict he believes entails an extreme moral pessimism. Schopenhauer is well-positioned against the background of his transcendental idealism to offer a momentous series of insights about the concept of free will and the morality of action, moral judgement and behaviour toward oneself and in social interaction with others, and the implementation of the concept of justice under the law. Schopenhauer's moral philosophy, like the metaphysics and epistemology on which it rests, testifies to the influence of Plato, Kant and the Asian religious traditions he admires. At the same time, it is highly original in its efforts to understand human nature from the unique standpoint afforded by his distinction between the world as Will and representation. The independence of Schopenhauer's ethics from his predecessors is indicated especially by his criticisms of Kant's moral philosophy.[2]

The suffering that characterizes all aspects of human life governed by the will to life, which is to say all aspects of human life except for those briefly available to the ascetic saint and aesthetic genius as islands of salvation, determines Schopenhauer's outlook on every aspect of moral value. The inevitable suffering experienced by willing subjects, in its metaphysical as well as psychological ramifications, colours Schopenhauer's conclusions concerning the concept of moral obligation, moral attitudes, decision-making in ethics, the nature of moral wrong, and of justice and the good. He proposes to explain all facets of morality from the standpoint of intuited feelings of compassion. His ethics can thus be regarded as a secular theoretization of the Buddha's pronouncement that we are to act from compassion for all living things, transposed in

Schopenhauer's thought from a religious sentiment into a comprehensive abstract moral principle.

The moral motivation of all action is purely egoistic. Whatever is done that can be rationally explained is intended for the individual agent's personal benefit, even if only subconsciously. This is appropriate and possibly unavoidable in all consistency for Schopenhauer, given his commitment to the deeper nature of thing-in-itself as Will and its objectifications in the world as representation. For it is as objectifications of thing-in-itself that all individual psychologies are set at opposition competitively against one another in all their activities. The world as Will dictates that its objectifications must look out for their own interests. They must be naturally moved in whatever they do, however they may try to resist the urge in observance of culturally approved values, by whatever is perceived egoistically as contributing to their individual benefit. Schopenhauer does not judge the self-interest that drives action as necessarily morally good or bad. On the contrary, through his metaphysics of thing-in-itself and its hidden inner character as the insatiably hungry Will, Schopenhauer does not imagine that things could possibly be otherwise. There is no choice but for each person to be motivated by egoistic considerations. This is not to say, however, that all actions are motivated or rationally explainable. Morally praiseworthy actions, as we shall see, constitute an important exception.

Since there are many distinct objectifications of thing-in-itself as Will, including many different individual thinking subjects, all of whom are motivated egoistically by self-love to attain whatever they can for themselves, Schopenhauer believes that moral wrong occurs when one agent infringes upon another's will to life. Moral wrong, as such, is a positive thing, not as a matter of moral value, but logically or metaphysically. It is the positive doing of something that we ought not to do. What makes it wrong is that, in killing or stealing, for example, we limit the natural expansion of another subject's will to life for the sake of our own. We recall that will to life is the phenomenal psychological objectification of the common core of pure willing, the Will that underlies each willing subject. It follows that for Schopenhauer moral right and ethical good, from a logical or metaphysical rather than valuational standpoint, can only be something negative. Moral right is the negation of moral wrong, which is itself the gratification of one individual's will to life at the expense of that of another. The suffering in the phenomenal world that comes about through the imposition of one will to life on another as the hungry Will feeds on itself is in turn an occasion for compassion. Through egoistic concern for our own suffering, we can, if we are morally enlightened, and we should, as an implication of the only moral principles Schopenhauer thinks are capable of metaphysical justification, show compassion for the sufferings of others by acting mercifully to whatever extent we can to relieve their distress.

The effect, especially when seen in contrast with Kant's elaborate moral philosophy, produces a highly simplified moral code. Schopenhauer argues, without the heavy trappings of philosophical dogma, that we are to avoid harming others and to try within the limits of our abilities to help them. The beauty of the principle is its straightforward and immediately understandable formulation. The principle can be taught to the youngest children capable of moral guidance, and yet offers a useful standard for persons at any stage of life concerned with questions about what it is morally right or wrong to do. The principle is also very much in keeping with Schopenhauer's epistemic distinction between intuitive and abstract knowledge. One of the examples by which he illustrates the distinction when he first introduces it is that of the person who through theoretical pedantry does not simply know what is right or wrong, as everyone should, but finds it necessary to consult a system of rules or exact set of laws for conduct. Instead of being able to proceed intuitively with an immediate grasp of the requirements of morality, the pedant needs to look up the answer provided by a theory. Here Schopenhauer is clearly casting barbs at Kant's categorical imperative, as well as targeting all efforts to replace a sound intuitive understanding of moral right and wrong with explicit rules for behaviour that try to forecast any eventuality and prescribe a particular behaviour or restraint of behaviour in the form of an explicit code.

We must all know intuitively what it is morally right and wrong to do. The task for a philosophical moral theory is to abstract from our intuitive knowledge the underlying theoretical principles, as Schopenhauer says in all such cases, for convenience in communication and application. What a moral philosophy can properly try to do is to work out a concise theoretical expression of the intuited knowledge embodied in a particular area of human activity, whether in ethics, music composition or logical reasoning skills. Schopenhauer seems to think that in Western philosophy there has occurred a corruption and over-intellectualization of the natural intuition guiding moral behaviour. The implicit morality is represented by a recognition that life is suffering and that we ought to try to avoid, prevent and alleviate the sufferings of others to whatever extent possible. Asian ethical traditions in philosophical religion have remained more faithfully in touch with these basic truths, and at the same time have evinced a crude grasp of the distinction between reality and the world of appearance, mythologized as the veil of Maya. Schopenhauer sees it as part of his mission, while still addressing a scientific philosophical audience, to restore these intuitive attitudes toward ethical conduct in the form of the modest requirements of a correct moral philosophy.

The first requirement in approaching what Schopenhauer calls the two basic problems of moral philosophy is to understand the nature of human freedom as a prerequisite to responsible action. Schopenhauer denies that there is any such thing as freedom in the way it is usually conceived, and in this he again stands at least partially in agreement with Kant. He rejects Kant's theory of freedom as moral autonomy in the course of refuting the rationalistic scaffolding of Kant's ethics, and in particular Kant's doctrine of the categorical imperative. It is for this reason that Schopenhauer, both in "Criticism of the Kantian Philosophy", the Appendix to *The World as Will and Representation*, and in *The Two Fundamenetal Problems of Ethics*, deals first with the metaphysics and moral implications of the concept of human free will, and only thereafter turns to problems of moral reasoning, moral values and the elaboration of a philosophically adequate moral philosophy.

Schopenhauer's analysis of freedom

We should expect that Schopenhauer is especially well placed to investigate the problem of free will. It is in his thought especially that willing and thing-in-itself as Will are most prominently thematized among the vital concerns of philosophy. He acknowledges the essential connection between freedom and thing-in-itself in Kant's critical idealism as providing the springboard to his own transcendental idealism. He maintains that the metaphysics of freedom, and the concept of freedom or lack thereof of willing moral agents, depend on how thing-in-itself is understood:

> The solution of the third antinomy [freedom and a special "causality of freedom" is required to explain some of the appearances of nature and there is no causal freedom from the laws of nature], whose subject was the Idea of freedom, merits special consideration, in so far as for us it is very remarkable that Kant is obliged precisely here, in connexion with the *Idea of freedom*, to speak in greater detail about the *thing-in-itself*, hitherto seen only in the background. This is very easy for us to understand after we have recognized the thing-in-itself as the *will*. In general, this is the point where Kant's philosophy leads to mine, or mine springs from his as its parent stem. (WWR 1: 501)

He takes the opportunity again to portray Kant as having only dimly grasped what is better understood from the standpoint of a more properly conceived distinction between the world as Will and representation, and in particular from the vantage of an identification of thing-in-itself as Will. The question of human freedom for Schopenhauer is thus tightly bound up in interesting ways with his metaphysics of Will.

The clue to Kant's perceptive but still clouded understanding of free will is the fact that Kant, perhaps without himself fully understanding why, finds it necessary to discuss thing-in-itself immediately upon presentation of the Third Antinomy, affirming and denying the existence of human freedom in different senses and for different reasons.[3] What Schopenhauer proposes to do is to make these conceptual connections clear, to draw sharper distinctions on the basis of his discovery that thing-in-itself is Will, and from this platform to explain the senses of free will that are available and unavailable to human moral agents. The problem of free will in its relation to thing-in-itself is regarded as so important to Schopenhauer that he mentions it in this context from opposite perspectives as the Kantian point of departure for the development of his own philosophy.

For two reasons, there can be no meaningful human freedom in Schopenhauer's system. First, the actions undertaken by moral agents, like all events in the phenomenal world, are governed by the fourfold root of the principle of sufficient reason, and in particular by causal laws. In so far as freedom of will is opposed to physical determinism, there can be no possibility in Schopenhauer's philosophy for the decisions and actions of human agents to be free in the sense of being contracausally undetermined. Secondly, Schopenhauer regards the character of each willing subject as an individual essence, comparable to thing-in-itself construed as Will, the hidden inner nature of reality that transcends the world as representation. Schopenhauer believes that just as the character of the world, the Will as thing-in-itself in perpetual self-conflict, can never be changed or altered in any way, so by analogy the character of each person is unalterable, incapable of change. Thus, a thief or a murderer is necessarily a thief or a murderer for all his or her life, and cannot change from being such by any act of will or effort at reform.[4] To an extent, this conclusion of Schopenhauer's echoes Socrates' argument in Plato's dialogue the *Meno*. There Socrates is asked whether virtue can be taught or is bestowed by nature, or acquired in some other way. Socrates reasons that virtue cannot be taught, since there are no teachers who can competently train others to be virtuous as though they were imparting a technical skill. He further argues that virtue is not the product of nature, which, if it were, could be discerned among infants to distinguish between those who are destined later to be virtuous and those who will later become vicious. He suggests at the very end of Plato's dialogue that virtue must therefore be a gift of the gods (BM: 187–8).[5]

Schopenhauer does not suppose that moral character has a divine origin. At most, he sometimes interprets references to God or the gods as a metaphor for the transcendence of thing-in-itself as mind-independent reality. He nevertheless agrees with Socrates that virtue cannot be taught, and more particularly that it cannot be altered within an individual's character by training or resolve leading either to improvement or corruption. We cannot change what we are, just as the character of thing-in-itself, the hungry Will in constant struggle and strife, cannot change. The unalterability of the character of the willing subject deprives the moral agent of a certain type of freedom: the freedom to change. If Schopenhauer is right, then we can never become something different, change from being virtuous to vicious, or the reverse, or reform ourselves through force of will and dedication of effort to alter the kinds of people we are. We can never remake ourselves morally after another image of what we would rather become, to exert control over the course of our lives by modifying the deepest aspects of our personalities from within. This, Schopenhauer maintains, is impossible, thereby denying the possibility of another morally relevant type of freedom.

We can neither shape our destinies by deliberately transforming our characters, which are fixed and unchangeable, nor defy the rigid nomic necessity of cause and effect by which our bodies, including our brains and all our actions, are determinately ruled by the laws of causality. What, then, if anything, remains of the sense of human freedom? Is it real or illusory? If free will is only illusory, what implications does it have for moral responsibility, the meaning of moral judgement, and moral value? The first problem Schopenhauer faces in the *Essay on the Freedom of the Will* is to explicate a concept of freedom that is compatible with his commitment to causal determinism and the fixed nature of human character. As he also says of the concept of moral right, freedom is something essentially negative. He distinguishes between three broad categories of physical, intellectual and moral freedom in everyday and philosophical thought and discourse, arguing that all three are negative concepts involving the absence of obstruction or restraint. We are physically free when we are not physically restrained from doing what we want to do, and similarly with respect to intellectual and moral freedom.

Schopenhauer refers to the physical concept of freedom as the "popular" sense. With great sensitivity to the term's occurrence in many different contexts, he lists a large number of ordinary ways in which the expressions "free" and "freedom" are ascribed even to non-living things when their physical motion is not physically inhibited. He extends the concept of freedom in a morally extraneous sense to animals and human beings when they act wilfully. We are free in what Schopenhauer calls the superficial sense when we are not physically prevented from doing what we choose to do. If we consider slavery as the opposite of freedom in the political meaning of the word, including the physical restraints by which a slave's freedom to do as he or she wills are sometimes prevented, by shackles, locks and keys, then Schopenhauer is clearly right in classifying political freedom as a type of physical freedom (FW: 4).

Proceeding from the popular sense of freedom, Schopenhauer categorizes intellectual and moral freedom as philosophical subtypes. He defers discussion of intellectual freedom to the end of the essay, to the "Appendix, Supplementing the First Section", where he interprets intellect as the "medium" of moral motivation. Intellectual freedom enables a willing subject to entertain reasons for acting, and to engage in practical inference by connecting together means with ends. It is the forum where we evaluate ends in terms of our larger purposes and values, making reference to what it is rational and practically feasible to do. Intellectual freedom obtains when we are not prevented from exercising normal abilities to reason about what to do and how to do it. In keeping with the theory of freedom as a negative concept, the absence of obstruction or restraint, Schopenhauer provides an idea of the kinds of restraints that might otherwise inhibit the intellect's free exercise. "The intellectual freedom is *suspended*", he writes:

> either through the permanent or temporary derangement of the medium of motives, the faculty of cognition, or by a faulty apprehension of motives which is caused by external circumstances in the particular case. The former is the case in madness, delirium, paroxysm, and heavy drowsiness; the latter occurs when a decisive but innocent mistake has been made ... when instead of medicine poison is administered, or a servant entering at night is mistaken for a burglar and shot, and so on. (FW: 89)

The preliminary discussion and distinction of these irrelevant senses of freedom clears the ground for a topic that more properly interests Schopenhauer in the analysis of moral freedom. Schopenhauer understands moral freedom in what he takes to be the sense of the term intended by the Norwegian Society essay competition. The topic, originally formulated in Latin, is contained in the question, "Can the freedom of the human will be demonstrated from self-consciousness?" (FW: 3). He answers, as we should now be able to predict from what we know about his transcendental idealism, that free will in the moral sense of freedom cannot be demonstrated from self-consciousness. His reasons are instructive for the further light they shed on his metaphysics and epistemology, and in grounding his theory of ethics.

Moral free will, for Schopenhauer, is related to, but metaphysically different from, physical freedom. The main confusion with which Schopenhauer charges popular thinking about the nature of freedom is its assumption that we are free provided that we can do what we want, whatever it is we may will to do. Schopenhauer has already defined the concept of physical freedom in such a way as to distinguish it from moral freedom. The exact manner in which the two are sometimes jumbled together is worth disentangling because of the prevalence of misinterpretations.

Suppose that there is no obvious compulsion driving a person to act in a certain way. Schopenhauer eliminates from his thought experiment any factors that would prevent or force the agent to do or refrain from doing something. If we try to answer the problem of free will by appealing to self-consciousness, we can only superficially approach the question of whether we have free will by consulting our wishes and desires. We examine our phenomenal will and acts of willing, which Schopenhauer identifies with the will to life, whereupon we may conclude that our will is free provided that we can do whatever we want. Schopenhauer insists that we need to look beyond the question of whether or not we can do what we want to the further and deeper question of whether we have the freedom to will what we want, or whether the will itself is subject to such predeterminations that what might otherwise pass as acts of free will are in fact predetermined.

He pinpoints the error in conventional efforts to address the metaphysical problem of free will by addressing the will and asking whether or not it can do what it wants. He answers the essay question in the negative for an obvious reason. Any such effort to solve the free will problem from Schopenhauer's perspective merely forces the issue back to what he has already distinguished as the very different concept of physical as opposed to moral freedom. He continues, in the most frequently cited and enthusiastically admired passage in the essay:

> As a result of the empirical concept of freedom we have: "I am free if I can *do what I will*," and the freedom is already decided by this "what I will." But now since we are asking about the freedom of *willing* itself, this question should accordingly be expressed as follows: "Can you also *will* what you will?" This appears as if the willing depended on yet another willing lying behind it. And supposing that this question were answered in the affirmative, there would soon arise the second question: "Can you also will what you will to will?" and thus it would be pushed back to infinity, since we would always think of *one* willing as being dependent on a previous or deeper willing, and thus in vain endeavor to arrive ultimately at a willing that we were bound to conceive and accept as being dependent on absolutely nothing. (FW: 6)

The regress that Schopenhauer projects begins with efforts to understand free will as being able to do what one wills. It gains momentum when we ask about the freedom or unfreedom of what it is we will. If the principle of sufficient reason is true, then anything we offer as a reason for anything else in turn must have a sufficient reason why it is, and so on, indefinitely. The same is true for psychological phenomena such as an act of willing as for the movements of the planets and stars. All are equally subject to deterministic laws of causality. The mere fact that we find ourselves engaged in an endless regress of asking whether we are free to will what we will in willing anything at all indicates that we are asking the wrong kinds of questions and looking in the wrong places for answers. The mistake, as Schopenhauer diagnoses the problem, is in confining attention exclusively to the "empirical" concept of freedom. Rejecting the entire issue of empirical freedom paves the way for Schopenhauer's deeper transcendental investigation of freedom, in which he brings the analysis of free will back around to the metaphysics of thing-in-itself. In this way, he draws together two fundamental metaphysical problems that he remarks are only implicitly interrelated in Kant's examination of the Third Antinomy.[6]

The enquiry leads Schopenhauer away from the inadequacies of the empirical concept of free will. He remains firmly within the treatment of freedom as something negative, as the absence of necessity in acts of willing. "The original, empirical concept of freedom, a concept drawn from doing, thus refuses to enter into a direct connection with that of willing", he comments.

> Therefore to be able to apply to the will the concept of freedom, one had to modify it by grasping it in a more abstract way. This was done by conceiving through the concept of *freedom* only the absence of all *necessity* in general. Here the concept retains the *negative* character which I had assigned to it at the very beginning.   (FW: 6)

Pursuing the investigation in this framework, Schopenhauer is led to the problem of understanding the nature of necessity. As one approach is rejected, making the remaining alternatives stand out more clearly, he is obliged to look more carefully into what is meant by necessity and the conditions of its application to willing.

Schopenhauer does not interpret necessity modally as the negation of impossibility, but epistemically, in terms of the principle of sufficient reason. Absence of necessity in Schopenhauer's language means that every aspect of the will does not fall under the fourfold root. There are, in other words, truths about willing that cannot be explained. Explanation fails in such cases not merely for practical reasons, but because the nature of will is such that there exists no possible explanation of all its properties. "We therefore ask what is meant by *necessary*", Schopenhauer continues:

The usual explanation that "necessary is that the opposite of which is impossible, or which cannot be otherwise," is merely verbal, a paraphrase of the concept which does not increase our insight. But as the real definition I give the following: *necessary is that which follows from a given sufficient ground.* (FW: 6)

The will is free only in so far as it is not subject to necessity, where necessity is interpreted as lawlike explanatory governance under the principle of sufficient reason. As individual willing subjects, we are free in that there is something about our willing that in principle cannot be explained. We know that for Schopenhauer many aspects of phenomenal willing can be explained in terms of logic, mathematics, causation and motivation. There are reasons why we will as we do and why we will to do specific things. A chain of inferences accounts motivationally for all acts of willing, just as there are causal explanations for all aspects of the phenomenal will in behavioural psychology and neurophysiology.

On the empirical side of willing, there is no moral freedom in Schopenhauer's sense, because all phenomenal action and decision-making is necessary. The phenomenal willing subject is under as much lawlike explanatory necessity as any other aspect of the physical universe. It is causally and in other ways explanatorily fully determined. Schopenhauer is a materialist in his philosophy of mind. He identifies the representing mind with the brain, itself a represented object. The fact that both phenomenal mind and brain are objectifications of thing-in-itself enables Schopenhauer to articulate a coherent account of the world as representation existing idealistically in each representing subject's thoughts, and governed by the necessity of causal and other types of explanation under the principle of sufficient reason.

In the second edition of *The World as Will and Representation*, referring to idealism's burden to explain the creation of past time within the occurrent thinking of a representing subject, Schopenhauer asks: "How can he, a transient and ephemeral being hurrying past, to whom is permitted only a fleeting glance into such a world, judge apodictically, beforehand, and without experience, about this world, about the possibility of its existence and origin?" (WWR 2: 46). "The solution of this riddle," he says:

is that the man is concerned merely with his own representations, which as such are the work of his brain; therefore their conformity to law is merely the mode or manner in which the function of his brain alone can be carried out, in other words, the form of his representing. (WWR 2: 46–7)

If the representing subject were not also something representational, namely, the phenomenal brain by which the representing subject perceives the world, intuits the represented objects and empirical facts of the world, then the world as representation would not be explainable, and would not be subordinate to the principle of sufficient reason. The world would then be removed from all possibility of explanation by virtue of existing idealistically in the non-phenomenally representing subject's thoughts. "He therefore judges only about his own *brain-phenomenon*," Schopenhauer concludes, "and states what goes into its forms, time, space, and causality, and what does not. He is then perfectly at home, and speaks apodictically" (WWR 2: 47). Were it otherwise, the subject would be unable to attribute any certainty or apodicticity to pronouncements about the logical, mathematical, causal or motivational necessity of occurrences in the world as representation. The judgements and their explanatory necessity are thinkable for Schopenhauer only because they apply to the representing subject's own representations, occurring within the representing subject's representational brain. The mind, in Schopenhauer's metaphysics, in so far as it represents the world, is itself a representation, a concrete physical objectification of thing-in-itself. This is to say that the representing subject is nothing other than the brain. It follows that whatever occurs in thought, by virtue of the mind's identity with the representational brain, and including the world as representation in its entirety, is subject to the same explanatory necessity as any represented object.

We recall that Schopenhauer takes a dual-aspect approach to the nature of the willing subject. The willing subject has not only a representing mind = representational brain, but also a transcendent underlay of pure willing or Will. As we think away the will's phenomenal trappings, the pure willing at its core is entirely uncaused, unmotivated, objectless, subjectless and therefore unindividualizable and unexplainable. Pure willing or Will as such stands entirely outside the principles of individuation and sufficient reason, satisfying the epistemic and metaphysical requirements of Kantian thing-in-itself. The pure willing underlying individual will lacks individual personality, and for that reason is incapable of being destroyed along with the body. The Will that transcends each willing subject, the centre of each thinker that constitutes his or her impersonal immortality, by virtue of its independence from the explanatory necessity of logical, mathematical, causal and motivational law, is metaphysically free in what Schopenhauer considers to be the only morally relevant sense.

Free will and the contents of consciousness

To address fully the Norwegian Royal Society's essay topic, Schopenhauer needs to say whether or not the moral freedom of the will can be "demonstrated from self-consciousness". He answers the question in the negative, holding that self-consciousness by itself is inadequate to establish the freedom of pure willing.

His reason has primarily to do with the exact definition of the concept of self-consciousness. He claims that as a special source of empirical knowledge it is insufficient to prove that there is transcendent freedom of the will. The negative sense of free will that Schopenhauer describes is implied by the unindividualizability and causal and other inexplicability of Will as thing-in-itself. The freedom of will, transcending representation, cannot be demonstrated from the phenomenal content of self-consciousness. Schopenhauer first distinguishes between self-consciousness as consciousness of the self and consciousness of other things about which we may be conscious. Consciousness of self or self-consciousness is only a minor part of consciousness generally, the greater proportion of which is concerned with things other than the self in the external world (FW: 9).

The expectation is defeated when Schopenhauer enquires into the knowledge constituted by self-consciousness. He argues that self-consciousness considered in and of itself as consciousness of the self and not of other things is inherently incapable of establishing the necessary relation between the will and things outside itself. It is incompetent, consequently, to judge whether or not the will is free of the necessity of lawlike explanation, for its discoveries depend entirely on the applicability of the principle of sufficient reason. Self-consciousness as consciousness of the self takes only the phenomenal, empirical half of the nature of will into account. Hence, self-consciousness cannot possibly render knowledge of the transcendent aspect of will that Schopenhauer considers essential in proving its freedom (FW: 19).

What is needed, in addition to the data of self-consciousness, according to Schopenhauer, is a form of Kantian transcendental reasoning. He describes what is needed to establish the freedom of will as pure understanding for the faculty of reason:

> Now the question of the Royal Society would really be answered, and in fact in the negative, by the discussion contained in this section, although only in the main, since this exposition of the state of affairs in self-consciousness will be rendered even more complete by what follows ... Thus if we now turn with our question to that authority to which, as the only competent one, we were previously referred, namely to the pure understanding, to the faculty of reason

193

reflecting on the latter's data, and to experience which results from both, and if their decision proved to be that a *liberum arbitrium* in general did not exist, but that human conduct, like everything else in nature, in every given case ensued as a necessarily occurring effect, then this would give us the assurance that in immediate self-consciousness *there could not possibly be found* data from which the *liberum arbitrium* we are inquiring about could be established.

(FW: 21)

We might wonder whether the Norwegian Royal Society had ever imagined that reason would not also be involved in proceeding from the data of self-consciousness to an inference in support of free will. For Schopenhauer to conclude that self-consciousness as consciousness of the self in and of itself cannot establish the freedom of the will because reason is also required does not at first seem to be a relevant, let alone exciting or original, reply to the essay question.

Schopenhauer misstates the force of his solution in two ways. It is not merely reason or pure understanding in addition to the empirical data of self-consciousness that is required in order to determine that the will is free. It is Kantian transcendental reasoning in particular by which the Will as thing-in-itself can be intuited as beyond the scope of the principle of sufficient reason, and hence of explanatory necessity. The limitation of self-consciousness that prevents it from being able to demonstrate that the will is free is not merely its empirical status. It is the fact that by itself self-consciousness, as Schopenhauer defines the concept, provides data only of the self, and not of the knowledge of its relation to other things. Yet it is only knowledge of how self-consciousness relates to pure willing or Will as thing-in-itself that can prove the freedom of the will in the negative sense of being non-subservient to the necessity of explanatory law.

In the last section of his *Essay on the Freedom of the Will*, Schopenhauer presents his "Conclusion and Higher View", indicating that:

the negative reply to the question set by the Royal Society, that was established directly and actually, and hence *a posteriori*, above with the investigation of self-consciousness, is now also established indirectly and *a priori*. For that which does not exist at all cannot have in self-consciousness data from which it could be demonstrated.

(FW: 81)

Here he provides another way of describing the limits of self-consciousness in trying to prove the freedom of the will. He argues that the freedom of the phenomenal will as opposed to Will as thing-in-itself cannot be demonstrated from the data of self-consciousness or any other empirical source, with or without the assistance of inference. The reason is simple, because there is no such thing, no freedom of the phenomenal will, to be proved. The phenomenal will is not free. It is only the transcendental Will as thing-in-itself that is free of all necessity of explanatory law, which for that very reason is such that its existence and freedom cannot be established from the data of self-consciousness.

This is Schopenhauer's official answer to the Norwegian Royal Society's prize essay question. It may nevertheless be doubted whether he might not have reached a different conclusion by allowing that the data of self-consciousness, while not sufficient to determine the freedom of the will, are nevertheless the enquiry's only possible starting-point. It is by consulting the data of self-consciousness, and in particular the phenomenal will, that Schopenhauer arrives through a process of abstraction at pure willing or Will as thing-in-itself, which he concludes is free in the sense of being removed from the force of explanatory law and from the necessity of the principles of individuation and sufficient reason. The data of self-consciousness in that case are admittedly not sufficient in and of themselves to prove the freedom of the will. They are nevertheless indispensable in proving the transcendent negative explanatory freedom of the Will that lies identically at the heart of every phenomenal act of will. Self-consciousness, while incapable alone of proving that the will is free, is essential to Schopenhauer's proof. It is only from the fact of self-conscious willing as empirical raw material for the right application of transcendental reasoning that the will's freedom is demonstrated. In that sense and with these qualifications, could Schopenhauer not have answered the prize essay question in the affirmative?

Transcendental freedom of will

The problem of whether the will is free, of whether there is such a thing as free will, is complex. It can have two different answers, depending on exactly how the question is supposed to be understood. We are free and we are not free, unparadoxically, once we have properly disambiguated the question according to Schopenhauer's distinction between the world as Will and representation.

Schopenhauer considers direct and indirect modes of enquiry into the question of free will. The duality of method is dictated by the basic division that governs all aspects of his philosophy, especially his metaphysics. The direct investigation is a matter of consulting self-consciousness at a superficial level to see whether it discloses any information that might be used to

decide the problem of free will. The indirect approach follows the methodology Schopenhauer proposes to prove that thing-in-itself is Will. He begins
with the phenomenal data of willing in self-consciousness and abstracts from
them the essence of pure willing in order to recognize thing-in-itself as Will.
It is only the Will in turn that is immortal and independent of all law and
necessity, and therefore free in the negative sense he requires.

The empirical will is not free, because its acts are subject to the same
lawlike explanatory necessity as every other phenomenon in the world as
representation. The transcendental Will at the core of phenomenal will is
as morally free as it is immortal, and for precisely the same reason. Every
willing subject is potentially morally responsible for the actions decided upon
and undertaken by the phenomenal will, which, considered only in itself, is
neither free nor morally responsible, nor, of course, immortal. As Schopenhauer states in *The World as Will and Representation*: "The will in itself is
absolutely free and entirely self-determining, and for it there is no law. First
of all, however, before we embark on the aforesaid discussion, we must
explain and define more precisely this *freedom* and its relation to necessity"
(WWR 1: 285).

The will is free only because the Will is free. The Will is free because it is
subject to no lawlike necessity. The only necessity to be found pertains to the
world as representation, where individuation and the principle of sufficient
reason govern all represented objects, states of affairs and occurrences. The
Will as thing-in-itself exists outside all explanation and explanatory necessity.
The Will is free, and the phenomenal will is free to the extent that it contains
within it Will as its most basic transcendental foundation, in the same way and
for the same reason that the phenomenal will is immortal by virtue of containing Will as thing-in-itself at its core. Schopenhauer adds:

> That the will as such is *free*, follows already from the fact that,
> according to our view, it is the thing-in-itself, the content of all
> phenomena. The phenomenon, on the other hand, we recognize as
> absolutely subordinate to the principle of sufficient reason in its four
> forms. As we know that necessity is absolutely identical with
> consequent from a given ground, and that the two are convertible
> concepts, all that belongs to the phenomenon, in other words all that
> is object for the subject that knows as an individual, is on the one
> hand ground or reason, on the other consequent, and in this last
> capacity is determined with absolute necessity; thus it cannot be in
> any respect other than it is.   (WWR 1: 286)

If the willing subject is immortal only in the sense that thing-in-itself
identified as Will underlying each act of will is beyond individuality and

explanation, then we are left at best with an uncomforting concept of impersonal survival that does not carry the soul through the event of death to the other side of eternity. Might the same not be said now about the limitations of treating Will rather than the empirical will as free, especially where the concept is supposed to be related to the moral responsibility attributed to agents for actions performed within the world as representation?

We must ask whether Schopenhauer provides a sufficiently robust sense of free will to uphold the possibility of moral responsibility, of moral judgement and moral values. Is the freedom of Will, the freedom of thing-in-itself, which in Schopenhauer's analysis it possesses only by standing outside explanatory necessity, adequate by itself to sustain a sufficiently interesting sense of moral responsibility for the requirements of theoretical ethics? The answer, unsurprisingly, once again, is yes and no, depending on what we mean by morality and what we expect of moral philosophy. As usual, Schopenhauer regards his philosophical rivals as only partially grasping the significance of the intuition by which morality is related to freedom of the will. The transcendent freedom of that part of phenomenal willing identical to Will is, he believes, the only possibility of establishing the existence of freedom, in a sense that, correctly understood, provides the foundation needed for the only logically coherent moral philosophy.

The relation of the intellect to acts of will in motivating action pertains only to the phenomenal will, which, in any case, Schopenhauer does not regard as free. The same relation leaves the pure willing or Will as thing-in-itself underlying every act of phenomenal will untouched and unnecessitated by any law or explanatory principle. Schopenhauer accordingly writes, in the concluding paragraphs of his *Essay on the Freedom of the Will*:

> In a word, a human being always does only what he wills, and yet he necessarily does it. This is owing to the fact that he already *is* what he wills; for from what he is all that he ever does follows of necessity. If we consider his actions *objectively*, i.e., from without, we recognize apodictically that, like the actions of every being in nature, they must be subject to the law of causality in all its strictness. *Subjectively*, on the other hand, everyone feels that he always does only what he *wills*. But this means merely that his actions are the pure manifestation of his very own essence. Therefore if it could feel, every being in nature, even the lowest, would feel the same thing.
>
> *Freedom*, then, is not suspended by my treatment of the matter, but merely moved up from the domain of individual actions, where it obviously is not to be found, into a higher region, which, however, is not so easily accessible to our cognition; in other words, freedom is transcendental. (FW: 88)

Moral character: empirical, intelligible and acquired

The parallelism between the world and the individual willing subject encourages Schopenhauer to posit the existence of the character of every individual willing subject, just as he identifies the character of thing-in-itself in speaking of the insatiably hungry Will. He holds that the character of an individual willing subject is as unchanging and unalterable as the character of the world as Will.

He distinguishes between *empirical*, *intelligible* and *acquired character*. All three are of interest in understanding the moral nature of human agents. Roughly, empirical character is the quality of a personal psychology, among the many objectifications of thing-in-itself in the world as representation, reflected in the individual's actions and behaviour, and unalterable in its distinctive features. Intelligible character is the empirically hidden nature of Will as thing-in-itself, the blind urging that transcends all individual willing subjects, that is only known through the appropriate exercise of Kantian transcendental reasoning. Acquired character is the changeable first-person knowledge of an individual's good and bad qualities, of what he and others can and cannot expect as a result of what we ordinarily speak of as moral character, the virtues a person possesses or his or her lack thereof. The concept of character, and especially of intelligible character, is crucial to Schopenhauer's moral philosophy. His thesis that moral character is unalterable, but comes to express itself differently under different circumstances over time, is especially noteworthy. It is the individual's character, moreover, to which Schopenhauer attaches all moral responsibility.[7]

Transcending the empirical character is the intelligible character, identical to Will construed as thing-in-itself. It is the intelligible character that is free and incidentally immortal, because it alone is independent of explanatory law. The freedom of will is also transcendental, as a consequence, and does not directly make itself known as such in phenomenal psychology. Schopenhauer describes the intelligible character as the conditioning transcendental ground of an individual's empirical character (FW: 86). The freedom of intelligible character is the negative sense of the term Schopenhauer develops as the Will's not being subject to explanatory necessity of any type, standing outside the principles of individuation and sufficient reason. "This freedom, however," he reminds us, "is *transcendental* ... it does not emerge in the appearance but is present only insofar as we abstract from the appearance and all its forms in order to arrive at that which, outside all time, is to be thought of as the inner essence of the human being in himself" (FW: 86). As inner being or moral essence, the Will in its transcendental freedom is the source of every aspect of the empirical character it objectifies. It is also for this reason the ground of every attribution of morally responsible action to the empirical character in phenomenal psychology (FW: 86). The relation between the empirical and intelligible character in an individual willing subject is the same as that between the world as representation and Will as thing-in-itself (FW: 86–7). This is true not merely by analogy, but in a strict and literal sense in Schopenhauer's metaphysics, in so far as the empirical character is one among various phenomenal objectifications of thing-in-itself, intelligible character is identical with Will, and Will is thing-in-itself (BM: 111–12).[8]

In addition to the empirical and intelligible characters of moral agents, Schopenhauer identifies a third type, which he calls acquired character. It is to this sense of character that most people refer when they speak of the virtuous or unvirtuous nature of a moral agent. A character is acquired through constant interaction with other objectifications of Will in the world as representation, by means of the accidental circumstances through which the empirical character is shaped and moulded in reacting and adjusting to the contingencies of existence. "Besides the intelligible and empirical characters", Schopenhauer relates in *The World as Will and Representation*:

> we have still to mention a third which is different from these two, namely the *acquired character*. We obtain this only in life, through contact with the world, and it is this we speak of when anyone is praised as a person who has character, or censured as one without character. (WWR 1: 303)

Although empirical and intelligible character are unalterable, Schopenhauer allows, even as the name suggests, that acquired character is malleable, subject to change over time.

The alterability of acquired character contributes to the illusion that willing moral agents are able to change themselves, to transform the persons they really are in another sense of character, through experience, training, incentive, punishment, deliberation or resolve. The acquired character of a moral agent in particular is the most superficial and ephemeral part of a subject. Because of its propensity to change the exact manner in which its underlying empirical and intelligible characters express themselves behaviourally, acquired character cannot possibly be the source of moral responsibility to which decision-making and action are properly attributed. Schopenhauer makes similar remarks in taking up the distinction between empirical, intelligible and acquired character in the *Essay on the Freedom of the Will*, where he remarks:

> Only a precise knowledge of his own empirical character gives a human being what is called an *acquired character*. It is possessed by

the human being who knows precisely his own qualities, both good and bad, and thus knows for certain what he may and may not count on and expect from himself. (FW: 43)

It is through this kind of knowledge that moral agents proceed confidently on the basis of superficial self-knowledge.

We can misjudge ourselves where acquired character is concerned. As to empirical character, ironically, it is less easily empirically determined. It is difficult to know which features of acquired character are among the true signs of a willing subject's empirical character objectified as intelligible character in the world as representation, where it is subject to errors of judgement. Intelligible character itself, however, if we have a correct understanding of it as Will, cannot be misjudged. The inference is trivial, in a way, because there is nothing substantive to know concerning thing-in-itself except that it is Will. The Will's intelligible character, which is equally the character of every individual willing subject, is the blind urging of a hungry beast, bent on consuming itself by proxy through its objectifications in the world as representation. There is a greater chance of misunderstanding the acquired character of individuals in the empirical world, where we can always suffer illusion or be deceived, misread the clues we encounter, jump to hasty conclusions, and exercise faulty inductive reasoning. The empirical character of a willing subject or moral agent, according to Schopenhauer, is nevertheless fixed, permanent and unchanging.

Schopenhauer relies in part on folk wisdom about persons not changing their natures or characters, but at most making only shallow adjustments of their acquired characters. Once a thief, always a thief, is the popular cliché. "We can obtain confirmation of this truth from daily experience", Schopenhauer allows:

> but the most striking is obtained when after twenty or thirty years we meet an acquaintance again and soon spot in him precisely the same old tricks as before. – Many a human being, of course, will deny this truth in words; yet he himself presupposes it in his actions, for he never again trusts anyone whom he has *once* found to be dishonest, whereas he relies on the one who has previously shown himself to be honest. (FW: 44)

Schopenhauer assumes that in so far as we fail to trust someone again after we have once been betrayed, or on the contrary return for assistance to the same person repeatedly after we have once been befriended, we evince an implicit understanding of the thesis he believes follows from the proposition that empirical character can never be changed. If we do not expect people to alter their ways, then we agree with Schopenhauer in taking this assumption as evidence for the proposition that moral character, empirical rather than acquired, never changes in the life of any person from birth to death, but is manifested over time in different ways and in different circumstances as modifications of acquired character.

Finally, Schopenhauer attaches transcendental freedom and the concept of empirical character to moral responsibility. It is only the concept of empirical character, he believes, that connects the body's physical behaviour in action to a willing subject as a morally responsible agent. The transition from freedom to responsibility in its most general terms is found in almost any ethical philosophy. In Schopenhauer, there is a finely nuanced linkage by which the two concepts are related. "[T]here is still a fact of consciousness," he writes, "which, to avoid disturbing the course of our investigation, I have so far entirely disregarded. This is the perfectly clear and certain feeling of *responsibility* for our actions – a feeling that rests on the unshakable certainty that we ourselves are *the doers of our deeds*" (FW: 83). Morality functions superficially in certain judgements we make in episodes of phenomenal psychology. Schopenhauer wants to explain how we can justify attributions of moral responsibility as we pronounce an agent's actions morally right or wrong.

"On the strength of that consciousness", he says:

> it never occurs to anyone, not even to someone who is fully convinced of the necessity (previously discussed) with which our actions occur, to make use of this necessity as an excuse for a transgression, and to throw the blame on the motives because their appearance rendered the deed inevitable. (FW: 83–4)

The explanatory necessity of moral decision-making and action is never reasonably cited as an excuse for wrongful behaviour. We can say on Schopenhauer's behalf that it makes no sense to try to avoid blame on grounds that would apply to any and every moral agent. All willing subjects are in the same boat in that all their actions are necessitated by lawlike explanatory principles, including causal and motivational laws. Schopenhauer argues that the conditions by which an action is determined have only a subjective necessity, stemming from the contingent fact that the individual is determined involuntarily to be one particular individual willing subject rather than another:

> For he sees quite well that this necessity has a *subjective* condition, and that here *objectively* it depended on the latter alone; in other words, in existing circumstances and hence under the influence of the motives that have determined him, an entirely different action,

in fact the very opposite of his, was quite possible and could have happened, *if only he had been another person.*   (FW: 84)

The same could be said, of course, by any other agent. "Because he is this person and not another," Schopenhauer adds:

> because he has such-and-such a character, naturally no other action was possible for *him*; in itself, however, and thus *objectively*, it is possible. Therefore the *responsibility* of which he is conscious concerns the deed only in the first instance and ostensibly, but at bottom it concerns his *character*; it is for the latter that he feels himself responsible.   (FW: 84)

The agent implicitly intuits the basic facts about the nature of free will that Schopenhauer codifies as abstract theoretical knowledge. In practice, Schopenhauer argues, moral agents behave as though they understand and accept his analysis. This is just the corroboration he seeks, the only sort he thinks he needs. "And for the latter he is also made responsible by others," he elaborates, "since their judgment turns at once from the deed to ascertain the qualities of the doer. 'He is a bad human being, a rogue,' or 'he is a scoundrel,' or 'he is a petty, false, mean soul' – such is their verdict, and their reproaches recur to his *character*" (FW: 84).

The intuitive conduct of those who stand in moral judgement of others provides powerful evidence for Schopenhauer's theory. When someone acts wrongly, the misdeed is attributed to the agent, which is to say the character of the perpetrator. Although he chooses a wrongful action to illustrate the point, the same might be said of someone who acts rightly and thereby earns moral respect or praise. The credit for morally right or wrong actions, in either case, Schopenhauer emphasizes, redounds to the agent's character. The empirical rather than the acquired character is not only the seat of moral responsibility, but it is that which alone is transcendentally free. Schopenhauer in this way forges the required conceptual connection between freedom of the will and moral responsibility. Morality presupposes the free will and responsibility of moral agents for their actions, without which attributions of moral right and wrong lack meaningful application. Schopenhauer locates the freedom of will transcendentally in Will as thing-in-itself, where the pure willing of a willing subject exists outside the necessity of law. He assigns responsibility for action to the unalterable empirical character of the subject, from which all free-will moral decision-making proceeds.[9]

CHAPTER SEVEN

Compassion as the philosophical foundation of morality

Boundless compassion for all living things is the firmest and surest guarantee of pure moral conduct, and needs no causistry. Whoever is inspired with it will assuredly injure no one, will wrong no one, will encroach on no one's rights; on the contrary, he will be lenient and patient with everyone, will forgive everyone, will help everyone as much as he can, and all his actions will bear the stamp of justice, philanthropy, and loving-kindness.   (BM: 172)

Origin of morality

Schopenhauer's "Prize Essay", *On the Basis of Morality*, in fact won no prize. It was written in response to the Royal Danish Society of Scientific Studies competition, like the Norwegian prize essay contest on freedom of the will, on a topic concerning the psychology of moral reasoning. The essay question contains a lengthy preamble, the main thrust of which is to ask:

Is *the source and foundation of morality to be looked for* in an idea of morality which lies immediately in consciousness (or conscience), and in the analysis of the other principal notions of morality springing from this, or is it to be sought in another ground of knowledge?
(BM: 38)

Critique of Kant's ethics

Schopenhauer begins his essay, following a brief general introduction, with a long section criticizing Kant's moral philosophy, covering roughly half the length of the book. He maintains that, despite being profoundly indebted to Kant's critical idealism, and in particular to the distinction between appearance and thing-in-itself, he is everywhere in disagreement with Kant's ethics and with what Kant calls the groundwork of the metaphysics of morals.

The analysis of free will and its relation to moral responsibility are among the respects in which Schopenhauer believes he has improved over Kant's moral philosophy. Impressed as he is with the opening sections of Kant's *Critique of Pure Reason* on the Transcendental Aesthetic, and especially with Kant's theory of space and time as the representing subject's pure forms of intuition, Schopenhauer does not accept at face value Kant's distinction between the world of appearance and thing-in-itself, and he regards Kant's argument for the existence of thing-in-itself as logically incoherent. He rejects the architectonic system of twelve Aristotelian categories in Kant's Analytic of Concepts, and takes issue with Kant's doctrine of the transcendental unity of apperception in his theory of self-consciousness. Most importantly, Schopenhauer believes he has surpassed the limitations of Kant's metaphysics and epistemology of noumenal thing-in-itself, which he is convinced he has correctly identified as Will.

These are among the most important differences between Schopenhauer and Kant. Nevertheless, they pale in comparison with the repugnance Schopenhauer feels for every aspect of Kant's moral theory. Schopenhauer devotes a relatively short final section of the "Criticism of the Kantian Philosophy", the Appendix in the first volume of *The World as Will and Representation*, to Kant's ethics. As he remarks even in the book's second edition, it is in *On the Basis of Morality* that he offers the most detailed critique of Kant's ethics, in the long, 70-plus-page chapter, "Criticism of Kant's Basis of Ethics". This extended polemic can be understood as the more complete continuation of the Appendix evaluation of Kant's moral philosophy. Schopenhauer makes explicit both his intellectual debt to and disagreements with Kant in declaring that: "[T]he criticism of Kant's foundation of morals will be in particular the best preparation and guide – in fact the direct path – to my own foundation of morals, for opposites illustrate each other, and my foundation is, in essentials, diametrically opposed to Kant's" (BM: 47).

In criticizing Kant's moral philosophy Schopenhauer prepares the way for the presentation of his own ideas. He identifies important themes and problems, and distances himself from Kant as an influential precursor whose conclusions he rejects. He establishes the need for another hopefully improved solution, reflecting the difficulties and shortcomings of the system under review. To properly understand Schopenhauer's criticisms of Kant's moral philosophy, and the differences between Kant's and Schopenhauer's ethics, we should therefore first examine the basic principles of Kant's metaphysics of morals.[1]

Kant's moral philosophy

In his *Grounding for the Metaphysics of Morals*, Kant lays down purely rationalist foundations. He disavows all empirical elements in ethics, which he regards as theoretical impurities. When ethics is completely purged of empirical factors, Kant stands ready to reject consequentialist moralities based on the experience of pleasure or inclination.

Kant is so convinced of the fundamental distinction between ethics and empirical psychological factors that he argues that we cannot be known without qualification to act in a morally correct way when there is any possibility of a conflicting motivation of desire. He formulates this conclusion in the thesis that the only thing that is unqualifiedly good is a good will. He proposes to identify synthetic *a priori* judgements that constitute the proper subject matter of the metaphysics of morals, as they do for him in any branch of metaphysics. He distinguishes between hypothetical imperatives and the categorical imperative as the one and only purely rational principle of ethics. Hypothetical imperatives are obligations we incur only conditionally, if we want to achieve some other end, such as promoting the general happiness. The categorical imperative is unconditional, requiring that we act always according to whatever moral maxims we can will at the same time to be universal principles of conduct for all rational beings. In four applications, Kant makes it clear that violations of the categorical imperative involve rules of conduct that we cannot will to be followed universally; when we try to do so, we encounter logical contradictions. The implementation of the categorical imperative through the logical consistency or inconsistency encountered in efforts to universalize a maxim of action makes Kant's ethics a formalist theory of moral value. The reductions to contradiction in some of Kant's illustrations of how the categorical imperative is supposed to be practically applied are not always immediately convincing. The categorical imperative is meant to be an unconditional principle of moral action, in any case, one that imposes a duty on every rational being simply by virtue of being rational.

Kant proposes to establish a special type of freedom that he believes is needed to make sense of moral responsibility by distinguishing between moral autonomy and heteronomy. Autonomy is freedom in the sense of self-governance or self-rule, while heteronomy is governance by something other than or outside the self. Kant's grounding of the metaphysics of morals, like

Schopenhauer's, postulates a transcendental sense of freedom, but as a kind of moral autonomy that is presupposed by the possibility of moral responsibility. Moral autonomy is achieved when reason, as that which is essential to every morally responsible agent, gives the moral law to itself, which can only occur when a rational agent accepts the categorical imperative. Moral heteronomy as something inconsistent with the requirements of moral responsibility occurs when a moral law is given to reason by something other than reason, standing outside itself. A rational agent can be heteronomously ruled by passion, emotion, inclination or such empirical considerations as the desire to promote happiness or pleasure. When reason accepts the moral law of reason in the form of the categorical imperative, Kant believes, the agent is free by virtue of being self-governing, and hence morally responsible.

The categorical imperative takes several forms under several interpretations. Kant insists that there is only one principle of unconditional moral duty that can be viewed from different perspectives. An important interpretation of the categorical imperative holds that we are always to treat rational beings as intrinsically valuable ends in themselves, and never merely as instrumentally valuable means to another end. We violate this implication of the categorical imperative, for example, when we act in such a way as to advance the moral consequentialist goal of promoting the greatest good or greatest happiness for the greatest number. This is the moral objective defended later in the history of ethics in John Stuart Mill's utilitarianism, among other hedonistic moral systems advocating the values of pleasure that Kant vehemently rejects. Kant projects a utopian ideal state of humankind, which he calls the Kingdom of Ends, in which every rational being treats every other rational being in accordance with the categorical imperative as ends in themselves rather than merely as means to another end. There would theoretically be no violations of the moral rights of others in the Kantian Kingdom of Ends. It instantiates what Kant hopes will result in a state of perpetual peace, in which all conflict and violence is overcome in the moral equivalent of a perfectly just reign in an ethical heaven on earth.

Schopenhauer's objections

Schopenhauer takes issue with all of these components of Kant's moral philosophy. At the beginning of the Appendix to *The World as Will and Representation*, he states with specific reference to Kant, that "It is much easier to point out the faults and errors in the work of a great mind than to give a clear and complete exposition of its value" (WWR 1: 415). In his assessment of Kant's ethics in *On the Basis of Morality*, Schopenhauer tries to do a little of both. However, he places greater weight by far on the objections by which he seeks to demolish Kant's theory, in order to make room for his own.

In his "Introduction" to *On the Basis of Morality*, Schopenhauer admits:

> I therefore confess the particular pleasure with which I set to work to remove the broad cushion from ethics, and frankly express my intention of proving Kant's practical reason and categorical imperative are wholly unjustified, groundless, and fictitious assumptions, and of showing that even Kant's ethics lacks a solid foundation.
>
> (BM: 48)

He begins by undermining Kant's fundamental idea that the purpose of philosophical ethics is to give reasons for what ought to happen, even if it never actually happens, disputing the *a priori* orientation of Kant's ethics. One can see, in light of Schopenhauer's commitment to moral motivation as one of the four roots of the principle of sufficient reason, that he would expect an adequate theory of ethics to concern the real behaviour of human agents here and now in the world as representation where all action takes place. He argues that:

> *moral* laws, apart from human ordinance, State institution, or religious doctrine, cannot be assumed as existing without proof. By this anticipation Kant is, therefore guilty of a *petitio principii*, which appears all the bolder because he adds at once . . . [in] the Preface that a moral law ought to imply *"absolute necessity"*.   (BM: 53)

Kant errs, according to Schopenhauer, right from the start, when he begins by stating without demonstration that the purpose of ethics is to articulate necessary principles of morality. Schopenhauer not only faults Kant with the circular assumption that there must be such principles, leaving open the possibility that the proposition could be adequately defended, but claims further and more pointedly that the entire realm of ethics is not in fact necessary but only contingent. "[S]uch necessity is everywhere characterized by the inevitability of the resulting effect", he argues. "Now how can we speak of absolute necessity in the case of these alleged moral laws, as an example of which [Kant] mentions *Du sollt* [*sic*] *nicht lügen* [Thou shalt not lie]. For as we know and as he himself admits, they remain frequently, indeed as a rule, ineffective" (BM: 53).

Although Schopenhauer offers additional criticisms against Kant's quest for necessary *a priori* moral principles, the above reason does not seem particularly persuasive. There is generally no objection to supposing that necessary principles can imply logically or causally contingent consequences, provided that at least some additional assumptions are contingent. The opposite inference would of course be modally invalid, but to derive merely possible or contingent propositions from necessary and contingent assumptions is no failure of reasoning. The fact that a moral rule against lying is ineffective in practice, and in that sense is not logically or causally necessary, is no count against a defender of Kant who might reply that the rule nevertheless remains morally necessary in the sense that whether or not it is actually observed it is necessary if true at all within Kant's system that one ought not to lie. Would Schopenhauer similarly dispute the causal necessity of the proposition that a golden globe ten miles in circumference would have a certain gravitational attraction solely on the grounds that as a matter of fact there nowhere exists such an immense gold orb? Why not interpret Kant's demand for *a priori* moral principles in the same charitable subjunctive fashion? Why not say that if a person were never to lie, despite the fact that all persons do lie, then that person would be acting rightly according to an idealized moral principle?

Schopenhauer understands Kant's emphasis on moral duty, especially as it is formulated in the categorical imperative, as a kind of disguised theological morality. He may in fact have his finger on the beating pulse of Kant's implicit reasoning in ethics, but the argument again is not clearly conclusive (BM: 56–7). His objection to what he perceives as the hidden theological presuppositions of Kant's moral philosophy is a recurrent theme in his criticism. Kant's own attitude toward religion is ambivalent, while Schopenhauer, despite expressing great interest in the philosophical ideas concealed in religion, is undoubtedly an atheist. Here he regards any effort to cast ethics in the form of a code as duties or imperatives, in effect, in the way that a "Thou shalt X" or "Thou shalt not Y" assumes the existence of another will to which the individual to whom the duty applies is subject and subservient (BM: 57–8).[2]

There is no good reason why such constructions as the form of moral obligation should not be construed as a moral agent's dictating the requirements of moral law to herself. This is particularly true of Kant's categorical imperative, which does not explicitly depend essentially on the "Thou shalt" formula. "Act always ... etc." is, after all, not far afield from "Thou shalt". While it addresses the moral agent as though in another voice, it need not be so construed, but might be understood instead as a reminder of an ethical principle that a person can issue to himself. It has a form something like "Rotate your tyres every six months", from which no reference to a deity is necessarily inferred. It can be understood instead as the voice of impersonal reason. When Schopenhauer's own moral principle finally surfaces in the exposition, it appears in much the same formulation, which can easily be translated without addition or loss of meaning as either "Act always" or

"Thou shalt". Schopenhauer avoids the implication by surrounding his moral principle with disclaimers to the effect that it offers at most a moral guideline rather than a strict duty or command. The point is that the mere linguistic form in which a moral principle is presented is no certain indication of whether or not it is supposed to have a theological foundation.

Schopenhauer further disputes Kant's assumption that the essence of a moral agent is reason, and that therefore the freedom of will and moral responsibility, along with all morality, must somehow be connected to the agent's reason in a correct moral philosophy. Schopenhauer believes, on the contrary, that willing is the essence of moral agency, and that rationality is relatively superficial, belonging only to the world as representation where it is subject to the principle of sufficient reason. We know this first from Schopenhauer's epistemology, in which he gives second place to abstract knowledge in deference to intuited insight and pre-theoretical understanding, and also from his secondary treatment of intellectual freedom as an afterthought to physical and moral freedom in the *Essay on the Freedom of the Will*, where the role of reasoning in matching means to ends in practical judgement is assigned only to the Appendix (BM: 64).

We could hardly hope for a more revealing statement of Schopenhauer's disagreements with Kant. Kant, although a critical idealist in metaphysics and epistemology, strives to be a pure rationalist in ethics. Schopenhauer no doubt already sees this as a betrayal of critical idealism and a symptom of deep incoherence in Kant's philosophy. The opposition between regarding moral agents as essentially wilful by contrast with the view of people as essentially rational makes an enormous difference in the outlook toward human nature reflected in a thinker's moral philosophy. Kant appeals to reason in the form of the categorical imperative and as the source of that freedom whereby it is possible for rational agents to be morally responsible. Schopenhauer regards reason, cognitive and intellectual faculties generally as secondary phenomena. Transcendental freedom for Schopenhauer is implied instead by the fact that each willing subject contains a common core of pure willing or Will as thing-in-itself that is non-individualizable and inexplicable, whose actions consequently are not subject to causal or motivational law. Schopenhauer, in this sense, if we can be permitted such a barbarism, believes that he out-transcendentalizes Kant.

In keeping with his denial of Kant's starting-point, Schopenhauer rejects the purpose of ethics as an articulation of *a priori* necessary principles of moral duty and obligation. He disputes Kant's view of ethics as what ought in principle to be done, even if such actions are never actually performed. He detaches reason from moral virtue and vice, as these qualities are actually instantiated in the world as representation. "Only after Kant," Schopenhauer observes with a touch of sarcasm, "for then virtue was supposed to spring from pure reason, did the virtuous and the reasonable become one and the same; this despite the usage of all languages, which is not accidental, but the work of universal human, and therefore coherent and consistent knowledge" (BM: 83). Far from supposing that reason is the basis of morality, Schopenhauer holds that the greater the powers of reasoning, the more harm and havoc an evil will can wreak in the world. Nor does he suppose that a good moral will must necessarily coincide with sound reasoning, but instead believes that it can motivate the charitable of heart to acts of unreason and even practical stupidity.

It is not astonishing, then, that Schopenhauer should also dispute not only the form but the content of Kant's categorical imperative as the foundation of his moral theory. At one point he objects that:

> Moreover, there is the fact that, considered merely as a formula, [the categorical imperative] is only a paraphrase, an obscure and disguised expression of the well-known rule, *Quod tibi fieri non vis, alteri ne feceris* [Do not to another what you do not wish to be done to you], if, that is, by repeating this without *non* and *ne*, we remove the defect of containing only the duties of rights or law and not of love. (BM: 92)

Unfortunately, Schopenhauer in this passage indicates that he misunderstands Kant's categorical imperative in equating it as he does here with the so-called Golden Rule. In formulating the categorical imperative, Kant does not say that we are to act only in such a way toward other persons as we would like in turn to be acted toward ourselves. That would be to make morality a matter of inclination and empirical psychology, of what agents want or wish or will to have happen to them as a consequence of the actions of others, which Kant emphatically disavows. The focus in Kant's categorical imperative is instead on whether we *can* logically consistently will that the maxims of our actions become universal principles to be followed by all rational beings. If, without falling into logical contradiction, we can will the maxims of our actions to be universalized, then the categorical imperative commands that the actions be done. If we cannot consistently will our maxims to be universally applied, then the categorical imperative forbids our performing the respective actions. It is not at all a question for Kant of what we will to do, but of what we logically can will. This is, naturally, what is supposed to make Kant's ethics purely formal, and what is supposed to make his groundwork for the metaphysics of morals an exercise in pure *a priori* reason with a purely rational justification that depends only on logical contradiction or non-contradiction.

Schopenhauer should know better. He should have based his critique of Kant's moral philosophy on a more accurate interpretation of the categorical imperative. He takes aim at the further implication of the principle according to which we are to treat all rational beings as ends in themselves and never merely as means to another end. Schopenhauer claims that the concept of something's being an end in itself is in the first place conceptually incoherent. "Kant ... slips through his strange definitions to the proposition", he writes. "'Man, and in general every rational being, exists *as an end in himself.*' But I must say frankly that *'to exist as an end in oneself'* is an unthinkable expression, a *contradictio in adjecto*" (BM: 95). The reason is that:

> To be an end or aim means to be willed. Every aim or end in view exists only in reference to a will, and is the end of the will, that is (as I have said) the direct motive of it. Only in this relation has the concept *end* any meaning, which it loses as soon as it is torn away. But this essential relation necessarily excludes all *in itself*.   (BM: 95)

Schopenhauer ridicules the idea of an end in itself in a series of comparisons: "'End in itself' is exactly like saying 'friend in himself, enemy in himself, uncle in himself, north or east in itself, above or below in itself,' and so on. Basically, however, the case is the same with 'end in itself' as with the 'absolute ought'" (BM: 95).

There has often been thought to exist a distinction in value enquiry between intrinsic and extrinsic or instrumental value. It is the difference between things that are valuable in and of themselves or for their own sake, as opposed to those that are valuable merely as the means to another end. Schopenhauer challenges the distinction with the charge that the concept is logically inconsistent, a contradiction in terms. His objection is that to be an end is by definition to stand in some relation to an act of will or to be undertaken for some purpose. Thus, we cannot simply sheer off the purpose for which the thing in question is supposed to be valued. The comparisons with other inherently relational concepts such as "uncle in itself", which Schopenhauer raises, have a certain rhetorical force, making the idea seem absurd; but are they the right way to think about the concept of an end in itself?

Let us suppose that Schopenhauer is correct to hold that the concept of an end only makes sense in relation to an act of will by which the end is defined. Does this entail that an end must always have something other than itself as that for the sake of which it is an end? We can grant that all ends are willed and that they cannot be understood in themselves in any sense that would entail their detachment from every act of will. Still, does it not make sense, and is it not what Kant, Aristotle in *Nicomachean Ethics*, and other philosophers mean by invoking the distinction between intrinsic and

211

instrumental value? Is there not a distinction between ends that are willed only because they are valuable as contributing to some further end, and things that are willed because they are deemed valuable even if they do not contribute to any further end? Is the question of whether or not things that are thought to be ends in themselves are supposed to be understood independently of any act of will not simply a red herring in Schopenhauer's criticism? Does it not confuse the issue of the distinction between different ways in which willed ends can assume value, either for their own sake, as something we would choose even if they did not produce anything else of value, and those we choose only because they are the means to obtaining something else of value other than themselves?

Schopenhauer questions the conclusion whereby rational beings alone have intrinsic value in the sense of constituting ends in themselves according to one of Kant's interpretations of the categorical imperative. Kant is committed to the position that non-rational beings lacking intrinsic value do not need to be treated with anything like the same moral respect as rational agents. This position is distinctly at odds with Schopenhauer's doctrine of moral compassion. He agrees in this respect with the teachings of Buddhism, Hinduism and other Asian religious traditions, concerning moral conduct toward all sentient beings. He praises these values in opposition to what he takes to be the anthropocentric ethics of Judaism, Islam, Christianity, and Kant's formalist deontology, in their blithe disregard for the sufferings of non-human animals (BM: 96). His moral indignation is aroused by the Kantian suggestion that our obligations extend only to other rational beings. This is the kind of unenlightened ethical outlook that animal rights advocates have sometimes referred to with some justice as species chauvinism. Why, indeed, should beings equally capable of suffering as ourselves be treated so differently simply on the basis of whether or not they are also capable of reasoning?

For Schopenhauer, whose moral principles depend on intuited compassion for the sufferings of other objectifications of Will in the world as representation, there can be no philosophical justification for prejudice against the suffering of any creatures. Kant, on the other hand, is committed to preferential moral attitudes only toward rational beings, since it is only by virtue of possessing reason that he believes a being has moral value as an autonomous morally free agent and end in itself. Everything else in the universe, according to Kant's viewpoint, can be used with perfect moral impunity merely as a means to any other chosen end. Schopenhauer, perhaps wishing not unduly to offend the prize essay judges, refers only obliquely to the Book of Genesis assertion that God gave humankind "dominion" over all the beasts of the field, fowl of the air and fish of the sea. He thinks that no such division in the basic principles of morality can possibly be correct.

He is appalled at the practices encouraged by moral theories that regard only rational agents as morally valuable, allowing non-rational animals to be used for the benefit of rational beings without moral concern for their pain and suffering.

Finally, following the development of moral principles in Kant's exposition, Schopenhauer turns at last to the utopian Kingdom of Ends. He had previously indicated that he regards the concept of an end in itself as logically incoherent. Moreover, we know that any such ideal is incompatible with Schopenhauer's moral pessimism, based on his metaphysics of the hungry Will as thing-in-itself, endlessly feeding on itself through its objectifications in the world as representation. We moral agents, considered in terms of our phenomenal psychologies or empirical and acquired characters, are part and parcel of the phenomenal world, and as such are equally among the objectifications of thing-in-itself as Will that, of necessity, are constantly at war with one another. Strife rules the world as representation, according to Schopenhauer's moral pessimism, even when we are personally victorious, and even when we can afford to relax temporarily through periods of plenty, repose and détente. The world as a whole can never attain the sort of perpetual peace that Kant projects for a Kingdom of Ends, even as a philosophical fiction or ideal state of affairs that it would make sense to try to attain. The Kantian idea of perpetual peace in a Kingdom of Ends is not merely unfounded optimistic pie in the sky, as far as Schopenhauer is concerned, but it is philosophically inconceivable in light of the world's transcendental reality. The world we live in can never be free of conflict between moral agents because the world is the objectification of Will as thing-in-itself, the insatiably hungry and inherently self-conflicted Will that necessarily manifests its character in endless collisions of individual phenomenal wills.

Schopenhauer rehearses his objections to the category of an end in itself as a prelude to refuting Kant's Kingdom of Ends. "However, Kant propounds a second and entirely new class of actions occurring without any interest and thus without motive," he writes in exasperation, "and these were supposed to be actions of justice and charitableness!" (BM: 100). "To refute this monstrous assumption," he adds:

> it was necessary merely to reduce the assumption to its real meaning, which was concealed by the play on the word *interest*. Meanwhile Kant celebrates ... the triumph of his autonomy of the will in the setting up of a moral Utopia with the name of a *kingdom of ends*, which is populated with nothing but *rational beings in abstracto*, who one and all constantly will without willing *anything* (i.e., without interest). The one thing they will is that they all constantly will in accordance with *one* maxim (i.e., autonomy). (BM: 100)

Schopenhauer tries in this way to criticize Kant's concept of the Kingdom of Ends on logical rather than ideological grounds, referring again to the nonsense of an unwilled end.

We have already raised the issue of whether Schopenhauer's objection to the concept of intrinsic value is misplaced. If there could be a Kingdom of Ends, its members, each a monarch in his or her own right by virtue of possessing absolute moral autonomy, could presumably will many things. In particular, they could will to use each other as means to other ends, provided that they never will to use each other *merely* as means to another end. The royalty of the Kingdom of Ends could will many other things besides, concerning the use of non-rational beings and non-living entities for other ends. The only moral restriction they must observe is never to violate one another's moral rights by treatment incompatible with the moral respect implied by the categorical imperative. Again, this does not mean without relation to will, as Schopenhauer would have it, but more specifically as not willing to treat other rational beings merely as instruments for the satisfaction of practical needs, merely as means to another end rather than always as ends in themselves. Whatever other defects may plague Kant's categorical imperative, it cannot responsibly be said that Kant advocates an unintelligible concept of ends in themselves or of rational beings as ends in themselves in an ideal Kingdom of Ends.

After harsh criticism of Kant, it is interesting to see that Schopenhauer credits him with important contributions to moral philosophy. He opens Chapter II of *On the Basis of Morality*, with the sincere acknowledgment that: "Kant has the great merit of having purged ethics of all *eudaemonism*" (BM: 49). He appreciates the fact that in his misguided efforts to cleanse moral reasoning of all empirical elements, Kant rejects the ancient Greek concept of moral reasoning and right action as directed toward securing *eudaimonia*, a happy life, or living in accord with the principles of morality regardless of the vicissitudes of life. Schopenhauer is at pains even in the first edition of *The World as Will and Representation* to distinguish the suffering–salvation axis of his moral philosophy from that of the Stoics and Epicureans, who sought to achieve happiness in the absence of pain. We shall see below how Schopenhauer attacks such moral philosophies, beginning with Aristotle and continuing through Hellenistic and Graeco-Roman Stoic and Epicurean moral philosophy.

Near the end of *On the Basis of Morality*, Schopenhauer writes:

> justice requires that I not leave this subject without recalling Kant's greatest and most brilliant merit in the service of ethics. This consists in the doctrine of the coexistence of freedom and necessity, which he expounds first of all in the *Critique of Pure Reason* . . .; yet an even

clearer presentation of the discussion is given in the *Critique of Practical Reason* .... (BM: 109)

Needless to say, Schopenhauer, while lauding this achievement of Kant's, approaches the compatibility of moral freedom and causal necessity with respect to the transcendental ground of moral responsibility in a very different way than Kant. Just as Schopenhauer credits Kant's critical idealist epistemology and metaphysics with invaluable insights that he transposes in modified form as principles of his transcendental idealism, so he now does the same with respect to Kant's doctrine of the compatibility of moral freedom and causal necessity. There is, moreover, an essential connection between these two borrowings from Kant's metaphysics of morals in Schopenhauer's transcendental idealism.

"I regard Kant's doctrine of the coexistence of freedom and necessity as the greatest of all achievements of the human mind", Schopenhauer writes with heartfelt enthusiasm. "With the Transcendental Aesthetic it forms the two great diamonds in Kant's crown of fame, which will never become extinct" (BM: 111). The eulogy allows Schopenhauer to end, as he begins this section of the essay, on a positive note of praise for his philosophical predecessor. He diplomatically avoids mentioning that he completely rejects Kant's way of reconciling freedom with necessity by means of Kant's concept of moral autonomy. Nor does he repeat his complaints about the limitation of Kant's ethics to rational beings. We are free, according to Kant, only in so far as we rationally choose to adopt the categorical imperative, which Schopenhauer rejects in both form and content. He perceives an interesting connection between Kant's notion of transcendental freedom, and the Kantian noumenal thing-in-itself. "The *thing-in-itself* underlying the phenomenon is outside space and time and free from all succession and plurality of acts", he states, "it is one and unchangeable" (BM: 110). He then inserts his own analysis of the concept of transcendental freedom related to the Will and relevant to moral responsibility, stretching Kant's thing-in-itself to cover the distinction between intelligible and empirical character. "Its constitution *in itself* is the *intelligible character*", he writes:

which is equally present in all the actions of the individual and is stamped on every one of them, like the signet on a thousand seals. The *empirical character* of this phenomenon, manifesting itself in time and in the succession of acts, is determined by the intelligible. Hence this phenomenon must show the constancy of a natural law in all its manifestations, which are brought about by the motives; and thus all its acts ensue with strict necessity. (BM: 110)

Schopenhauer thereby reconciles transcendental freedom and phenomenal necessity in a significantly different way than Kant had proposed. He does so, moreover, in what he undoubtedly sees as a more thoroughly grounded comprehensive transcendental idealism. He interprets thing-in-itself as Will, underlying or existing at the core of every individual willing subject of action, and hence of every morally responsible agent. Finally, he argues that Will is free by virtue of falling outside the principle of individuation and explanatory lawlike necessity under the principle of sufficient reason.

Egoism as the ultimate motivation of morality

Having worked through the main principles of Kant's ethics, and criticizing what he finds inadequate in the theory, Schopenhauer is now ready to square off against the Danish prize essay question. Chapter 3 of the book, approximately as long as the "Criticism of Kant's Basis of Ethics", is developed in several parts under the title "The Foundation of Ethics".

Schopenhauer first argues that the motivation for action is primarily but not exclusively egoistic. He distinguishes between three kinds of motives, but believes that ultimately most actions are motivated by self-love. The idea that people generally act self-interestedly is by no means new or original to Schopenhauer's ethics. We may think of cynics who regard persons willing to donate money to charity as doing so only for selfish motives because it makes them feel better about themselves. Or of even the most apparently altruistic behaviour as somehow indirectly self-benefiting, if only we can untangle the ulterior reasons why people do what they do. Schopenhauer does not go quite this far or in quite this direction, although he maintains that: "The chief and fundamental incentive in man as in the animal is *egoism*, that is, the craving for existence and well-being" (BM: 131).

Where it is important to explain the motivations for actions, considering what is done as a phenomenal occurrence adhering to the principles of individuation and sufficient reason, Schopenhauer argues that the incentive to act is always egoistic. It follows that all moral motivation is ultimately a matter of self-interest or self-love. This is to say that all worldly motivated action is undertaken for the sake of egoistic satisfaction, even when the agents in question do not recognize the fact and even if they would positively deny that they were acting to promote their own personal self-interests. Schopenhauer argues that in the absence of self-love moral agents can never be sufficiently motivated to act, a fact that follows directly as a function of the kinds of explanations available for actions within the world as representation. He nevertheless believes that egoism is opposed to morality, and that all actions motivated by self-aggrandizement have no moral value. "Morality without argumentation and reasoning, that is, mere moralizing, cannot have any effect, because it does not motivate", he says in *The World as Will and Representation*, adding:

> But a morality that *does* motivate can do so only by acting on self-love. Now what springs from this has no moral worth. From this it follows that no genuine virtue can be brought about through morality and abstract knowledge in general, but that such virtue must spring from the intuitive knowledge that recognizes in another's individuality the same inner nature as in one's own.
>
> (WWR 1: 367–8).

When individuals act non-egoistically, their deeds can have moral value, although in such cases what they choose to do is by definition unmotivated and hence cannot be rationally explained. Morally worthy actions in Schopenhauer's philosophy as a result are always, in his technical sense of the word, mysterious.

Why do we then sometimes act altruistically, and why do we make sacrifices for others, as Schopenhauer recognizes people sometimes do? We do so literally for no reason, or, more specifically, with no motivation. The only motivation we can possibly have for our actions as objectifications of the hungry Will in the world as representation is self-interest. When we act altruistically through compassion for the suffering of others, we do so by virtue of a mysterious transcendental intuition. We recognize that all people in their intelligible characters, the pure willing or Will in each individual, are identical beneath their representational guises. We help others even when doing so does not directly benefit us, because we intuit that the intelligible character of another thinking subject distinct from us in space, time and personality, is really strictly identical to ourselves, to our own intelligible character. There is in the end only one such intelligible character. There is only one strictly identical Will as thing-in-itself, transcending the empirical distinctions among individuals objectified in the world as representation. We help others, when we do, according to Schopenhauer, through self-love, because we at least implicitly know that all willing subjects are at bottom identical, that all are really the one and only intelligible character, which is thing-in-itself construed as Will.

To repeat, the explanation of all action in human beings and non-human animals for Schopenhauer can only involve egoistic motivations. "In the animal as in man this egoism is most intimately connected with their innermost core and essence", Schopenhauer writes; "in fact, it is really identical with essence. As a rule, therefore, all man's actions spring from egoism, and we must always first try to explain a given action with this in mind" (BM: 131). Like the Will that it objectifies, the essence of an individual animal or human being has potentially unlimited desires, needs and wants, which its egoistic motivations seek to gratify, necessarily, in the long run, if not more immediately, at the expense of others. This is the source of at least a good part of the suffering that takes place in the phenomenal world, as we objectifications of Will struggle against and attempt in effect to eat each other and take valuable things away from each other.

Why are we so? Not because we fell from a state of grace through an act of disobedience to God in the Garden of Eden. Nor because we have succumbed to malevolent influences perpetuated in a materialistic culture through a series of historical accidents. It is for one reason only, according to Schopenhauer – because we are all objectifications of an insatiably hungry Will. We cannot help ourselves, as creatures inhabiting the world as representation, in so far as our actions are motivated and hence explainable according to causal and motivational laws. Schopenhauer remarks that: "Everything opposing the strivings of [a person's] egoism excites his wrath, anger, and hatred, and he will attempt to destroy it as his enemy" (BM: 131–2). This is motivation indeed. When individuals feel that their vital interests are threatened, they act in every way to defend themselves, and, with emotions at their peak, actively engage in efforts to obtain whatever the ego demands (BM: 142–3).

From a rational rather than emotional point of view, most individuals recognize that their needs and interests are no different from, and no less valuable to themselves than, those of the countless other persons who also populate the world. "Now while in his subjective view a man's own self assumes these colossal proportions," Schopenhauer says, "in the objective view it shrinks to almost nothing, to a thousand millionth part of the present human race" (BM: 132–3). Knowing that there are others with whom the ego is in competition for the goods it desires only intensifies the struggle, and thereby the suffering (BM: 133). It is exclusively this kind of unmotivated and literally inexplicable mysterious leaping across the egoistic gulf that divides one human being from another in the act of aiding them or relieving their suffering that Schopenhauer regards as possessing moral value. The philosophical basis of morality can accordingly be sought only in the transcendental understanding of Will as thing-in-itself. The origin of moral principles and rules of behaviour in the world as representation are explained by Schopenhauer along the lines of something like a social contract, although he does not quite adopt this theory or terminology. He argues, citing Thomas Hobbes's *Leviathan* and thinkers with similar insights about the need to control the violence of unbridled egoism, that:

218

where egoism is not opposed either by external force, which must also include all fear whether of human or supernatural powers, or by a genuine moral incentive, it pursues its purposes without reserve. Therefore, without such checks and in view of the infinite number of egoistic individuals, the *bellum omnium contra omnes* [war of all against all] would be the order of the day, to the undoing of all. And so reflecting reason very soon invented the machinery of the State which, springing from mutual fear of mutual violence, obviates the disastrous consequences of universal egoism, as far as this can be done in the *negative* way. (BM: 133)

The untrammelled egoistic pursuit of gain is restrained by external force within the social contract for the greater benefit of all people. Individuals must seek their fortunes and strive to fulfil their ambitions within a framework of religious or political laws designed to prevent the chaos of every person trying to satisfy their egoistic desires by whatever violent or unjust means they might otherwise choose. In this account of the origins of law and civil government, Schopenhauer merely echoes, as he acknowledges, what many political theorists have speculated before him. The doctrine receives special emphasis in the context of his transcendental idealism, where egoistic pursuits by many individuals in potentially endless conflict are objectifications of the insatiably hungry Will. The egoism of societies banding together for the sake of promoting the interests of their members in Schopenhauer's philosophy inevitably conflict with one another at the tribal and national level in trade and war, where even then there are often rules for the management of collective self-serving egoism.

Moral value of compassion

All moral value, according to Schopenhauer, stands in stark opposition to egoism. Although he limits motivational explanation of actions to egoistic considerations, he characterizes this only as the primary type of action for the sake of self-love undertaken by most people most of the time. There are important exceptions in the realm of ethics, just as there are in aesthetics for the rare individual possessed of aesthetic genius. The ascetic saint is such a person in the moral sphere. Falling short of genuine saintliness, there are many small acts of benevolence and charity, loving kindness and altruism. These for Schopenhauer are the only preciously few morally worthy acts that contradict all egoistic motivations in the vast majority of actions that human beings undertake in doing the things they do, especially with or to each other.

Standing out among the common throng of individuals in egoistic pursuit of selfish interests, there are also persons of genuine morality. These are individuals who mysteriously and unmotivatedly dedicate some part of their energy and resources to helping others for no other reason than the fact that those persons are suffering and need someone to help. "I believe there are those who have, as it were, an *inborn* principle of giving others their due, who therefore do not intentionally hurt anyone's feelings, who do not unconditionally seek their own advantage, but who in this connection also consider the rights of others" (BM: 138–9). Schopenhauer acknowledges the statistically limited numbers of persons who behave morally toward others. He characterizes such individuals notably as benefiting others without thought of egoistic benefit or self-love, and hence inexplicably without motivation. "In the case of obligations mutually undertaken," Schopenhauer elaborates:

> they see not only that the other man *does* his part, but also that he *receives* his due, since it is their sincere desire that whoever has dealings with them may not be the loser. These are the *people of true integrity*, the few *aequi* (just) among the numberless host of *iniqui* (unjust); but there are such. (BM: 139)

The restriction of moral value to unegoistic actions is now made explicit in Schopenhauer's ethics. He writes: "It is, therefore, only actions of the kind just described to which we attribute real *moral worth*. We find that their characteristic feature is the exclusion of that class of motives whereby all human actions are otherwise prompted, namely, those of *self-interest* in the widest sense of the term" (BM: 139). The slightest taint of self-interest does not morally invalidate an action in Schopenhauer's moral philosophy, as in Kant's. Rather, an action is altogether lacking in moral value if it is undertaken entirely and exclusively for egoistic motives. "If a self-interested motive is the only one," Schopenhauer explains, "its discovery entirely destroys the moral worth of an action; and if such a motive acts as an accessory, the moral worth of the action is reduced by its discovery. The absence of all egoistic motivation is, therefore, *the criterion of an action of moral worth*" (BM: 139–40).

Non-egoistic action for Schopenhauer is compassionate. Compassion is the emotional capacity for sharing vicariously in the sufferings of others (BM: 144). There is a kind of identification with another person when we are emotionally moved to an act of compassion. The word "compassion" means literally to have passion *with* another, which is also true of the preposition particle "*mit*" in Schopenhauer's German term *Mitleid*. We may strongly feel a unity with the person for whom we experience the psychological phenomenon of compassion, for which Schopenhauer in due course offers a deeper, transcendental, metaphysical understanding. Ultimately, the feeling of compassion is a recognition that another individual is literally identical with ourselves, not in the superficial sense of ego, personality, or empirical or acquired character, but in the sense of intelligible character, the Will as thing-in-itself, which all phenomenally willing subjects have identically within themselves, transcending or underlying all superficially distinct acts of will. We are all one in this sense. As willing subjects, we are all objectifications of the same Will. We share equally in the identical intelligible character on which our distinctive empirical and acquired characters are founded and on which they metaphysically depend.

If it is only actions inspired by compassion rather than egoistically motivated by considerations of self-interest that are morally valuable, what, then, is an acceptable principle of ethical conduct? What is an appropriate rule of moral behaviour for people who want to do the right thing and live their lives in accordance with a correct set of moral rules? Schopenhauer roundly rejects both the form and content of Kant's categorical imperative. Kant, in any case, contrary to Schopenhauer, regards compassion as antithetical to morality. Schopenhauer believes just the opposite, holding that it is only compassionate action that is morally justified. Where Kant insists that we are to act always according to that maxim which we can will at the same time to be a universal law for all rational beings, what does Schopenhauer offer instead? Previously, in his criticism of Kant's basis for ethics, Schopenhauer announces his counter-principle. He formulates a simplified moral rule of guidance in this way, contrasting it with Kant's categorical imperative misintepreted as the Golden Rule:

> But this rule, *Quod tibi fieri*, etc. [Do not do to another what you do not wish to be done to you], is again only a circumlocution or, if it is preferred, a premise of the proposition that is laid down by me as the simplest and purest expression of the mode of conduct unanimously demanded of all systems of morality, *Neminem laede, imo omnes quantum potes, juva* [Injure no one; on the contrary, help everyone as much as you can]. This proposition is and remains the true and genuine substance of all morality. (BM: 92)

What could at the same time be simpler or more profound? Schopenhauer's principle of morality, not to injure but to try to help others, vibrates with a deeply felt sense of what it is right and wrong to do.

The principle has two complementary components. *Neminem laede*, harm or injure no one, is negative in specifying what we ought not to do. Schopenhauer introduces the rule, although he has not yet said why it would be wrong to injure another or why compassion for others and in particular for their sufferings dictates that we ought to avoid injuring them. The second component of the rule, *omnes quantum potes, juva*, obligates us to help others as much as possible. This part of the principle is positive, instructing or advising us to do whatever advances the interests of others in avoiding pain and suffering. Compassion supports not only the justice of refraining from injuring other sentient beings, but helping to alleviate their suffering whenever and to whatever extent we can. "[A]nother's suffering in itself and as such directly becomes my motive by means of *compassion*," Schopenhauer reminds us:

> which was previously shown to be a fact, although of mysterious origin. This second degree is clearly distinguished from the first by the *positive character* of the actions resulting from it, since compassion now not only restrains me from injuring another, but even impels me to help him.   (BM: 163)

Schopenhauer, in sharp contrast with Kant's limitation of moral responsibility to rational beings, regards compassion for all suffering beings, including human beings and non-human animals, as morally obligatory. "The moral incentive advanced by me as the genuine", Schopenhauer holds:

> is further confirmed by the fact that *the animals* are also taken under its protection. In other European systems of morality they are badly provided for, which is most inexcusable. They are said to have no rights, and there is the erroneous idea that our behavior to them is without moral significance, or, as it is said in the language of that morality, there are no duties to animals. All this is revoltingly crude, a barbarism of the West ...   (BM: 175)

Although Schopenhauer is not a consequentialist like James Mill, John Stuart Mill, Jeremy Bentham or the later utilitarians, he is clearly closer in spirit to them in acknowledging these implications of his moral philosophy than he is to Kant's purely rationalist formal deontology. Schopenhauer is generally concerned for the suffering of any sentient being, and analyses moral value in terms of justice and mercy or loving kindness toward others.[3]

Schopenhauer explains the psychology of compassion in *The World as Will and Representation*:

> That we are moved to tears not by our own sufferings, but by those of others, happens in the following way; either in imagination we put ourselves vividly in the sufferer's place, or we see in his fate the

lot of the whole of humanity, and consequently above all our own fate. Thus in a very roundabout way, we always weep about ourselves; we feel sympathy with ourselves. This seems also to be a main reason for the universal, and hence natural, weeping in cases of death. It is not the mourner's loss over which he weeps; he would be ashamed of such egoistical tears, instead of sometimes being ashamed of not weeping. In the first place, of course, he weeps over the fate of the deceased; yet he weeps also when for the deceased death was a desirable deliverance after long, grave, and incurable sufferings. In the main, therefore, he is seized with sympathy over the lot of the whole of mankind that is given over to finiteness. In consequence of this, every life, however ambitious and often rich in deeds, must become extinct and nothing.   (WWR 1: 377)

The morality of compassion is further explained in Schopenhauer's treatise as something that approximates a morally acceptable form of egoism that might be called alter-egoism. We recognize ourselves in the sufferings of other persons, so that in alleviating their sufferings we are in a sense acting in our own interests (WWR 1: 379). While Schopenhauer's anti-egoistic treatment of the subject in *On the Basis of Morality* is not strictly incompatible with his earlier account of why compassion is morally valuable, he more clearly distances himself from any taint of egoism in addressing the prize essay question. Here he now distinguishes:

There are generally only *three fundamental incentives* of human action, and all possible motives operate solely through their stimulation:

a) Egoism: this desires one's own weal (is boundless).

b) Malice: this desires another's woe (goes to the limits of extreme cruelty).

c) Compassion: this desires another's weal (goes to the length of nobleness and magnanimity).

Every human action must be attributable to one of these incentives, although two can also act in combination. Now as we have assumed that actions of moral worth are given facts, they too must result from one of these fundamental incentives. But by virtue of the eighth premise, they cannot spring from the *first*, still less from the *second*; for all actions that arise from the second are morally bad, while the first incentive produces actions that, from a moral point of view, are in part neither good nor bad. They must, therefore, come from the *third* alternative; and this will receive its confirmation a posteriori in what follows.   (BM: 145)

To fulfil this final promise, Schopenhauer must try to explain precisely how it is that compassion is related to morality. Why is it that compassion, and compassion alone, is morally valuable? What is wrong with egoism, especially if its unrestrained expression is harnessed by a social contract in a system of laws by which violence and aggression are sublimated for the better good of the commonwealth? If egoism is such a powerful motivation to action, should we not rather see it as a source of moral good? Is it not the case that most if not all of the substantive benefits accruing to a society ultimately derive from individuals pursuing their own interests in a way that has the indirect effect of making life better for others? Schopenhauer proposes to prove the dependence of morality on compassion in the essay by explaining the concepts of moral right and wrong.

Moral right and wrong

The next step for Schopenhauer is to give substance to moral value and moral judgement. He proceeds by recalling his "supreme principle of ethics", that we are not to injure others, but on the contrary to try to help them in practice to whatever extent we can. He has not tried to justify the principle, but indicates only that he has previously "laid down the rule".

Schopenhauer acknowledges two parts, positive and negative, into which the rule divides, and accordingly divides up the discussion of moral right and moral wrong into the same two moments:

> I now turn to the derivation of actions of genuine moral worth from
> the source already indicated [compassion]. In the previous section
> I laid down the rule as the universal maxim of such actions and
> consequently as the supreme principle of ethics: *Neminem laede;*
> *imo omnes, quantum potes, juva.* As this maxim contains *two*
> clauses, the actions that correspond to them automatically fall into
> two classes.   (BM: 147)

We can expect that Schopenhauer will find it morally wrong to injure others and morally right to help others as much as possible. What remains to be seen is why he wants to make these identifications in the analyses he proposes and in his defence of what it is he believes constitutes moral right and wrong.

Schopenhauer gives an account of the concept of moral wrong in *The World as Will and Representation*, which he presupposes in *On the Basis of Morality*. The idea is that an egoistic action that thwarts another individual's pursuit of his or her interests is morally objectionable. It is morally wrong

because it takes away from someone something that belongs most personally to them. Schopenhauer says that such actions by a wrongdoer in effect
deprive an individual of the body's "powers" for the sake of increasing the
wrongdoer's own body powers proportionately without compensation for
something that had belonged to the victim. It is not difficult to see what he
means by taking away another's body powers for the sake of one's own
benefit, or why he construes it as something that is morally wrong. In terms
of his transcendental idealism, Schopenhauer regards egoistic action against
another person as the wrongdoer's affirming his or her own will while
denying the will of the other. We must nevertheless ask why any of this is
supposed to be morally wrong, when Schopenhauer maintains that:

> The will of the first breaks through the boundary of another's
> affirmation of will, since the individual either destroys or injures this
> other body itself, or compels the powers of that other body to serve
> *his* will, instead of serving the will that appears in that other body.
> Thus if from the will, appearing as the body of another, he takes away
> the powers of this body, and thereby increases the power serving *his*
> will beyond that of his own body, he in consequence affirms his own
> will beyond his own body by denying the will that appears in the body
> of another. This breaking through the boundary of another's affir-
> mation of will has at all times been distinctly recognized, and its
> concept has been denoted by the word *wrong* (*Unrecht*). For both
> parties instantly recognize the fact, not indeed as we do here in
> distinct abstraction, but as feeling.   (WWR 1: 334)

The closest Schopenhauer comes to explaining the judgement that it is
wrong to act egoistically against the interests of another sentient being,
denying that individual's will to life at the same time and to the same extent
that we amplify our own, is that this is simply what we call moral wrong-
doing. We can say more charitably with respect to his attempt to clarify these
concepts that his theory stands or falls holistically in so far as it seems to shed
light on the ideas and language used to describe moral and immoral conduct.
Schopenhauer might reply that this is all we can expect of any moral
philosophy, and that his analysis in particular has the virtue of fitting com-
patibly into a much larger system of metaphysics and epistemology of the
world as representation and thing-in-itself. Ultimately, it seems, Schopenhauer understands moral wrong as the causing of pain. He further interprets
any egoistic action, enhancing one's own will to life at the expense of that
of another, as causing pain (WWR 1: 334–5, 339).

The descriptive nature of Schopenhauer's ethics is clear in his admission
that he has derived the fundamental principle of his moral philosophy not

to injure others but to try to help them as much as possible. This is perfectly justified contextually if his purpose throughout is to account for how people think and talk about moral values, which in turn agrees with his criticism of the *a priori* goals of Kant's theoretical ethics (WWR 1: 272). If moral philosophy is supposed to take its starting-point from empirical evidence, from moral reasoning, judgement and practice, as it actually occurs, then Schopenhauer's method of trying to justify what is morally wrong about egoistic behaviour and what is morally right about compassionate behaviour has much to recommend it, even if counter-considerations should finally countermand his conclusions in the court of philosophical criticism (WWR 1: 362–3).

Schopenhauer considers the negative part of his fundamental moral principle in "The Virtue of Justice", *On the Basis of Morality* §17, and the positive part in "The Virtue of Loving-Kindness", §18. "[T]he maxim, *Neminem laede*", he begins, "arises in noble dispositions from the knowledge, gained once for all, of the suffering which every unjust action necessarily brings to others and which is intensified by the feeling of enduring wrong, that is, of someone else's superior strength" (BM: 150). Thus far, Schopenhauer recapitulates his discussion of moral wrong in *The World as Will and Representation*. He now adds the negative concept of a moral right, which is the right not to be injured by another: "Rational reflection", he continues, "raises noble dispositions to the firm resolution, grasped once for all, of respecting the rights of everyone, of never allowing themselves to encroach on them, of keeping themselves free from the self-reproach of being the cause of another's suffering" (BM: 150).

The concept of a moral right is the right not to have others interfere with one's individual will to life. We can almost imagine persons having a kind of sphere of personal space surrounding them, metaphorically speaking, which others cannot penetrate without causing suffering and pain. It is significant that Schopenhauer believes that the concept of another individual's right not to have their will to life infringed upon by others can and should be "grasped once for all". We either understand that others have such a right, or we do not. This is not the kind of thing we need to learn gradually over time through a number of different encounters, but the kind that we can be expected to intuit as something any other person is due. We might possibly do so through a feeling similar to compassion. We extend the same right not to have pain and suffering imposed on others by our actions that we believe ourselves to deserve as a result of what we find objectionable about surrendering any part of our needs or wants in order for others to enhance their own will to life at our expense.

What is fascinating about Schopenhauer's analysis of the concept of moral wrong and the right to avoid injury from others is the extent to which it reinforces his abiding moral pessimism. Schopenhauer sees pain and suffering as something extremely negative. It is the basis of all moral wrong and moral badness in the behaviour of moral agents. Most philosophers would probably agree. Schopenhauer is unique among other thinkers in that he regards the reality of the world, thing-in-itself, as the insatiably hungry Will that through its objectifications in the world as representation is the source of all suffering. Suffering is bad. Causing others to suffer is morally wrong. All persons have a moral right not to have suffering imposed upon them egoistically by others trying to improve their own situation and gratify their will to life. It is the world itself, the reality that transcends the phenomenal appearances of things, that is the non-causal basis for all suffering. We cannot simply connect the dots in Schopenhauer's moral philosophy by concluding that the hungry Will as thing-in-itself is morally bad or morally wrong. Thing-in-itself does not cause anything to happen, nor is the Will motivated egoistically or in any other way to produce suffering in the world. We cannot intelligibly blame the world for the suffering it contains, even though it is its character to objectify itself in such a way that pain and suffering are inevitable. We can nevertheless agree that for Schopenhauer the moral pessimism he admits makes the world as representation the dismal theatre of suffering. It is only the noblest moral natures who, through altruistic acts of compassion in their actions toward others, rise above their own interests and desires in order to alleviate suffering, while defending others against moral wrongs that threaten to be perpetrated by third parties (BM: 152–3).

The positive part of Schopenhauer's fundamental moral principle concerns compassion toward others, and enjoins us to help others to whatever extent we can. We are not required by the principle to sacrifice our own interests for the sake of others, but only to help them when, where and to whatever degree is reasonable. Schopenhauer explicitly links this part of his principle to the Asian philosophical religions whose metaphysical tenets he admires. The connection between intuited idealisms concerning the nature of the world and a compassionate attitude in morality cannot be accidental. It stems from a common tacit recognition that the nature of the world beyond the reality-shrouding veil of Maya makes all persons in reality one and the same. It implies that we as psychologically individual thinkers are no different from any other suffering beings on this planet. In reality, we are all indistinguishable objectifications of the same Will as the one and only thing-in-itself. When I look at someone suffering in pain, Schopenhauer maintains, in agreement with the moral stance of Christians, Buddhists and Hindus, I am really looking at myself. Schopenhauer now turns from questions of justice, covered by the first half of his fundamental moral principle, to questions of compassion and loving kindness.[4]

The positive doctrine of Schopenhauer's fundamental moral principle supports many of the ethical duties and obligations that have traditionally been promoted by religions and the practical wisdom of family and civic values. "Thus in that direct participation," he reports, "resting on and requiring no arguments, is to be found the only true origin of loving-kindness, *caritus*, αγαπη [*agape*], in other words, that virtue whose maxim is *Omnes, quantum potes, juva*" (BM: 163). All moral duties to others can be traced to compassion. It is only through compassion that actions respecting moral rights in acts of justice or benefiting others altruistically can possibly have moral value (BM: 167).[5]

Idealist metaphysics of compassion

Let us now consider Schopenhauer's reasoning concerning the metaphysics of compassion. How can people have compassion toward others? Schopenhauer asks: "how is it possible for a suffering which is not *mine* and does not touch *me* to become just as directly a motive as only my own normally does, and to move me to action?" (BM: 165). There is, admittedly, a problem here to be solved.

Schopenhauer cannot expect altruistic moral conduct, inspired by compassion, to be motivated in anything like the same way as egoistically gratifying actions. The difficulty is in understanding why the sufferings of another person should lead one to offer assistance, to help relieve their pain. In one's own case the explanation is obvious. We act in order to diminish our sufferings because we want to avoid pain. Why, however, should we devote any of our own precious time and treasure to help another person experiencing discomfort? "As I have said," Schopenhauer resumes, "only by the fact that although it is given to me merely as something external, merely by means of external intuitive perception or knowledge, I nevertheless *feel it with him, feel it as my own*, and yet not *within me*, but in *another person*" (BM: 165). Schopenhauer gestures toward a phenomenology of compassion. When we experience compassion we feel another person's suffering, not, so to speak, within our own skin, but perceptibly as though our sensations were extended to another's body. When we feel compassionately toward another person, this is what it can feel like. We may wince and look away, clutch at ourselves or undergo other kinds of visceral reactions, even though the pain is not physically within us. The desire to relieve such pain and suffering in another can therefore approximate even if it does not exactly duplicate the motivation to do so in the case of pain we are ourselves immediately suffering.

Schopenhauer remarks that for such an explanation to make sense there must be an identification between the compassionate person and the person in pain. "[T]his presupposes that to a certain extent I have identified myself with the other man, and in consequence the barrier between the ego and non-ego is for the moment abolished; only then do the other man's affairs, his need, distress, and suffering, directly become my own" (BM: 166). The identification of self and other must be such that the compassionate person understands at some level that the suffering of the person toward whom compassion is directed is only superficially another person. "I no longer look at him as if he were something given to me by empirical intuitive perception, as something strange and foreign, as a matter of indifference, as something entirely different from me", Schopenhauer says. "On the contrary, I share the suffering *in him*, in spite of the fact that his skin does not enclose my nerves. Only in this way can *his* woe, *his* distress, become a motive *for me*; otherwise it can be absolutely only my own" (BM 166). How, then, in the end, does the compassionate person literally make the sufferings of another person his or her own? Schopenhauer admits, as he must, given the limits of motivational explanation, that such behaviour is a mystery: "I repeat that this *occurrence is mysterious*, for it is something our faculty of reason can give no direct account of, and its grounds cannot be discovered on the path of experience" (BM: 166).

Schopenhauer opens the way for an idealist metaphysics of compassion. The basis of compassion is not empirically discoverable or explainable. It involves the transcendental identity of the unitary intelligible character of all willing subjects. Moral agents are spatiotemporally physically individuated one from another only phenomenally within the world as representation as distinct objectifications of Will. In reality, they are metaphysically numerically identical, the single unitary pure willing that is deep within every willing subject (BM: 166). The transcendental ground of Schopenhauer's metaphysics of compassion is indicated in these terms as essential for a complete moral philosophy (BM: 200). That there is a serious need for a metaphysics of compassion, and, more generally, for a metaphysical foundation of ethics, is recognized by Kant as well as Schopenhauer. Schopenhauer, in particular, disagreeing so radically with Kant with respect to the superstructure of morality, believes that without a properly transcendental metaphysics of morals we cannot explain compassion as the only morally valuable motivation for the two components of his most fundamental moral principle. The solution to the problem is indicated by Schopenhauer as the metaphysical identity or shared intelligible character of both compassionate and suffering individuals (BM: 205–6).

Advancing from mere possibility to the conclusion that all thinking willing subjects are actually identical, Schopenhauer argues that the compassionate moral agent and the suffering person whose pain is to be relieved, or whose moral right to justice is respected by the only morally valuable motivation for any action, are in reality identical.

> This doctrine teaches that all plurality is only apparent; that in all the individuals of this world, however infinite the number in which they exhibit themselves successively and simultaneously, there is yet manifested only one and the same truly existing essence, present and identical in all of them. (BM: 207)

Schopenhauer maintains:

> Accordingly, if plurality and separateness belong only to the *phenomenon*, and if it is one and the same essence that manifests itself in all living things, then that conception that abolishes the difference between ego and non-ego is not erroneous; but on the contrary, the opposite conception must be. We find also that this latter conception is described by the Hindus as *Maya*, i.e., illusion, deception, phantasm, mirage. It is the former view which we found to be the basis of the phenomenon of compassion; in fact, compassion is the proper expression of that view. Accordingly, it would be the metaphysical basis of ethics and consist in *one* individual's again recognizing in *another* his own self, his own true inner nature.
> (BM: 209)

The question remains why Schopenhauer's mystical solution to the metaphysics of compassion is not after all egoistic. When I witness the sufferings of another person I am in a sense really seeing myself in pain, in the sense that I recognize however implicitly in another human body the objectification of the same thing-in-itself as Will or intelligible character that every willing subject, myself included, embodies at bottom, transcending every willing subject alike. If that is why I am inclined at my own expense in time and trouble to help another individual, why is my motivation in that case not also at least a disguised form of egoism? The answer is that for Schopenhauer the word "ego" does not apply to the intelligible character or thing-in-itself, but only to the superficial phenomenal psychological willing subject also known as the empirical or acquired character, the self, soul or person, with which we associate our individual personalities. If this is ego for Schopenhauer, then his metaphysics of compassion as a moral motivation for helping others in need clearly transcends egoism, just as the intelligible character of every willing subject, the one and only Will as thing-in-itself, transcends the phenomenal psychological or phenomenological ego.[6]

230

Ethics Prize decision

The Danish Royal Society did not award its prize to Schopenhauer, even though his essay was the only submission. Their reasons are sociologically rather than philosophically interesting, but are an important part of Schopenhauer's intellectual biography. The essay is so skilfully composed and carefully argued that it is hard to see how the Danish committee could have rejected it on purely objective grounds.

What they officially maintain is that Schopenhauer fails to deliver what the essay topic requires, while offering instead more in the essay's final section than entrants were asked to write about in expounding the relation between ethics and metaphysics. The unknown judges dispute the relevance of what Schopenhauer has to say about the origin of ethics as originating in compassion rather than as belonging immediately to conscience or consciousness. It is clear, however, that Schopenhauer's essay taken as a whole directly answers the essay question, holding that morality owes its basic principles to conscience in the sense of compassion as the feeling we may have for the pain and suffering of others. We have seen that Schopenhauer mentions both conscience and consciousness, and that his excursion into the metaphysics of compassion is meant to prove that superficial psychological considerations of consciousness and conscience alone are not adequate for the philosophical foundations of morals.

The committee seems to have objected that Schopenhauer, in developing his own systematic principles of ethics, skirts the essay question rather than addressing it directly. This is an uncharitable interpretation of what Schopenhauer sets out to do in the essay. Without stretching things, his purpose can just as easily be understood as providing the necessary context for claiming that the foundations of morals in one sense belong to phenomenal consciousness and conscience in the form of compassion, while in yet another sense the foundations of morals transcend empirical psychology. The complete grounding of ethics in the metaphysics of Will as thing-in-itself identifies the intelligible character that willing subjects share in common, by virtue of which all individuals in reality are identical. It further recognizes that compassion, while mysterious, can be intuitively understood as one's own personal suffering that only appears superficially to be distributed in different physical bodies in different places in space and time. These aspects of Schopenhauer's essay are not superfluous, but immediately relevant to what could and perhaps should have seemed a legitimate effort directly to answer the prize essay question.

The report of the committee states:

> For by omitting what had been asked first and foremost, [the author, Schopenhauer] thought it was a question of laying down some

principles of ethics. Therefore that part of the essay in which he discusses the connection between the ethical principle laid down by him and his metaphysics has been expounded by him only in an appendix. Here he submitted more than had been required, whereas the theme had asked for just such an investigation in which, first and foremost, the connection between metaphysics and ethics would be clearly discussed.   (BM: 216)

The essay question, however, says nothing whatsoever about metaphysics, but mentions only consciousness and conscience. It leaves open to the author whether or not in answering that part of the question in the negative it is appropriate to offer an account that in principle might but need not delve into metaphysics in order to uncover the theoretical basis of morals. The committee complains that: "when the author attempts to show that compassion is the foundation of morality, he has not satisfied us by the form of his essay, nor has he in point of fact shown that this foundation is adequate" (BM: 216). If the committee was never looking for moral principles in the first place, but limited the essay question to the problem of the psychological origins of morality, how can they object that Schopenhauer fails to provide them? They add that: "On the contrary, he saw himself obliged even to admit the very opposite" (BM: 216). Again, Schopenhauer by no means hesitates to proclaim his fundamental principle of ethics adequate. He thinks that he has correctly formulated the only possible basis of morality in the two-part requirement of justice by which all willing subjects are morally obligated not to injure others, and to show mercy and loving kindness in trying to alleviate their suffering. He acknowledges that compassion is mysterious, but this is only because according to his theory it cannot be empirically motivated. He believes that the transcendental ground of morality in the identity of the compassionate and suffering individual is thoroughly upheld by his transcendental idealism and doctrine of Will as thing-in-itself.

It is in their parting comment that the committee seems to give away its real reason for withholding the prize from Schopenhauer's essay. "Finally," they say, almost offhandedly, "we cannot pass over in silence the fact that several distinguished philosophers of recent times are mentioned in a manner so unseemly as to cause just and grave offense" (BM: 216). Here we may have a better clue as to the prize committee's decision. Hegel, Fichte and Schelling are criticized by Schopenhauer at different points in the essay with his usual vitriolic scorn. He cannot help indulging his bad humour concerning these rival exponents of post-Kantian idealism with whom he is so diametrically opposed, and whose writings in philosophy he thinks are so utterly confused as to be fraudulent. Moreover, he is envious of the attention and accolades they have received, especially from the popular press. We may naturally wonder why the committee should have taken such offence at Schopenhauer's castigating especially recent philosophers, as opposed to his lengthy diatribe against Kant's ethics. What difference can it possibly make whether Schopenhauer has attacked recent as opposed to long-deceased philosophers, unless he has thereby ruffled the feathers of some of the followers of these post-Kantian thinkers active at the time in Denmark or recruited to serve on the committee? Even if Schopenhauer has gone over the top in embroidering his criticisms with indelicate polemics, one might reply that the committee's purpose should have been to evaluate the truth and strength of Schopenhauer's objections, rather than reacting to the admittedly unscientific animus with which he sometimes criticizes his opponents. The committee no doubt believed that it would be inappropriate to sanction what they perceived as Schopenhauer's uncivil pronouncements about these well-respected ideologues by awarding him the prize, thereby lending his acid criticisms of these figures their implicit approval.

It is possible to dismiss the committee's rejection of Schopenhauer's submission to the contest as philosophically incompetent or academically political. Schopenhauer's discussion of theoretical ethics and its practical applications as based on compassion constitute a cogent, even brilliant, original answer to the prize essay question. In lieu of another more successful submitted contribution, it seems only reasonable, regardless of whether we agree or disagree with Schopenhauer's moral philosophy, that his essay should have won the prize. Undeterred by the essay's rejection, Schopenhauer soon published it together with his winning entry for the Norwegian Royal Society's previous year's competition. He includes a statement of the Danish Society's justification for their verdict for readers to judge the merits of the decision for themselves. He also attaches a lengthy preface in which he discusses the scandal and replies in detail to the committee's conclusion that he had spoken in an unseemly fashion of recent philosophers in such a way as to give "grave offense". The incident provides yet another example of Schopenhauer's ill-considered invective delivered against his philosophical adversaries without concern for its possible repercussions. As such, the episode constitutes another set piece in Schopenhauer's biography to be placed alongside his decision to hold his lectures at the same time as Hegel's. It reflects an unflappable conviction that when he believes himself philosophically in the right, nothing else matters. He thinks it is worth any risk to test the waters as dramatically as possible for the sake of achieving a possible stunning victory over his ideological opponents. At best, through such puerile tokens of disapproval, Schopenhauer might have hoped to win a minor Pyrric victory over his adversaries. In the end, he was repeatedly denied even that sort of trophy during his lifetime.

CHAPTER EIGHT

Schopenhauer's legacy in the philosophy of Nietzsche, Heidegger and the early Wittgenstein

Not to my contemporaries or my compatriots, but to mankind I consign my now complete work, confident that it will not be without value to humanity, even if this value should be recognized only tardily, as is the inevitable fate of the good in whatever form ... Accordingly, as the history of literature testifies throughout, every-thing of value needs a long time to gain authority ...

(WWR 1: xviii)

Years of neglect and posthumous triumph

To his dismay, Schopenhauer's philosophy was largely neglected during his lifetime. He did not obtain serious recognition for his ideas until relatively late in his career, and then only from a few enthusiastic but relatively uninfluential thinkers. His books were not well received and sold only a few copies, they were seldom and then almost always indifferently or unsympa-thetically reviewed, and they went out of print without his knowledge or permission. The scant recognition he finally began to receive toward the end of his life was not enough, and not timely enough, to satisfy him. Schopen-hauer should have recognized in this situation precisely the kind of sufferings of will that his own metaphysics entailed, and it is conceivable that he may have appreciated the irony.[1]

While Schopenhauer writes that he is not interested in popular acclaim, that he is in pursuit of truth rather than fame, the very opposite of the lionized heroes of philosophy in his day, Hegel, Fichte and Schelling, there is no doubt that he was disappointed by the lack of any meaningful recognition. However unknown he remained during his life, the first signs of interest in his work that began to emerge in his twilight years were

234

indications of a tsunami that began to sweep the artistic, literary and philosophical worlds of Europe, where Schopenhauer's thought was about to exert an enormous, powerful and long-lasting influence. Schopenhauer's aesthetics in particular was important in shaping attitudes toward art that guided Romantic and Symbolist movements in painting and poetry. His metaphysics of music had a powerful impact on many musicians, especially Richard Wagner, who considered himself a Schopenhauerian and sought to compose music to immediately objectify Will.[2]

If we were simply to list the important thinkers, writers, musicians and artists who owe an intellectual or inspirational debt to Schopenhauer from the end of the nineteenth century through the twentieth century to the present, we would need to mention at least such figures as Nietzsche, Sigmund Freud, Martin Heidegger, Wittgenstein, Wagner, Leo Tolstoy, Anton Chekov, Ivan Turgenev, Guy de Maupassant, Thomas Hardy, Émile Zola, Edgar Allan Poe, Charles Baudelaire, Joseph Conrad, Eugene Delacroix, Thomas Mann, Gustav Mahler, Marcel Proust, Rainer Maria Rilke, Thomas Bernhard, Odilon Redon, Gustave Moreau, Maurice Denis, Luigi Pirandello, Felix Feneon, Gustav Kahn, J. K. Huysmans, William Butler Yeats, Max Horkheimer, Samuel Beckett, T. S. Eliot, Somerset Maugham, Jorge Luis Borges, and directly or more or less indirectly everyone influenced in turn by them, including the burgeoning industry of professional Schopenhauer scholarship that flourishes today.[3]

We get a sense of the way in which Schopenhauer's moral pessimism struck a chord with several generations of poets and novelists by considering the Portuguese writer Fernando Pessoa's enigmatic collection of vignettes, the *Livro do Desassossego* [*The Book of Disquiet*], discovered in manuscript scribbled on scraps of paper in a trunk after his death in 1935. Pessoa's name is not often mentioned in connection with Schopenhauer's idealism, but the similarities between so many of his passages and Schopenhauer's reflections on the human condition are too striking to be coincidental. This is true despite or perhaps as further evidence of the fact that Pessoa says repeatedly that he is not pessimistic, merely "sad". In the first long part of the book, "A Factless Autobiography", offered under the assumed name of one of his numerous imaginary literary personae, Bernardo Soares, an assistant bookkeeper in a Lisbon fabric company, Pessoa writes:

> The way I see it, plagues, storms and wars are products of the same blind force, sometimes operating through unconscious microbes, sometimes through unconscious waters and thunderbolts, and sometimes through unconscious men. For me, the difference between an earthquake and a massacre is like the difference between murdering with a knife and murdering with a dagger. The monster immanent in

things, for the sake of his own good or his own evil, which are apparently indifferent to him, is equally served by the shifting of a rock on a hilltop or by the stirring of envy or greed in a heart. The rock falls and kills a man; greed or envy prompts an arm, and the arm kills a man. Such is the world – a dunghill of instinctive forces that nevertheless shines in the sun with pale shades of light and dark gold.

To oppose the brutal indifference that constitutes the manifest essence of things, the mystics discovered it was best to renounce. To deny the world, to turn our backs on it as on a swamp at whose edge we suddenly find ourselves standing. To deny, like the Buddha, its absolute reality; to deny, like Christ, its relative reality; to deny . . .[4]

In music, literature and the arts, Schopenhauer's ideas found an exceptionally receptive audience and fertile ground for expression. The process was painfully slow during Schopenhauer's lifetime, and non-philosophers, who are seldom trained in the methods of rigorous argumentation, inevitably found what they wanted and were predisposed selectively to find among Schopenhauer's ideas. Often they focused exclusively on the aesthetics and analysis of human nature in Schopenhauer with which many persons especially of artistic temperament can readily identify. They frequently fastened onto these implications independently of the epistemic and metaphysical foundations of Schopenhauer's transcendental idealism, without which his ethics and aesthetics cannot be fully understood and appreciated. The idea of Will as thing-in-itself is often confused in many of these Schopenhauerian traditions with the phenomenal will or will to life, rather than as the Kantian thing-in-itself.

What, then, of the philosophers who read and came to be influenced by Schopenhauer? There are many such thinkers who were capable of grasping the complexities of Schopenhauer's writings and were shaped in their own philosophical contributions by his ideas. For the sake of convenience, we shall concentrate on three of the most important: Nietzsche, Heidegger and Wittgenstein.

Nietzsche's critique of Schopenhauer

The story of Nietzsche's introduction to Schopenhauer's philosophy typifies the thinker's unpopularity at the time. Because Schopenhauer's books were not taught in the universities, anyone who became interested in his thought had to stumble upon it accidentally. This is what happened to Nietzsche. He was serving in the Prussian cavalry and had fallen from his horse, hurting his leg. While recuperating, he found the two volumes of the second edition of Schopenhauer's *The World as Will and Representation* at a used book stand, and, purely out of curiosity, bought them to read and pass the time.[5]

What occurred at first was a rapid and enthusiastic conversion to Schopenhauer's philosophy in Nietzsche's mind. He describes the awakening he experienced as one in which Schopenhauer had suddenly revealed the true nature of the world and provided a set of concepts in terms of which for the first time he could see behind the surface of phenomena to understand every aspect of existence. Nietzsche was particularly impressed with Schopenhauer's account of the nature of human life and the significance of art. With his prior interests in classical literature and aesthetics, it was this component of Schopenhauer's thought that had the greatest impact on Nietzsche. For some time thereafter, Nietzsche apparently considered himself to be a Schopenhauerian. The effect lasted at least until the 1872 publication of his first book, *The Birth of Tragedy*, a predominantly Schopenhauerian account of the origins of tragedy in classical Greece. By 1887, when he came to write *On the Genealogy of Morality*, Nietzsche had completely reversed his devotion to Schopenhauer. He then began to describe Schopenhauer as his spiritual "antipode", and continued a kind of love–hate relationship with Schopenhauer's ideas throughout the period of his philosophical activity.[6]

The Birth of Tragedy relates the origin of tragedy to music, and the origin of music in turn to a Dionysian expression of desire interpreted roughly along the lines of a Schopenhauerian conception of Will. Nietzsche identifies two trends in Western culture, mythologized as the spirit of Apollo, the ancient Greek god of reason, calculation, moderation and planning, and also of music, in contrast with that of Dionysus, god of wine and sexual frenzy. Later in his philosophy, after he had abandoned his fondness for Schopenhauer, Nietzsche reconciles and finds polytheistic accommodation for both Apollo and Dionysus in the pantheon of art. In *The Birth of Tragedy*, he sees these two forces as fundamentally opposed, and throws in his preference for that side of human nature represented by Dionysus, representing the forces of emotion and desire, rather than the Apollonian restraint of intellect. He associates the Apollonian strain he wants to see subordinated in art with the rationalist philosophy of Socrates, who in Plato's dialogue the *Republic* argues that justice is a state of the individual soul in which reason prevails over spiritedness and the carnal appetites.

In his early writings, Nietzsche believes that the fine arts flourish only when cold Apollonian reason is superseded by hot-blooded Dionysian passion. "Music and tragic myth", Nietzsche explains, near the end of *The Birth of Tragedy*:

are equally expressive of the Dionysiac talent of a nation and cannot be divorced from one another. Both have their origin in a realm of art which is beyond the Apollonian; both shed their transfiguring light on a region in whose rapt harmony dissonance and the horror of existence fade away in enchantment.[7]

"Thus," Nietzsche adds, "the Dionysiac element, as against the Apollonian, proves itself to be the eternal and original power of art, since it calls into being the entire world of phenomena".[8] Here we clearly see in Nietzsche's study the elements of a modified Schopenhauerian metaphysics and philosophy of art. Schopenhauer had similarly distinguished between intuition and abstract knowledge, which in some ways maps directly onto Nietzsche's exaggerated emphases on these characteristics personified respectively by Dionysus and Apollo. Schopenhauer anticipates Nietzsche's portrayal of the aesthetic attitude toward the sublime as one in which the audience suspends concern for the will to life, or, as Nietzsche prefers more flamboyantly and with a significant shift of emphasis to say, experiences "the horror of existence".

Nietzsche reports his indebtedness to Schopenhauer's aesthetics more explicitly earlier in the text, when he maintains, "In accordance with Schopenhauer's doctrine, we interpret music as the immediate language of the will, and our imaginations are stimulated to embody that immaterial world, which speaks to us with lively motion and yet remains invisible."[9] We find Schopenhauer's technical philosophical terminology scattered throughout Nietzsche's *Birth of Tragedy*, for example, when Nietzsche writes: "Apollo embodies the transcendental genius of the *principium individuationis*; through him alone is it possible to achieve redemption in illusion. The mystical jubilation of Dionysos, on the other hand, breaks the spell of individuation and opens a path to the maternal womb of being".[10] He embellishes the same point in adding:

> Among the great thinkers there is only one who has fully realized the immense discrepancy between the plastic Apollonian art and the Dionysiac art of music. Independently of Greek religious symbols, Schopenhauer assigned to music a totally different character and origin from all the other arts, because it does not, like all the others, represent appearance, but the will directly. It is the metaphysical complement to everything that is physical in the world; the thing-in-itself where all else is appearance (*The World as Will and Idea*, I).[11]

In *The Birth of Tragedy*, Nietzsche even manages to put in a sympathetic word for Buddhism, when he theorizes that:

Apollo, the founder of states, is also the genius of the *principium individuationis*, and neither commonwealth nor patriotism can subsist without an affirmation of individuality. The only path from orgiastic rites, for a nation, leads to Buddhism, which, given its desire for Nirvana, requires those rare moments of paroxysm that lift man beyond the confines of space, time, and individuation. These paroxysms, in turn, require a philosophy which teaches how the drab intermediate phases can be triumphed over with the aid of the imagination.[12]

How different things were soon to become. In a few years Nietzsche made a dramatic turn away from every part of Schopenhauer's philosophy. The rejection of Schopenhauer seems to have come about near the end of 1876, as documented by a letter he wrote in that year to Richard and Cosima Wagner. Thereafter, Nietzsche criticizes and distances himself increasingly from Schopenhauer, beginning with his next book, *Human, All Too Human* (1878–80), and proceeding through his middle-period writings, *Daybreak* (1881), *The Joyful Science* (1882), *Beyond Good and Evil* (1886), and finally to the *Genealogy*.

A most valuable resource for investigating Nietzsche's complex relation to Schopenhauer, what he borrowed from Schopenhauer's thought and how he later came to reject all he had learned, is Christopher Janaway's collection, *Willing and Nothingness: Schopenhauer as Nietzsche's Educator* (1998). Of special interest is the book's opening essay by Janaway, "Schopenhauer as Nietzsche's Educator" and the Appendices, including Janaway's translation of Nietzsche's 1868 essay, "On Schopenhauer", and list of "Nietzsche's References to Schopenhauer", culled from all of Nietzsche's writings. In his introduction to the volume, Janaway asks:

> How much of Nietzsche's thought is shaped by the effort to rid himself of Schopenhauerianism, and how much is the persistence of Schopenhauerian elements in disguise? A collection of pieces addressing such questions is timely, given that many discussions of Nietzsche these days make only glancing reference to Schopenhauer – which is, at best, *Hamlet* without the Ghost.[13]

Popular philosophical discussions of Nietzsche in recent years have proceeded largely in a vacuum because they have not paid sufficient heed to the Schopenhauerian background of Nietzsche's thought. They have tended to downplay or simply ignore both the period when Nietzsche considered himself a follower of Schopenhauer, and later when he decided that Schopenhauer was pointing humanity in an altogether wrong direction.[14]

Nietzsche characterizes what has become a non-Schopenhaurian quest in the *Genealogy* as one of investigating the "value of morality". Put this way, the problem presupposes that morality itself is identifiable. We know what morality is, and the question is only what value it has or how we are to think of it. Nietzsche's project is remarkable for daring to ask whether what passes for morality is in another possibly higher sense truly or genuinely moral. He wants to know whether the morality that he finds preached and practised by others around him, the conventional ethics that informs the lives and attitudes, decisions and actions of the surrounding culture, has any authentic moral value, and if so, what that value is and what it means. He specifically mentions Schopenhauer's philosophy in this connection, citing his influence:

> The issue for me was the *value* of morality – and over this I had to struggle almost solely with my great teacher Schopenhauer, to whom that book, the passion and the secret contradiction of that book, is directed, as if to a contemporary (– for that book, too, was a "polemic"). In particular the issue was the value of the unegoistic, of the instincts of compassion, self-denial, self-sacrifice, precisely the instincts that Schopenhauer had gilded, deified, and made otherworldly until finally they alone were left for him as the "values in themselves," on the basis of which he *said "no"* to life, also to himself.[15]

Nietzsche says that he struggled with Schopenhauer's ideas. This is not, presumably, because they were so difficult to grasp, but because for a time he had fallen under Schopenhauer's sway, and had to make an effort to free himself from his impact as he later found himself rebelling. He expresses a high degree of passion in his ambivalence and finally antipathy toward Schopenhauer's thought.

Eventually, Nietzsche came to recognize something profoundly unacceptable pervading Schopenhauer's philosophical outlook. Schopenhauer and the mature Nietzsche are polar opposites in their philosophical approaches to ethics and the meaning of life. Nietzsche is so repulsed by Schopenhauer's philosophy, despite its initial attraction, that he finds it natural to go further and further in a direction diametrically opposed to Schopenhauer's views.

We can summarize the difference that eventually emerges between Nietzsche and Schopenhauer in Nietzsche's own terms as one in which Nietzsche says "yes" where Schopenhauer says "no" to life. For reasons we have now considered, Nietzsche rightly interprets Schopenhauer as espousing a life-denying philosophy that Nietzsche came to see as intellectually and morally unhealthy. He proposes to counter Schopenhauer's nihilism with a more life-affirming philosophical outlook. It is clear from what little Nietzsche relates in the passage that Schopenhauer's saying "no" to life is based on the ethics of self-denial and self-sacrifice, which Schopenhauer, according to Nietzsche, regarded as pure moral values, values in themselves. Nietzsche, on the contrary, identifies any self-limiting attitudes as life-denying.

Nietzsche increasingly denounces Schopenhauer's "morality of compassion". This is a significant objection for Nietzsche to make, since the conventional morality that is reflected even in Schopenhauer's ethical system understands compassion as the foundation of moral judgement and conduct. Nietzsche insists that the opposite is true, that compassion for others is life-denying, and that it leads finally to a nihilistic embrace of nothingness. He protests:

> But against precisely *these* instincts there spoke from within me an ever more fundamental suspicion, an ever deeper-delving skepticism! Precisely here I saw the *great* danger to humanity, its most sublime lure and temptation – and into what? into nothingness? – precisely here I saw the beginning of the end, the standstill, the backward-glancing tiredness, the will turning *against* life, the last sickness gently and melancholically announcing itself: I understood the ever more widely spreading morality of compassion – which seized even the philosophers and made them sick – as the most uncanny symptom of our now uncanny European culture, as its detour to a new Buddhism? to a Buddhism for Europeans? to – *nihilism?*[16]

Nietzsche characterizes the affirmation of compassion in popular sentiment and in Schopenhauer's moral philosophy as a kind of European Buddhism. One of the world's most widely respected religions, Buddhism is known for its emphasis on moral compassion for all living things. Nietzsche speaks of a Buddhism for Europeans, by which he derides the morality of compassion that he believes has taken hold of European ethics. It is reasonable to suppose that Nietzsche is thinking also and perhaps more specifically of Christianity, another major world religion that stresses compassion, exemplifying the modern European "Buddhist" morality he rejects as inimical to the full development of human potential.

He also objects to the Buddhist ideal of achieving nirvana. The state of nirvana is one of total annihilation, of quieting all desire and exiting from the wheel of dharma or endless cycle of birth, death and rebirth. Nietzsche reacts violently to this ego-less self-denying religious concept as the desire for nothingness he denounces as nihilistic. He does not assume that the

Europeans of his day are literally converting to Buddhism, although some of them then just as today were no doubt attracted to its principles and practices. He complains that through the influence of self-denying compassion, moral thinkers like Schopenhauer have created an objectionable intellectual climate, whose continued proliferation he hopes to reverse, and which he describes as Buddhism rhetorically as a way of registering his strong disapproval.

In keeping with the avowed purpose of his project as a polemic, indicated in the book's subtitle, Nietzsche reviles compassion, maintaining a steady barrage of complaints against it as life-denying. The defenders of a compassionate morality are likely to reply that feeling compassion and acting from compassionate motives toward less fortunate individuals are life-affirming rather than life-denying, and that caring for others also enhances one's own life. If Nietzsche is to raise a convincing criticism of moral compassion, he needs to make a powerful case against the popular conception that sees compassion as an ethical virtue. He proposes to do so, and he has no hesitation in identifying the feeling of compassion for others as a symptom of what he finds objectionable in conventional morality. Caring for others and their welfare, being moved emotionally by their suffering, and trying to help them, oddly enough, Nietzsche regards as tantamount to a self-denying embrace of nothingness. Why should this be so?

Nietzsche understands moral compassion as a relatively new development in European philosophy. He insinuates that it is an aberration that does not reflect the underlying spirit of European morality. He suggests that to resist compassion is not contrary to the real moral orientation of Western philosophy, but rather a return to its true nature. It is probably for this reason also that he labels moral compassion in non-Western terms as a grafting of Asian religion onto European stock. He now explains:

> For this preferential treatment and overestimation of compassion on the part of modern philosophers is something new: until this point philosophers had agreed precisely on the *worthlessness* of compassion. I name only Plato, Spinoza, La Rochefoucauld, and Kant, four spirits as different from each other as possible, but united on one point: their low regard for compassion.[17]

The rationalist philosophers Nietzsche names on the whole do in fact consider reason to be more important in moral theory than compassion. They emphasize logic, the analysis of concepts and practical reasoning over feeling, and generally consider compassion to be inessential to morality. This is clear especially in Kant, who discounts emotion, along with inclination and desire, as morally irrelevant and inimical to autonomy. What constitutes moral duty for Kant is the categorical imperative, a principle of pure reason, rather than the psychological factor of whether or not an agent feels sorry for other people and wants to do something to help them. If compassion as an empirical psychological factor is permitted to influence moral decision-making, then, Kant believes, the moral agent will lack freedom in the sense of autonomy, and hence be deprived of moral responsibility. Schopenhauer, in contrast, as Nietzsche observes, regards compassion as the basis for morality and the only proper motivation for ethical behaviour, for putting into practice what a correct morality requires in theory.

Although Nietzsche is right to argue that rationalist philosophers downplay the role of such emotions as compassion in moral obligation, it is questionable whether it is accurate also to say that compassion is a particularly new development in European thought. If we think of European philosophy as heavily influenced by Christian theology, then it is a more difficult proposition to agree with Nietzsche that compassion is something new on the philosophical horizon in the Europe of his day. On the contrary, it might be historically more accurate to conclude that compassion is part of the very fibre of European morality, at least from the time of the late Roman Empire. What is new or old is a relative matter. It is worth noting that to the extent that Nietzsche regards a morality of compassion as a novelty in European thought, he is presumably thinking back almost two thousand years to a time before the rise of Christianity.

After struggling with and finally overcoming his initial infatuation over Schopenhauer's system, Nietzsche declares that Schopenhauer's philosophy must be rejected as detrimental to a healthy life-affirming outlook. Where compassion governs morality, individual will to power (*Wille zur Macht*) is denied and sacrificed for the sake of others, contributing ultimately to self-denial. Schopenhauer is the central figure in Nietzsche's critique of nihilistic European Buddhism. Nietzsche, for reasons we are now in a position to understand, criticizes Schopenhauer's philosophy precisely on these grounds. Schopenhauer would not be embarrassed in the least by this conclusion. He is fully confident that a correct philosophical account of the human condition ought to entail that life and the will to life are worthless except as something to be resisted and overcome for the sake of knowledge. Nietzsche for his part, on the other hand, thoroughly rejects Schopenhauer's metaphysics and moral philosophy, which he abominates as spiritually unwholesome. He is repelled by Schopenhauer's subjugation of the will in a very visceral way, at a deep level of intuition that precedes argument and signals fundamental irreconcilable differences in their respective outlooks on life.

After a powerful flirtation with Schopenhauerianism, Nietzsche comes to regard himself as anti-Schopenhauerian. He argues, not only in the *Genealogy*, but in all of his writings after this time, that Schopenhauer's denial of life, his exaltation of suffering and salvation, has had a deleterious effect not only on philosophy but on the course of human development. He believes that it is vital to resist the kinds of attitudes that inform Schopenhauer's idealism and moral pessimism for the good of the human species. It is only through unlimited reign of the individual will to power, Nietzsche's non-transcendentalist version of Schopenhauer's concept of the will to life, that Nietzsche believes our species can realize its full potential. To deny the will to life in Nietzsche's view is like keeping a sprouted acorn under a bushel so that it cannot receive the light it needs in order to thrive and grow into an oak tree. Denial and renunciation of the will to life, in effect of life itself, in Schopenhauer, is seen by Nietzsche as profoundly unhealthy because it is contrary to nature.

Regardless of how much he has learned from Schopenhauer, Nietzsche finally opposes him on virtually every key point of his philosophy. It is possible to object that in repudiating Schopenhauer's ethics and his rejection of the will to life even as the positive therapeutic effect of fine art, Nietzsche goes too far, swinging the pendulum as far as it can go in the opposite direction. He advocates giving full vent to the will to power for the sake of allowing human potential to flower without any restraint. The much-disputed break in relations between Nietzsche and Wagner, who lived together for a time and were in close intellectual sympathy and collaboration for eight years, is in large part a result of Nietzsche's mounting disaffection for Schopenhauer and Wagner's continuing commitment to the truth of Schopenhauer's philosophy. It is nevertheless significant testimony to the importance of Schopenhauer's later prestige years after his death that a thinker as passionate as Nietzsche should have found it necessary to take his bearings from Schopenhauer and criticize his ideas so vehemently in developing his own philosophy, as though one pole of a very powerful magnet had repelled another as far and as violently as possible in the opposite philosophical direction.[18]

Heidegger on *Da-sein, Sorge, Zuhandenheit, Gelassenheit*

Looking ahead from the late-nineteenth century to the middle of the twentieth century, Martin Heidegger is a more recent Schopenhauerian whose existentialist ontology bears many signs of Schopenhauer's influence. It is possible to interpret Heidegger's philosophy as a synthesis of the method of transcendental phenomenology developed by his teacher, Edmund Husserl, informed in a modified and distinctively Heideggerean language by what are still recognizably Schopenhauerian ideas concerning the philosophical meaning of human life.

Julian Young begins his essay "Schopenhauer, Heidegger, Art, and the Will" (1996), with the words:

> The question of the relationship between Schopenhauer and Heidegger has been, in English at least, virtually untouched. This is somewhat odd given the evident fact that Heidegger read Schopenhauer and the rather striking affinities between the two. No doubt this neglect has been encouraged by the fact that Heidegger's explicit references to Schopenhauer are, almost without exception, contemptuous.[19]

Young is right to cite the few and virtually unanimously derogatory references to Schopenhauer in Heidegger as a reason for the topic of their relationship having been so largely neglected in philosophical commentary on Heidegger. Another reason, in the same way that Janaway complains about the lack of appreciation of Schopenhauer's positive and negative influence on Nietzsche, is that contemporary scholars of Heidegger, as of Nietzsche for the most part, have not studied Schopenhauer in depth, and hence are unprepared to notice the most important of Schopenhauer's ideas reflected and transformed in the work of or reacted against by these more widely discussed thinkers.

In Heidegger's case, it is possible to trace back to Schopenhauer virtually all of the most distinctive concepts of *Da-sein* (human existence, literally being-there), *Sorge* (care or concern), *Zuhandenheit* (literally to-handed-ness, an attitude of seeing everything in the world as a raw material or tool for human use) and *Gelassenheit* (an attitude of leaving things alone, non-interference with what is found that could otherwise be put to use for human needs and wants). Protagoras, in the pre-Socratic world of ancient Greece, said that "Man is the measure of all things, of those that exist and those that do not exist". Heidegger seems to take this motto as his own for the phenomenology of existence that he undertakes to articulate in his 1927 masterwork, *Being and Time* (*Sein und Zeit*). As a student of Husserl, Heidegger argues that the only method of ontology is phenomenology. From this starting-point, he proposes to analyse the concept of being in its most general terms, and to answer the question of being, of what it means for something to exist, along with the problem of why there is something rather than nothing. When he enters phenomenologically into the concept of being, he observes that all existence, seen unavoidably through the ontologist's human eyes, can only be understood in human terms, from the standpoint of human interests, which he refers to as *Da-sein*. He adapts and typographically modifies the German word *Dasein* for this purpose, whose original meaning is simply "being there" or literally "there-being", in the sense of manifest presence, confronting the perceiver with its undeniable reality, giving it a particularly anthropocentric interpretation more specifically as human being-in-the-world.[20]

The phenomenological method of exploring the fundamental question of being encourages Heidegger to discover within himself that all things are tinged with human concern. Existence needs to be understood from the perspective of what he characterizes as a kind of anxiety, related to every entity's potential uses for human purposes. The things we own and the things we encounter even if we do not have any special responsibility toward them, according to Heidegger, are always seen or understood in terms of our care or concern (*Sorge*). We feel as though they need to be handled and maintained, and we feel distress over the prospect of their deteriorating to the point of becoming useless for our needs. More directly, Heidegger believes that we experience the world of objects from the standpoint of to-handedness or *Zuhandenheit*, considering everything as something we might be able to use, to pick up and manipulate, even if we cannot physically do so with our bare hands, but for which we may require powerful machines to manually guide and control.

The connection to Schopenhauer is obvious if we read into Heidegger's theory of *Sorge* and *Zuhandenheit* Schopenhauer's concept of the will to life. In setting forth additional points of agreement and disagreement between Schopenhauer and the early and later Heidegger on the relation of art and the individual will, we find in the early Heidegger an ontic conception of the differences among things as stemming from the standpoint of the perceiver's will and purposive preoccupations. This yields a Schopenhauerian anticipation of Heidegger's key notions of ready-to-handedness and human being-in-the-world. The two philosophers, despite many differences, emphasize a kind of idealistic outlook on the world. They assume the perspective of an individual phenomenological investigator beginning with perceptual data as something given in the represented world, and trying to abstract philosophical principles from intuitive knowledge. In presenting their findings, Schopenhauer and Heidegger arrive at a number of conclusions that are so similar as to be due either to coincidence in the investigation of similar problems by similar methods, or, as is more likely, because Heidegger, through his reading, was directly influenced by Schopenhauer's idealism. Where Schopenhauer recommends denial of the will to life, either through the renunciation of the ascetic saint or transcendent rapture in the experience of beauty or the sublime of aesthetic genius, as the only salvation from the suffering incurred by the will to life, so Heidegger describes a kind of salvation from the care and concern of *Zuhandenheit* in *Gelassenheit*, an attitude of simply leaving things alone.

Young explains Heidegger's turn from the early to the later philosophy as a recognition of the need to alter his system to make room for something like Schopenhauer's account of salvation through aesthetic experience. Heidegger defines being-in-the-world by reference to time, and to social circumstances in particular. What Heidegger, expanding on Schopenhauer's concept, calls the assertive will in modern technological society creates a pathological attitude toward the world that reduces nature to a mere supply store for human wants. The later Heidegger is convinced that only art, in somewhat the way Schopenhauer conceived it as a release from individual willing, can save us from this deplorable state of things through a return to metaphysical at-homeness. Young further finds that Heidegger's theory of *techné* provides the basis for two criticisms of Schopenhauer's aesthetics. The aesthetic condition is not necessarily opposed to will without qualification, as Schopenhauer maintains, but more specifically to what Heidegger calls the self-assertive will. The will in general, moreover, is not essentially excluded from aesthetic activity, but can be embodied in a proper mode of production, and even in an entire culture.[21]

The spirit of Schopenhauer's philosophy pervades Heidegger's *Being and Time* in these and other ways, despite Heidegger's efforts to separate his existential ontology from Schopenhauer's moral pessimism. Heidegger, much like Schopenhauer, thinks that we can learn to overcome the alienation from authentic existence that occurs as a result of seeing the world primarily as a warehouse of things to satisfy our wants. Heidegger is also often compared to Schopenhauer on the basis of Schopenhauer's proto-phenomenological understanding, in ways that are preminiscent of Merleau-Ponty's *The Phenomenology of Perception*. Merleau-Ponty similarly thematizes a sense of place and interaction with the world that occurs through proprioception, body knowledge and the range and limits of activity available to a human agent.[22] This concept is much in agreement with if not actually derivative from Heidegger's concept of *Da-sein* as human being-in-the-world, revealed by phenomenology as a potentially endless succession of time horizons for alternative courses of action. The idea in both Heidegger and Merleau-Ponty is related indirectly to Schopenhauer's second way of knowing the body intuitively through wilful direction and control of its actions.

There is also a methodological epistemic analogy between Schopenhauer and Heidegger. Schopenhauer suggests, in his first effort to prove that thing-in-itself is Will, that desire and other manifestations of phenomenal will to life is the Trojan horse by which knowledge can penetrate the fortress wall that separates the world as it appears and as transcendental reality. The empirical will for Schopenhauer allows metaphysics to peek behind the veil of Maya to discover that thing-in-itself is pure willing or Will. There we discover it to be blind, objectless and therefore subjectless, uncaused and unmotivated urging, undirected striving. Heidegger similarly glimpses the nature of being phenomenologically through the eyes of temporally situated personal experience, and in particular as *Da-sein*, or specifically human being-in-the-world. It, too, is therefore a kind of Trojan horse that enables us to unlock the mystery posed by the question of being that Heidegger hopes to resolve. Young maintains:

> Heidegger divided his philosophy into early and late in terms of a "turning" (*die Kehre*) that occurred in about 1930. While there is a great deal of debate as to the radicalness and uniqueness of this "turning," a rough and ready division of his philosophy into early and late is universally accepted ... I want to postulate an extremely bold two-part hypothesis. (i) Early Heidegger, in particular the Heidegger of *Being and Time* (1927) = the Schopenhauer of, roughly, Books I and II of *The World as Will and Representation*. In a different sense of "early" one could speak of "early" Schopenhauer and say that early Heidegger = "early" Schopenhauer. (ii) Late Heidegger = the result of adding Books III and IV of *The World as Will*, in particular, the discussion of art, to Books I and II. (Late Heidegger = "late" Schopenhauer.)[23]

Young does not believe that these identifications are strictly true; in fact, he denies their validity. "This hypothesis is certainly false", he continues. "There is, however, enough truth in it to make its exploration fruitful both in terms of illuminating the affinities between the two philosophers and in terms of illuminating the issues themselves with which both are concerned."[24] Whether and to what extent such correlations between Heidegger and Schopenhauer can be substantiated, and to whatever degree they shed light on the ideas each develop, Young usefully calls attention to a sufficiently strong basis of contact between the two thinkers to make the comparison worth exploring.

By making phenomenology the methodological foundation of ontology, rather than the other way around, Heidegger, like Schopenhauer before him, investigates the nature of being from the standpoint of the knower's felt condition. For Schopenhauer, this is intuition concerning the phenomenal will or will to life, while for Heidegger it is phenomenology of *Da-sein*, construed as human being-in-the-world. The difference, and the reason why Schopenhauer's pre-Husserlian phenomenological starting-point in metaphysics is more excusable than Heidegger's, is that Schopenhauer, unlike Heidegger, is clearly involved in an empirical enquiry into introspective clues about the nature of reality, of Will as Kantian thing-in-itself, and not, like Heidegger, attempting rigorously to establish the meaning of a concept *a priori* before proceeding to its application.[25] Schopenhauer undoubtedly

248

influences Heidegger's thinking about the question of being, the concept of *Da-sein*, interpreted in terms of a Schopenhauerian understanding of human will. Schopenhauer's moral pessimism is translated into Heidegger's concept of care, concern and ready-to-handedness, which Heidegger regards also as a regrettable fact about the world. It is something to be resisted, by a contravening ethics of leaving-things-alone, just as Schopenhauer proposes that salvation from the sufferings produced by the demands of the phenomenal will to life can only be attained by not giving in to such pressing urges but by overcoming will for the sake of knowledge in ascetic renunciation or aesthetic rapture.

To attribute a lineage to Heidegger's ideas, going back to Schopenhauer and Husserl, in no way detracts from the originality of Heidegger's philosophy, any more than it does so in the case of Schopenhauer to trace sources of his distinctions and philosophical principles to Plato, Kant and the *Vedas* and *Upanishads*. In his existentialist ontology, Heidegger offers a remarkable transcription of Schopenhauer's philosophy into a twentieth-century idiom of Husserlian phenomenology and a concern with the ethics of technology. Heidegger's methodology and its distinctive field of applications could not have arisen for Schopenhauer in quite the same way, given changes in the twentieth-century intellectual context that became prevalent only many years after he died. Nor could Schopenhauer have approached these problems with the same sense of urgency as Heidegger following the accelerated development of technological culture from the end of the nineteenth century. The differences between Schopenhauer and Heidegger should nevertheless not obscure the definite points of contact they share.

Wittgenstein's early Schopenhaurianism

It is not only among continental thinkers like Nietzsche and Heidegger that Schopenhauer's idealism exerted influence. He was also enormously important especially in the early philosophical thinking of young Wittgenstein. Wittgenstein, as one of the seminal founders of analytic philosophy at the beginning of the twentieth century, testifies to the wide philosophical appeal of Schopenhauer's thought and his continuing significance in many branches and traditions of philosophy.

What, exactly, did Wittgenstein learn from Schopenhauer, and how are Schopenhauer's ideas transformed by Wittgenstein in his two earliest surviving writings, the *Tractatus Logico-Philosophicus* and *Notebooks 1914–1916*? There is hearsay evidence that Wittgenstein, like many other Austrian intellectuals near the end of the nineteenth century, discovered in Schopenhauer's moral pessimism a touchstone for his own sense of adolescent *Weltschmerz.* G. H. von Wright, a student of the later Wittgenstein at Cambridge in the 1930s, writes in his book, *Wittgenstein* (1982): "If I remember rightly, Wittgenstein told me that he had read Schopenhauer's *Die Welt als Wille und Vorstellung* in his youth and that his first philosophy was a Schopenhauerian epistemological idealism."[26] A. J. Ayer, another later acquaintance of Wittgenstein's, although not a member of his inner circle of students, similarly recounts:

> Wittgenstein was not entirely dismissive of the philosophers of the past, but his reading of them was markedly eclectic. As a boy he was strongly influenced by Schopenhauer's principal work, *The World as Will and Representation*, and we shall see that this influence persists in the *Tractatus*, though the only philosophers to whom he acknowledges a debt in the *Tractatus* are Frege and Russell. The book contains a passing reference to Kant and has been thought by some critics to display a Kantian approach, but there is no evidence that Wittgenstein made any serious study of Kant's writings and his knowledge of Kant was probably filtered through Schopenhauer.[27]

Ayer seems unaware of the fact that Wittgenstein had made a close study of Kant's *Critique of Pure Reason.* He did so with Ludwig Hänsel and Michael Drobil while a prisoner of the Italians at the end of the First World War in the castle at Monte Cassino. It seems reasonable also to infer that Wittgenstein's first interest in Kant may have been stirred by his prior reading of Schopenhauer.[28]

Wittgenstein's aphoristic style, first perfected in the *Notebooks, Proto-Tractatus* and *Tractatus*, and later modified in *The Blue and Brown Books, Philosophical Investigations* and virtually all of the posthumous manuscripts, seems in part at least to have been inspired by Schopenhauer, as many commentators have assumed.[29] Wittgenstein was probably stylistically influenced to a limited degree by Schopenhauer, particularly if he was familiar not only with *The World as Will and Representation* but also with the second volume of Schopenhauer's *Parerga and Paralipomena*. This, unfortunately, is a possibility that no Wittgenstein or Schopenhauer scholar seems to have convincingly demonstrated. Von Wright, in his addendum to Norman Malcolm's *Ludwig Wittgenstein: A Memoir with a Biographical Sketch by Georg Henrik von Wright*, argues that it is Georg Christoph Lichtenberg in his *Aphorisms*, written in numerous notebooks and in the margins of accounting ledgers up to the time of his death in 1799, rather than Schopenhauer, that Wittgenstein may have adopted as his admired literary model. As further corroboration, Wittgenstein also seems to have adopted some of

Lichtenberg's ideas concerning the relation between mathematics and the world of nature.[30]

Wittgenstein himself later denied any strong impact by Schopenhauer on his own early thinking. M. O'C. Drury reports a conversation with Wittgenstein as follows:

> WITTGENSTEIN: My fundamental ideas came to me very early in life.
> DRURY: Schopenhauer?
> WITTGENSTEIN: No; I think I see quite clearly what Schopenhauer got out of his philosophy – but when I read Schopenhauer I seem to see to the bottom very easily. He is not deep in the sense that Kant and Berkeley are deep.[31]

It may be surprising to find Wittgenstein mentioning Berkeley as deep, especially in comparison with Schopenhauer. Nevertheless, we know that Wittgenstein was often as reluctant to acknowledge predecessors as he was jealous especially of his later ideas not being plagiarized by such later contemporaries as Gilbert Ryle, Rudolf Carnap and Friedrich Waismann. The oral history may be ambiguous, and we can only hope to resolve the question by considering Wittgenstein's own writings to decide whether it is reasonable to attribute to him a Schopenhauerian strand in his early thought.

If we agree with many recent commentators that in the *Tractatus* and *Notebooks* Witgenstein is a kind of semantic and logical transcendentalist, then there may be a sound basis for identifying Schopenhauer's distinction between the world as Will and representation as somehow at work in Wittgenstein's philosophy. There are several respects in which Wittgenstein evinces Schopenhauerian transcendentalism in the *Tractatus*. He notably distinguishes between sign and symbol, when he writes "The sign is the part of the symbol perceptible to the senses".[32] The distinction is crucial to Wittgenstein's efforts to provide a general semantics for the possibility of determinate meaning in any logically possible language. Wittgenstein is as aware as Gottlob Frege and Bertrand Russell that ordinary language is rife with conceptual confusions, and in particular with ambiguities in which single terms have more than one referent or no referent at all, as well as multiple terms with difference senses but the same reference.

Unlike Frege and Russell, Wittgenstein is unwilling to take refuge in an ideal language or *Begriffsschrift*. He recognizes that formal technical and mathematical languages from a historical point of view derive from pre-existent natural languages in which it is already possible to express determinate meaning. It does not contribute to Wittgenstein's purpose of understanding the semantics of languages generally to turn his back especially on colloquial languages. As many commentators have observed, this is one important respect in which Russell in his introduction to the *Tractatus* seriously misunderstands Wittgenstein's intentions.[33] It is only by distinguishing between two aspects of language, the perceptible sign part of a symbol and its transcendent imperceptible part, that Wittgenstein is able to explain the logic and picture theory semantics of all genuine languages despite their superficial confusions and ambiguities. Whereas colloquial language disguises the meanings of thoughts, its transcendent symbolism expresses definite meaning by picturing an existent or non-existent state of affairs in a one–one correspondence between the fully analysed elements of a sentence in the linguistic order and the fully reduced elements of a state of affairs in the ontic order.[34] The colloquial sentence "It is raining" does not picture precipitation in its sign aspect at the superficial level of its orthographic appearance in conventional English. It does so, rather, according to Wittgenstein, in its transcendent imperceptible symbolic level as a truth function of elementary propositions corresponding to the co-presence of relevant atomic facts or states of affairs, and in the one–one picturing of simple names concatenated in each elementary proposition with the simple objects correspondingly juxtaposed in each pictured atomic fact or state of affairs.[35]

The sign-aspect of language is Wittgenstein's semantic version of Schopenhauer's concept of the world as representation. It is that part of language that is perceptible to intuition and represented in thought. The transcendent symbol-aspect of language is Wittgenstein's semantic version of Schopenhauer's concept of thing-in-itself, understood as the transcendent reality underlying the world of appearances or representations. Wittgenstein does not need to posit the existence of an ideal language if every language already has an ideal transcendent aspect by virtue of which it expresses meaning. Similarly, therefore, he has no need to abandon conventional colloquial language for the sake of limiting semantic theory only to an ideal language. If we compare Plato to Frege and Russell and Wittgenstein to Kant and Schopenhauer, then we can see how Wittgenstein's prior reading and interest in Schopenhauer might have prepared him later in his study of Whitehead and Russell's logic in *Principia Mathematica* (1910–13). He need not construct an ideal language in order to understand the meaning of language generally, if all languages have a Schopenhauerian transcendental aspect in which ambiguities are avoided and meaning functions pictorially in a metaphysics of logical atomism.

Where Plato posits two worlds, the changing phenomenal world of Becoming and the real unchanging world of Being, of appearances and the realm of eternal Forms or Ideas, Frege and Russell posit two categories of languages. They distinguish between ordinary languages with a natural history developed through accidental contingencies of expression in linguistic communities, and ideal languages such as that to which Frege's *Begriffsschrift* and Whitehead and Russell's *Principia Mathematica* aspire. Similarly, where Kant and Schopenhauer postulate a single unified world with two aspects, as perceptually intuited representation and transcendent thing-in-itself, there Wittgenstein posits a single linguistic order, for all colloquial and artificial languages, each of which has a dual aspect. All languages in Wittgenstein's *Tractatus* can be understood from the standpoint of their perceivable signs and imperceivable transcendent symbols. It is with respect to their symbolic aspect alone that Wittgenstein argues that meaning is grounded in the one–one picturing of fully analysed elements in language and in the states of affairs that the sentences in a language picture. Within the nineteenth-century German logic and semantic tradition, Bernard Bolzano in his *Wissenschafts-lehre* had previously distinguished in similar Kantian fashion between sentences (*Sätze*) and sentences-in-themselves (*Sätze an sich*). The latter are evidently supposed to be the linguistic equivalent of Kant's or Schopen-hauer's thing-in-itself, which Bolzano designates by a choice of term that unmistakably recalls Kant's *Ding an sich*.[36]

There is nevertheless an important difference between Bolzano's and Wittgenstein's dual aspect treatment of the semantics of sentences and Kant's and Schopenhauer's metaphysics of the world as phenomenon and thing-in-itself. Whereas for Kant and Schopenhauer there is only one thing-in-itself, to which the *principium individuationis* does not apply, for Wittgenstein and Bolzano there are as many transcendent meanings, symbol aspects of colloquial sentences for Wittgenstein, *Sätze an sich* for Bolzano, as there are meaningful sentences in all possible languages. Wittgenstein argues that one–one picturing relations, pictorial and representational form and logical form, are all transcendent. The division is the basis for his important further distinction between what can be said and what can only be shown. The showing of which Wittgenstein speaks is not perceptual or intuitive in Schopenhauer's sense, but takes place only in the transcendent order where the symbolic aspect of language stands in one–one correspond-ence with the fully analysed atomic components of whatever states of affairs a sentence transcendentally pictures in the "great mirror" or "logical scaf-folding" of language.[37]

Wittgenstein accordingly writes: "Logic is not a theory but a reflexion of the world. Logic is transcendental."[38] The perceptible part of language and the states of affairs in logical space that constitute a world for early Wittgenstein are the equivalent of Schopenhauer's world as representation. Logical form, pictorial and representational form, among other items of interest, in turn transcend the world of facts, where alone they show them-selves. They do not exist as objects or states of affairs in what Schopenhauer would call the world as representation, but stand outside all facts and objects, comprising a transcendent logical structure of the world in which pictorial

meaning relations obtain. It is possible in this light to understand Wittgenstein's picture theory of meaning as a Schopenhauerian semantics in which
the distinction between the world as representation and as thing-in-itself is
applied on a limited scale to language, for the sake of interpreting the
meanings expressed by sentences in similarly dual – perceptible and transcendent – aspects.

Wittgenstein's reasoning in the *Tractatus*, furthermore, takes the form of
a Kantian transcendental argument. Just as Kant begins with something
given, a datum, and asks transcendentally what must be true in order for the
given to be possible, so similarly, although less explicitly, Wittgenstein begins
with the fact that we can use language to express determinate meaning, or
that genuine uses of language are determinately meaningful, and asks in
effect what must be true in order for such a thing to be possible.[39] What he
concludes, with all the assurance of any of Kant's or Schopenhauer's *a priori* synthetic pronouncements, is that in order for the determinate meaning-
fulness of language to be possible it must be the case that sentences in a
language stand in one–one picturing relations with the states of affairs that
sentences picture. The picturing relation obtains only in the transcendental symbolic aspect of language, and only when fully analysed as concatena-
tions of simple names possessing the same structures of the simple objects
they name in the corresponding facts as sentence pictures. There is scarcely
any other way to understand the theory of the *Tractatus* than in these
Kantian–Schopenhauerian terms, as Erik Stenius, Allan Janik and other
commentators have urged.[40]

It is not only logical, pictorial and representational form that transcends
the empirical world of facts, according to the *Tractatus*. Wittgenstein places
value, ethics and aesthetics (identified as one) outside the world, by which
attempts to express value are relegated to the extrasemantic category of
literal nonsense. Value thereby joins representational form, logical form, the
metaphysical subject, and whatever cannot be said but only shown. This
includes, as Wittgenstein subsequently adds, the mystical, *das Mystische*,
interpreted Spinozistically as religious or spiritual experience of the world
considered as a whole as though from the Godlike perspective of eternity,
sub specie aeterni.[41] Moral and aesthetic value transcends the world. The
elimination of value from the world implies that ethics, including attempts
at ethical judgement in theory and practice, is nonsense, since, according to
the logic and semantics of the *Tractatus*, only logically contingent statements
of fact convey meaning.[42]

> 6.41   The sense of the world must lie outside the world. In the
>   world everything is as it is and happens as it does happen. *In*
>   it there is no value – and if there were, it would be of no value.

> If there is a value which is of value, it must lie outside all happening and being-so. For all happening and being-so is accidental.
> What makes it non-accidental cannot lie *in* the world, for otherwise this would again be accidental.
> It must lie outside the world.
> 6.42 Hence also there can be no ethical propositions.
> Propositions cannot expess anything higher.
> 6.421 It is clear that ethics cannot be expressed.
> Ethics is transcendental.
> (Ethics and aesthetics are one.)[43]

Wittgenstein locates undifferentiated value outside the world. He explains the semantic implications of transcendence for the ineffability of ethics and the pseudopropositional status of efforts to express ethical value. Finally, he concludes with an intriguing identification of ethics and aesthetics as one.[44] The transcendence of value and identification of ethics and aesthetics are explicit also in the *Notebooks*, when Wittgenstein writes: "The work of art is the object seen *sub specie aeternitatis*; and the good life is the world seen *sub specie aeternitatis*. This is the connexion between art and ethics".[45]

The discussion of transcendence in the *Tractatus* does not draw directly on the transcendence of the metaphysical subject as transmitting transcendence to value by constituting the transcendental ground of subjective valuation, as in one of Wittgenstein's *Notebooks* arguments on the topic. In the *Notebooks* entry for 2 August 1916, Wittgenstein writes, in distinctively Schopenhauerian terms:

> And this consciousness is life itself.
> Can there be any ethics if there is no living being but myself?
> If ethics is supposed to be something fundamental, there can.
> If I am right, then it is not sufficient for the ethical judgment that a world is given.
> Then the world in itself is neither good nor evil.
> For it must be all one, as far as concerns the existence of ethics, whether there is living matter in the world or not. And it is clear that a world in which there is only dead matter is in itself neither good nor evil, so even the world of living things can in itself be neither good nor evil.
> Good and evil only enter through the *subject*. And the subject is not part of the world, but a boundary of the world.
> It would be possible to say (a la Schopenhauer): It is not the world of Idea that is either good or evil; but the willing subject.[46]

The *Tractatus* develops Wittgenstein's concept of the subject's transcendence even more fully than the *Notebooks*, but leaves the connection between the subject's transcendence and the transcendence of value unstated.[47]

What does Wittgenstein mean in *Tractatus* 6.421 by identifying ethics and aesthetics as one? Ethics and aesthetics are not identical merely because both are transcendent, unsayable and non-discursive.[48] The same is true of pictorial form, logical and mathematical form, and sheer nonsense like "There is only one 1" (4.1272) or "Socrates is identical" (5.473, 5.4733). Wittgenstein does not lump all of these together as one in the realm of *Unsinn* [nonsense] in the way that he specifically identifies ethics and aesthetics. We can be reasonably certain that Wittgenstein does not mean anything so quotidian as that morality reduces in practice to the duty to create, preserve and appreciate beauty, or that the life of the artist is somehow supposed to be a fulfilment of every type of moral obligation.

The *Notebooks* entries for July and August 1917, in which these parts of the *Tractatus* are first drafted, preserve Wittgenstein's reflections on Schopenhauer's idealist metaphysics, ethics and aesthetics. The difficult parenthetical pronouncement of *Tractatus* 6.421 might be understood by considering Schopenhauer's doctrine that aesthetic genius involves the moral duty to place knowing above willing and to perfect natural forms in art. Schopenhauer's hints at an identification of ethics and aesthetics in turn go back to Plato's Pythagorean concept of justice as a harmony of the parts of the soul, and Socrates' portrayal of the moral wrongdoer as "unmusical".[49]

We do not discover Schopenhauer anywhere explicitly stating, as Wittgenstein does, that ethics and aesthetics are one. He does, however, relate ethics to aesthetics indirectly by describing the will-less attitude of aesthetic absorption in nature or in a work of great beauty or the sublime as a mode of salvation, with evident moral overtones. Wittgenstein has not bought into all of Schopenhauer's metaphysical apparatus by which this conclusion is upheld, but he does seem for similar reasons to regard ethics and aesthetics as indistinguishable.

Ethics and aesthetics are one for Wittgenstein in the *Tractatus* because the requirements of art are moral obligations. They make demands upon an artist's actions that are not merely like but indistinguishable from the moral attitude of a responsible craftsperson. He regards all actions as works of art, which we can perform skilfully and stylishly, which is to say morally, or unskilfully and unstylishly, which is to say irresponsibly. There is an art to everything, because every action as a human doing is an artifact rather than something that merely occurs naturally in non-human or extrahuman reality. We are good or bad artists in every action we undertake. Wittgenstein, accordingly, can discern no meaningful difference between ethics and aesthetics because they are merely different ways of emphasizing what persons choose to do or not to do. The actions in which ethics and aesthetics are one include but are not limited to the making of art and artifacts as narrowly conceived, in painting, sculpting, writing or reciting poetry, drafting a novel, designing a work of architecture, composing a sonata or whistling a tune. There is an indistinguishable ethics–aesthetics for all other less obviously artistic actions as well; in diapering a baby, having a conversation with a friend, negotiating a treaty, serving in the military or deciding whether or not violently to avenge a perceived wrong. The ethical terms we use in judging the merits of such behaviour are equally aesthetic, and the aesthetic vocabulary by which we assess the merits of artistic endeavours are equally pronouncements of the artist's morality. To be a good or bad conductor of an orchestra is no different in principle, although the applicable criteria are highly specialized, than to be a good or bad soldier, husband, mother or prime minister.

To conclude that value transcends the world makes an important contribution to our understanding both of value and the world. The implication of identifying ethics and aesthetics is that there is no theoretical task for ethics, and therefore no philosophical discipline in the category of what is commonly called metaethics. This is in keeping with Wittgenstein's levelling of the presumed hierarchy of traditional philosophical domains, eliminating metaphilosophy, metamathematics and metaphysics. There is only a single flatland dimension of moral and aesthetic attitudes toward states of the world, including facts about what people do. Beyond this, according to Wittgenstein, there is no prospect for meaningful speculation about moral or aesthetic value. Wittgenstein brands all attempts to express value propositionally as logically meaningless. This negative semantic categorization does not preclude the moralist or aesthete from appreciating and cultivating value in enlightened theoretical silence, as prescribed by *Tractatus* 7. This is in sharp contrast with those who accept the possibility of a theoretical or philosophical ethics or metaethics. Ethics and aesthetics considered as one are literal nonsense according to the picture theory of meaning. Value in moral and aesthetic judgement for Wittgenstein is nevertheless immensely important, arguably even among the most important kinds of nonsense.

In the *Tractatus* Wittgenstein is committed to what he calls the general form of proposition. The principle holds that all language is constructible as a truth function of the elementary propositions. It establishes the full range of meaningful expression, distinguishing meaning from nonsense. In defence of the general form of proposition, Wittgenstein is induced to reject the existence of the psychological subject and propositional attitudes. His application of Ockham's razor to eliminate whatever is not strictly logically needed from theory rescues his commitment to the general form of proposition from a host of counter-examples. If we say or write "I believe that p", then it appears we have produced a genuine sentence of a language that is not simply a truth function of p. For the truth of "I believe that p" does not depend on the truth or falsehood of p. Wittgenstein argues that the meaningful content of propositional attitude sentences, such as "I believe that p", "I doubt that p", "I fear (hope, etc.) that p", all reduce simply to the content of the sentence p. His reasons are complex, and whether or not his argument is correct would require extended discussion. If the reduction is successful, then Wittgenstein has no further obstacle to limiting all proposition-building to purely truth-functional operations on the elementary propositions, as the general form of proposition prescribes.

With the elimination of propositional attitude contexts from a correct logical notation, as the transcendental aspect of every genuine language, Wittgenstein eliminates propositional attitudes or psychological states themselves, and therewith all psychological subjects. He speaks of phenomenal mental states in Schopenhauerian fashion as belonging to "contemporary superficial psychology". Like Hume in *A Treatise of Human Nature*, but in an importantly different way, in a single stroke Wittgenstein rids philosophy of the psychological subject, and thereby defends the general form of proposition. The logical and metaphysical economy he achieves in this way creates an opportunity for him to articulate some remarkably penetrating, often Schopenhauerian observations about the pretensions of *a priori* knowledge (5.634), the problem of solipsism (5.62, 5.64–5.641), and the concept of death (6.431–6.4312).[50] Thus, he writes:

> 5.631 The thinking, presenting subject; there is no such thing.
> If I wrote a book "The world as I found it", I should also have therein to report on my body and say which members obey my will and which do not, etc. This then would be a method of isolating the subject or rather of showing that in an important sense there is no subject: that is to say, of it alone in this book mention could *not* be made.
> 5.632 The subject does not belong to the world but is a limit of the world.
> 5.633 *Where* in the world is a metaphysical subject to be noted?

And, one page later:

> 5.641 There is therefore really a sense in which in philosophy we can talk of a non-psychological I.
> The I occurs in philosophy through the fact that the "world is my world".
> The philosophical I is not the man, not the human body or

the human soul of which psychology treats, but the metaphysical subject, the limit – not a part of the world.[51]

What in Wittgenstein is called the superficial psychological subject is
merely a coordination of picturing occurrences. In effect, it is the con-
currence of scaffold-like alignments of the internal logical structures and
analytically logically isomorphic facts, plus an act of will that one fact
represent another. The subject is a technically meaningless formal coordination of elements that shows itself in but adds no further sayable facts to the
world.

The philosophy of mind that underwrites the theory of meaning in the
Tractatus is complex. In Schopenhauerian fashion, Wittgenstein passes along
the extrasubjectivity of thought and thinking to the extrasubjectivity of a
transcendent *will to represent* as the ultimate reality of language. Wittgenstein does not speak of the will to represent as such, but the picture theory
of meaning requires a way of establishing directional lines of projection from
picturing facts to analytically isomorphic pictured facts' constituents. It fits
the requirements of his semantic philosophy to attribute this picturing role
to a transcendental will to represent as the function of what he introduces
as the metaphysical subject or philosophical "I", to which no other office is
ascribed. A Wittgensteinian–Schopenhauerian will to represent cannot
picture facts, because it transcends the world of facts. The metaphysical
subject or philosophical I can nevertheless will that facts be represented. It
can manifest its will directly in language use as lines of projection extending from pictures to pictured facts. In so doing, it provides the transcendental
ground underlying the epiphenomenal phenomenological will of superficial
psychological subjects who express facts in language, whenever we make to
ourselves pictures of facts.

Wittgenstein maintains that semantic picturing requires thinking the sense
of a proposition. If there is thinking, there is something that thinks – a thinking subject. There is no psychological subject, if Wittgenstein's use of
Ockham's razor in defending the general form of proposition is correct. He
accordingly fills the gap at precisely this juncture by introducing his concept
of the metaphysical subject or philosophical I. The metaphysical subject
seems to serve no other purpose than to ground what we have called the will
to represent that is required by any picturing relation. The will to represent
has no direct access to facts to use in picturing other facts. Schopenhauer's
concept of the transcendent Will nevertheless provides the blind Schopenhauerian will (or "Will") to express ideas by which thought at some deeper
transcendental rather than superficial psychological level is enabled to
picture facts. The unidirectional projection of meaning from pictures to
whatever they are meant to picture is conditioned by the will to represent.

The transcendence of the metaphysical subject or philosophical I is then no obstacle to its supplying the necessary will that drives representation transcendently, as in Schopenhauer, from behind the scenes.[52]

By willing representation, the metaphysical subject makes it possible extrasubjectively for finite consciousnesses like ourselves to make to ourselves pictures of facts. Picturing facts are pictorially unidirectionally related to the facts they picture in a transcendental act of willing, which is not the willing of any phenomenal or superficial psychological subject. The metaphysical subject or philosophical I thinks the sense of every proposition by transcendently willing to represent. Thinking, after all, does not cease to exist, when, as in Hume, it is no longer regarded as the thinking of a psychological subject. Wittgenstein finds it necessary to ground willing to represent in a subject, and, when logic discounts the existence of a psychological subject, he turns to the metaphysical subject as the only alternative, in a Schopenhauerian kind of "Will" that transcends the phenomenal world of facts.[53]

The passage quoted from Wittgenstein's *Notebooks 1914–1916* is the only place in that early source where he mentions Schopenhauer by name. If our reading of the *Tractatus* is correct, then Wittgenstein's philosophy is run through with Schopenhauer's influence. It is an almost palpable presence in the semantic theory, from the distinction between sign and symbol, to the theory of aesthetics and ethics as one, the transcendence of logic, mathematics and all semantic form, and the concept of the metaphysical subject or philosophical I. Limited as all of Wittgenstein's Schopenhauerianism seems to be in the early philosophy to logic, semantics and their implications for philosophy generally, the parallel concept in Wittgenstein is not quite Schopenhauer's Will, but what we have characterized in modified terms as the will to represent. Alternatively, the will to represent, even though the term does not appear in Wittgenstein, can be understood as nothing other than Schopenhauer's Will objectifying itself in this among so many other ways in language whereby meaning is projected pictorially onto states of affairs.

In his later philosophy, Wittgenstein is by no means as Schopenhauerian as he appears in the *Tractatus*. In *Philosophical Investigations*, he declares that meaning can be understood in terms of language games with a certain point and purpose, and that all we need to do is offer a perspicuous representation of the way in which the rules for language games are praxeologically grounded in a complex network of linguistic and extralinguistic activities that constitute a form of life. Wittgenstein writes:

> 435. If it is asked: "How do sentences manage to represent?" – the answer might be: "Don't you know? You certainly see it, when you use them. For nothing is concealed."

> How do sentences do it? – Don't you know? For nothing is hidden.
> But given this answer: "But you know how sentences do it, for nothing is concealed" one would like to retort, "Yes, but it all goes by so quick, and I should like to see it as it were laid open to view."[54]

With the firm conviction that in semantics nothing is hidden, the later Wittgenstein turns away from Schopenhauer's transcendentalism in the theory of meaning. Whether and to what extent if any Wittgenstein remains indebted in more subtle ways by his early immersion in Schopenhauer's idealism is as interesting and important a question in coming to terms with Wittgenstein's valuable contributions to philosophy as it is in understanding Nietzsche's early devotion to and later rejection of Schopenhauerianism. The movement constitutes a philosophical reversal that in some ways, in a very different sphere of application and with very different results, anticipates Wittgenstein's similar experience almost a century later. Wittgenstein's later philosophy, like Nietzsche's, after losing affection for Schopenhauer's transcendental idealism, would not have been what it became if it had not first been seasoned in a system of thought that emphasized a transcendental reality, of thing-in-itself as Will, including all that this might be regarded as implying for ethics and aesthetics, and, in Wittgenstein's example more immediately, for logic, semantics and the limits of philosophy.[55]

Schopenhauer's philosophical achievement

In taking the measure of Schopenhauer's accomplishments, it is difficult not to exaggerate the brilliance of his philosophy. He succeeds in so many areas where his predecessors and contemporaries did not attain the same high standard of rigorous argumentation, synthesis of science, religion, metaphysics, ethics, history, art and aesthetic theory.

To such an extent did Schopenhauer excel in providing more adequate grounds for similar conclusions reached by Kant, that his writings *On the Fourfold Root of the Principle of Sufficient Reason* and *Essay on the Freedom of the Will* in particular have been esteemed by generations of analytic philosophers who otherwise have no interest in or sympathy with Schopenhauer's transcendental idealism. If we think of analytic philosophy as a method of careful reasoning and clarification of concepts in the service of scientific knowledge broadly conceived, then there can be no objection to including Schopenhauer as a practitioner of proto-analytic philosophy.

We should try to imagine Schopenhauer as a young man, convinced that he has discovered that Kant's thing-in-itself is Will, and beginning to grasp the full implications of his metaphysics. He reads science, religion, history and works of mysticism, and everywhere, even in the newspapers, he finds confirmation of his basic thesis. He writes constantly when he is not travelling or attending the theatre. He keeps extensive notebooks, chap-books and journals, in which he records new discoveries in science, along with curiosities that find their proper place in his grand philosophical scheme. He publishes these or collects them for future use; he leaves a certain part of them behind at his death, active in his work until the very end. In this way, he prepares the second edition of *The World as Will and Representation*. He publishes further corroborations of his metaphysics in science in *On the Will in Nature*. He gathers further verification, especially of his ethical and aesthetic ideas, in the extensive *Parerga and Paralipomena*. He composes essays on related topics concerning the freedom of will and the basis of morality, that fit together like the parts of a well-oiled machine.

Schopenhauer's philosophy compartmentalizes all disciplines according to its fundamental distinction between the world as representation and Will as thing-in-itself. Within these categories Schopenhauer allows a purer approach to the kind of methods and conclusions they sustain. As a result, he is more empirical than most empiricists, at least where the world as representation is concerned, for he is not only or primarily an empiricist. He is also more transcendental than most transcendentalists, because he is not only or primarily a transcendentalist. Nor, for that matter, is he merely a German idealist philosopher, a European or Western thinker, although he is all of these to an exceptional degree and in an exceptionally pure form. Integrating Plato, Kant and the great Asian religious philosophies, Schopenhauer is at home intellectually as much on the banks of the Main-Fluß as the Ganges.

The compartments into which he divides the world and all knowledge or understanding are watertight. The same cannot be said, as Schopenhauer critically observes, of Kant's original use of the prior distinction between noumena and phenomena. This gives Schopenhauer's system a special strength. It does so only, however, at the price of making it difficult for him to explain the exact relationship between thing-in-itself and the phenom-enal world. He is in many ways no better off than Kant, explaining thing-in-itself merely as the transcendental ground of appearance, or than Plato, positing two worlds rather than a single world possessing two aspects, hold-ing that the world of Becoming imitates or participates in the world of Being, consisting of abstract Ideas. The basic categories of Schopenhauer's meta-physics are in other ways more flexible and adaptable than those of his major primary sources. The fact that he recognizes a wide range of grades of the

Will's objectification in the world as representation permits him to reorganize the phenomenal data of other philosophical theories, notably in ethics and aesthetics, but also for the empirical side of metaphysics generally, in philosophy of science. He also readily makes allowance for a sense of the world's historical progress, regress and developmental apotheosis in a more fine-grained way than other systems such as Kant's or Hegel's.

There is much to admire in Schopenhauer's philosophy. He offers penetrating insight into some of philosophy's deepest and most long-standing problems. If we agree with his methods and the distinctions he draws, together with their implications, then he can help us to understand such puzzling occurrences as matter and causation, the methods of science, logic and mathematics, life and death, the value of art, the vast panorama of conflict, disappointment, the nature and fragility of existence, the inevitability of suffering and natural evil in the lived world, and the possibility of salvation and the paradoxical saintly life that renounces life. If we want to understand why the world is perpetually divided into opposing camps, into communists and capitalists, Jews and Gentiles, Muslims and Infidels, Catholics and Protestants, carnivores and vegetarians, feminists and chauvinists, liberals and conservatives and so on, why not look to Schopenhauer? He, almost alone in the history of philosophy, provides a powerful and immensely intriguing, if still controversial, answer to these kinds of questions within a single unified system of metaphysical and epistemological distinctions that purport to cover, in their peculiar way, every truth of existence. He offers a vision of the world with an empirical and metaphysical aspect that finds a place for every fact and the transcendental justification of every fact concerning the physical, biological and human social world. He proposes a metaphysics of compassion as the basis for all morality. He defends the possibility of a qualified sense of immortality in which the impersonal essence of each person survives death without supposing that there exists an immaterial spirit or soul. He relates and integrates all of these stunning conclusions, finally, in terms of the concept of pure willing in each of us as thing-in-itself. It is the transcendent Will that is deep within each willing subject that makes us what we truly are in our empirical and acquired characters at the heart of moral responsibility.

Schopenhauer's writings are rich and beautiful works of genius. His distinctions are crisp and clear; his arguments have hard sharp edges, like those we value in the work of the best analytic philosophers. If we do not always agree with his conclusions, that hardly distinguishes his work from that of other great thinkers. We almost always know exactly what Schopenhauer is saying and why he finds it necessary or expedient to defend the positions he takes. We can generally see where we think he may have taken a false step, and the criticisms it would be useful to raise. The philosophical stature of Schopenhauer's achievement depends equally not only on his impact on professional philosophers but on the fine arts and literature in Europe and throughout the world.

What is most astonishing, perhaps, is that during his lifelong programme of philosophical activity, from the beginning Schopenhauer never once deviated from the course he set. Contrary to the philosophers he most deeply influenced, Nietzsche, Heidegger and Wittgenstein, Schopenhauer's work does not fall into an early and later period in which he changed his mind or made a drastic turn away from previous commitments to philosophical principles. He remains true to the "single thought" that he says in the Preface to the First Edition of *The World as Will and Representation* (WWR 1: xii) informs all his reflections, and which all his later writings in different ways and from different perspectives develop at length, like the spokes radiating from the hub of a wheel. The very fact that Schopenhauer exerted such a marked effect on the course of both so-called continental and analytic traditions indicates the extent of his universality and depth of insight. The many points of interest in his system that have inspired the imagination of some of the most important thinkers in Western philosophy, to which he also introduces or defends the philosophical merits of Asian religions, testifies to his greatness, independently of whether or not in the end he arrives at final truths.

Notes

Introduction: Schopenhauer's life and times

1. The most authoritative biographies include A. Hübscher, *Schopenhauer: Biographie eines Weltbildnis* (Stuttgart: Reclam, 1967); W. von Gwinner, *Schopenhauers Leben* (Leipzig: F. A. Brockhaus, 1878); H. Zimmern, *Schopenhauer: His Life and His Philosophy* (London: Allen & Unwin, 1876), rev. edn 1932; R. Safranski, *Schopenhauer and the Wild Years of Philosophy*, E. Osers (trans.) (Cambridge, MA: Harvard University Press, 1990). A new resource, *Schopenhauer: A Biography* (Cambridge: Cambridge University Press), is currently in preparation by D. E. Cartwright.
2. In the *Manuscript Remains*, Schopenhauer writes: "I regard my inheritance as a consecrated treasure which is entrusted to me simply for the purpose of being able to solve the problem set me by nature and to be for myself and humankind what nature intended me to be. I regard it as a charter without which it would be useless to humankind and would perhaps have the most wretched existence a man of my nature ever had" (HN 4: 503).
3. "Schopenhauer's way of expressing himself reminds me here and there a little of Goethe, but otherwise he recalls no German model at all. For he understands how to express the profound with simplicity, the moving without rhetoric, the strictly scientific without pedantry: and from what German could he have learned this?" (F. Nietzsche, "Schopenhauer as Educator", in *Untimely Meditations*, R. J. Hollingdale (trans.), 125–94 (Cambridge: Cambridge University Press, 1983), 134). See also J. Snow, "Schopenhauer's Style", *International Philosophical Quarterly* 33 (1993), 401–12 and P. Bridgwater, *Arthur Schopenhauer's English Schooling* (New York: Routledge, 1988), 322–48.
4. See P. Abelsen, "Schopenhauer and Buddhism", *Philosophy East and West* 43 (1993), 255–78; B. Nanajivako, *Schopenhauer and Buddhism* (Kandy, Ceylon: Buddhist Publication Society, 1970); H. Dumoulin, "Buddhism and Nineteenth Century German Philosophy", *Journal of the History of Ideas* 4 (1981), 457–70; R. K. Das Gupta, "Schopenhauer and Indian Thought", *East and West* 13 (1962), 32–40; C. Muses, *East–West Fire: Schopenhauer's Optinism and the Lanhavatara Sutra* (Indian Hills, CO: Falcon's Wing Press, 1970); and D. Dauer, *Schopenhauer as Transmitter of Buddhist Ideas* (Berne: Herbert Lang, 1969).
5. F. Nietzsche, *On the Genealogy of Morality*, M. Clark and A. J. Swenson (trans.) (Indianapolis, IN: Hackett, 1998), 2.
6. The episode is amusingly recounted by W. Wallace, *Life of Arthur Schopenhauer* (London: W. Scott, 1890), 149–50. For analysis of Schopenhauer's objections to Hegel's philosophy, see A. Schmidt, *Idee und Wertwille: Schopenhauer als Kritiker Hegels* (Munich: Carl Hauser, 1988). Schopenhauer's later considered opinions on the limitations of academic philosophy are discussed in PP 1: 137–97.
7. An example of Schopenhauer's misanthropy in the manner of one who does not suffer fools gladly is found in his tirade against the mindless distractions of the greater part of mankind:

"But purely intellectual pleasures are not accessible to the vast majority of men. They are almost wholly incapable of the pleasure to be found in pure knowledge; they are entirely given over to willing ... this need for exciting the will shows itself particularly in the invention and main-tenance of card-playing, which is in the truest sense an expression of the wretched side of humanity" (WWR 1: 314). See K. Pfeiffer, *Arthur Schopenhauer: Persönlichkeit und Werk* (Leipzig: A. Kröner, 1925) and Wallace, *Life of Arthur Schopenhauer*, 151–5. Also: "At one o'clock [Schopenhauer] dines in the *Englischer Hof*. Of the company at the *table d'hôte* he does not think highly. It was noticed that for some time he had each day put down on the table a gold coin, which he afterwards replaced in his pocket, but it was not easy to guess the import of the action. It turned out that it was in consequence of a wager he made to himself to pay the sum over to the poor-box the first day the officers dining there talked of anything besides horses, dogs, and women. Schopenhauer's idea was probably not original: a book of sketches of travel (*Bilder aus Helvetien*, &c.) by the poet [Friedrich von] Mattisson, published in 1816, tells the same story of an Englishman at Innsbruck in 1799" (Wallace, *Life of Arthur Schopenhauer*, 171). A version of the account appears in Saltus, *The Philosophy of Disenchant-ment* (New York: AMS Press, 1995), 163.

8. Hübscher, *Schopenhauer-Bildnisses: Eine Ikonographie* (Frankfurt: Waldemar Kramer, 1968) and Wallace, *Life of Arthur Schopenhauer*, 205–6.

Chapter 1: Schopenhauer's idealism

1. Schopenhauer introduces his idealist concept of the representing subject early in WWR: "That which knows all things and is known by none is the *subject*. It is accordingly the supporter of the world, the universal condition of all that appears, of all objects, and it is always presup-posed; for whatever exists, exists only for the subject. Everyone finds himself as this subject, yet only in so far as he knows, not in so far as he is object of knowledge" (WWR 1: 5).
2. I limit discussion here to Kant's B-edition refutation of idealism in CPR, B275–6. Kant offers anticipations of the argument in A368–80, in the Fourth Paralogism: Of Ideality (in Regard to Outer Relation), in what he calls the Critique of the Fourth Paralogism of Transcendental Psychology. See also the Preface to the Second Edition, Bxxxix–xli, note a. Kant maintains (Bxxxvii–xlii) that the only real addition to the second edition of CPR is the section "The Refutation of Idealism"; yet the new material is supposed to constitute only a "method of proof", with no substantive doctrinal innovations.
3. For a more complete exposition and criticism of Kant's argument see D. Jacquette, "Of Time and the River in Kant's Refutation of Idealism", *History of Philosophy Quarterly* 18 (2001), 297–310.
4. CPR, A19–B73; on thing-in-itself, see B67–6 and *passim*.
5. The standard references are Galileo, "*Il Saggiatore* [The Assayer]", in *Le Opere de Galileo Galilei*, 20 vols, A. Favaro (ed.) (Florence: S.A.G. Barbèra Editore, 1929–39); R. Descartes, *The Philosophical Works of Descartes*, 2 vols, E. S. Haldane & G. R. T. Ross (trans.) (Cam-bridge: Cambridge University Press, 1975), 1, §§188–203; R. Boyle, *The Origin of Forms and Qualities* [1666], volume 3 in *The Works of the Honourable Robert Boyle*, 6 vols (London: J. and F. Rivington, 1772); and J. Locke, *An Essay concerning Human Understanding* [1700], P. H. Nidditch (ed.) (Oxford: Clarendon Press, 1975), Bk 2, Ch. 8.
6. G. Berkeley, *Three Dialogues Between Hylas and Philonous*, *The Works of George Berkeley Bishop of Cloyne*, vol. 2, A. A. Luce & T. E. Jessop (eds) (London: Thomas Nelson, 1949), 184–254. See J. Bennett, "Berkeley and God", *Philosophy* 40 (1965), 207–21; I. C. Tipton, *Berkeley: The Philosophy of Immaterialism* (London: Methuen, 1974), 320–50; and D. Jacquette, "Berkeley's Continuity Argument for the Existence of God", *The Journal of Religion* 65 (1985), 1–14. On Berkeley's distinction between ectypal and archetypal existence of sensible things as congeries of ideas as the basis for his objective idealism, see D. Jacquette, "Reconciling Berkeley's Microscopes in God's Infinite Mind", *Religious Studies* 29 (1993), 453–63.
7. See R. A. Tsanoff, *Schopenhauer's Critique of Kant's Theory of Experience* (New York: Longmans, Green & Co, 1911) and C. Janaway, *Self and World in Schopenhauer's Philosophy* (Oxford: Clarendon Press, 1989), 37–83. Also P. Guyer, "Schopenhauer, Kant, and the Methods

of Philosophy", in C. Janaway (ed.), *The Cambridge Companion to Schopenhauer* (Cambridge: Cambridge University Press, 1999), 93–137.

8. Kant discusses the concept of an object-in-itself as an abstraction: "The understanding, when it entitles an object in a [certain] relation mere phenomenon, at the same time forms, apart from that relation a representation of an *object in itself*, and so comes to represent itself as also being able to form *concepts* of such objects. And since the understanding yields no concepts additional to the categories, it also supposes that the object in itself must at least be *thought* through these pure concepts, and so is misled into treating the entirely *indeterminate* concept of an intelligible entity, namely, of a something in general outside our sensibility, as being a *determinate* concept of an entity that allows of being known in a certain [purely intelligible] manner by means of the understanding" (CPR: B306–7).

9. "Deep sleep, while it lasts, is in no way different from death, into which it constantly passes, for example in the case of freezing to death, differing only as to the future, namely with regard to the awakening. Death is a sleep in which individuality is forgotten; everything else awakens again, or rather has remained awake" (WWR 1: 278).

10. See P. Welsen, *Schopenhauers Theorie des Subjekts: ihere transzendentalphilosophischen, anthropologischen und naturmetaphysischen Grundlagen* (Würzburg: Königshausen & Neumann, 1995), 156–238 and B. Magee, *The Philosophy of Schopenhauer* (Oxford: Clarendon Press, 1997), 105–18.

11. On Schopenhauer's critique of Fichte, see Janaway, *Self and World in Schopenhauer's Philosophy*, esp. 203–7.

12. See R. E. Aquila, "On the 'Subjects' of Knowing and Willing and the 'I' in Schopenhauer", *History of Philosophy Quarterly* 10 (1993), 241–60.

13. "The entire *centre of the world* is in every living being, and therefore its own existence is to it all in all. On this rests also *egoism*. To imagine that death annihilates it is absolutely absurd as all existence proceeds from it alone" (PP 2: 95 (Chapter IV, "Observations on the Antithesis of the Thing-in-Itself and the Phenomenon", §66)).

14. A useful exposition of Schopenhauer on these topics is offered by B. Bykhovsky, *Schopenhauer and the Ground of Existence*, P. Moran (trans.) (Amsterdam: R. R. Grüner, 1984). See also S. S. Colvin, *Schopenhauer's Doctrine of the Thing-in-Itself and his Attempt to Relate it to the World of Phenomena* (Providence, RI: Franklin Press, 1897); and see F. C. White, "The Fourfold Root", in Janaway, *Cambridge Companion to Schopenhauer*, 63–92.

15. Schopenhauer's place in the German idealist tradition is discussed by S. G. Neeley, *Schopenhauer: A Consistent Reading* (Lewiston, NY: Edwin Mellen Press, 1994). An early appreciative account of his influence and relation to the idealists he criticizes is presented by W. Caldwell, *Schopenhauer's System in its Philosophical Significance* (Edinburgh: Blackwood, 1896). See also D. Snow and J. Snow, "Was Schopenhauer an Idealist?", *Journal of the History of Philosophy* 29 (1991), 633–55 and M. Kelly, *Kant's Philosophy as Rectified by Schopenhauer* (London: Swan Sonnenschein, 1909).

Chapter 2: Empirical knowledge of the world as representation

1. F. C. White, *On Schopenhauer's Fourfold Root of the Principle of Sufficient Reason* (New York: E. J. Brill, 1992), 1–11, 152–3 and R. Taylor, "Introduction", in *The Fourfold Root of the Principle of Sufficient Reason*, E. F. J. Payne (trans.), ix–xviii (LaSalle, IL: Open Court, 1974), ix–xi.

2. Schopenhauer adopts Christian Wolff's Latin formulation: *nihil est sine ratione cur potius sit quam non sit* (for which he offers no exact source).

3. CPR A592/B620–A603/B631 (Transcendental Dialectic, Book 2, Chapter 3, The Ideal of Pure Reason, Section 4, "The Impossibility of an Ontological Proof of the Existence of God").

4. P. Gardiner, *Schopenhauer* (Harmondsworth: Penguin, 1967), 69–77.

5. Aristotle, *Metaphysics*, in *The Complete Works of Aristotle*, 2 vols, the revised Oxford translation, J. Barnes (ed.) (Princeton, NJ: Princeton University Press, 1984), 1013a24–1014a25.

6. See A. Phillips Griffiths, "Wittgenstein on the Fourfold Root of the Principle of Sufficient Reason", *Proceedings of the Aristotelian Society*, supplementary volume 50 (1976), 1–20.

7. In his *Letters from a Stoic* [*Epistulae Morales ad Lucilium*], R. Campbell (trans.) (Harmondsworth: Penguin, 1969), Seneca similarly speaks of the "plays on words, syllogisms, sophistries and all the other toys of sterile intellectual cleverness" (*Letters From a Stoic*, 204). See also *ibid.*, 97–9.
8. See WWR 1: 60 on pedantry as a form of folly.
9. WWR 1: 76, n.28 similarly criticizes Spinoza's *more geometrico* in the *Ethics* as an abstract theoretical construction of intuited conclusions.
10. See note 2 above. The translation is from Schopenhauer's preferred formulation of the principle in Wolff.
11. D. W. Hamlyn, *Schopenhauer* (London: Routledge & Kegan Paul, 1980), 11 and "Schopenhauer on the Principle of Sufficient Reason", in *Reason and Reality*, Royal Institute of Philosophy Lectures 5, 1970–1971, G. N. A. Vesey (ed.), 145–62 (London: Macmillan, 1972); and Griffiths, "Wittgenstein and the Fourfold Root".
12. Hamlyn, *Schopenhauer*, 12.
13. Schopenhauer refers to *Metaphysics* III [Γ], 6 [1011a3–17], and *Posterior Analytics*, I, 3 [72b5–73a20].
14. "[W]ith the exception of the Kantian which is directed not to the validity but to the a priori nature of the law of causality" (FFR: 32); and "I have attempted to show that the principle of sufficient reason or ground is a common expression for four entirely different relations each of which rests on a particular law that is given a priori (for the principle of sufficient reason is synthetical a priori)" (FFR: 231).
15. Aristotle's distinction between demonstration and the irreducible axioms of demonstration suggests an independent foundation for Schopenhauer's contention that there can and need be no proof of the sufficient reason principle. Schopenhauer writes: "[E]very proof is a reduction of something doubtful to something acknowledged and established, and if we continue to demand a proof of this something, whatever it may be, we shall ultimately arrive at certain propositions which express the forms and laws and thus the conditions of all thinking and knowing. Consequently, all thinking and knowing consist of the application of these; so that certainty is nothing but an agreement with those conditions, forms, and laws, and therefore their own certainty cannot again become evident from other propositions" (FFR: 32). Schopenhauer must show not only in a general way (as Aristotle does) that all proofs and explanations have unprovable conceptual foundations, but that the principle of sufficient reason in particular is foundational. This is why he advances the circularity argument, attempting to establish the sufficient reason principle as the unprovable basis of every proof, causal explanation, or scientific justification.
16. CPR: Axv–xvii, Bix–xi, A58/B82–A61/B86.
17. Hamlyn, *Schopenhauer*, 11.
18. This conclusion contradicts Hamlyn's claim that the sceptic who doubts the truth of the sufficient reason principle is refuted by Schopenhauer's circle not merely by denial, but by engaging or attempting to engage in argument. "In the case of the principle of sufficient reason … the sceptic would have to do more than speak; he would have to argue. An unargued scepticism about the principle of sufficient reason might be gratuitous, but it would not be incoherent in the way that a denial of the principle of contradiction might be held to be" (Hamlyn, *Schopenhauer*, 11). If the defence of scepticism presented here is sound, then the sceptic is free not only to deny the principle of sufficient reason, but also to argue against it by demanding proof and refusing to accept the principle in the absence of satisfactory proof, without falling into logical inconsistency.
19. F. Bacon, *Novum Organon*, translated in 1863 as *The New Organon and Related Writings*, J. Spedding, R. L. Ellis & D. Denon Heath (trans.), F. H. Anderson, (ed.) (Indianapolis, IN: Bobbs-Merrill, 1960), Aphorisms (Book One) I, 39; XIX, 43; XXII, 43–4. See L. K. Luxembourg, *Francis Bacon and Denis Diderot: Philosophers of Science* (Copenhagen: Munksgaard, 1967), 72–108. J. Martin, *Francis Bacon: The State and the Reform of Natural Philosophy* (Cambridge: Cambridge University Press, 1992), 141–71.
20. Hume, *A Treatise of Human Nature* [1739–40], 2nd edn, with text revised and notes by P. H. Nidditch and analytical index by L. A. Selby-Bigge (Oxford: Oxford University Press, 1978), Bk 1, Pt 3, Sec. 2, 73–8.

Chapter 3: Willing and the world as Will

1. Magee does not seem to understand that Schopenhauer deliberately avoids speaking of thing-in-itself as noumenon or noumenal. See Magee, *The Philosophy of Schopenhauer*, esp. 96, 210–11.

2. "See human beings as though they were in an underground cavelike dwelling with its entrance, a long one, open to the light across the whole width of the cave. They are in it from childhood with their legs and necks in bonds so that they are fixed, seeing only in front of them, unable because of the bond to turn their heads all the way around. Their light is from a fire burning far above and behind them. Between the fire and the prisoners there is a road above, along which we see a wall, built like the partitions puppet-handlers set in front of the human beings and over which they show the puppets . . . [D]o you suppose such men would have seen anything of themselves and one another other than the shadows cast by the fire on the side of the cave facing them?" (Plato, *Republic* 514a3–515a8).

3. WWR 1: Appendix: Criticism of the Kantian Philosophy, 421–2 and C. Janaway, "Will and Nature", in Janaway, *Cambridge Companion to Schopenhauer*, 138–70.

4. "[Kant] did not deduce the thing-in-itself in the right way, as I shall soon show, but by means of an inconsistency; and he had to pay the penalty for this in the frequent and irresistible attacks on this principal part of his teaching. He did not recognize the thing-in-itself directly in the will, but made a great and original step towards this knowledge, since he demonstrated the undeniable moral significance of human conduct to be quite different from, and not dependent on, the laws of the phenomenon, to be not even capable of explanation according to them, but to be something directly touching the thing-in-itself" (WWR 1: 422); and "I now return to Kant's great mistake, already touched on above, namely that he did not properly separate knowledge of perception from abstract knowledge; from this there arose a terrible confusion which we have now to consider more closely. If he had sharply separated representations of perception from concepts thought merely *in abstracto*, he would have kept these two apart, and would have known with which of the two he had to deal in each case" (*ibid.*: 437).

5. Schopenhauer explains motivational laws in FFR. He argues that motivation is "causality seen from within" (FFR: 214). The subject of willing is known from within, and can never become a represented object, according to FFR: 207, 210–14.

6. "Finally, the knowledge I have of my will, although an immediate knowledge, cannot be separated from that of my body. I know my will not as a whole, not as a unity, not completely according to its nature, but only in its individual acts, and hence in time, which is the form of the body's appearing, as it is of every body. Therefore, the body is the condition of knowledge of my will. Accordingly, I cannot really imagine this will without my body" (WWR 1: 101–2). See also "Meanwhile it is to be carefully noted, and I have always kept it in mind, that even the inward observation we have of our own will still does not by any means furnish an exhaustive and adequate knowledge of the thing-in-itself . . . In the first place, such knowledge is tied to the form of the representation; it is perception or observation, and as such falls apart into subject and object . . . Hence even in inner knowledge there still occurs a difference between the being-in-itself of its object and the observation or perception of this object in the knowing subject" (WWR 2: 196–7). The point is that thing-in-itself is not directly encountered in introspection of any act of phenomenal willing. Inner sense of phenomenal willing provides only the starting-point for enquiry, from which it is necessary to arrive at a grasp of thing-in-itself as pure willing or Will only by a process of abstraction or thinking away the cause, motivation, object and subject of phenomenal willing to arrive at something that on reflection is understood as not governed by the principles of individuation and sufficient reason.

7. See, for general reference, J. E. Atwell, *Schopenhauer on the Character of the World: The Metaphysics of the Will* (Berkeley, CA: University of California Press, 1995); Janaway, *Self and World in Schopenhauer's Philosophy*; Bykhovsky, *Schopenhauer and the Ground of Existence*; Colvin, *Schopenhauer's Doctrine of the Thing-in-Itself*; A. Hübscher, *The Philosophy of Schopenhauer in its Intellectual Context: Thinker Against the Tide* (Lewiston, NY: Edwin Mellen Press, 1989).

8. "Thus everyone in this twofold regard is the whole world itself, the microcosm; he finds its two sides whole and complete within himself. And what he thus recognizes as his own inner being also exhausts the inner being of the whole world, of the macrocosm. Thus the whole

world, like man himself, is through and through will and through and through representation, and beyond this there is nothing" (WWR 1: 162).

9. Plato, *Republic*, 595a–602b.

10. Janaway challenges the historical accuracy of Schopenhauer's theory of Platonic Ideas, in *Self and World in Schopenhauer's Philosophy*, 9, 27, 277.

11. See J. D. Chansky, "Schopenhauer and Platonic Ideas: A Groundwork for an Aesthetic Metaphysics", in E. von der Luft (ed.) *Schopenhauer: New Essays in Honor of his 200th Birthday*, 67–81 (Lewiston, NY: Edwin Mellen Press, 1988); and T. G. Taylor, "Platonic Ideas, Aesthetic Experience, and the Resolution of Schopenhauer's Great Contradiction", *International Studies in Philosophy* 19 (1987), 43–53.

Chapter 4: Suffering, salvation, death and renunciation of the will to life

1. Alfred Lord Tennyson, "In Memoriam, A.H.H." (1850). In his 1844 essay, Darwin wrote: "[The Swiss botanist Alphonse] De Candolle, in an eloquent passage, has declared that all nature is at war, one organism with another, or with external nature. Seeing the contented face of nature, this may at first be well doubted; but reflection will inevitably prove it is too true. The war, however, is not constant, but only recurrent in a slight degree at short periods and more severely at occasional more distant periods; and hence its effects are more easily overlooked" (*The Works of Charles Darwin: vol. 10, The Foundations of the Origin of Species: Two Essays Written in 1842 and 1844*, P. H. Barrett & R. B. Freeman (eds) (London: William Pickering, 1986), "Natural means of Selection", 68).

2. See G. Goedert, "Schopenhauer: Ethik als Weltüberwindung", *Schopenhauer-Jahrbuch* 77 (1996), 113–31; V. J. McGill, *Schopenhauer: Pessimist and Pagan* (New York: Haskell House, 1977); I. Murdoch, *Metaphysics as a Guide to Morals* (Harmondsworth: Penguin, 1992), 57–80; and F. Paulsen, *Schopenhauer, Hamlet, Mephistopheles: drei Aufsätze zur Naturgeschichte des Pessimismus* (Berlin: Cotta Verlag, 1901), 45–81, 97–176.

3. "[L]ife may certainly be regarded as a dream and death as an awakening. But then the personality, the individual, belongs to the dreaming and not to the waking consciousness; and so death presents itself to the former as annihilation" (PP 2: 272 ("On the Doctrine of the Indestructibility of Our True Nature by Death")).

4. "And now ... as man is nature herself and indeed as the highest degree of her consciousness; moreover, as nature is only the will-to-live together with the phenomenon of this, it is appropriate for man, as long as he is the will (or nature), to console himself about his own death and the death of his friends by looking back at the immortal life of nature, which he himself is, – the will-to-live objectified" (HN 1: 370).

5. Quoted in WWR 2: 588. Greek mythology offers a legend that strikingly affirms Schopenhauer's philosophy of death. Herodotus in his *Histories* and Plutarch in *Lives*, among others, recount the story of Cleobis and Biton, two young sons of a priestess of Argos. When the oxen that were supposed to draw their mother's cart more than five miles to the temple of Hera at Delphi were late in arriving, the boys piously took the animals' place and pulled the cart all the way themselves. The priestess in gratitude to her sons prayed to the goddess to grant them the greatest possible blessing, whereupon, the boys, who apparently were not consulted in the matter, died peacefully in their sleep that night within the temple. Their memory is enshrined in two kouros statues carved in the seventh–sixth centuries BCE, and currently housed in the Delphi museum. The idea of a painless uneventful death even at so tender an age as the greatest gift the gods can bestow is much in the spirit of Schopenhauer's moral pessimism.

6. "Death is the great reprimand that the will-to-live, and more particularly the egoism essential thereto, receive through the course of nature; and it can be conceived as a punishment for our existence" (WWR 2: 507). In the asterisk footnote, Schopenhauer adds: "Death says: You are the product of an act that ought not to have taken place; therefore, to wipe it out, you must die". Also, "For with the empirical consciousness we necessarily have not only sinfulness, but also all the evils that follow from this kingdom of error, chance, wickedness and folly, and finally death. Death is, so to speak, a debt contracted through life, as are also the other evils that are

determined with less certainty (*haec est conditio vivendi*). The Bible and Christianity through the fall of man rightly introduce into the world death and the troubles and miseries of life" (HN 1: 74). See J. E. Atwell, *Schopenhauer: The Human Character* (Philadelphia, PA: Temple University Press, 1990), 202–4.

7. W. James, *The Varieties of Religious Experience: A Study in Human Nature*. The Gifford Lectures on Natural Religion 1901–1902 (London: Longmans, Greene & Co., 1935), 145–7. James refers to Theodule Armand Ribot's original sense of *anhedonia* as an indifference to life resulting from liver disorders in Ribot's *Psychologie des sentiments* (1897), 54.

8. One might compare the idea of a will to death complementing Schopenhauer's concept of the will to life with the present complementary suggestion concerning a will to death with Freud's (Schopenhauerian) distinction between (in reverse order) the pleasure principle and the death wish (*eros* and *thanatos*), as reflected in the difference of outlook from the time of *Interpretation of Dreams* (1899) to *Beyond the Pleasure Principle* (1920). See S. Gardner, "Schopenhauer, Will, and the Unconscious, in Janaway, *Cambridge Companion to Schopenhauer*, 375–421. Freud consistently maintained that he had not read Schopenhauer or Nietzsche until many years after making his foundational clinical discoveries and formulating the basic principles of psychoanalysis.

9. Epicurus, *Letter to Menoeceus*, in Diogenes Laërtius, *Lives and Opinions of Eminent Philosophers*, 10.27.

10. A. Camus, *The Myth of Sisyphus and Other Essays*, J. O'Brien (trans.) (New York: Vintage, 1955), 3.

11. "It might be thought that in view of this grim picture of human life, Schopenhauer would recommend suicide; but, though he refused to recognise any valid moral reason for condemning suicide, he considered that it is no real solution to life's tragedy" (F. Copleston, *Schopenhauer: Philosopher of Pessimism* (London: Burns, Oates, & Washburne, 1946), 91).

12. "On the whole, we shall find that, as soon as a point is reached where the terrors of life outweigh those of death, man puts an end to his life. The resistance of the latter is nevertheless considerable; they stand, so to speak, as guardians at the gate of exit. Perhaps there is no one alive who would not already have made an end of his life if such an end were something purely negative, a sudden cessation of existence. But it is something positive, namely the destruction of the body, and this frightens people back just because the body is the phenomenon of the will-to-live" (WWR 1, 324–5; PP 2, 310 ("On Suicide")).

13. I. Kant, *Foundations of the Metaphysics of Morals*, L. White Beck (trans.) (New York: Macmillan, 1959), 39–40.

14. "If criminal law condemns suicide, that is not an ecclesiastically valid reason and is, moreover, definitely ridiculous; for what punishment can frighten the man who seeks death? If we punish the *attempt* to commit suicide, then we are simply punishing the want of skill whereby it failed" (PP 2: 307).

15. "I have expounded in my chief work, volume one, §69, the only valid moral reason against suicide. It lies in the fact that suicide is opposed to the real salvation from this world of woe and misery one that is merely apparent. But it is still a very long way from this aberration to a crime, such as the Christian clergy would like to stamp it" (PP 2: 309). See G. Simmel, *Schopenhauer and Nietzsche*, H. Loiskandl, D. Weinstein & M. Weinstein (trans.) (Amherst, MA: University of Massachusetts Press, 1986), 131–2.

16. "The question whether Schopenhauer's higher view of death could be consoling is a difficult one. He tries to inculcate the thought that one's own death has no great significance in the order of things. But if one accepted his reasons for taking this attitude, ought one not to think that one's life has just as little significance? And is that a consoling thought? Schopenhauer appears to think so" (C. Janaway, *Schopenhauer* (Oxford: Clarendon Press, 1984), 89). See D. E. Cartwright, "Schopenhauer on Suffering, Death, Guilt, and the Consolation of Metaphysics", in von der Luft, *Schopenhauer: New Essays*, 51–66.

17. Schopenhauer further criticizes suicide as a puerile metaphysical gamble: "Suicide can also be regarded as an experiment, a question we put to nature and try to make her answer, namely what change the existence and knowledge of man undergo through death. But it is an awkward experiment, for it abolishes the identity of the consciousness that would have to listen to the answer" (PP 2: 311).

18. "Between this voluntary death springing from the extreme of asceticism and that resulting from despair there may be many different intermediate stages and combinations, which are indeed hard to explain; but human nature has depths, obscurities, and intricacies, whose elucidation and unfolding are of the very greatest difficulty (WWR 1: 402). I develop these themes at greater length in D. Jacquette, "Schopenhauer on Death", in Janaway, *Cambridge Companion to Schopenhauer*, 293–317 and "Schopenhauer on the Ethics of Suicide", *Continental Philosophy Review* 33 (2000), 43–58.

19. "Whoever has perceived the true nature of the world, sees life in death, but also death in life; the two are only different but inseparable aspects of the objectification of the will" (HN 1: 369). And "But just as death is essential to life, yet it is the distressing side of life, that in which the inner emptiness and unreality of the will-to-live most frequently expresses itself, the identity of life and suffering. Considered in this way, there is in exchange for death only one consolation, namely that, just as the phenomenon of the will-to-live must come to an end, this will itself can freely come to an end. If the will itself has ended, in other words has turned, then death is no longer a suffering, because a will-to-live no longer exists" (HN 1: 370–71).

20. "In rejecting suicide while affirming the motivation to negate the will, Schopenhauer must evade the fact that suicide removes the individual organism, which is the only tool for producing suffering, without any trace or potential for further suffering ... The renunciation of life and ascetic resignation from all desire that Schopenhauer proposed as the perfection and sanctification of the soul are too comprehensive and fundamental to be motivated merely by suffering, even if the metaphysical unity of the world translates all suffering into the personal soul. We rarely find that this is the motivation for renouncing the will by the holy penitents and ascetes of all religions, who Schopenhauer deems to be the embodiments of his ideal" (Simmel, *Schopenhauer and Nietzsche*, 133). See R. A. Gonzales, *An Approach to the Sacred in the Thought of Schopenhauer* (Lewiston, NY: Edwin Mellen Press, 1992); and B. V. Kishan, *Schopenhauer's Theory of Salvation* (Visakhapatnam: Andrea University Press, 1978).

21. Copleston, *Schopenhauer: Philosopher of Pessimism*, 91. See Simmel: "The annihilation of will does, indeed, remove the possibility of suffering, but this procedure is unnecessary if the annihilation of the phenomenon completely cuts off the reality of will ... The weakness of Schopenhauer's argumentation in this case is obvious, especially as it pertains to life's suffering, because in the instance of suicide alone, the treatment of the symptoms is as radically potent as is the internal annihilation of the will to live ... Though it might seem paradoxical, suicide might seem to be justified in less radical cases, whereas it would not be a proper remedy for a profound and total distaste with life. In the case of radical ennui Schopenhauer is correct and shows profound perception, though weak argumentation, in claiming that an external annihilation of life would be a totally useless and contradictory expression of an inner separation of life from itself" (Simmel, *Schopenhauer and Nietzsche*, 132–3). See also Saltus, *The Philosophy of Disenchantment*, 36–76.

22. The life-denying moral stance that Schopenhauer represents is also attributed to several other philosophers in Leo Tolstoy's remarkable *Confession*, D. Patterson (trans.) (New York: Norton, 1983). Tolstoy summarizes the same "nihilistic" outlook in the following passages:

> Thus we have the direct answers that human wisdom has to give when it answers the question of life.
>
> "The life of the body is an evil and a lie. And so the destruction of the life of the body is a blessing, and we should long for it," says Socrates.
>
> "Life is what it should not be, an evil; and a passage into nothingness is the only blessing that life has to offer," says Schopenhauer.
>
> "Everything in the world – both folly and wisdom, wealth and poverty, joy and sorrow – all is vanity and emptiness. A man dies and nothing remains. And this is absurd," says [King] Solomon [in the Old Testament].
>
> "It is not possible to live, knowing that suffering, decrepitness, old age, and death are inevitable; we must free ourselves from life and from all possibility of life," says the Buddha.
>
> And the very thing that has been uttered by these powerful minds has been said, thought, and felt by millions of people like them. I too have thought and felt the same way. (Tolstoy, *Confession*, 48)

Chapter 5: Art and aesthetics of the beautiful and sublime

1. Nietzsche, "Schopenhauer as Educator", 160.
2. Plato, *Republic*, 514a–b4.
3. I. Kant, "Analytic of the Beautiful", in *The Critique of Judgement*, J. C. Meredith (trans.) (Oxford: Clarendon Press, 1952), 41–89 and "Analytic of the Sublime", in *The Critique of Judgement*, 90–203.
4. Plato, *Parmenides*, 130e.
5. "For the beauty with which . . . objects present themselves rests precisely on the pure objectivity, i.e., disinterestedness, of their perception" (WWR 2: 374). Kant had earlier written: "Now, where the question is whether something is beautiful, we do not want to know, whether we, or any one else, are, or even could be, concerned in the real existence of the thing, but rather what estimate we form of it on mere contemplation (intuition and reflection) . . . Every one must allow that a judgement on the beautiful which is tinged with the slightest interest, is very partial and not a pure judgement of taste" ("Critique of Aesthetic Judgement", in *The Critique of Judgement*, 42–3).
6. Kant, "Critique of Aesthetic Judgement", 94–117.
7. Rousseau offers an evocative image of the sublime in describing the waterfalls at Chailles, near the Pas de l'Échelle, in *The Confessions*, J. M. Cohen (trans.) (Harmondsworth: Penguin, 1953), Book Four (1732), 167–8.
8. In *A Treatise of Human Nature*, Hume explains the sublime in terms of the triumph of the imagination over the challenges of great distances in space and time or the terrifying. Hume writes: "'Tis a quality very observable in human nature, that any opposition, which does not entirely discourage and intimidate us, has rather a contrary effect, and inspires us with a more than ordinary grandeur and magnanimity. In collecting our force to overcome the opposition, we invigorate the soul, and give it an elevation with which otherwise it wou'd never have been acquainted. Compliance, by rendering our strength useless, makes us insensible of it; but opposition awakens and employs it" (*A Treatise of Human Nature*, 433–4).
9. Kant, "Critique of Aesthetic Judgement", 109–14.
10. Plato, *Republic*, 514a–b4; H. Hein, "Schopenhauer and Platonic Ideas", *Journal of the History of Philosophy*, 4 (1996), 133–44; Chansky, "Schopenhauer and Platonic Ideas", 67–81; Taylor, "Platonic Ideas, Aesthetic Experience", 43–53; J. Engelmann, "Schönheit und Zweckmäßigkeit in der Architektur", *Schopenhauer-Jahrbuch* 65 (1984), 157–69.
11. I. Knox, "Schopenhauer's Aesthetic Theory", in *Schopenhauer: His Philosophical Achievement*, M. Fox (ed.), 132–46 (Brighton: Harvester Press, 1980), 132–46.
12. See WWR 1: 126–7 for Schopenhauer's references to Augustine's denunciation of the carnal in *City of God*, XI, 28.
13. "[T]he most excellent works of any art, the noblest productions of genius, must eternally remain sealed books to the dull majority of men, and are inaccessible to them. They are separated from them by a wide gulf, just as the society of princes is inaccessible to the common people . . . [The *Idea*] is never known by the individual as such, but only by him who has raised himself above all willing and all individuality to the pure subject of knowing. Thus it is attainable only by the man of genius, and by him who, mostly with the assistance of works of genius, has raised his power of pure knowledge, and is now in the frame of mind of the genius" (WWR 1: 234). See also PP 2: 71–87 and Hamlyn, *Schopenhauer*, 62.
14. "By virtue of his objectivity, the genius with *reflectiveness* perceives all that others do not see. This gives him as a poet the ability to describe nature so clearly, palpably, and vividly, or as a painter, to portray it. On the other hand, with the *execution* of the work, where the purpose is to communicate and present what is known, the *will* can, and indeed must, again be active, just because there exists a *purpose*" (PP 2: 418–19).
15. Nietzsche, *On the Genealogy of Morality*, 63.
16. *Ibid.*, 71.
17. *Ibid.*, 72.
18. *Ibid.*, 73. The anti-erotic elements of Schopenhauer's aesthetics are discussed by Murdoch, *Metaphysics as a Guide to Morals*, 61–2, 67–70.
19. Nietzsche, *On the Genealogy of Morality*, 73.

20. See P. Alperson, "Schopenhauer and Musical Revelation", *The Journal of Aesthetics and Art Criticism* 40 (1982), 155–66; M. Budd, *Music and the Emotions: The Philosophical Theories* (London: Routledge & Kegan Paul, 1985), 76–7, 115, 176, 181; T. J. Diffey, "Schopenhauer's Account of Aesthetic Experience", *The British Journal of Aesthetics* 30 (1990), 132–42; C. Foster, "Schopenhauer's Subtext on Natural Beauty", *The British Journal of Aesthetics* 32 (1992), 21–32 and "Ideas and Imagination: Schopenhauer on the Proper Foundation of Art", in Janaway, *Cambridge Companion to Schopenhauer*, 213–51; L. Goehr, *The Imaginary Museum of Musical Works: An Essay in the Philosophy of Music* (Oxford: Clarendon Press, 1992), 148–75; D. Jacquette, "Schopenhauer on the Antipathy of Aesthetic Genius and the Charming", *History of European Ideas* 18 (1994), 373–85 and "Schopenhauer's Metaphysics of Appearance and Will in the Philosophy of Art", in D. Jacquette (ed.), *Schopenhauer, Philosophy, and the Arts*, 1–36 (Cambridge: Cambridge University Press, 1996); C. Janaway, "Knowledge and Tranquility: Schopenhauer on the Value of Art", in Jacquette, *Schopenhauer, Philosophy, and the Arts*, 39–61; A. Kanovitch, *The Will to Beauty: Being a Continuation of the Philosophies of Arthur Schopenhauer and Friedrich Nietzsche* (New York: Henry Bee Company, 1923), 17–18, 116–17; I. Knox, *The Aesthetic Theories of Kant, Hegel, and Schopenhauer* (New York: Humanities Press, 1958), 123–66; U. Pothast, *Die eigentlich metaphysische Tätigkeit: über Schopenhauers Ästhetik und ihre Anwendung durch Samuel Beckett* (Frankfurt: Surkamp, 1982), 33–44, 95–107; J. Taminiaux, "Art and Truth in Schopenhauer and Nietzsche", *Man and World* 20 (1987), 85–102; and J. Young, "The Standpoint of Eternity: Schopenhauer on Art", *Kant-Studien* 78 (1987), 424–41.

Chapter 6: Transcendental freedom of will

1. Atwell, *Schopenhauer: The Human Character*, 32–43 and *Schopenhauer on the Character of the World*, 132–4, 163; and S. G. Neeley, "A Re-Examination of Schopenhauer's Analysis of Bodily Agency: The Ego as Microcosm", *Idealistic Studies* 22 (1992), 52–67.
2. BM 49–119. See D. E. Cartwright, "Kant, Schopenhauer, and Nietzsche on the Morality of Pity", *Journal of the History of Ideas* 45 (1984), 83–98; P. F. H. Lauxtermann, *Schopenhauer's Broken World-View: Colours and Ethics Between Kant and Goethe* (The Hague: Kluwer, 2000), 135–96; M. Kelly, *Kant's Ethics and Schopenhauer's Criticism* (London: Swan Sonnenschein, 1910); and M. Nicholls, "The Kantian Inheritance and Schopenhauer's Doctrine of Will", *Kant-Studien* 85 (1994), 257–79.
3. CPR A445/B473–A452–B480. The antinomy states: "*Thesis* Causality in accordance with laws of nature is not the only causality from which the appearances of the world can one and all be derived. To explain these appearances it is necessary to assume that there is also another causality, that of freedom. *Antithesis* There is no freedom; everything in the world takes place solely in accordance with laws of nature".
4. "Is it possible that ethics, in discovering the moral incentive, is also capable of setting it in motion? Can ethics transform the man who is hardhearted into one who is compassionate, and thereby just and humane? Certainly not; the difference of characters is innate and ineradicable. The wicked man is born with his wickedness as much as the serpent is with its poisonous fangs and glands; and he is as little able to change his character as the serpent its fangs" (BM: 187).
5. Schopenhauer refers to Plato's *Meno* as corroboration for his thesis that empirical and acquired character is unalterable.
6. "For we cannot accept as possible a final contradiction between the immediate utterances of self-consciousness and the results from the fundamental principles of the pure understanding together with their application to experience; ours cannot be so mendacious a self-consciousness. It must be observed here that even the alleged antinomy advanced by *Kant* on this topic is not supposed to result, even for him, from the thesis and antithesis from different sources of cognition, one possibly from the utterances of self-consciousness, and the other from the faculty of reason and experience. On the contrary, thesis and antithesis both rationalize from allegedly objective grounds" (FW: 21).
7. "That relation, explained by *Kant*, between the empirical and intelligible character rests entirely

on what constitutes the fundamental trait of his entire philosophy, namely the distinction between appearance and thing in itself; and as with him the complete *empirical reality* of the world of experience coexists with its *transcendental ideality*, so does the strict *empirical necessity* of acting coexist with its *transcendental freedom*" (FW: 86). See Janaway, *Self and World in Schopenhauer's Philosophy*, 84–97, 208–47.

8. See D. E. Cartwright, "Schopenhauer's Axiological Analysis of Character", *Revue Internationale de Philosophie* 42 (1988), 18–36.

9. "Freedom appertains not to the empirical character but only to the intelligible. The *operari* of a given person (what he does) is necessarily determined from without by motives, and from within by his character; hence everything that he does necessarily takes place. In his *esse* (what he is), however, the freedom lies. He could have *been* a different man, and guilt or merit lies in what he *is*" (BM: 112).

Chapter 7: Compassion as the philosophical foundation of morality

1. Schopenhauer considers Kant's *Grundlegung* as the primary source for Kant's metaphysics of morals. "I take as my guide in the present criticism the first-mentioned *Foundations of the Metaphysics of Morals*, and request the reader to note that that all page numbers mentioned by me without further addition refer to that work. I shall consider the other two works [*Critique of Practical Reason* and *Metaphysical Principles of the Doctrine of Virtue*] only as accessory and secondary" (BM: 51).

2. See J. Young, "Schopenhauer's Critique of Kantian Ethics", *Kant-Studien* 75 (1984), 191–212.

3. "The circumstance of John the Baptist coming before us quite like an Indian sannyasi, yet clad in the skin of an animal, could be viewed as an odd *symbol* of the defect in Christian morality . . ., in spite of its otherwise close agreement with the Indian. We know, of course, that to every Hindu such a thing would be an abomination. Even the Royal Society of Calcutta received their copy of the Vedas only on their promising not to have it bound in leather, in the European style; it is therefore to be seen bound in silk in their library" (BM: 178–9). Devout Muslims similarly will not use silk prayer rugs for their devotions on the grounds that silk worms must be killed in the processing of silk when their cocoons are boiled in water.

4. It is worthwhile in this context to consider the frequently raised question of whether Schopenhauer is a misanthrope. He pushes a seamstress down the stairs, writes venomous things about Hegel and other philosophical contemporaries, and expresses contempt for the human race. Does he therefore simply despise the species? The answer is complex. Alongside the evidence for his hatred of mankind, we must consider also the fact that he places human beings at the apex of the pyramid of Platonic Ideas as the highest grade of the Will's objectification in the world as representation, that he regards the human form as the greatest subject of art and recommends compassion for all suffering humanity. Schopenhauer seems to exalt human possibilities while decrying the failure of the vast majority of the species as failing to live up to their potential. The enormous individuality of human beings that places them at the highest grade of the Will's objectivity implies every possible degree of ability and accomplishment, including genius, sainthood and the common run of humanity. The sense in which the sufferings of human beings deserve our loving kindness is no different for Schopenhauer than that which we equally morally owe non-human animals. Suffering must always be met with compassion, no matter what species of willing subject suffers, because all willing subjects as pure willing or Will are transcendentally identical.

5. See Abelsen, "Schopenhauer and Buddhism", 255–78; A. Barua, *The Philosophy of Arthur Schopenhauer* (New Delhi: Intellectual Publishing House, 1992); Dauer, *Schopenhauer as Transmitter of Buddhist Ideas;* Muses, *East–West Fire;* Nanajivako, *Schopenhauer and Buddhism*; and G. Son, *Schopenhauers Ethik des Mitleids und die Indische Philosophie: Parallelität und Differenz* (Freiburg im Breisgau: Verlag K. Alber, 2001), 62–95, 122–51, 173–336.

6. J. E. Atwell, "Schopenhauer's Account of Moral Responsibility", *Pacific Philosophical Quarterly* 61 (1980), 396–404 and *Schopenhauer: The Human Character*, 67–142; D. E. Cartwright, "Compassion", in *Zeit der Ernte: Festschrift für Arthur Hübscher zum 85. Geburtstag*, 60–69

(Stuttgart and Bad Cannstatt: Frommann-Holzboog, 1982), "Kant, Schopenhauer, and Nietzsche", 83–98, "Schopenhauer as Moral Philosopher: Toward the Actuality of his Ethics", *Schopenhauer-Jahrbuch* 70 (1989), 54–65, "Schopenhauer's Compassion and Nietzsche's Pity", *Schopenhauer-Jahrbuch* 69 (1988), 557–67, "Schopenhauer's Narrower Sense of Morality", in Janaway, *Cambridge Companion to Schopenhauer*, 252–92; Goedert, "Schopenhauer: Ethik als Weltüberwindung"; Lauxtermann, *Schopenhauer's Broken World-View*, 135–96; and M. Maidan, "Schopenhauer on Altruism and Morality", *Schopenhauer-Jahrbuch* 69 (1988), 265–72.

Chapter 8: Schopenhauer's legacy in the philosophy of Nietzsche, Heidegger and the early Wittgenstein

1. Safranski, *Schopenhauer and the Wild Years*, 327–49.
2. B. Magee, *Wagner and Philosophy* (Harmondsworth: Penguin, 2000), 126–73; R. Gray, "The German Intellectual Background". In *The Wagner Companion*, P. Burbridge & R. Sutton (eds), 34–59 (London: Faber, 1979); B. Nelson, "Wagner, Schopenhauer, and Nietzsche: On the Value of Human Action", *The Opera Quarterly* 6 (1989), 24–32.
3. See S. Atzert, *Schopenhauer und Thomas Bernhard: zur literarischen Verwendung von Philosophie* (Freiburg: Rombach, 1999), 104–25. See also the papers collected in the volume edited by J. T. Baer, *Arthur Schopenhauer und die russische Literatur des späten 19. und frühen 20. Jahrhunderts*, *Slavistische Beiträge*, vol. 140 (Munich: Verlag Otto Sagner, 1980); A. Baillot, *Influence de la philosophie de Schopenhauer en France, 1860–1900* (Paris: Vrin, 1927); C. S. Durer, "Moby Dick's Ishmael, Burke, and Schopenhauer", *The Midwest Quarterly* 30 (1989), 161–78; Knox, *The Aesthetic Theories of Kant*; L. Krukowski, *Aesthetic Legacies* (Philadelphia, PA: Temple University Press, 1992), 41–64, 109–17; P. Lefew-Blake, *Schopenhauer, Woman's Literature, and the Legacy of Pessimism in the Novels of George Eliot, Olive Schreiner, Virginia Woolf, and Doris Lessing* (Lewiston, NY: Edwin Mellen Press, 2001), esp. 13–34, 69–88; Magee, *Wagner and Philosophy*, 205–27; T. J. Diffey, "Metaphysics and Aesthetics: A Case Study of Schopenhauer and Thomas Hardy", in Jacquette, *Schopenhauer, Philosophy, and the Arts*, 229–48; S. McLaughlin, *Schopenhauer in Russland: zur literarischen Rezeption bei Turgenev* (Wiesbaden: Harrassowitz Verlag, 1984), esp. 15–44; Nelson, "Wagner, Schopenhauer, and Nietzsche", 24–32; N. Pangopoulus, *The Fiction of Joseph Conrad: The Influence of Schopenhauer and Nietzsche* (New York: Peter Lang, 1998); K. Pfeiffer, *Zum höchsten Dasein: Goethes Faust im Lichte der Schopenhauerschen Philosophie* (Berlin: Walter de Gruyter, 1949); A. Philonenko, *Schopenhauer: Une Philosophie de Tragedie* (Paris: Vrin, 1980); B. Sorg, *Zur literarischen Schopenhauer-Rezeption im 19. Jahrhundert* (Heidelberg: Winter Verlag, 1975); C. Wulf, *The Imperative of Narration: Beckett, Bernhardt, Schopenhauer, Lacan* (Brighton: Sussex Academic Press, 1998), 21–5, 63–78, 130–37; S. Doss-Davezac, "Schopenhauer According to the Symbolists: The Philosophical Roots of Late Nineteenth-Century French Aesthetic Theory, in Jacquette, *Schopenhauer, Philosophy, and the Arts*, 249–76.
4. F. Pessoa, *The Book of Disquiet*, R. Zenith (ed. and trans.) (Harmondsworth: Penguin, 2001), 120.
5. C. Janaway, "Schopenhauer as Nietzsche's Educator", in C. Janaway (ed.), *Willing and Nothingness: Schopenhauer as Nietzsche's Educator*, 13–36 (Oxford: Clarendon Press, 1998), 16–19.
6. F. Nietzsche, *Nietzsche contra Wagner*, *Werke: Kritische Studienausgabe*, 4 (Berlin: Walter de Gruyter, 1967), 425.
7. F. Nietzsche, *The Birth of Tragedy and The Genealogy of Morals*, F. Golffing (trans.) (Garden City, NY: Doubleday, 1956), 145.
8. *Ibid.*
9. *Ibid.*, 109.
10. *Ibid.*, 97.
11. *Ibid.*
12. *Ibid.*, 124–5.
13. C. Janaway, "Introduction", in Janaway, *Willing and Nothingness*, 1–17, esp. 1.

14. See the papers collected in W. Schirmacher (ed.), *Schopenhauer, Nietzsche, und die Kunst* (Vienna: Passagen Verlag, 1991); Simmel, *Schopenhauer and Nietzsche*; C. S. Taylor, "Nietzsche's Schopenhauerianism", *Nietzsche-Studien* 17 (1988), 45–73; D. Touey, "Schopenhauer and Nietzsche on the Nature and Limits of Philosophy", *Journal of Value Inquiry* 32 (1998), 243–52; M. Clark, "On Knowledge, Truth, and Value: Nietzsche's Debt to Schopenhauer and the Development of his Empiricism", in Janaway, *Willing and Nothingness*, 37–78; K. M. Higgins, "Schopenhauer and Niezsche: Temperament and Temporality", in Janaway, *Willing and Nothingness*, 151–77; I. Soll, "Schopenhauer, Nietzsche, and the Redemption of Life Through Art", in Janaway, *Willing and Nothingness*, 79–115.
15. Nietzsche, *On the Genealogy of Morality*, 4.
16. *Ibid.*
17. *Ibid.*
18. Cartwright, "Kant, Schopenhauer, and Nietzsche", 83–98 and "Nietzsche's Use and Abuse of Schopenhauer's Moral Philosophy for Life", in Janaway, *Willing and Nothingness*, 116–50; D. Berman, "Schopenhauer and Nietzsche: Honest Atheism, Dishonest Pessimism", in Janaway, *Willing and Nothingness*, 178–95; D. E. Cooper, "Self and Morality in Schopenhauer and Nietzsche", in Janaway, *Willing and Nothingness*, 196–216.
19. J. Young, "Schopenhauer, Heidegger, Art, and the Will", in Jacquette, *Schopenhauer, Philosophy, and the Arts*, 162–80, esp. 162.
20. M. Heidegger, *Being and Time: A Translation of Sein und Zeit*, J. Stambaugh (trans.) (Albany, NY: SUNY Press, 1996), esp. 132–7, 141–86 on disclosedness (*Erschlossenheit*), and 121–7, 171–230 and *passim* on care (*Sorge*). See also 113–30, 161–4, 237–8, 263–4, 270–72, 280–83, on the concept of *Mitda-Sein*.
21. Young, "Schopenhauer, Heidegger, Art", esp. 164–6, 169–71.
22. See M. Merleau-Ponty, *The Phenomenology of Perception*, C. Smith (trans.) (New York: Humanities Press, 1962), esp. 67–199, on the concept of the lived-body.
23. Young, "Schopenhauer, Heidegger, Art", 163.
24. *Ibid.*
25. Heidegger, *Being and Time*, 6.
26. G. H. von Wright, *Wittgenstein* (Minneapolis, MN: University of Minnesota Press, 1982), 18.
27. A. J. Ayer, *Wittgenstein* (Chicago, IL: University of Chicago Press, 1985), 13.
28. See R. Monk, *Wittgenstein: The Duty of Genius* (Harmondsworth: Penguin, 1990), 158.
29. The case for Schopenhauer's stylistic influence is made by A. S. Janik and S. Toulmin, *Wittgenstein's Vienna* (New York: Simon & Schuster, 1973), 74, 164.
30. "It may appear strange that Schopenhauer, one of the masters of philosophic prose, did not influence Wittgenstein's style. An author, however, who reminds one, often astonishingly, of Wittgenstein is [Georg Christoph] Lichtenberg. Wittgenstein esteemed him highly. To what extent, if any, he can be said to have learned from him I do not know. It is deserving of mention that some of Lichtenberg's thoughts on philosophic questions show a striking resemblance to Wittgenstein's" (G. H. von Wright, "Biographical Sketch", in Malcolm (1958: 21–2)). Compare von Wright (1942: 201–17); Janik and Toulmin, after describing Schopenhauer's "epigrammatic punch" and "elegant literary style" (*Wittgenstein's Vienna*, 164) as influencing the early Wittgenstein and such writers as Karl Kraus, whom Wittgenstein admired; citing von Wright, they also acknowledge the importance of Lichtenberg (*ibid.*, 176).
31. Drury in R. Rhees (ed.) *Recollections of Wittgenstein*, rev. edn (Oxford: Oxford University Press, 1984), 158.
32. *Tractatus* 3.32. All references are to the Ogden edition of the *Tractatus*: L. Wittgenstein, *Tractatus Logico-Philosophicus*, C. K. Ogden (ed.) (London: Routledge & Kegan Paul).
33. "Mr. Wittgenstein is concerned with the conditions for a logically perfect language – not that any language is logically perfect, or that we believe ourselves capable, here and now, of constructing a logically perfect language, but that the whole function of language is to have meaning, and it only fulfils this function in proportion as it approaches to the ideal language which we postulate" (Bertrand Russell, "Introduction", in *Tractatus*, 8). Compare "All propositions of our colloquial language are actually, just as they are, logically completely in order" (*Tractatus* 5.5563).
34. Wittgenstein writes: "Colloquial language is a part of the human organism and is not less

complicated than it. From it it is humanly impossible to gather immediately the logic of language. Language disguises the thought; so that from the external form of the clothes one cannot infer the form of the thought they clothe, because the external form of the clothes is constructed with quite another object than to let the form of the body be recognized" (*Tractatus* 4.002).

35. I develop an account of Wittgenstein's early picture theory of meaning as involving a kind of Kantian–Schopenhauerian transcendence of symbol over linguistic sign in D. Jacquette, *Wittgenstein's Thought in Transition* (West Lafayette, IN: Purdue University Press, 1998), 35–58. See also R. Haller, "Was Wittgenstein a Neo-Kantian?", in *Questions on Wittgenstein*, R. Haller (ed.), 44–56 (Lincoln, NE: University of Nebraska Press, 1988); and D. Jacquette, "Haller on Wittgenstein and Kant", in *Austrian Philosophy Past and Present: Essays in Honor of Rudolf Haller*, K. Lehrer & J. C. Marek (eds), 29–44, Boston Studies in the Philosophy of Science (Dordrecht: Kluwer, 1997).

36. B. Bolzano, *Theory of Science: Attempt at a Detailed and in the Main Novel Exposition of Logic with Constant Attention to Earlier Authors*, R. George (ed. and trans.) (Berkeley, CA: University of California Press, 1972), esp. 20–31, 171–80.

37. Wittgenstein, *Tractatus* 3.42, 4.023, 4.121, 5.511, 5.514, 6.124.

38. *Ibid.*, 6.13.

39. See, *inter alia,* E. Stenius, *Wittgenstein's "Tractatus": A Critical Exposition of its Main Lines of Thought* (Ithaca, NY: Cornell University Press, 1960), 214–26.

40. A. S. Janik, "Schopenhauer and the Early Wittgenstein", *Philosophical Studies* (Ireland) 15 (1966), 76–95; M. S. Engel, "Schopenhauer's Impact on Wittgenstein", *The Journal of the History of Philosophy* 7 (1969), 285–302; A. Phillips Griffiths, "Wittgenstein, Schopenhauer, and Ethics", in *Understanding Wittgenstein*, Royal Institute of Philosophy Lectures, vol. 7, 96–116 (London: Macmillan, 1974); D. A. Weiner, *Genius and Talent: Schopenhauer's Influence on Wittgenstein's Early Philosophy* (Rutherford, NJ: Farleigh Dickinson University Press, 1992), esp. 15–21, 46–79; N. Garver, *This Complicated Form of Life: Essays on Wittgenstein* (LaSalle, IL: Open Court, 1994), 91–101; H.-J. Glock, "Schopenhauer and Wittgenstein: Representation as Language and Will", in Janaway, *The Cambridge Companion to Schopenhauer*, 422–58.

41. Wittgenstein, *Tractatus*, 2.151, 2.172, 2.18, 4.12–4.1211, 4.461, 6.22, 5.541–5.5422, 5.631–5.641, 6.432–6.45, 6.522. On the saying–showing distinction, see especially 4.12–4.1212.

42. *Ibid.*, 3.3, 4.01, 4.021–4.023, 4.06, 4.2.

43. *Ibid.*

44. Ethics is identified with aesthetics in the final statement of *Notebooks 1914–1916*, 2nd edn, G. H. von Wright & G. E. M. Anscombe (eds), G. E. M. Anscombe (trans.) (Oxford: Basil Blackwell, 1979), 24.7.16, p. 77e. See also, in connection with Wittgenstein's extension of the relation between ethics and happiness, his remark that: "the beautiful *is* what makes happy" (21.10.16, p. 86e).

45. Wittgenstein, *Notebooks 1914–1916*, 7.10.16.

46. Wittgenstein, *Notebooks 1914–1916*, 79e; C. Barrett, *Wittgenstein on Ethics and Religious Belief* (Oxford: Basil Blackwell, 1991), 30, also 60–63. And: "Ethics does not treat of the world. Ethics must be a condition of the world, like logic" (Wittgenstein, *Notebooks 1914–1916*, 77e).

47. There is substantial distance between *Tractatus* 5.5421, in the last passage of which the transcendence of the metaphysical subject is explicitly discussed, and *Tractatus* 6.41, where Wittgenstein's remarks on the transcendence of value appear. Wittgenstein makes no attempt to connect the two or to prove the transcendence of value by the transcendence of the metaphysical subject.

48. Most commentators on the *Tractatus* do not hazard interpretations of Wittgenstein's reasoning in 6.421. M. Black, for example, in *A Companion to Wittgenstein's Tractatus* (Ithaca, NY: Cornell University Press, 1964), offers no interpretation or concordance, nor does he even include mention of the final parenthetical identification of ethics and aesthetics in the passage.

49. Plato, *Republic*, 410a7–412a6.

50. "For my part, when I enter most intimately into what I call *myself*, I always stumble on some particular perception or other, of heat or cold, light or shade, love or hatred, pain or pleasure. I never can catch *myself* at any time without a perception, and never can observe any thing but the perception" (Hume, *A Treatise of Human Nature*, 162).

51. Wittgenstein, *Tractatus*, 5.5421. In an earlier draft of the *Tractatus*, Wittgenstein's elimination of propositional attitude contexts (and criticism of Russell's relational theory of judgement) in 5.54–5.5423, originally came immediately after the statement of the general form of proposition. See L. Wittgenstein, *Prototractatus: An Early Version of Tractatus Logico-Philosophicus*, B. McGuinness, T. Nybert & G. H. von Wright (eds), D. Pears & B. McGuinness (trans.) (Ithaca, NY: Cornell University Press, 1971), 6.001–6.0051, 196–201. The concept of the self as the vanishing point is taken from the (Schopenhauerian) analogy of the eye as excluded from the visual field in *Tractatus* 5.6331. In 5.64, Wittgenstein explains: "Here we see that solipsism strictly carried out coincides with pure realism. The I in solipsism shrinks to an extensionless point [*schrumpft zum ausdehnungslosen Punkt*] and there remains the reality co-ordinated with it". Wittgenstein's concept of transcendence precludes the application of identity principles by which things in the world of facts are individuated. This makes it nonsense to consider the possibility of there being more than one transcendent subject. The world may be "my" world, as Wittgenstein states in *Tractatus* 5.641, but it is not mine as opposed to yours. The world does not belong to any particular personal empirical subject of superficial psychology, but to the impersonal undifferentiated extraworldly transcendent subject, the metaphysical, not the phenomenological "I", at the limit of the world.

52. See D. Jacquette, "Wittgenstein on Thoughts as Pictures of Facts and the Transcendence of the Metaphysical Subject", in *Wittgenstein and the Future of Philosophy: A Reassessment After 50 Years/Wittgenstein und die Zukunft der Philosophie. Eine Neubewertung nach 50 Jahren*, R. Haller & K. Puhl (eds), 160–70 (Vienna: Öbv&Hpt, 2002). Wittgenstein's famous metaphor of the ladder is also prefigured in Schopenhauer. Wittgenstein writes: "My propositions are elucidatory in this way: he who understands me finally recognizes them as senseless [*unsinnig*], when he has climbed out through them, on them, over them. (He must so to speak throw away the ladder, after he has climbed up on it. He must surmount these propositions; then he sees the world rightly" (*Tractatus* 6.54). Compare Schopenhauer: "However, for the man who studies to gain *insight*, books and studies are merely rungs of the ladder on which he climbs to the summit of knowledge. As soon as a rung has raised him one step, he leaves it behind" (WWR 2: 80).

53. Wittgenstein's statement that the existence of ethics is logically independent of whether or not the world is inhabited by living things seems to presuppose some more fundamental chain of reasoning in his thought. The identification of a Kantian thesis as a source for the independence of the existence of ethics from life has the advantage of linking Wittgenstein's work to the critical idealist tradition through well-documented connections with Schopenhauer. R. B. Goodman, "Schopenhauer and Wittgenstein on Ethics", *Journal of the History of Philosophy* 17 (1979), 437–47.

54. Wittgenstein, *Philosophical Investigations*.

55. See also E. M. Lange, *Wittgenstein und Schopenhauer: logisch-philosophische Abhandlung und Kritik des Solipsismus* (Cuxhaven: Junghaus-Verlag, 1989), 3–52; B. R. Tilghman, *Wittgenstein, Ethics and Aesthetics: The View from Eternity* (Basingstoke: Macmillan, 1991), 51–5, 74–8; J. S. Clegg, *On Genius: Affirmation and Denial from Schopenhauer to Wittgenstein* (American University Studies, Series V, Philosophy, vol. 158) (New York: Peter Lang, 1994), 7–38; J. Young, "Wittgenstein, Kant, Schopenhauer and Critical Philosophy", *Theoria* 50 (1984), 73–105.

Bibliography and recommended reading

Arthur Schopenhauer (1788–1860) collected works

Schopenhauers sämtliche Schriften, 7 vols, Arthur Hübscher (ed.) (Wiesbaden: Eberhard Brockhaus Verlag, 1946–1958).

1: *Schriften zur Erkenntnislehre*
2: *Die Welt als Wille und Vorstellung I*
3: *Die Welt als Wille und Vorstellung II*
4: *Schriften zur Naturphilosophie und zur Ethik*; *Über den Willen in der Natur*; *Die beiden Grundprobleme der Ethik*
5: *Parerga und Paralipomena I,*
6: *Parerga und Paralipomena II*
7: *Über die vierfache Würzel des Satzes vom zureichenden Grunde*;*Gestrichene Stellen*; *Zitate und fremdsprachige Stellen*; *Namen- und Sachregister*

Schopenhauer's writings in translation

1966. *The World as Will and Representation*, 2 vols, E. F. J. Payne (trans.). New York: Dover Publications. [Originally published 1819, 1844, 1859, 1919.]

1974. *The Fourfold Root of the Principle of Sufficient Reason*, E. F. J. Payne (trans.). LaSalle, IL: Open Court. [Originally published 1813, 1847.]

1974. *Parerga and Paralipomena*, 2 vols, E. F. J. Payne (trans.). Oxford: Clarendon Press. [Originally published 1851.]

1988. *Arthur Schopenhauer: Manuscript Remains in Four Volumes*, E. F. J. Payne (trans.). Oxford: Berg.

1992. *On the Will in Nature: A Discussion of the Corroborations from the Empirical Sciences that the Author's Philosophy has Received Since its First Appearance*, E. F. J. Payne (trans.), D. E. Cartwright (ed.). Oxford: Berg. [Originally published 1836.]

1994. *On Vision and Colors: An Essay*, E. F. J. Payne (trans.), D. E. Cartwright (ed.). Oxford: Berg. [Originally published 1816.]

1995. *On the Basis of Morality*, E. F. J. Payne (trans.), with an introduction by D. E. Cartwright. Indianapolis, IN: Hackett. [Originally published 1840.]

1999. *Prize Essay on the Freedom of the Will*, E. F. J. Payne (trans.), G. Zöller (ed.). Cambridge: Cambridge University Press. [Originally published 1839.]

Secondary philosophical literature

Abelsen, P. 1993 "Schopenhauer and Buddhism", *Philosophy East and West* 43, 255–78.

Acton, H. B. 1970. *Kant's Moral Philosophy*. New York: St. Martin's Press.

Allison, H. E. 1996. *Idealism and Freedom: Essays on Kant's Theoretical and Practical Philosophy*. New York: Cambridge University Press.

Alperson, P. 1982. "Schopenhauer and Musical Revelation", *The Journal of Aesthetics and Art Criticism* 40, 155–66.

Aquila, R. E. 1993. "On the 'Subjects' of Knowing and Willing and the 'I' in Schopenhauer", *History of Philosophy Quarterly* 10, 241–60.

Aristotle 1984. *The Complete Works of Aristotle*, 2 vols, the revised Oxford translation, J. Barnes (ed.). Princeton, NJ: Princeton University Press.

Atwell, J. E. 1980. "Schopenhauer's Account of Moral Responsibility", *Pacific Philosophical Quarterly* 61, 396–404.

Atwell, J. E. 1986. *Ends and Principles in Kant's Moral Thought*. Dordrecht & Boston: Martinus Nijhoff.

Atwell, J. E. 1990. *Schopenhauer: The Human Character*. Philadelphia, PA: Temple University Press.

Atwell, J. E. 1995. *Schopenhauer on the Character of the World: The Metaphysics of the Will*. Berkeley, CA: University of California Press.

Atwell, J. E. 1996. "Art as Liberation: A Central Theme of Schopenhauer's Philosophy". See Jacquette (ed.) (1996), *Schopenhauer, Philosophy, and the Arts*, 81–106.

Atzert, S. 1999. *Schopenhauer und Thomas Bernhard: zur literarischen Verwendung von Philosophie*. Freiburg: Rombach.

Aune, B. 1979. *Kant's Theory of Morals*. Princeton, NJ: Princeton University Press.

Ausmus, H. J. 1996. *A Schopenhauerian Challenge of Nietzsche's Thought: Towards a Restoration of Metaphysics*. Lewiston, NY: Edwin Mellen Press.

Ayer, A. J. 1985. *Wittgenstein*. Chicago, IL: University of Chicago Press.

Bacon, F. 1960. *Novum Organon*, translated in 1863 as *The New Organon and Related Writings*, J. Spedding, R. L. Ellis & D. Denon Heath (trans.), F. H. Anderson, (ed.). Indianapolis, IN: Bobbs-Merrill.

Baer, J. T. (ed.) 1980. *Arthur Schopenhauer und die russische Literatur des späten 19. und frühen 20. Jahrhunderts, Slavistische Beiträge*, vol. 140. Munich: Verlag Otto Sagner.

Baillot, A. 1927. *Influence de la philosophie de Schopenhauer en France, 1860–1900*. Paris: Vrin.

Barrett, C. 1991. *Wittgenstein on Ethics and Religious Belief*. Oxford: Basil Blackwell.

Barua, A. 1992. *The Philosophy of Arthur Schopenhauer*. New Delhi: Intellectual Publishing House.

Beer, M. 1914. *Schopenhauer*. London: T.C. & E.C. Jac.

Bennett, J. 1965. "Berkeley and God", *Philosophy* 40, 207–21. Reprinted in *Locke and Berkeley: A Collection of Critical Essays*, C. B. Martin & D. M. Armstrong (eds), 350–99 (Notre Dame, IN: University of Notre Dame Press, 1968).

Berkeley, G. 1949. *Three Dialogues Between Hylas and Philonous*, *The Works of George Berkeley Bishop of Cloyne*, vol. 2, A. A. Luce & T. E. Jessop (eds). London: Thomas Nelson.

Berman, D. 1998. "Schopenhauer and Nietzsche: Honest Atheism, Dishonest Pessimism". See Janaway (ed.) (1998), *Willing and Nothingness*, 178–95.

Birnbacher, D. (ed.) 1996. *Schopenhauer in der Philosophie der Gegenwart*. Würzburg: Königshausen & Neumann.

Black, M. 1964. *A Companion to Wittgenstein's Tractatus*. Ithaca, NY: Cornell University Press.

Bolzano, B. 1972. *Theory of Science: Attempt at a Detailed and in the Main Novel Exposition of Logic with Constant Attention to Earlier Authors*, R. George (ed. and trans.). Berkeley, CA: University of California Press.

Boyle, R. 1772. *The Origin of Forms and Qualities* [1666]. Volume 3 in *The Works of the Honourable Robert Boyle*, 6 vols. London: J. and F. Rivington.

Braun, P. 2000. *Vernunft und Endlichkeit: eine kritische Auseinandersetzung mit dem Problem der Endlichkeit des Daseins in der Philosophie Arthur Schopenhauers unter besonderer Berücksichtigung alternativer Reflexionsätze*. Essen: Verlag die Blaude Eule.

Bridgwater, P. 1988. *Arthur Schopenhauer's English Schooling*. New York: Routledge.

Brinkmann, K. 1958. *Die rechts- und staatslehre Schopenhauers*. Bonn: H. Bouvier.

Budd, M. 1985. *Music and the Emotions: The Philosophical Theories*. London: Routledge & Kegan Paul.

Bykhovsky, B. 1984. *Schopenhauer and the Ground of Existence*, P. Moran (trans.). Amsterdam: R.R. Grüner.

Caldwell, W. 1896. *Schopenhauer's System in its Philosophical Significance*. Edinburgh: Blackwood.

Camus, A. 1955. *The Myth of Sisyphus and Other Essays*, J. O'Brien (trans.). New York: Vintage.

Cartwright, D. E. 1982. "Compassion". In *Zeit der Ernte: Festschrift für Arthur Hübscher zum 85. Geburtstag*, 60–69. Stuttgart and Bad Cannstatt: Frommann-Holzboog.

Cartwright, D. E. 1984. "Kant, Schopenhauer, and Nietzsche on the Morality of Pity", *Journal of the History of Ideas* **45**, 83–98.

Cartwright, D. E. 1998. "Nietzsche's Use and Abuse of Schopenhauer's Moral Philosophy for Life". See Janaway (ed.) (1998), *Willing and Nothingness*, 116–50.

Cartwright, D. E. 1989. "Schopenhauer as Moral Philosopher: Toward the Actuality of his Ethics", *Schopenhauer-Jahrbuch* **70**, 54–65.

Cartwright, D. E. 1988. "Schopenhauer on Suffering, Death, Guilt, and the Consolation of Metaphysics". See von der Luft (ed.) (1988), *Schopenhauer: New Essays*, 51–66.

Cartwright, D. E. 1988. "Schopenhauer's Axiological Analysis of Character", *Revue Internationale de Philosophie* **42**, 18–36.

Cartwright, D. E. 1988. "Schopenhauer's Compassion and Nietzsche's Pity", *Schopenhauer-Jahrbuch* **69**, 557–67.

Cartwright, D. E. 1999. "Schopenhauer's Narrower Sense of Morality". See Janaway (ed.) (1999), *The Cambridge Companion to Schopenhauer*, 252–92.

Cartwright, D. E. forthcoming. *Schopenhauer: A Biography*. Cambridge: Cambridge University Press.

Chansky, J. D. 1988. "Schopenhauer and Platonic Ideas: A Groundwork for an Aesthetic Metaphysics". See von der Luft (ed.) (1988), *Schopenhauer: New Essays*, 67–81.

Clark, M. 1998. "On Knowledge, Truth, and Value: Nietzsche's Debt to Schopenhauer and the Development of his Empiricism". See Janaway (ed.) (1998), *Willing and Nothingness*, 37–78.

Clegg, J. S. 1994. *On Genius: Affirmation and Denial from Schopenhauer to Wittgenstein* (American University Studies, Series V, Philosophy, vol. 158). New York: Peter Lang.

Colvin, S. S. 1897. *Schopenhauer's Doctrine of the Thing-in-Itself and his Attempt to Relate it to the World of Phenomena*. Providence, RI: Franklin Press.

Cooper, D. E. 1998. "Self and Morality in Schopenhauer and Nietzsche". See Janaway (ed.) (1998), *Willing and Nothingness*, 196–216.

Copleston, F. 1946. *Schopenhauer: Philosopher of Pessimism*. London: Burns, Oates, & Washburne.

Darwin, C. 1986. *The Works of Charles Darwin: vol. 10, The Foundations of the Origin of Species: Two Essays Written in 1842 and 1844*, P. H. Barrett & R. B. Freeman (eds). London: William Pickering.

Dauer, D. 1969. *Schopenhauer as Transmitter of Buddhist Ideas*. Berne: Herbert Lang.

Descartes, R. 1975. *The Philosophical Works of Descartes*, 2 vols, E. S. Haldane & G. R. T. Ross (trans.). Cambridge: Cambridge University Press.

Desmond, W, 1988. "Schopenhauer, Art, and the Dark Origin". See von der Luft (ed.) (1988), *Schopenhauer: New Essays*, 101–22.

Diffey, T. J. 1990. "Schopenhauer's Account of Aesthetic Experience", *The British Journal of Aesthetics* **30**, 132–42.

Diffey, T. J. 1996. "Metaphysics and Aesthetics: A Case Study of Schopenhauer and Thomas Hardy". See Jacquette (ed.) (1996), *Schopenhauer, Philosophy, and the Arts*, 229–48.

Döring, W. O. 1947. *Schopenhauer*. Hamburg: Hansischer Gildenverlag.

Doss-Davezac, S. 1996. "Schopenhauer According to the Symbolists: The Philosophical Roots of Late Nineteenth-Century French Aesthetic Theory. See Jacquette (ed.) (1996), *Schopenhauer, Philosophy, and the Arts*, 249–76.

Dumoulin, H. 1981. "Buddhism and Nineteenth-Century German Philosophy", *Journal of the History of Ideas* **42**, 457–70.

Durer, C. S. 1989. "Moby Dick's Ishmael, Burke, and Schopenhauer", *The Midwest Quarterly* **30**, 161–78.

Engel, M. S. 1969. "Schopenhauer's Impact on Wittgenstein", *The Journal of the History of Philosophy* 7, 285–302.

Engelmann, J. 1984. "Schönheit und Zweckmäßigkeit in der Architektur", *Schopenhauer-Jahrbuch* 65, 157–69.

Ferrara, L. 1996. "Schopenhauer on Music as the Embodiment of Will". See Jacquette (ed.) (1996), *Schopenhauer, Philosophy, and the Arts*, 183–99.

Fleischer, M. 2001. *Schopenhauer*. Freiburg im Breisgau: Herder.

Foster, C. 1992. "Schopenhauer's Subtext on Natural Beauty", *The British Journal of Aesthetics* 32, 21–32.

Foster, C. 1996. "Schopenhauer and Aesthetic Recognition". See Jacquette (ed.) (1996), *Schopenhauer, Philosophy, and the Arts*, 133–49.

Foster, C. 1999. "Ideas and Imagination: Schopenhauer on the Proper Foundation of Art". See Janaway (ed.) (1999), *The Cambridge Companion to Schopenhauer*, 213–51.

Fox, M. 1980. *Schopenhauer: His Philosophical Achievement*. Totowa, NJ: Barnes & Noble.

Fromentin, E. 1981. *The Masters of Past Time: Dutch and Flemish Painting from Van Eyck to Rembrandt*. Ithaca, NY: Cornell University Press.

Galileo 1929–39. "*Il Saggiatore* [The Assayer]". In *Le Opere de Galileo Galilei*, 20 vols, A. Favaro (ed.). Florence: S.A.G. Barbèra Editore.

Gardiner, P. 1967. *Schopenhauer*. Harmondsworth: Penguin.

Gardner, S. 1999. "Schopenhauer, Will, and the Unconscious". See Janaway (ed.) (1999), *The Cambridge Companion to Schopenhauer*, 375–421.

Garver, N. 1994. *This Complicated Form of Life: Essays on Wittgenstein*. LaSalle, IL: Open Court.

Glock, H.-J. 1999. "Schopenhauer and Wittgenstein: Representation as Language and Will". See Janaway (ed.) (1999), *The Cambridge Companion to Schopenhauer*, 422–58.

Goedert, G. 1996. "Schopenhauer: Ethik als Weltüberwindung", *Schopenhauer-Jahrbuch* 77, 113–31.

Goehr, L. 1992. *The Imaginary Museum of Musical Works: An Essay in the Philosophy of Music*. Oxford: Clarendon Press.

Goehr, L. 1996. "Schopenhauer and the Musicians: An Inquiry into the Sounds of Silence and the Limits of Philosophizing About Music". See Jacquette (ed.) (1996), *Schopenhauer, Philosophy, and the Arts*, 200–28.

Gonzales, R. A. 1992. *An Approach to the Sacred in the Thought of Schopenhauer*. Lewiston, NY: Edwin Mellen Press.

Goodman, R. B. 1979. "Schopenhauer and Wittgenstein on Ethics", *Journal of the History of Philosophy* 17, 437–47.

Gray, R. 1979. "The German Intellectual Background". In *The Wagner Companion*, P. Burbridge & R. Sutton (eds), 34–59. London: Faber.

Griffiths, A. P. 1974. "Wittgenstein, Schopenhauer, and Ethics". In *Understanding Wittgenstein*, Royal Institute of Philosophy Lectures, vol. 7, 96–116. London: Macmillan.

Griffiths, A. P. 1976. "Wittgenstein on the Fourfold Root of the Principle of Sufficient Reason", *Proceedings of the Aristotelian Society*, supplementary volume 50, 1–20.

Das Gupta, R. K. 1962. "Schopenhauer and Indian Thought", *East and West* 13, 32–40.

Guyer, P. 1996. "Pleasure and Knowledge in Schopenhauer's Aesthetics". See Jacquette (ed.) (1996), *Schopenhauer, Philosophy, and the Arts*, 109–32.

Guyer, P. 1999. "Schopenhauer, Kant, and the Methods of Philosophy". See Janaway (ed.) (1999), *The Cambridge Companion to Schopenhauer*, 93–137.

Haller, R. 1988. "Was Wittgenstein a Neo-Kantian?". In *Questions on Wittgenstein*, R. Haller (ed.), 44–56. Lincoln, NE: University of Nebraska Press.

Hamlyn, D. W. 1972. "Schopenhauer on the Principle of Sufficient Reason". In *Reason and Reality*, Royal Institute of Philosophy Lectures 5, 1970–1971, G. N. A. Vesey (ed.), 145–62. London: Macmillan.

Hamlyn, D. W. 1980. *Schopenhauer*. London: Routledge & Kegan Paul.

Hamlyn, D. W. 1999. "Schopenhauer and Knowledge". See Janaway (ed.) (1999), *The Cambridge Companion to Schopenhauer*, 44–62.

Heidegger, M. 1996. *Being and Time: A Translation of Sein und Zeit*, J. Stambaugh (trans.). Albany, NY: SUNY Press. [Originally published in 1953 by Max Niemeyer Verlag, Tübingen.]

Hein, H. 1996. "Schopenhauer and Platonic Ideas", *Journal of the History of Philosophy*, 4, 133–44.

Higgins, K. M. 1998. "Schopenhauer and Nietzsche: Temperament and Temporality". See Janaway (ed.) (1998), *Willing and Nothingness*, 151–77.

Hübscher, A. 1960. *Arthur Schopenhauer: Mensch und Philosoph in seinen Briefe*. Wiesbaden: F. A. Brockhaus.

Hübscher, A. 1967. *Schopenhauer: Biographie eines Weltbildnis*. Stuttgart: Reclam.

Hübscher, A. 1968. *Schopenhauer-Bildnisses: Eine Ikonographie*. Frankfurt am Main: Waldemar Kramer.

Hübscher, A. 1981. *Schopenhauer-Bibliographie*. Stuttgart: Fromann-Holzboog.

Hübscher, A. 1989. *The Philosophy of Schopenhauer in its Intellectual Context: Thinker Against the Tide*. Lewiston, NY: Edwin Mellen Press.

Hume, D. 1978. *A Treatise of Human Nature* [1739–40], 2nd edn, with text revised and notes by P. H. Nidditch and analytical index by L. A. Selby-Bigge. Oxford: Oxford University Press.

Jacquette, D. 1985. "Berkeley's Continuity Argument for the Existence of God", *The Journal of Religion* 65, 1–14.

Jacquette, D. 1992. "Schopenhauer's Circle and the Principle of Sufficient Reason", *Metaphilosophy* 23, 279–87.

Jacquette, D. 1993. "Reconciling Berkeley's Microscopes in God's Infinite Mind", *Religious Studies* 29, 453–63.

Jacquette, D. 1994. "Schopenhauer on the Antipathy of Aesthetic Genius and the Charming", *History of European Ideas* 18, 373–85.

Jacquette, D. (ed.) 1996. *Schopenhauer, Philosophy, and the Arts*. Cambridge: Cambridge University Press.

Jacquette, D. 1996. "Schopenhauer's Metaphysics of Appearance and Will in the Philosophy of Art". See Jacquette (ed.) (1996), *Schopenhauer, Philosophy, and the Arts*, 1–36.

Jacquette, D. 1997. "Haller on Wittgenstein and Kant". In *Austrian Philosophy Past and Present: Essays in Honor of Rudolf Haller*, K. Lehrer & J. C. Marek (eds), 29–44. Boston Studies in the Philosophy of Science. Dordrecht: Kluwer.

Jacquette, D. 1998. *Wittgenstein's Thought in Transition*. West Lafayette, IN: Purdue University Press.

Jacquette, D. 1999. "Schopenhauer on Death". See Janaway (ed.) (1999), *The Cambridge Companion to Schopenhauer*, 293–317.

Jacquette, D. 2000. "Schopenhauer on the Ethics of Suicide", *Continental Philosophy Review* 33, 43–58.

Jacquette, D. 2001. "Of Time and the River in Kant's Refutation of Idealism", *History of Philosophy Quarterly* 18, 297–310.

Jacquette, D. 2002. "Wittgenstein on Thoughts as Pictures of Facts and the Transcendence of the Metaphysical Subject", *Wittgenstein and the Future of Philosophy: A Reassessment After 50 Years/ Wittgenstein und die Zukunft der Philosophie. Eine Neubewertung nach 50 Jahren*, R. Haller & K. Puhl (eds), 160–70. Vienna: Öbv&Hpt.

James, W. 1935. *The Varieties of Religious Experience: A Study in Human Nature*. The Gifford Lectures on Natural Religion 1901–1902. London: Longmans, Greene & Co.

Janaway, C. 1989. *Self and World in Schopenhauer's Philosophy*. Oxford: Clarendon Press.

Janaway, C. 1994. *Schopenhauer*. Oxford: Clarendon Press.

Janaway, C. 1996. "Knowledge and Tranquility: Schopenhauer on the Value of Art". See Jacquette (ed.) (1996), *Schopenhauer, Philosophy, and the Arts*, 39–61.

Janaway, C. 1998. "Schopenhauer as Nietzsche's Educator". See Janaway (ed.) (1998), *Willing and Nothingness*, 13–36.

Janaway, C. 1998. *Willing and Nothingness: Schopenhauer as Nietzsche's Educator*. Oxford: Clarendon Press.

Janaway, C. (ed.) 1999. *The Cambridge Companion to Schopenhauer*. Cambridge: Cambridge University Press.

Janaway, C. 1999. "Introduction". See Janaway (ed.) (1999), *The Cambridge Companion to Schopenhauer*, 1–17.

Janaway, C. 1999. "Will and Nature". See Janaway (ed.) (1999), *The Cambridge Companion to Schopenhauer*, 138–70.

Janaway, C. 1999. "Schopenhauer's Pessimism". See Janaway (ed.) (1999), *The Cambridge Companion to Schopenhauer*, 318–43.
Janik, A. S. 1966. "Schopenhauer and the Early Wittgenstein", *Philosophical Studies* (Ireland) 15, 76–95.
Janik, A. S. & S. Toulmin 1973. *Wittgenstein's Vienna*. New York: Simon & Schuster.
Kanovitch, A. 1923. *The Will to Beauty: Being a Continuation of the Philosophies of Arthur Schopenhauer and Friedrich Nietzsche*. New York: Henry Bee Company.
Kant, I. 1952. *The Critique of Judgement*, J. C. Meredith (trans.). Oxford: Clarendon Press.
Kant, I. 1959. *Foundations of the Metaphysics of Morals*, L. White Beck (trans.). New York: Macmillan.
Kant, I. 1965. *Critique of Pure Reason* [1781, 1787], N. Kemp Smith (trans.). New York: St. Martin's Press.
Keller, H. 1968. "Schopenhauer's 'Palestrina'", *The Listener*, 23 May, 79(2043), 676.
Kelly, M. 1909. *Kant's Philosophy as Rectified by Schopenhauer*. London: Swan Sonnenschein.
Kelly, M. 1910. *Kant's Ethics and Schopenhauer's Criticism*. London: Swan Sonnenschein.
Kishan, B. V. 1978. *Schopenhauer's Theory of Salvation*. Visakhapatnam: Andrea University Press.
Knox, I. 1958. *The Aesthetic Theories of Kant, Hegel, and Schopenhauer*. New York: Humanities Press.
Knox, I. 1980. "Schopenhauer's Aesthetic Theory". In *Schopenhauer: His Philosophical Achievement*, M. Fox (ed.), 132–46. Brighton: Harvester Press.
Krukowski, L. 1992. *Aesthetic Legacies*. Philadelphia, PA: Temple University Press.
Krukowski, L. 1996. "Schopenhauer and the Aesthetics of Creativity". See Jacquette (ed.) (1996), *Schopenhauer, Philosophy, and the Arts*, 62–80.
Lange, E. M. 1989. *Wittgenstein und Schopenhauer: logisch-philosophische Abhandlung und Kritik des Solipsismus*. Cuxhaven: Junghaus-Verlag.
Lauxtermann, P. F. H. 2000. *Schopenhauer's Broken World-View: Colours and Ethics Between Kant and Goethe*. The Hague: Kluwer.
Lefew-Blake, P. 2001. *Schopenhauer, Woman's Literature, and the Legacy of Pessimism in the Novels of George Eliot, Olive Schreiner, Virginia Woolf, and Doris Lessing*. Lewiston, NY: Edwin Mellen Press.
Locke, J. 1975. *An Essay Concerning Human Understanding* [1700], P. H. Nidditch (ed.). Oxford: Clarendon Press.
Luxembourg, L. K. 1967. *Francis Bacon and Denis Diderot: Philosophers of Science*. Copenhagen: Munksgaard.
Magee, B. 1997. *The Philosophy of Schopenhauer*. Oxford: Clarendon Press. [Revised and enlarged edition; originally published 1983.]
Magee, B. 1990. *Misunderstanding Schopenhauer*. London: University of London Institute of Germanic Studies.
Magee, B. 2000. *Wagner and Philosophy*. Harmondsworth: Penguin.
Maidan, M. 1988. "Schopenhauer on Altruism and Morality", *Schopenhauer-Jahrbuch* 69, 265–72.
Malcolm, N. 1958. *Ludwig Wittgenstein: A Memoir, with a Biographical Sketch by Georg Henrik von Wright*. Oxford: Oxford University Press.
Malter, R. 1988. *Der eine Gedanke: Hinführung zur Philosophie Arthur Schopenhauers*. Darmstadt: Wissenschaftliche Buchgesellschaft.
Malter, 1985. "Schopenhauers Transzendentalismus", *Schopenhauer-Jahrbuch* 66, 29–51.
Mann, T. 1947. "Schopenhauer", *Essays of Three Decades*, H. T. Lowe-Porter (trans.). New York: Knopf.
Martin, J. 1992. *Francis Bacon: The State and the Reform of Natural Philosophy*. Cambridge: Cambridge University Press.
McGill, V. J. 1977. *Schopenhauer: Pessimist and Pagan*. New York: Haskell House.
McLaughlin, S. 1984. *Schopenhauer in Russland: zur literarischen Rezeption bei Turgenev*. Wiesbaden: Harrassowitz Verlag.
Merleau-Ponty, M. 1962. *The Phenomenology of Perception*, C. Smith (trans.). New York: Humanities Press.
Monk, R. 1990. *Wittgenstein: The Duty of Genius*. Harmondsworth: Penguin.

Murdoch, I. 1992. *Metaphysics as a Guide to Morals*. Harmondsworth: Penguin.
Muses, C. 1955. *East–West Fire: Schopenhauer's Optimism and the Lanhavatara Sutra*. Indian Hills, CO: Falcon's Wing Press.
Nanajivako, B. 1970. *Schopenhauer and Buddhism*. Kandy, Ceylon: Buddhist Publication Society.
Neeley, S. G. 1992. "A Re-Examination of Schopenhauer's Analysis of Bodily Agency: The Ego as Microcosm", *Idealistic Studies* 22, 52–67.
Neeley, S. G. 1994. *Schopenhauer: A Consistent Reading*. Lewiston, NY: Edwin Mellen Press.
Neeley, S. G. 1996. "The Knowledge and Nature of Schopenhauer's Will", *Schopenhauer-Jahrbuch* 77, 85–112.
Nelson, B. 1989. "Wagner, Schopenhauer, and Nietzsche: On the Value of Human Action", *The Opera Quarterly* 6, 24–32.
Neymeyr, B. 1996. *Äesthetische Autonomie als Abnormalität: Kritische Analysen zu Schopenhauers Ästhetikk im Horizont seiner Willensmetaphysik*. Berlin: Walter de Gruyter.
Nicholls, M. 1994. "The Kantian Inheritance and Schopenhauer's Doctrine of Will", *Kant-Studien* 85, 257–79.
Nicholls, M. 1995. "Schopenhauer, Feeling and the Noumenon", *Schopenhauer-Jahrbuch* 76, 53–71.
Nicholls, M. 1999. "The Influence of Eastern Thought on Schopenhauer's Doctrine of the Thing-in-Itself". See Janaway (ed.) (1999), *The Cambridge Companion to Schopenhauer*, 171–212.
Nietzsche, F. 1967. *Kritische Studienausgabe: Werke*, 15 vols, G. Colli & M. Montinari (eds). Berlin: Walter de Gruyter.
Nietzsche, F. 1956. *The Birth of Tragedy and The Genealogy of Morals*, F. Golffing (trans.). Garden City, NY: Doubleday.
Nietzsche, F. 1974. *The Complete Works of Friedrich Nietzsche*, O. Levy (ed.). New York: Gordon Press.
Nietzsche, F. 1983. "Schopenhauer as Educator". In *Untimely Meditations*, R. J. Hollingdale (trans.), 125–94. Cambridge: Cambridge University Press.
Nietzsche, F. 1998. *On the Genealogy of Morality*, M. Clark & A. J. Swenson (trans.). Indianapolis, IN: Hackett.
Nussbaum, M. C. "The Transfigurations of Intoxication: Nietzsche, Schopenhauer, and Dionysus", *Arion*, 3rd series, 1, 75–111.
Nussbaum, M. C. 1999. "Nietzsche, Schopenhauer, and Dionysus". See Janaway (ed.) (1999), *The Cambridge Companion to Schopenhauer*, 344–74.
Odell, S. J. 2001. *On Schopenhauer*. Belmont, CA: Wadsworth.
O'Neill, O. 1989. *Constructions of Reason: Explorations of Kant's Practical Philosophy*. Cambridge: Cambridge University Press.
Pangopoulus, N. 1998. *The Fiction of Joseph Conrad: The Influence of Schopenhauer and Nietzsche*. New York: Peter Lang.
Paton, H. J. 1967. *The Categorical Imperative: A Study in Kant's Moral Philosophy*. New York: Harper & Row.
Paulsen, F. 1901. *Schopenhauer, Hamlet, Mephistopheles: drei Aufsätze zur Naturgeschichte des Pessimismus*. Berlin: Cotta Verlag.
Pessoa, F. 2001. *The Book of Disquiet*, R. Zenith (ed. and trans.). Harmondsworth: Penguin.
Pfeiffer, K. 1925. *Arthur Schopenhauer: Persönlichkeit und Werk*. Leipzig: A. Kröner.
Pfeiffer, K. 1949. *Zum höchsten Dasein: Goethes Faust im Lichte der Schopenhauerschen Philosophie*. Berlin: Walter de Gruyter.
Philonenko, A. 1980. *Schopenhauer: Une Philosophie de Tragedie*. Paris: Vrin.
Plato 1991. *The Republic of Plato*, 2nd edn, translated with notes, an interpretive essay and a new introduction by A. Bloom. New York: Basic Books.
Plato 1997. *Complete Works*, J. M. Cooper (ed.). Indianapolis, IN: Hackett.
Podro, M. 1972. *The Manifold in Perception: Theories of Art from Kant to Hildebrand*. Oxford: Clarendon Press.
Poggeler, O. 1960. "Schopenhauer und das Wesen der Kunst", *Zeitschrift für Philosophische Forschung* 14, 353–89.
Pothast, U. 1982. *Die eigentlich metaphysische Tätigkeit: über Schopenhauers Ästhetik und ihre Anwendung durch Samuel Beckett*. Frankfurt: Surkamp.

Preiffer, K. 1949. *Zum höchsten Dasein: Goethes Faust im Lichte der Schopenhauerschen Philosophie.* Berlin: Walter de Gruyter.

Rhees, R. (ed.) 1984. *Recollections of Wittgenstein*, rev. edn. Oxford: Oxford University Press.

Ross, W. D. 1954. *Kant's Ethical Theory: A Commentary on the Grundlegung zur Metaphysik der Sitten.* Oxford: Clarendon Press.

Rotenstreich, N. 1996. "Schopenhauer on Beauty and Ontology". See Jacquette (ed.) (1996), *Schopenhauer, Philosophy, and the Arts*, 150–61.

Rousseau, J.-J. 1953. *The Confessions*, J. M. Cohen (trans.). Harmondsworth: Penguin.

Safranski, R. 1990. *Schopenhauer and the Wild Years of Philosophy*, E. Osers (trans.). Cambridge, MA: Harvard University Press.

Saltus, E. 1995. *The Philosophy of Disenchantment.* New York: AMS Press.

Schirmacher, W. (ed.) 1988. *Schopenhauers Aktualität: ein Philosoph wird neu gelesen.* Vienna: Passagen Verlag.

Schirmacher, W. (ed.) 1991, *Schopenhauer, Nietzsche, und die Kunst.* Vienna: Passagen Verlag.

Schmidt, A. 1988. *Idee und Weltwille: Schopenhauer als Kritiker Hegels.* Munich: Carl Hauser.

Schwarzer, M. 1996. "Schopenhauer's Philosophy of Architecture". See Jacquette (ed.) (1996), *Schopenhauer, Philosophy, and the Arts*, 277–98.

Seneca 1969. *Letters from a Stoic*, R. Campbell (trans.). Harmondsworth: Penguin.

Simmel, G. 1986. *Schopenhauer and Nietzsche*, H. Loiskandl, D. Weinstein & M. Weinstein (trans.). Amherst, MA: University of Massachusetts Press.

Snow, D. & J. Snow 1991. "Was Schopenhauer an Idealist?", *Journal of the History of Philosophy* 29, 633–55.

Snow, J. 1993. "Schopenhauer's Style", *International Philosophical Quarterly* 33, 401–12.

Soll, I. 1998. "Schopenhauer, Nietzsche, and the Redemption of Life Through Art". See Janaway (ed.) (1998), *Willing and Nothingness*, 79–115.

Son, G. 2001. *Schopenhauers Ethik des Mitleids und die Indische Philosophie: Parallelität und Differenz.* Freiburg im Breisgau: Verlag K. Alber.

Sorg, B. 1975. *Zur literarischen Schopenhauer-Rezeption im 19. Jahrhundert.* Heidelberg: Winter Verlag.

Stenius, E. 1960. *Wittgenstein's "Tractatus": A Critical Exposition of its Main Lines of Thought.* Ithaca, NY: Cornell University Press.

Stratton-Lake, P. 2000. *Kant, Duty, and Moral Worth.* London: Routledge.

Sullivan, R. J. 1989. *Immanuel Kant's Moral Theory.* Cambridge: Cambridge University Press.

Taminiaux, J. 1987. "Art and Truth in Schopenhauer and Nietzsche", *Man and World* 20, 85–102.

Tanner, M. 1999. *Schopenhauer.* New York: Routledge.

Taylor, C. S. "Nietzsche's Schopenhauerianism", *Nietzsche-Studien* 17, 45–73.

Taylor, R. 1964. "Schopenhauer". In *A Critical History of Western Philosophy*, D. J. O'Connor (ed.), 365–83. New York: Free Press of Glencoe.

Taylor, R. 1974. "Introduction". In *The Fourfold Root of the Principle of Sufficient Reason*, E. F. J. Payne (trans.), ix–xviii. LaSalle, IL: Open Court.

Taylor, T. G. 1987. "Platonic Ideas, Aesthetic Experience, and the Resolution of Schopenhauer's Great Contradiction", *International Studies in Philosophy* 19, 43–53.

Tilghman, B. R. 1991. *Wittgenstein, Ethics and Aesthetics: The View from Eternity.* Basingstoke: Macmillan.

Tipton, I. C. 1974. *Berkeley: The Philosophy of Immaterialism.* London: Methuen.

Tolstoy, L. 1983. *Confession*, D. Patterson (trans.). New York: Norton.

Touey, D. 1998. "Schopenhauer and Nietzsche on the Nature and Limits of Philosophy", *Journal of Value Inquiry* 32, 243–52.

Tsanoff, R. A. 1911. *Schopenhauer's Critique of Kant's Theory of Experience.* New York: Longmans, Green & Co.

von der Luft, E. (ed.) 1988. *Schopenhauer: New Essays in Honor of his 200th Birthday.* Lewiston, NY: Edwin Mellen Press.

von Gwinner, W. 1878. *Schopenhauers Leben*, 2nd edn. Leipzig: F.A. Brockhaus.

von Wright, G. H. 1942. "Georg Lichtenberg als Philosoph", *Theoria* 8, 201–17.

von Wright, G. H. 1982. *Wittgenstein.* Minneapolis, MN: University of Minnesota Press.

von Wright, G. H. 1958. "Biographical Sketch", in *Ludwig Wittgenstein: A Memoir, with a*

Biographical Sketch by Georg Henrik von Wright, N. Malcolm, 1–22. Oxford: Oxford University Press.

Wagner, G. F. 1960. *Schopenhauer-Register*. Stuttgart: Frommann.

Wallace, W. 1890. *Life of Arthur Schopenhauer*. London: W. Scott.

Weimer, W. 1982. *Schopenhauer*. Darmstadt: Wissenschaftliche Buchgesellschaft.

Weiner, D. A. 1992. *Genius and Talent: Schopenhauer's Influence on Wittgenstein's Early Philosophy*. Rutherford, NJ: Farleigh Dickinson University Press.

Welsen, P. 1995. *Schopenhauers Theorie des Subjekts: ihre transzendentalphilosophischen, anthropologischen und naturmetaphysischen Grundlagen*. Würzburg: Königshausen & Neumann.

Whittaker, T. 1920. *Schopenhauer*. London: Constable.

White, F. C. 1992. *On Schopenhauer's Fourfold Root of the Principle of Sufficient Reason*. New York: E. J. Brill.

White, F. C. 1999. "The Fourfold Root". See Janaway (ed.) (1999), *The Cambridge Companion to Schopenhauer*, 63–92.

Wicks, R. 1993. "Schopenhauer's Naturalization of Kant's A Priori Forms of Empirical Knowledge", *History of Philosophy Quarterly* 10, 181–96.

Williams, T. C. 1968. *The Concept of the Categorical Imperative: A Study of the Place of the Categorical Imperative in Kant's Ethical Theory*. Oxford: Clarendon Press.

Wittgenstein, L. 1922. *Tractatus Logico-Philosophicus*, C. K. Ogden (ed.). London: Routledge & Kegan Paul.

Wittgenstein, L. 1966. *Philosophical Investigations*, 3rd edn, G. E. M. Anscombe (trans.). New York: Macmillan.

Wittgenstein, L. 1971. *Prototractatus: An Early Version of Tractatus Logico-Philosophicus*, B. McGuinness, T. Nybert & G. H. von Wright (eds), D. Pears & B. McGuinness (trans.). Ithaca, NY: Cornell University Press.

Wittgenstein, L. 1979. *Notebooks 1914–1916*, 2nd edn, G. H. von Wright & G. E. M. Anscombe (eds), G. E. M. Anscombe (trans.). Oxford: Basil Blackwell.

Wood, A. W. 1999. *Kant's Ethical Thought*. Cambridge: Cambridge University Press.

Wulf, C. 1998. *The Imperative of Narration: Beckett, Bernhardt, Schopenhauer, Lacan*. Birghton: Sussex Academic Press.

Young, J. 1984. "Schopenhauer's Critique of Kantian Ethics", *Kant-Studien* 75, 191–212.

Young, J. 1984. "Wittgenstein, Kant, Schopenhauer and Critical Philosophy", *Theoria* 50, 73–105.

Young, J. 1987. "The Standpoint of Eternity: Schopenhauer on Art", *Kant-Studien* 78, 424–41.

Young, J. 1987. *Willing and Unwilling: A Study in the Philosophy of Arthur Schopenhauer*. Dordrecht: Martinus Nijhoff.

Young, J. 1996. "Schopenhauer, Heidegger, Art, and the Will". See Jacquette (ed.) (1996), *Schopenhauer, Philosophy, and the Arts*, 162–80.

Zimmern, H. 1876. *Schopenhauer: His Life and His Philosophy*. London: Allen & Unwin. [Revised edition 1932.]

Zint, H. 1954. *Schopenhauer als Erlebnis*. Munich: E. Reinhardt.

Zöller, G. 1995. "Schopenhauer and the Problem of Metaphysics: Critical Reflections on Rudolf Malter's Interpretation", *Man and World* 28, 1–10.

Zöller, G. 1999. "Schopenhauer on the Self". See Janaway (ed.) (1999), *The Cambridge Companion to Schopenhauer*, 18–43.

Index